Uprising of Hope

CROSSROADS IN QUALITATIVE INQUIRY

SERIES EDITORS
Norman K. Denzin, University of Illinois, Urbana-Champaign
Yvonna S. Lincoln, Texas A&M University

ABOUT THE SERIES

Qualitative methods are material and interpretive practices. They do not stand outside politics and cultural criticism. This spirit of critically managing and pursuing a more democratic society has been a guiding feature of qualitative inquiry from the very beginning. The Crossroads in Qualitative Inquiry series will take up such methodological and moral issues as the local and the global, text and context, voice, writing for the other, and the presence of the author in the text. The Crossroads series understands that the discourses of a critical, moral methodology are basic to any effort to reengage the promise of the social sciences for democracy in the twenty-first century. This international series creates a space for the exploration of new representational forms and new critical, cultural studies.

SUBMITTING MANUSCRIPTS

Book proposals should be sent to Crossroads in Qualitative Inquiry Series, c/o Norman Denzin, Institute for Communication Studies, 810 S. Wright Street, University of Illinois, Champaign, Illinois 61820, or e-mailed to n-denzin@uiuc.edu.

BOOKS IN THIS SERIES

Volume 1: *Incarceration Nation: Investigative Prison Poems of Hope and Terror*, Stephen John Hartnett (2003)

Volume 2: *9/11 in American Culture*, edited by Norman K. Denzin and Yvonna S. Lincoln (2003)

Volume 3: *Turning Points in Qualitative Research: Tying Knots in a Handkerchief*, edited by Yvonna S. Lincoln and Norman K. Denzin (2003)

Volume 4: *Uprising of Hope: Sharing the Zapatista Journey to Alternative Development*, Duncan Earle and Jeanne Simonelli (2005)

Volume 5: *Ethnodrama: An Anthology of Reality Theatre*, edited by Johnny Saldaña (2005)

Uprising of Hope

Sharing the Zapatista Journey to Alternative Development

DUNCAN EARLE AND JEANNE SIMONELLI

*Children of Hope: Marta and Natalia.
Photo by Jeanne Simonelli.*

ALTAMIRA
PRESS

A Division of

ROWMAN & LITTLEFIELD PUBLISHERS, INC.

Walnut Creek • Lanham • New York • Toronto • Oxford

ALTAMIRA PRESS
A division of Rowman & Littlefield Publishers, Inc.
4501 Forbes Boulevard, Suite 200
Lanham, MD 20706

Estover Road
Plymouth PL6 7PY
United Kingdom

British Library Cataloguing in Publication Information Available

Library of Congress Cataloging-in-Publication Data

Earle, Duncan, 1952-
  Uprising of hope : sharing the Zapatista journey to alternative development / Duncan Earle and Jeanne Simonelli.
     p. cm. — (Crossroads in qualitative inquiry ; v. 4)
  Includes bibliographical references and index.
  ISBN 0-7591-0540-5 (alk. paper) — ISBN 0-7591-0541-3 (alk. paper)
  1. Chiapas (Mexico)—History—Peasant Uprising, 1994- 2. Mexico—Politics and government—1988- 3. Ejército Zapatista de Liberación Nacional (Mexico) 4. Indians of Mexico—Mexico—Chiapas—Government relations. 5. Mayas—Mexico—Chiapas—Government relations. I. Simonelli, Jeanne M. II. Title. III. Series.

F1256.E37 2005
972'.750836—dc22   2004017835

Printed in the United States of America

Contents

PART 4: HORIZONS OF HOPE

Foreword

JEANNE SIMONELLI AND DUNCAN EARLE have succeeded in their goal of sharing the Zapatista dreams with their students, fellow anthropological travelers, and what should be a wide readership with this book. En route, it provides an extraordinary insight into the Zapatistas, their neighbors in the Lacandon rain forest, the governments *de turno* (shifting regimes), and anthropological efforts into the theory and method of human lifeways. Their book may effectively change the way that ethnography is undertaken as well as written if their call for an activist approach to research and a collective effort in producing results is heeded.

The poetic images that the anthropologists utilize evoke, through the Zapatistas' own metaphors that are woven into the text, the reality of the lives of the colonizers who live in the rain forest. First we learn, along with the authors and their students, the reality of the hard work expended in subsistence and in cash crops and the often disappointing returns. Then we learn to appreciate the significance of the process of constructing autonomy as an alternative to neoliberal development. This connotes a degree of self-deprivation as Zapatistas reject the client-creating strategies embedded in policies employed by the government in the past. Finally, we learn, along with the students and the anthropologists themselves, about the process of learning itself. Anthropology has always called for a participatory experience, but in this ethnography we are asked to become part of the action, sharing the risks as well as the rewards of success. The compelling style of the narrative draws the reader into an odyssey that in itself creates a transformation in consciousness.

This is a far different reality from the postmodernist turn characteristic of ethnography in the past two decades. Posing as postcolonial subjects, anthropologists had become the central protagonists of a research project that they controlled from conception to the writing of a monograph. Jeanne Simonelli and Duncan Earle propose a collaboration with members of the communities they study that includes their help in framing the problem rather than simply providing answers to questions posed by the investigators. Although advocacy roles are part of the research design, dialogue often ensues in which a collaborative critique shapes the lines of inquiry.

Jeanne Simonelli arrived during President Zedillo's presidency, when he launched the massive militarization that promoted disruption and fragmentation of the Lacandon settlements. On February 9, 1995, at least 40,000 troops were added to the more than 30,000 that were deployed on the perimeter of the "conflict area" in the Lacandon. The long drive on the highway prepared for military caravans becomes even more aggravating with the *topes*—speed traps that can break the transmission of anything but a balloon-tired humvee. The community of "Miguel Hidalgo" that Jeanne Simonelli gained entrée to study was totally dismantled in the subsequent army sweep in 1998 that attempted to level Zapatista resistance during the tenure of Roberto Albores Guillén as governor of Chiapas. When Fox was inaugurated as president in 2000, the military presence receded to the margins of the settlements, and foreigners were no longer expelled as suspected subversives when they appeared in indigenous areas as had happened to Jeanne and her colleague Kate O'Donnell earlier.

Central to the investigation is the question as to whether the household organization of development is viable. Cash crops are an adjunct to food crops among Zapatistas of Cerro Verde, where Jeanne Simonelli concentrated her studies, as well as among highland Chamulas who colonized the settlement of Nuevo San Juan Chamula, where Duncan Earle had begun his study twenty-five years before. The monetary wealth provided by coffee cultivation in the 1980s no longer fueled the development instigated by the Party of the Institutional Revolution (PRI) in the waning days of its paternalistic intervention in indigenous affairs. Both Chamulas and Zapatistas had experienced the vicissitudes of neoliberal progress. They had also experienced the deceptions of the PRI government in failing to support the infrastructural supports that made market exchange viable in the jungle: roads were not built until the government decided to position an army of 40,000 to 70,000 soldiers in the vicinity of settlements. Credit to sustain the needed inputs for cash cropping was absent. Markets were still mediated by *coyotes*—wolves or voracious buyers—who cheated indigenous producers just as they had done in the colonial era. Yet Chamulas continued to compete with each other to attract a government pork barrel, while Zapatistas sought autonomy in defining their own goals.

At a more fundamental level, Zapatistas differ from traditional highland colonizers in the socialization of their children and their relations with their environment. Although both communities are made up of smallholders, Zapatistas are more consciously committed to living in balance with the ecosystem. Chamulas of Nuevo San Juan Chamula tried cattle and pig raising but admitted to the failure of these ventures, and the colony split into factions as they tried to maximize their share of the limited good. The path to individual wealth in Nuevo San Juan is reinforced by the adoption of distinct and competing Protestant cults that split the community and even family members. Zapatistas stress the collective base in production as well as consumption activities, a process that involves lengthy meetings in which everyone speaks and a consensus of sorts emerges. Zapatistas are actively searching for a new educational program that will cultivate multiskilled people who do not disdain the work of the milpa, even when they achieve leadership positions or acquire advanced education. This inspires the people of Cerro Verde to reject government supplies and professionals as they themselves construct a school and serve voluntarily as teachers.

Of course, this venture requires some outside help, and this is often made available by the nongovernment organizations that proliferated in the 1980s when an estimated 150,000 Guatemalans fled their country during the height of the massacres. Jeanne and her students worked with the United Nations agency called Development for Women (DESMU Desarrollo Mujeres AC), which was among the first nongovernmental organizations (NGOs) to arrive in the Lacandon area to attend to the needs of the self-exiled Guatemalans. Although DESMU was inspired by urban feminists with an agenda distinct from that of the Zapatistas, their activist organizers were willing to respond to the local scene.

The other major development initiative was provided by Marist Catholic priests who disseminated material and political assistance along with spiritual guidance. They were followed by deacons trained in the diocese by Bishop Samuel Ruíz, one of the most sensitive and informed church leaders to relate indigenous beliefs and customs to Christian teaching since the arrival of Fray Bartolomé de las Casas in the sixteenth century. As he made clear in his sermons and frequent personal appearances in the Lacandon communities, the Christian precept "Love your brother as you love yourself" has intensified meaning in a racist society: he who disparages his race disparages his mother as well as the work of God. He and the deacons he trained were probably the reason that the massacre that occurred in 1997 in Acteal, a highland indigenous hamlet of Chenalhó, did not result in hundreds instead of scores of dead. The bishop's wisdom was transmitted to the deacons he trained, and after his retirement in 1998, they continue to provide a model for intervention in crisis situations.

The resistance of the Zapatista communities is also expressed in their rejection of government handouts in every form, be it textbooks, medical supplies and interventions in immunization programs, and other programs that might well benefit the communities. Together Jeanne and Duncan introduced new facets to the emerging anthropological role as advocate, consulting with their Zapatista collaborators on the potential advantages to be gained from some government and NGO interventions, modifying the negative position that the Zapatistas had originally taken. They developed community guidelines for developers that would enable the communities to better assess the priorities of the interventions and how they would impact the people. These guidelines included assessments of how the project would enhance community harmony, whether the agency would work within the given political landscape of bottom-up and consensual democracy, the degree to which the project would promote diversification in production as a way of enhancing their autonomy, and how it might reinforce the ecological balance they valued. Was the mission of the agency clear? Did it reflect the joint planning and evaluation of the people and the project personnel?

Because of the strong emphasis on gender complementarity, women of the Zapatista communities reject projects that single out women as the recipients for grants. This provision has evolved during the thirty-five-year period in which aid assistance has been influenced by feminist thought, particularly in male-dominant societies. In such settings, experience had indicated that money given to men often did not reach domestic settings where women and children are at risk. Yet Zapatista women feel that they have achieved a degree of equality that enables them to work alongside men without fear of being preempted. "Coffee is not just a men's thing," the women explained when they took the money Jeanne and the students had raised for a bakery project. So long as alcoholism is not tolerated and the attendant abuse and violence toward women is actively prohibited by the community, this may be viable.

The autonomous communities have refined their structures to ensure the enactment of autonomy through the *Juntas de Buen Gobierno* (councils of good government) operating within the Caracoles—snail shells, a metaphor for the linkage between the past traditions and the present in regional headquarters. The time-consuming processes of consultation of the leaders with the bases—deplored by even the most sympathetic of the activists who have rallied to the Zapatista cause—have been perfected in the decade since the Zapatistas first congregated in San Andrés to dialogue with the government. Earle's twenty-five-year acquaintance with Maya traditions provides some parallels for communal consultation, although the process of consensus was limited to male heads of families.

Whereas the authority of the leaders in the traditional communities was ultimately sanctioned by elders who have filled all the offices in the course of a lifetime, the Zapatista authority is ultimately sanctioned by the unseen but felt presence of the military arm. So long as the threat of war from the federal troops that surround them exists, the presence of an armed Zapatista resistance is felt to be important. The army has continued to expel colonizers, especially in regions such as Montes Azules, where as recently as January 2004, thirty settlements were dislodged. As the megaprojects for the Plan Puebla Panama progress, the threat of dislocation for many more looms in the vicinity of proposed dams for hydroelectric power. The resistance of the communities is a daily rejection of the authority of the government. This is expressed in the colonizers' refusal to pay the exorbitant electrical charges for settlers of an area that produces over half the energy for the nation.

The entrance of the two anthropologists into the Caracol that was at the center of the command system was for them and the assembled council a *rite de passage* that surpasses most ethnographic accounts. For Jeanne it was like the passage from darkness to light when the twin heroes in the Popul Vuh go down to the underworld, where they challenge the lords of Ahkubal in a game of basketball, with one returning to the upper world transformed as a talking head.

In the early years of my research in Chiapas, we used to think of fieldwork as a liminal passage from our world to another. After a half century, the world has reached the rain forest, threatening an end to this reserve of biodiversity and the alternative social experiments it provided. The importance of the Zapatista resistance goes beyond the immediate survival of these settlements in their special environment. It extends to the world community that has yet to learn the finite limitations of resources and the implications for survival of human and animal species. As yet, the governing elites of Mexico and the powerful countries that force them to cede their national wealth to the world market cannot tolerate the Zapatista alternative.

Earle and Simonelli end their book with the image of the *topes*—bumps built into roads that slow traffic—with which they began their journey into the jungle. But this time the *topes* serve as a metaphor for the ever-present fear of the military and paramilitary troops, imprisonment, hunger, and the deprivation of medical and social services that inhibit development. As the Zapatistas attempt to overcome these deficiencies with their own resources and strategic assistance from international agencies, they are constructing an alternative form of survival in a world dominated by neoliberal market forces.

June Nash
April 15, 2004

Preface and Acknowledgments

THIS BOOK IS PART of a new series in experimental ethnography, and it is also the ethnography of an experiment, that of the Zapatista (r)evolution. It is the chronicle of a social movement seeking a path through the murky waters of twenty-first-century civilization so that our civilization might endure. We, as authors, have been privileged to be scribes of this process, and you, as readers, see it unfold here as you walk with our Zapatista *compañeros* and with us. Hence, you are witness to the day-to-day struggles of the Movement, to the hardship of building a new society. At the same time, you are witness to the process of cultural analysis, the experience of research, and the construction of the text that tells the story. You are with us as we spend six years of summer, winter intersession, and spring breaks going back and forth to Mexico, returning to the United States and our day jobs, feeling a little like migrant laborers. You are with us also through the process of writing, which as academics we do between classes and in the quiet hours just before dawn. You are with us as we arrive in Chiapas for the first time, and you are with the Zapatistas as they give us a logical point in history to conclude this portion of their tale.

This type of book would not have been possible without the support of those at AltaMira Press. We want to thank them for allowing us the space in which to solve some of our anthropological dilemmas in these pages: to produce a work that is scholarly while at the same time capturing the readers, drawing them into the experience, and, we hope, converting them in some small way to the dream that is *Zapatismo*. We wrap narrative in theory in the introduction, weave history through the early chapters, debate community development in the middle, and dream a shared future in the end.

Part of our task was to write this book as coauthors while often 2,000 miles apart. It is constructed of narrative produced from fieldwork that was at times done together and at other times separately. And often, as was our intent, we view the same events through different lenses. The varied voices of our community colleagues are present in the telling, and we are scribes of their lives. But, as occurs in all ethnography, we also tell the tale through our own eyes. Bear with us, then, as we narrate and analyze with many voices, a tale told singly, jointly, from within and from without, a spiraling caracol tale.

FROM JEANNE SIMONELLI

At dusk on December 15, 2003, my daughter Rachel and I lit a candle in the Escuela Autónoma Miguel Hidalgo, which was not an unusual act. The electricity was out in the school again, though it was working in the rest of the Cerro Verde enclave. But the candle wasn't for light this time; the candle was for hope, the candle was for thanks, and the candle was in memory of my Dad, Antonio Simonelli, to whom the school is dedicated and who died at dusk on December 15, 2000.

You will have to read this book to find out why a school in a tiny Zapatista community in the jungle of Chiapas, Mexico, is dedicated to a crotchety old Italian American, but at the outset I'd like to thank my Dad for making a lot of this possible. First, if he weren't a southern Italian male, good of heart, but with a desire to control everything, my Mom wouldn't have shouted *Basta!* at least twice a day, and the Zapatista cry would not have resonated so deep into my soul. Second, if he had not been so frugal all his life, mine would not now be as comfortable as it is, granting me the ability to travel and be involved in the experiment and experience described in these pages. So thanks, Dad. And thanks, Mom, for giving me the love of learning from other people's lives, beginning as a child with you in Puerto Rico in 1958. And thanks for passing, in 1998, leaving this earth as I stood on a San Cristóbal street and the thunder cracked and the rain fell, breaking one of the century's most deadly droughts, and I cried for you as I cried for the people of Tierra y Libertad.

And thanks to my daughter Rachel, who came to Chiapas to see what it was her crazy mother was doing there and came back, again and again, finding her own heart and her own scholarship as she did. And to my older daughter Elanor, whose life paralleled that of one of the women you will meet. We share the miracle of birth and the hope that our children and grandchildren might someday be friends in a better world. To Linda Randall, for keeping the home fires burning and the Springsteen playing back in Oneonta.

Thanks also to Lynn Payment, whose attention to and love of my parents and dogs made it possible for me to travel. I'll see you again on the other side of the blood river.

So many others are part of this story: Kate O'Donnell, without whom I would never have returned to or been thrown out of Mexico; Janet Schwartz, who brought Duncan and I together at Tonina; and Miguel Rolland de las Casas and Josefa Hernandez Perez, who helped confirm that all we were seeing was real. To Samuel García Ruíz and the Iglesia Autóctona for bringing me back into faith; Federico Gallardo Anaya and the other Frayba lawyers whose work, names, and picture eased our way through some difficult situations; to the Christines, Eber and Kovic, for their excellent fieldwork, analyses, and continuing moral support; and to Louanna Furbee for sharing a space and a few good journeys.

Mil gracias to June Nash, whose model of research and advocacy remains an inspiration to much of this work and whose San Cristóbal house became the research center she always hoped it would be. To the others I met there, Frank, Patty and Jan, as well. To John Ross, for all of his good words.

Thanks, too, to my own early mentors, Rich Pailes and Joe Whitecotton, who brought me into a love of Mexico and field research. Especially to Rich, whose generosity to a single mom during his own field program opened the door to my flexibility in constructing student programs. To the students of the Hartwick–Oneonta and the Wake Forest–University of Texas at El Paso programs who were part of the story and companions on the trail, sharing the amazement of discovery, learning, and even the deadly bat disease.

And, of course, to the four-leggeds of my life—my beloved dog Josa, to whom I bid farewell with each trip to Chiapas and who like Amarante Cordova was still there when I returned. After seventeen years, she has finally made her journey, joining O'Ryan, who went before. To Gandalf, Prozac, and Ofelia, who continue to provide fur therapy and motivation for walking and contemplation and who wonder if I'll ever stay home.

And to my fieldwork partner, Duncan, without whose good humor, language skills, great driving, analytical mind, and boundless energy this journey would not have been possible.

FROM DUNCAN EARLE

I recall with vivid clarity the scene, some years back, when my father, George Earle, decided he would come and visit me in the field and do some painting when I was doing research on community development impacts around the Lake Atitlan region. I was balancing a field school and my own research errands, one of which was a visit to Momostenengo to spend some time with my friend Andres Xiloj, the man who had given so much illumination to Barbara and Dennis Tedlock some years earlier. With me came some videographers who were putting together a series on the Maya and who I was getting to support Don Andres's new religious cargo in exchange for an interview. He was ill and had divined, as a K'iche' priest-shaman, that one of the obstacles had to do with me, that I had to make a *costumbre*, a ritual offering, to certain deceased diviners in the neighborhood where I first learned about such things, for his and my sake. This meant a trip well into the interior to the house of my *compadre* Lucas, so I brought my father along. I was nervous and self-conscious to show my nonreligious father all I was up to as the shaman's apprentice at an altar out in the cornfield. But when it was done and we watched the candles burn down, he said to me, "Son, you have penetrated the veil." He meant that in all his travels in Mexico in the 1930s—his time with Cardenas, Rivera, and painting and his many colorful adventures—he had not really grasped what the indigenous side of Mexico was all about. However, this chick of the brood picked up where he left off. As he continues to paint and write at ninety, I have to let him know I would not have done so without him. Or my now long-passed-on mother, Patricia Day, who gave me the gift of Spanish as her last unselfish act to me, a skill that has made what I do possible, every day. *Alla y aca.*

I have to thank Bill Isbell for first exposing me to Mesoamerica, Robert Carmack for taking me into the K'iche' project and teaching me the wiles of ethnohistory and social theory at the State University of New York at Albany, Lyle Campbell for exposing me to Maya linguistics along with John Mondlock, Peter Furst for opening my eyes to the vast universe of Mesoamerican imagery and meaning, and Billy Jean Isbell for showing me how meaning and power do their dance. Many other Albany people were also influential, but none more than Gary Gossen, who retrained me as a Chiapas ethnographer, taught me Tzotzil, and expected me to do whatever was necessary, even if it was getting him back from the fiesta. Many ideas of this and other works have been inspired by what Gary thinks.

The folks in anthropology at Dartmouth, Vanderbilt, and Texas A&M all put up with me for varying periods, and a thanks to them for it. Thanks also go to the Institute for Latin American Studies at the University of Texas at Austin, for their semester of support when I needed to think, and especially to the University of Texas at El Paso, where I hung my sombrero for six years, allowing me to continue my Chiapas research along with work on the other border, where I live. A nod is in order for my colleagues Howard Campbell, David Carmichael, and Josiah Heyman, who put up with me.

The Tedlocks, mentioned previously, have always been an inspiration, and I especially love the sensitivity by which Dennis not only brought my *compadre* to life but Tuncan as well. It has taken me a lifetime to understand it with clarity—after all, how often do people get to share their field sites with the pros? Along the way, many others have helped me intellectually develop: Michael Kearney, Carlos Velez-Ibañez, Jim Greenberg, Jan Rus, Robert Wasserstrom, Jan de Vos, Andre Aubrey, Neil Harvey, Christine Eber, Tim Knab, Chip Morris, Robert Laughlin, Shannan Mattiace, Gabriela Vargas, Igor Ayora, June Nash, the late Nancy Modiano, Kasuyasu Ochiai, and too many more to list them all. And thanks, Louanna, for telling us and our eager students about the miraculous saint baby. To my students, who believed and saw for themselves.

Everybody Jeanne mentioned, almost without exception, are people I knew or now know and care about, thanks to her, and she does this so much better, but thanks again. I had a great time traveling with her daughter Rache, over more *topes* than we would like to remember in a rental car with bad brakes. I want to mention and thank my two children, Maya and Tim, who have put up with much absentee Daddy in the making of this research. Also thanks to Judy Marcus, who has given so much so that I could be in the field. But biggest and most heartfelt thanks must go to Jeanne Simonelli, whose undaunted will, quick eye, and midnight plane fare surfing don't even begin to describe the talents, networks, ideas, and inspirations she brings into this partnership, not to mention a knack for turning a phrase, and many, many friends who care about her. I'm one.

Doing good fieldwork is time consuming, exhilarating, and exhausting. It is also expensive, and together we would like to thank all those who provided financial support for our forays into the jungle. A number of small grants through the State University College at Oneonta provided initial funding. Wake Forest University and especially the Archie Fund, the ProHumanitate Fund, the Reynolds Fund, the Mellon Foundation, and the Office of International Education were all contributors. The Carr Fund in Oneonta and the Taylor Foundation provided support for actual projects, backing the promise of autonomy. Editorial assistance was provided by Ginny Moench. Robert Vidrine worked with the maps, photos, and other artwork. He also solved uncountable computer problems, participating in an almost intergalactic hard-drive scan. Charlie Winters stepped in at the last minute to produce clean black-and-white prints from our gummy color negatives.

Thanks also to all the naysayers who strengthened our resolve in what we were doing, a theme you will see running through the Zapatista experience: the National Science Foundation for its critique of methodology, anonymous reviewers, and the Left for giving up on the promise and force of the Movement.

For all who bought cookies, embroideries, baby bibs, and honey, we're not done yet. Look for us on eBay with Café Comal or stuck in a ditch, singing hymns and show tunes, *cumbias* and *corridos*, on the road to Reality and to a rebellion the world cannot afford to lose.

But most of all, we want to thank the people of Chiapas, whose names and locales we have changed in this text, for having taught us, with humor and patience, about hope and life and sustainable dreams. For all the children, especially Natalia and Marta, and Cari. For the women, Camila and Alma and Ana. For Luz, beautiful Luz, with a strength that has sustained her family for decades; for Rodrigo and Davíd, growing from youth to elder; for

Ramón and Alejandro and Linda, for giving their lives to the Movement; to Don Antonio and Doña Dominga for their lives, their stories and their spirit; to Francisco and Carmen and their families for bringing us into this and for the best damn use of cookie money we've ever seen. To Ariana and Arturo, for sticking with it and with us. For Miguel and Veronica and the other pioneers of Ojo de Agua who trusted in the Mero Lucas from the beginning, twenty-five years ago. To all the others unnamed here, for their time and guidance, sweet coffee, and hospitality.

Special thanks, *koloval*, to Martín, for believing us, believing in us, and for opening the door. And finally, to the Zapatista rebellion for its continuing hope, insight, and incorporation of the absurd.

Winston-Salem, North Carolina
El Paso, Texas
April 15, 2004

Introduction: Lenses and Visions

THE ROAD TO RESEARCH

THERE ARE 113 *TOPES* ON THE ROAD between the colonial city of San Cristóbal de las Casas, Chiapas, Mexico, and the Maya archaeological site of Tonina, just fifty kilometers to the north. One hundred and thirteen concrete obstructions across the highway, designed to slow you down. There are round *topes*, flat *topes*, ribbed *topes*, wide *topes*, high *topes*, reversed *topes*, and if you try to pass through Chiapas oblivious to her ongoing struggle, your heart will be wrenched out, bent, folded, punctured, and you will slow down and see beyond the curtain of tropical flowers and the pyramids and palaces of the Maya past.

At first glance, these speed bumps seem like a good idea, protection for the pedestrians from the neighboring villages, keeping the visitor hordes from careening down the highways, hurrying in search of the true Chiapas. But in the absence of tourists, the *topes* are simply one more obstacle in the road, another illusion of assistance, like the basketball courts and empty clinic buildings found in nearby pueblos, gifts from a government trying to look constructive. They stand as a new round of stone monuments in a land where the stones are guardian to a complex and ancient history, concrete replies to living questions of human need.

Add to these constructions another type of *tope*, handcrafted by the communities[1] themselves from piles of debris, the excreta of government projects building freeways for nonexistent trade. These obstructions represent a somewhat futile attempt to gain control over what is passing through their previously isolated hamlets, a way of articulating their own perception of what it is they need. That need finally exploded into the Zapatista rebellion in 1994, startling Mexico and the rest of the world.

Ten years have passed since the chilly New Year's dawn when the world awakened to find an indigenous rebellion under way in Chiapas—Mexico's southernmost state. Coinciding with the signing of the North American Free

1

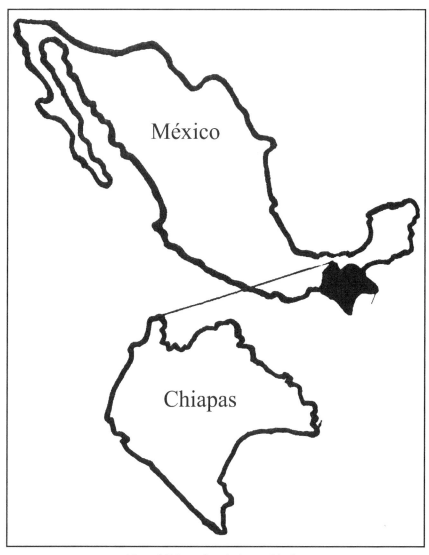

Map of Chiapas in relation to Mexico

Trade Agreement (NAFTA), the rebellion responded to long-standing pat-terns of exploitation and discrimination in this region of rich land and poor people. After ten days of fighting in 1994, a cease-fire led to stillborn peace ac-cords in 1996. Since that time, the struggle has merged low-intensity warfare with outright killing fields, exemplified by the massacre of forty-five women, children, and men in the village of Acteal in December 1997 and the breakup of four autonomous municipalities in 1998. A massive and intimidating mili-tary presence and a harassment policy against foreign activists and scholars

Map of principal cities of Chiapas

also characterized the height of the overt hostilities. Most recently, the shape of conflict has changed, as the Zapatistas work toward autonomy and democracy.

In spite of the continuing hostilities, in early January 1999 anthropologist Duncan Earle was asked to serve as an impromptu guide for American students traveling in Chiapas. The group was part of a service-learning program, jointly taught by Jeanne Simonelli and Kate O'Donnell, representing two small colleges in Oneonta, New York. As the travelers wound down the highway toward the ancient Maya complex at Tonina, they constructed a mental "topology" of speed bump shapes, counting and classifying, masking their apprehension about being in Chiapas at this point in history. As with so much else here, some *topes* were well worked and obvious, others hidden or insidious.

Earle is a cultural anthropologist with a twenty-five-year background of study linking the ancient Maya to their present-day descendants. On this trip, he provided an in-depth analysis of Tonina, a classic-era military outpost guarding the entrance to the Chiapas Cañadas region. It was a warm winter morning, and the students wandered freely, exploring the labyrinths and tunnels into the pyramid. On its top, Earle and Simonelli looked across the broad Ocosingo valley to where a once-small, contemporary army post had burgeoned into a huge military installation. It was a monster *tope*, replete with military and immigration checkpoints, blocking passage into the deeper canyons, much as Tonina had done 1,000 years before. The base was a legacy of the massive offensive that followed on the heels of the EZLN[2] uprising.

"So what ever possessed you to bring students here?" Duncan Earle asked Jeanne Simonelli, referring to the eight young women enjoying an exclusive visit to the archaeological zone. Tourism in Chiapas was way down.

"Trying to help Kate teach," she answered. "But I've begun fieldwork off on the other side of the state, near the Guatemalan border. I'm interested in community-authored development, and the ways in which NGOs have helped or hindered the process."

Duncan looked interested. "Where are you working?" he asked.

Jeanne shrugged. "You wouldn't know it. It's hours from the city of Comitán. The Rio Chayote valley."

Duncan broke into a broad grin. "I did my dissertation research there, almost twenty years ago. I studied cultural logic and ecology in community development. I know the region well."

Startled by the coincidence, Jeanne pulled out a map of Chiapas. Duncan smiled knowingly. There is no coincidence among the Maya, only seemingly serendipitous synchronicity. They sat down out of the wind on the backside of the pyramid and spread the map on the ground.

"There," said Duncan, indicating a place a few miles from the hamlet of Santa Elena, near a point where the Rio Chayote made a fast tumble toward the Guatemalan border.

Simonelli traced the river about twenty kilometers north, into the jungle foothills. "There," she said, indicating a region near the town of Rio Jade. "These are communities in resistance," she added.

"And these are a pro-government group of Tzoztil Maya immigrants," said Earle. "I haven't been back in ten years. I wonder how they are weathering the rebellion."

Thus, as is often the case in the field of anthropology, a research project was born, evolving out of mutual interests and complementary talents. Earle had easy rapport with the people and a great facility with languages. Simonelli had good organizational skills and the ability to scare up funding in the least likely places. A working partnership was the perfect solution to the problems of intellectual isolation and loneliness that often arise in the field, especially when complicated by the intricacies of doing ethnography in a conflict zone and the ambiguity of memory and senses.

This book is a product of that partnership, begun with the collaboration of the people of three communities in the Rio Chayote valley. The work is an examination of the daily life of indigenous campesinos who have, at this writing, survived over ten years of rebellion and resistance: children born into resistance, youths who became elders as they struggled to maintain their lives in relative peace without sacrificing their social and political values. As ethnography, it unites the details of life in Zapatista resistance communities in Chiapas with an analysis of their community development efforts. While focusing largely on two communities, Cerro Verde and Tulan, and Tierra y Libertad, the autonomous municipality they belong to, as the fieldwork and analysis continued during a five-year period, we were privileged to participate in the evolution of Zapatista civil organization. Thus, as Tierra y Libertad became part of a multimunicipal Junta de Buen Gobierno, surrounded by the symbolic and actual infrastructure of its related Caracol, the focus widened to include these regional changes. In addition, the work also provides comparative information from Ojo de Agua, a non-Zapatista community in the same region, and adds a look at neighboring settlements and settlement neighbors with contrasting visions of Mexico's future and their own.

In the final analysis, this book is a testimony to the strength and hope of Zapatismo, a twenty-first-century experiment in democracy and development. Like the ancient Maya ancestors for whom the sea was a dreamtime boundary between two creations, the Zapatista vision described in the following pages also crosses a sea that separates two distinct worlds. It leaves behind a place bounded by a 500-year legacy of exploitation and poverty and moves toward one where the rural economy is viable and the dream of self-sufficiency is gradually becoming reality.

UNDERSTANDING THE ZAPATISTA REBELLION

There have been a myriad of books about the Zapatistas and the conflict in Chiapas, many of these exhaustive analyses tying social, political, and economic conditions to the current conflict. For instance, Collier and Quartiello's *Basta!* (1994) is a comprehensive background to the rebellion. Neil Harvey's *The Chiapas Rebellion* (1998) provides a detailed chronicle of the struggle for land, and June Nash's *Mayan Visions* (2001) is an exhaustive survey of the attempt to achieve indigenous autonomy.

Some of these works, including Lynn Stephen's *Zapata Lives!* (2002) and Shannan Mattiace's *To See with Two Eyes* (2003), simplify the areas of contradiction and ambiguity surrounding the Zapatista movement. For instance, Mattiace gives the impression that indigenous nationalism in Mexico arose in large part after the 1994 rebellion. This echoes the increasing number of analyses that claim that class issues were replaced with a social movement based on ethnicity, seeking to pigeonhole the Zapatistas on one side of a dichotomy that in-depth field research does not support.

Other popular books have told of the activities of leaders or large groups, major participants on all sides of the conflict. John Ross's *Rebellion from the Roots* (1995) and *The War against Oblivion* (2000) are comprehensive and readable pieces of investigative journalism. We are introduced to the charismatic Zapatista spokesperson Subcomandante Insurgente Marcos, to the now-retired radical Catholic bishop Samuel Ruíz García, and Mexican presidents Salinas and Zedillo, all key figures in the story. Andres Oppenheimer's *Bordering on Chaos* (1996) places the conflict into the context of Mexico's financial woes and describes events as reported to him by official sources in the Mexican and American governments. These are the histories of presidents and subcomandantes, of bishops and organizations, locked in lethal rivalry.

In contrast, the goal of *Uprising of Hope* is to be an easily readable ethnography of how these larger struggles play out on the ground in the lowland jungle, in a place both marginal and critical to the Chiapas revolt, and how they affect families and communities trying to construct a political third space. This is the view from the base, the jungle, the people who live out the day-to-day struggles for a better tomorrow, a Zapatista movement conjoining class, ethnicity, caste, and faith in unity but also dividing it up. Some Zapatistas, within the same communities, are very traditional Mayas, and some are totally Mexicanized, secular or nominal Catholics, and ecumenical Protestants. It is these many roads to Zapatismo that this text explores, identifying a shared set of ideological *topes* that have brought them to the movement. All have some sense of disjuncture from the past, a profound distrust of the government based on repeated betrayals, a hope and faith that life can change with sacrifice to the larger social cause, and a profound love of the campesino smallholder lifestyle. The complementary contradictions are evident in Cerro Verde and Tulan, where the elders and the children clamor for Tojolobal Maya tales, the young adults ask for copies of *La Jornada* and *Proceso*, bringing the latest liberal news, and the adolescents want revolutionary folk singers, Zapatista heroes, and the latest soccer gear. In this presentation, the complexity of Zapatismo is revealed in the actions and stories of community members who toggle between ethnic and class identification in flexible response to time and place.

ETHNOGRAPHY AND CHIAPAS SCHOLARSHIP

A rich ethnographic tradition surrounds scholarship about Chiapas. As the fledgling field of anthropology developed in a number of universities, including Harvard, Columbia, Chicago, and the University of California, researchers from these institutions carved up the world, sending their students out to work in areas where their own interests lay. Chiapas was no exception. The Harvard-Chiapas project, under the direction of Evon Vogt, established a base of operations early on. The project produced a quantity of U.S.-written ethnographies about the Tzotzil–Tzeltal Maya area, including more than 100 master's theses and doctoral dissertations. Students learned indigenous languages and set about recording oral histories and analyzing social and cultural patterns in the highland communities surrounding San Cristóbal. These works supplemented numerous historical and ethnographic studies by Mexican researchers (see Rus 2003; Vogt 1994). Much of the work focused on aspects of Maya society that were not directly involved with the outside world and often reflected how Mayas were different from Mexicans.

In time, the field widened slightly as these students finished their dissertations, got jobs, married, and brought students and spouses back to Chiapas to work in other areas. As the discipline of anthropology changed in response to world conditions and conflicts, the focus of work also grew. The community studies of the 1950s gave way to analyses of ecological and political-economic relationships. Women researchers began writing about women's roles in an emerging global economy. The number of academic programs training anthropologists to work in Mexico and Central America also burgeoned as the first wave of anthropologists trained their own students at their own universities. A second wave of researchers began working at a time when Central American conflicts were escalating. Their studies were informed by conditions of war, genocide, and movements of people across borders in the wake of repressive and murderous regimes. The growing conflict in Chiapas stimulated a further round of investigations as newcomers joined the veterans studying the region under difficult conditions. Much of the new efforts engaged the conflict as part of their analyses.

While extensive, some of the fifty-year harvest of ethnography was restricted in scope. First, it focused on highland Maya who remained close to their traditions, both culturally and geographically. Second, as women emerged as important participants in the growing struggle, many of the resulting ethnographies dealt almost exclusively with the lives of women. Notable are Brenda Rosenbaum's *With Our Heads Bowed* (1993) and Christine Eber's *Women and Alcohol in a Highland Maya Town* (2000). This was an important addition to anthropological scholarship, but one with its own limitations since it downplayed the inherent complementarity in gender relations that was the positive side of Maya household life.

In *Uprising of Hope*, we try to fill certain gaps in the ethnographic literature by focusing on Maya migrants to the lowland jungles as they live out resistance, develop their communities, and seek autonomy a generation away from their traditions. We add to work by Hernández Castillo and Levya, both of which provide rich ethnographic data related to Lacandon rain forest colonization.[3] Moreover, we work to provide a balanced gender analysis, product of the access to information facilitated by our research partnership. What we do not try to do is rewrite the excellent and comprehensive analyses of Chiapas and the Chiapas conflict that already exist in several languages. Where appropriate, we direct the reader to them.

It is also important to note that this work is not the story of how all jungle communities have fared. In the autonomous municipality of Tierra y Libertad alone, there are forty resistance communities representing forty variations of an official Zapatista theme. We focus on three groups, each different from the other, highlighting the diverse routes and development styles that they have followed. In addition, the research process represents a coming to a new and renewed conscience on the part of the authors. Months of fieldwork in Chiapas erased personal skepticisms over the possibility of self-sufficiency and the viability of the rural economy, reservations intensified by the outright criticism of colleagues who see what we report as a fairy-tale construction imposed from the outside. It is only after years of conversation, observation, and the amused but firm guidance of our community partners that we are able to present a dissenting view of community development potential. This analysis counters the critique and criticism of the "tired left" and the impatient pessimism of some scholars of the region and much of the discipline. The vision of hope through autonomy that lies on the horizon on the far side of an ancient path penetrates the subtle desperation that our own well-endowed lives can sometimes provoke.

EL HORIZONTE

The quest for autonomy that has permeated the conflict in Chiapas since before the Zapatista uprising is the heart of the rebellion and the hope that dawns on the horizon. Both the EZLN and non-Zapatista civil society have struggled to define and implement alternative models of development and governance using administrative practice derived in part from indigenous customs. In theory, for the poor of Chiapas, autonomy means local and regional control of governance, resource extraction, development processes and projects, education, and health care, in a system that runs largely independent from the official Mexican model. Entwined in this are attempts to build self-sufficiency and revitalize the rural economy. The practice of peaceful civil resistance is a personal, familial, and community commitment to resist political, economic, and social entrapment that comes with participation in specific government programs and practices. This community-level resistance articulates with the work of autonomous municipal and emerging regional rebel governments that act to maintain order and adjudicate disputes based on traditional practices known as *usos y costumbres* [4] while at the same time providing models and training for alternative development and means of control over the development process.

Of all the autonomous administrative bodies in Chiapas, the municipality of Tierra y Libertad appears the most successful in helping communities implement services outside the government system. Though officially and violently dismantled by the PRI (Partido Revolucionario Institucional) government in 1998, the reconstituted leadership of this autonomous municipality continues to work out the practical implications of providing educational, community development, and health services for communities in resistance, including Cerro Verde and Tulan, and were key participants in the Zapatista civil reorganization announced in August 2003. Meanwhile, downriver, a different brand of autonomy prevails in Ojo de Agua as non-Zapatistas struggle with the same regional economic and geopolitical issues. And in Cerro Verde village, the government side of the town's schizophrenic, politically divided *ejido* has discovered its own road to resistance, even as it emerges from its own conflictive history.

THREADS OF INQUIRY

Late one evening in August 2002, Jeanne Simonelli sat with Martín Arevelo, then president of the municipality of Tierra y Libertad, and his young wife Camila. The couple looked exhausted, having just returned from a four-day health-training workshop in the Zapatista stronghold of Realidad. The rain was falling in sheets, drilling the lamina roof, and it was hard to hear Martín as he read aloud in Spanish from the book proposal just given to him. His Spanish was flawless, as was his Maya, and he stopped reading occasionally to translate a word into English. He had an extensive vocabulary but dreadful pronunciation since English speakers were hard to come by in the jungle. He was learning rapidly, improving with periodic practice sessions, as he learned media mild from Duncan (dog) and Brooklynese from Jeanne (dawg). Martín looked up from the four-page document.

"I like this," he said, referring to the Spanish translation of our description of our book project. "I like the idea of telling what it is like to be a mother in a support community or a president of an autónomo. Not another book about Marcos. But I have one reservation, and it has to do with language, with words, which are not always what they seem."

He handed the proposal to Camila and took a drink of the cup of sweet, dark coffee she'd brought him.

"It's like this. Suppose we say the word tierra . . . land. You might think we mean suelo . . . soil. Yet we are not talking about dirt, but about the heart of our life, something sacred, about something you die for. How would you know that you got the meanings right?"

Jeanne took a deep breath, getting the Spanish arranged to tell a story, a story about getting the words wrong in a draft of her book about the Navajo—how it was translated into Navajo before it was published and read to the elders so the people could make corrections to conceptual errors.

Martin was silent. He took the proposal back from Camila, folded it, and put it into an envelope.

"Do you need the answer now?" he asked.

"No, when we come back is fine," lied Jeanne, once again marveling at the shape that twenty-first-century ethnographic fieldwork was taking. The proposal for *Uprising of Hope* disappeared into a process of community and municipal reflection that could take longer than the review process for a refereed journal.

The communities we work with are no longer the benign recipients of anthropological scrutiny. We have been asked to give up part of the control of the research endeavor, to learn and document together, to return with what we write. For some anthropologists, this loss of power has not been accepted easily. Do we study others, or do we learn from them? Do they consent to be part of our researches, or are we given permission to remain in their villages? As much as we would have liked to have a concrete research methodology for this work, ours became an ongoing process of observation, participation, and documentation that continues to this day. In the following chapters, this process of redefinition and negotiation between anthropologist and communities is an important part of the story.

ANALYTICAL LENSES

In addition to detailing the day-to-day efforts of families of families trying to live and work together peacefully in the lowland jungles of Chiapas, *Uprising of Hope* raises theoretical and ethical issues in anthropology. Theoretically, the book focuses on the notion of "agency" and, deriving from this, the act of giving agency to those to be "studied" as a creative response to the colonial experience, of which anthropology was a part. We have helped them build another platform from which they could speak. This perspective means that, methodologically, the authors shared the inquiry process of research with community members. The authors' experience in gaining permission to document and do research in the municipality allows consideration of the complex relationship between anthropological research and informed consent in field settings and between applied research and theoretical analysis, addressing a further anthropological dilemma, namely, can an objective anthropology and advocacy coexist?

A recent debate in anthropology centers on the role of nonanthropologists in the research process and the place of advocacy in anthropology. Gross and

Plattner (2002) maintain that anthropologists are not trained to be advocates and that community members are not adequately trained to be anthropologists. They argue that field research designs cannot be developed with our community colleagues as equal partners because that would "virtually erase the role of training, expertise, theory and methodology in anthropological research." Further, they contend that the "practical issues" of interest to members of a study community fall outside the purview of the "theoretical issues arising from the development of the discipline." We could not disagree more.

Giving agency to those to be "studied" as part of an equal partnership does not mean that we cease doing those things that we are trained to do. In working in Chiapas, it has meant that we bring to the partnership those skills that each of us has and from this derive a modified research design that emphasizes symmetry in the research endeavor and attention to community concerns surrounding how and when information should be shared. Moreover, our shared practical concerns tie in directly with our theoretical interests.

Gross and Plattner note that "good research can strengthen advocacy." But they say that anthropologists don't have the "wisdom" to advocate. Yet those fields that are traditionally defined as "advocacy disciplines" have learned that our methods of ethnographic research are the only way that they can gain the understanding they need in order to advocate. Anthropology's contribution to the body of knowledge concerning the overall human experience derives from our ability to accurately characterize the intersection of local-level phenomenon with the larger global forces that influence individual daily life. The continuing dilemma lies between doing nothing with our extensive field-based knowledge and doing something that may ultimately be harmful since we fear that we don't have the wisdom. We are able to see the problems but refrain from suggesting solutions, fearing "unintended consequences." Anthropology stands aloof as other disciplines and practitioners adopt our research models and our cultural insights, while we stay in the background often espousing theory incomprehensible to the uninitiated.

To counter this, in doing the work described in this book, we have aimed at praxis, the combination of knowledge, theory, and action. Our involvement in community and municipal discussion and planning provided the opportunity to document autonomous development as a social experiment. The subsequent analysis of these practical expressions of human action informs the construction of theory concerning development and social change. Their continuing real-life practical dilemmas, successes, and failures serve as tests of our theoretical concepts. As social scientists, we seek to clarify the process of autonomous development while allowing analytic space for our partners to speak to the same issue. We join concerns over authorial (top-down) development that transforms knowing subjects into preconceived objects to be "helped," with ways to empower those community voices. Encapsulated in these concerns are the academy's ideas about informed consent.

On college campuses, institutional review boards oversee the legal and ethical aspects of research. Using a "one size fits all" model, the researcher is asked to obtain a written informed consent from all those who participate in research. We are often expected to produce in advance a list of questions we will ask those who consent to be a part of our "study." Each of these "subjects" is asked to sign a waiver that explains the intent of the work and assures them that at any time they can decide to withdraw from the project. Derived from clinical trials, one purpose is to protect the unsuspecting from unethical behavior on the part of the researcher. A second is to protect the institution from possible litigation. Many anthropologists use modified, verbal versions of this process, arguing that written documents in politically volatile situations and among semiliterate people simply won't work. Moreover, individual agreements in collectively governed communities are not part of the local cultural logic.

In our work in Chiapas, communities saw it in their interest to help the research process because it helped in their larger project in life. In the final analysis, we received informed permission to be scribes of portions of their social experiments, but not until we were made fully aware of the responsibilities associated with our collaboration. At the same time, community members began to learn methods of research that continue to be useful to them (Simonelli and Earle 2003b).

Zapatistas March for World Peace, January 1, 2003

As the Zapatistas reached consensus concerning regional and local development in late July 2003, the EZLN announced sweeping changes in their external and fiscal policy as part of this internal reorganization. Spearheaded by the regional councils of the autonomous indigenous municipalities, they were striving to achieve a more equitable and effective development plan, and they spoke out about it. It's not often that the recipients of development and humanitarian aid speak out about the well-intentioned, uneven, and mission-directed assistance that arrives to "help" them. As spokesperson for the autonomous councils, in mid-July 2003, Subcomandante Insurgente Marcos provided a five-part critique of development aid, stating that

> the Zapatista communities are the responsible parties in their projects (more than a few NGOs can testify to this), they make them go, make them produce and in this way make improvements for the collectivity, not just for individuals. . . . With the passing of the Aguascalientes[5] there also dies the "Cinderella syndrome" [an attitude of deprecating charity; providing castoffs to the poor relations] of some civil society types and the paternalism of some national and international NGOs. . . . At least they die for the Zapatista communities, that, from this moment onward the communities will not receive leftovers nor permit the imposition of projects.

As will be seen in later chapters, for the first time the results of our synergistic reflections and methods were becoming visible beyond the late-night discussions in the Cerro Verde and Tulan kitchens in specific policies revealed during the reorganization. Our prior views were both confirmed and advanced.

THE DIALECTIC OF CONQUEST AND THE ZAPATISTA VISION

Many scholars of the ancient and living traditional Maya have difficulty placing them in the context of their ongoing oppression by the structures that were introduced in the colonial period and remain today in a transformed state. Other scholars have dedicated their attention to the exploited state of the Maya without much understanding of their local cultural logics and Mesoamerican cosmovision. These camps are often at odds with each other, one focused on culture and the other on socioeconomic and political relations. The Maya live in both worlds, and understanding them means understanding both their culture and the history of their sociopolitical relations and current economic position.

No understanding of the lives of the people of Chiapas is complete without acknowledging the historical experiences that connect the pre-Hispanic past to the current realities of indigenous life. The most defining historical experience for them is Conquest, not simply as an event or an invasion but as a new political condition of their "collective enterprise of survival" (Farris 1984). Conquest as a dialectic between the power and culture of those who conquer and those who resist becomes an ongoing process, a tension as yet unresolved between the legitimacy of the first inhabitants and the desire for profit and gain by those who have invaded. The invading culture seeks justification for its position of superiority, while the invaded one seeks techniques of resistance and reinterpretation of the dominant system that gives them a more equal position, rejecting the legitimacy of their conquerors. As Scott (1985) notes, the "weapons" that the weak can marshal rarely involve direct confrontation, and that only when other avenues are exhausted. Most of the resistance to conquest in Mesoamerica has been oblique and subtle, but the struggle continues today, and in that sense the conquest is ongoing and permeates social relations in indigenous areas.

Racism is still prominent in much of Mexico. It derives some of its power from the failure to resolve the contradiction between the legitimacy of the preconquest peoples and their encounter with the "civilized" Spanish Europeans, who sought legitimacy for their acts in religion and law. Any in-depth understanding of the current people must take into account this history and its imprint not just on the living indigenous people but also on the nonindigenous, the Ladino or mestizo. Like a dark secret revealed in the procedures of therapy, the national psyche confronts the de facto "*seguimiento*," the continuing sagas of the structures and processes of conquest, and the *llanto*, the call of pain of those oppressed by this conquest. With the uprising of Zapatismo and the new Mayanism of the indigenous in Guatemala, both nations have had to confront their "Indian question." For the indigenous, of course, it was always the Ladino question: how the "naturals" could get along with them without getting killed or beaten. Chiapas appeared out of the obscurity of the regions of periphery and internal colonialism. The deadly angel of free trade and the condescending repudiation of a more socialist Mexican past by what had been its standard-bearing political party was for many a clear betrayal. Zapatismo spoke with a revitalization message evoking Emiliano Zapata, that hero of the glorious Mexican revolutionary past, that defender of the indigenous claim to land and liberty, then as now in Chiapas. Or so goes the mental equation of the movement.

Claiming revolutionary high ground by wrapping autonomy in the Mexican flag and calling forth the names and ideals of the legitimate national political ancestors for validation of the cause was an astute political line for the Zapatistas to take, in a movement so much about the hidden and the silenced. A revitalized national vision is a way to appropriate the symbolic icons and enduring concepts of the revolution and place Indianness at the center of this whole question of where we place ourselves with regard to the nation's ancestral heroes and the revolutionary Constitution. It calls forth ancestral apotheosized demigods. Zapata becomes a postrevolutionary santo, with Bishop Samuel Ruiz the "pastor," or shepherd. Marcos is the son, the Jesus figure in the posture of sacrifice, who dies, yearly and by degrees, in the mud and damp of the jungle for the sake of the Zapatista campesinos. In all this, Mexico, as a nation, woke up to its own racist past and the legitimacy of an illegal, politically autonomous revolt given the 500 years of abuse and colonialist control.

Nationalistic ideology allows inclusion, opening bridges of solidarity between the indigenous and the mestizo and other Europeanized peoples rather than declaring an ideology of ethnicity. To do so would have been inherently exclusionary and suspect of separatist interests along the lines of an "Indian nation," a terror to Mexican nationalism. Within this comes the whole global engagement, where sibling-like political kinship, *hermanamiento*, is promoted between communities and international supporters of the communities, the framework for direct linkages between people inside and supporters of the *autónomo* movement. This kind of recruitment of diverse sites of political alignment and solidarity can be available to a movement only if it has the ability to speak on a larger scale, even at the universal one. The voice of legitimacy from below, from the native people and others whose lives are tied to the earth, has a deep and powerful resonance with the people in the hyperinformed world of the modern.

The revindication, the return of the voice of the Other colonized by invasion, is salutory and relevant. It is the dialectic of conquest and resistance, and Zapatismo has made this utterly clear and utterly relevant, as they weave together *usos y costumbres* with resistance to NAFTA, globalization at the expense of the rural, and critiques of neoliberalism at many levels. With this interesting trope of nation in step with revindication, underwritten by ideologies of Christian universalism and indigenous egalitarianism, Zapatismo has been able to leap onto the global stage to propose an alternative model of resistance and an alternative model of society that all can in turn appropriate and make their own. They offer us hope.

SELF-SUFFICIENCY AS RESISTANCE

The struggle for autonomy in rural Chiapas is as much an actual struggle as a tension between competing worldviews, one that strives for self-sufficiency while the other protests that the rural economy is inefficient, irrational, and doomed. Thus, an additional question raised through the text of *Uprising of Hope* is the consideration of how and if informed autonomous control over the development trajectory can become a viable indigenous response to economic conquest and provide an alternative to armed conflict and/or depopulation through out-migration.

Contrary to going wisdom concerning small-scale "postpeasant" producers, the household still remains a viable focus of socially organized production. If true community development is in fact defined by control at the local level, then the control of this global articulation is at the core of the issue. We seek to understand in what ways and at what levels smallholders can affiliate so as to maintain control and yet be buffered from the worst troughs of global capitalism's market fluctuations. The level of individual, family and household, and immediate community is important, but not sufficient given the powers outside these, as we can see from what follows. None of these immediate alliances is capable of creating political space sufficient to endow communities with autonomy. To control articulation impacts (see Kearney 1996, 73–113), as defined by development theorists, one has to have a large organization beyond the face-to-face community, one with a flexible structure within its organization. This larger grouping has the force to confront state power on an insurrectional scale, a sufficient body of troops in arms to take noticeable spaces, if only briefly and symbolically, and to maintain strategic marginal spaces in a pattern that continually suggests threat of arms. A force such as this creates the space for autonomy and by doing so becomes a constraint on hegemonic penetration. While in the real world we recognize that it is impossible to utterly arrest such imposed power, Zapatista representation shifts the terms of the engagement to enhance local control. The *compas* make the space for local autonomous development, both in the sense of what they promote in the numerous support bases and what they prevent or guard against, in the spaces of the political. Autonomous communities receive actual services from Zapatista centers and its politicomilitary organization, but the most important service is the creation of a space to develop. This is precisely why they are very contested spaces.

For the Zapatistas, the space of autonomy is the restraint on the hegemonic appetites of international development. The dual structure of a community and regional organization with a development arm and an army puts them in a position to better dictate the terms of global engagement. We may in fact argue for an entirely economic justifying logic of Zapatismo, quite apart from other virtues in the social, political, or moral realms. The irony of their anticapitalist movement is that capital may be on their side from a rational economic point of view. Moreover, for those who wish to arrest the flow of migration and help promote healthy communities in their current places of rural residence, there is no way to avoid the issue of economic viability of alternative forms of development.

If Zapatismo makes rural smallholder development viable and alternatives politically costly, it seems that here we have a profound motivation to work with them in their efforts, to dialogue with them when we can, and to offer up perspectives based on engagement to further this process of rural health. If articulation theory is about the asymmetries of global relations, then the only way to remedy this is with actual working alternative models. The Zapatistas seem to have one, and they are not alone in recognizing its value.

As Robert Netting (1993) has shown in his seminal study of small household-based landholding groups, "The characteristics of smallholder agricultural system . . . violate the conventional wisdom and contradict the industrial model of development shared by both socialists and capitalists" (321). Though the economic logic of scale would doom the small landholder as irrational and inefficient, Netting's extensive survey of smallholders around the globe pointed out that if efficiency is measured in terms of productivity of land, smallholders are in fact more efficient:

> Productivity per unit of land is inversely related to farm size. Smallholders use their fields more frequently and produce larger yields than larger landholders in the same environment and with the same technologies and crops . . . it is to the smallholder's advantage to produce in a more diversified, continuous, skilled labor-demanding manner in order to make fullest use of more restricted resources. (Netting 1993, 332)

In addition, Netting contends that these systems are more sustainable, rely on largely renewable resources, are a more efficient use of generally available labor, and tend to promote greater social equity. He concludes that the industrial model of agriculture is inappropriate for many areas of the world because of "its technical rigidity, its capital costs and labor savings, its energy inefficiency, its tendency to degrade natural resources, and its separation of ownership, management and labor." By contrast, smallholders "achieve high production, combine subsistence and market benefits, transform energy efficiently, and encourage practices of stewardship and conservation of resources" (Netting 1993, 320).

Most relevant to the Zapatista case is Netting's notion of power as expressed in autonomy, serving as a basis for a preferred form of life and ultimately as a goal of an alternative community development model. "Smallholders the world around emphasize their freedom to chart their activities and goals independently, to be their own bosses. Such autonomy as economic actors brings both market rewards and personal satisfaction" (Netting 1993, 332).

Such was the case in Cerro Verde in August 2003. The *comisariado* was worried. As titular head of the Cerro Verde *ejido*, it was his job to anticipate problems that might affect all 900 village resident/*ejido* members. The rains were a good month late, and everyone was in for trouble, he reasoned. Even though recent changes in land tenure law meant most of the *ejido*'s land was now privately titled, traditional practice dictated that they were still a landholding community, and he was its elected leader. He decided to test his authority, ordering each *ejidatario* to put an extra hectare of land in milpa.[6] Everybody pitched in a day or two to get the fields cleared and planted. The late rains meant that the corn would be late to harvest. All the villages would have to buy a little corn late in the year, when it was more expensive. A few extra hectares of corn, and Cerro Verde would have something to sell locally when the rest of the valley was out.

As a group of land-rich smallholders, they had the flexibility to make tactical changes in cropping strategies, something that the absentee landholders upriver could never do. Even though the *ejido* was politically divided, there was a unifying effect in the decision.

"Everyone decided it was a good idea, even the Zapatistas," said the *comisariado*. "Even those crazies, in resistance, like my own brother."

Netting quotes numerous authors who reached similar conclusions about the benefits of smallholder farming both in economic terms and in life-quality terms. "Everyone who has done careful research on farm size, residency of agricultural landowners, and social conditions in the rural community finds the same relationship: as farm size and absentee ownership increase, social conditions in the local community deteriorate" (Netting 1993, 333).

Case studies such as Netting's are contrary to the prevailing development ideology that says that bigger is better, or what E. F. Schumacher (1973, 66) once called the "idolatry of giantism," a notion reiterated by Scott twenty years later (1999). Writing in 1999, Scott shows how states can and have failed at agrarian change on a grand scale by using 1) an industrial, factory mentality or model in application to agricultural production; 2) a version of "high modernism" thinking through the top-down, scientific "rationalism" of elite experts; and 3) their authority in times of crisis or disorder to attempt to impose a new order. States favor "simplification and legibility" and therefore have sought in many cases to simplify and control agricultural production processes, with generally disastrous results, especially in the less developed areas of the world.

The ideology of large, simplified factories in the fields as rational, efficient, and productive systems, whether through capitalism or socialism, has not succeeded. Scott provides historical evidence for the failure of such models nearly everywhere they are constructed because of the way these efforts create unnatural ecosystems conducive to plagues ultimately requiring pesticides and fertilizers, ultimately becoming a costly and destructive addiction for large-scale agriculture. This design of food production is not geared to quality or nutrition but rather certain narrow conditions of the production process. Like Netting, Scott provides evidence for the relative success of small, traditional plots where complex multicropping favors biodiversity and long-term production.

With scientific research too distanced from the real variables present in the field and founded on neocolonial thinking rather than having positive results, the local people are once again reduced to ignorant obstacles to their own self-betterment and those writing about them considered to be unrealistic dreamers. It is then no surprise that assumptions of high modernism and the idolatry of giantism guide the thinking of the authors of imposed development models, as most recently described in the megadevelopment proposals of Plan Puebla Panamá (PPP), leading us to conclude that they are not concerned with issues of long-term productivity, conservation of resources, sustainability, or quality of life.

As Netting found, families of families, or communities can be an efficient production unit. In resistance communities, a legacy of involvement with Zapatista models is in the ability and inclination to organize and network, so a tiered social infrastructure exists that allows families to articulate with communities, communities with autonomous *municipios*, and *municipios* with regional groups of *municipios*, thus taking advantage of their own version of economies of scale (see Murdoch 2000). This organizational integration allows for the flow of relevant information about a multitude of issues from production to health care and has even begun to serve as the basis for establishing regional cooperative stores for the purchase of commonly consumed household goods. Here, scale efficiencies do not require the shift to centralized ownership, and overall management becomes a negotiated process involving the voices of the primary producers so important for a responsive organization (see Brokensha 1989).

Moreover, in the equation used to figure a point of equilibrium above which production is "profitable," the strengths of small-scale production replace conventional inputs. Household/community-based production includes extensive attention to environmental issues and microenvironmental knowledge that makes "wasteland" arable and labor-intensive conservation efforts practicable. Smallholders can exploit lands that are marginal to agroindustry and deemed inaccessible or useless. And, as noted previously, these production units are infinitely flexible. For instance, in Cerro Verde, lacking adequate roads to take trees to become lumber, the trees were processed into beams on the spot, where they were cut with a handsaw, carried on people's backs some miles to the closest road, and there loaded onto small trucks. Labor, which is abundant, displaces the high capital costs of roads and large trucks, with their attendant specialists, and has the side effect that there is less environmental destruction than roads inevitably bring to rain forest environments. These are producers who envision themselves as lifelong residents in their fragile ecosystem rather than temporary investors and so have a long-term interest in the environmental health and viability of the lands that sustain them (Earle 1984).

Though this work remains labor intensive, it is a rational alternative to cash-heavy capitalist models for countries such as Mexico and states such as Chiapas. To use systems of production and distribution that require expensive infrastructure is foolish at a time when cash continues to be at a premium. And even if financing was possible, indebtedness is not a rational answer, locally or nationally. Community members are still willing to maximize their labor inputs, provided that the returns to their labor, in terms of family and community social organization and a way of life responsive to their social and political values, is part of the profit. As the very recent experiences of Rio Chayote communities will show, the debts associated with borrowing capital can be dangerous when income is irregular and credit is based on the alienability of property.

ZAPATISMO AS AN EXPERIMENT IN ALTERNATIVE LOGIC

One way of looking at the Zapatista movement is as an alternative to industrial stratification and the urban order. The logic of the political class of Mexico, as shared by much of the intelligentsia, is a form of social evolutionism that imagines the rural smallholder as a peasant and peasants as a part of a stage of capitalist development (feudal) that is by its nature "behind" the more modern forms in capitalism. The inevitable conclusion of this approach is the need to transform the archaic form to the modern so that development as a concept comes to mean capitalist penetration. The changing of agrarian forms of "use-value" into the civilized world of "exchange value" so that everyone can work and go shopping, so that urban life can receive its new recruits to come in at the bottom of the power pyramid, and the logic of capital, whether we are pro or con, can finally wipe the feudal from the map.

To consider this semi-Marxian progressive evolutionism as an unerring inevitability is simplistic. Our analysis echoes the work of Bodley (1999), who provides extensive evidence of the virtues of smaller-scale societies in terms of ecological responsiveness and stewardship skills. We add to Netting's concept that smallholding rural production works as an alternative route to economies of scale via organization and flexibility connected with swift information systems as well as certain reshaped and deeply held beliefs, an ideology of hope, a religion of landscape, of the land. Such subject identification, encapsulated in descriptions of solidarity economics (Desmi, AC, 2001), creates identity and an absence of alienation as Marx predicted, only this version is without the trauma associated with putting up with capitalism, urbanism, and its marginalization for the campo exiles. With each passing month, Zapatismo reiterates that paying that price for proletarian consciousness or participation in the fruits of urbanism is too high and, these days, unnecessary.

Envisioning civilization without urbanism is outside the acceptable alternatives of the evolutionist political ideology of the urban, the "North," both left and right. In it, the revolution in information enables rural smallholders to organize across large spaces, organize the delivery of knowledge without migration to cities, and raise global participation capacities without complete stratification. This means the people can maintain the domestic mode of production, the milpa adaptation, while at the same time improving their position in the global system under more independent terms than selling their labor. We have called it capitalism with socialist goals, or social capitalism. But it is also an adaptation especially suited to the uncertain times and high market flux that the future is likely to visit on us all. This is because the highly flexible extended kin community formations we see among the groups we visit are able to shut down, pull back, and live at subsistence levels in bad political or climactic moments or when all their market-dependent production activities are not worth it, as is now the case with coffee. Further, the nature of their demography attaches labor to family. In bad times, the labor is still there to make subsistence work, so vital to the survival of the group.

This adaptation lends itself to a life that integrates the specific and the general, knowledge and skill specialization with the generalized knowledge of milpa and related agricultural and communitarian practices, including such things as the building and care of paths. Zapatista training models seek to produce multiskilled members, as evidenced in their proposal for a training center to "give capacity," as they say, in a center of *capacitación* in skills ranging from auto mechanics to accounting and construction to small-appliance repair. We meet to discuss these proposals in jungle rooms where the computer and the newly hatched turkeys share an office, where machetes and floppy disks are watched over by the living symbols of Maya life. This vision of technology and technical capacity without urbanism or a complete division of labor challenges our ideas about the inevitability of the urban model and its hegemonic understandings of smallholders and their precious lands. It breaks with the historic projection of development as size and imagines an intermediate place that is adaptively "in the middle." Mayas herald the power of the midmost place, the center, where there is balance. It is smallholders who truly live in balance with their ecosystem, who will rescue this planet's last lungs and allow all of us to breathe. Who will hold the wisdom of cultural diversity that both understands the global and cleaves to the traditions and heritage of the local, if not the smallholder, dwelling in the middle? At minimum, all people of conscience should take a good gaze at this experiment and let it proceed, the demonstration model for alternative development. Let us see the fruits of this hope before we declare its impossibility or its supposed anachronism. The responsibility of the ethnographer is to show the local vision. Just as we see those with whom we work as members of less developed societies, they view us as part of the "overdeveloped" world, in the specific sense of too much extraction and inefficient use of energy and the destruction of both ecosystems and cultural diversity. Like the Blob of science fiction fame, overdevelopment continues encroaching on the resources of small-scale peoples, enveloping them in globalized maquiladoras, sweatshops, and urban slums. There is nothing in this that speaks of hope for those whose labor fuels the process.

When our anthropological forebears wrote of a folk–urban continuum, they could not see around the corner, visualize a process that served only to deepen domination and control from without, driving apart the kin unit, the ideology of the collective, the unity of vision, replacing it with the ideology of the individual. An alternative development must have alternative goals, ones other than the growth of capital, even if capital is a means to that end. And should such an alternative be operative, even with faults and defects, we as social scientists should be studying how it works, how it self-regulates, evolves, deals with crises, and serves the interests of its constituents. Zapatismo is a laboratory of social experimentation with alternatives to a dismal probability of urban life. It puts the folk back into the continuum. To hope for its success is to be partisan in favor of humanity in the long run.

THE ROSE-COLORED SHOE: CONTRADICTIONS OF DEVELOPMENT AND HUMANITARIAN AID

While building on the ideas of Netting, Scott, Bodley, and others concerning the continued viability of the small farmer in the face of imposed globalization, a final focus of this book is an analysis of why development efforts designed to help these *campesinos* and their communities often fail. Helping without hurting fragile experiments in community development is a central theme (Earle and Simonelli 2000). Indeed, viewing top-down development as irresponsible social experimentation, our community partners provide a lively commentary about governmental and nongovernmental attempts to provide aid, leading to a series of guidelines for responsible community-authored development (Simonelli and Earle 2003a, 2003b; for details, see chapter 8).

A half century ago, the arrogant, paternalistic model of progress emerging from the top was largely unquestioned as a part of a deep-seated ethnocentric theory of cultural evolution that informed the concept of development (Mead 1961; Nunez del Prado 1973). The transformation of the agrarian way of life was seen as inevitable, if not entirely good, and in this process applied anthropologists were sometimes enlisted to be culturally skilled delivery agents of change. Within this dominant and unitary ideology of modernization, all participants would be able to benefit from the prosperity of the wealthy nations of the industrialized north. Our work in applied anthropology was to clear the path of cultural and social obstacles (Foster 1962; Goodenough 1970). This ideology of "culture as obstacle" penalized people for their own heritage and, in the manner of secular missionaries, sought to "convert" the locals away from aspects of their social organization deemed contrary to their progress. This attitude is still with us in the vast industry of humanitarian and development aid and reflects one of its principal shortcomings (Farmer 2003; Linden 1976).

With the rise of dependency theory and other political-economic critiques of Third World development, including articulation theory, the modernist promise of evolutionary prosperity was replaced by one of conflict. In this, the industrialized north prospered at the expense of the dependent and recolonized south, against which the latter needed to resist (Cardoso 1981; Stavenhagen 1981). Community development was at best seen as a palliative, at worst as an agent of capitalist penetration and increased pauperization of the poor (Lappe, Collins, and Rosset 1998). The us/them dualism of prosperity and poverty was preserved, but now it was reformulated to envision the former as the cause of the latter (see Kearney 1996).

Recently, such critiques of modernist assumptions about progress and concern with discursive constructions of reality have led to a contrast between "development anthropology" and "anthropology of development." In development anthropology, one is still directly engaged in application. As an active critique of the community development "project," a more interactive fieldwork has promoted a reciprocal and respectful approach to involvement in community development. In contrast, the anthropology of development is "primarily concerned with the socio-scientific analysis of development as a cultural, economic, and political process," about the significance of the typical "discourses of development" and what they tell us about the "development gaze" that prevents us from an honest and authentic encounter with the "subaltern subject" (Escobar 1991, 1995; Grillo 1997, 2). These critiques about hidden cultural values and agendas that underlie development projects and serve political purposes are important to the field (Ferguson 1994). They deepen our understanding of the ethnocentrism of development efforts, their sociopolitical manifestations, and their ideological texts, yet they still do not provide for practical solutions. In fact, for some social scientists they have served to put a halt to involvement with what is seen as a flawed development enterprise.

Without disengaging from development anthropology entirely, over the decades others have considered alternative approaches to the issue, involving local knowledge (Brokensha, Warren, and Werner 1980; Crewe 1997), local participation (Croll and Parkin 1992), and identity issues (Mueller 1986). The problem, as Earle's (1984) original research in the area maintained, can be reduced to a standoff between doing nothing and doing something that might ultimately be harmful. Said another way, the issue is whether the development projects are part of the solution to the difficulties of the poor or contributors to the problem (Escobar 1995).

In Chiapas as elsewhere, it is NGOs that frequently serve as practical arms of the development endeavor. On the one extreme, many development NGOs internalize the notion that their programs are short-term bridges on the long road to privatization, promoting economic opportunities that are seen as part of the process of liberalization (Duffield 1997, 174). At the other extreme, the organizations act as spokespersons for civil society in rebellion, seeing their alternative development initiatives as ways to subvert and circumvent the system (Burgerman 1998; Nash 2003).

Clearly, for us, abdicating is not an answer, any more than the promotion of projects that are not in the interest of the people they are to serve. Thus, the process of informed development revolves around control. From Earle's dissertation in 1984 to the recent comments of Subcomandante Marcos, the same theme emerges, namely, that rural people seek to maintain, regain, or increase their control over their land, economy, ecology, health, education, decision making, and destiny. The actions and words of the people of Cerro Verde, Tulan, and Ojo de Agua are testimony to this.

Since 1998, we've watched the Zapatistas work as an informal NGO, providing services and training to its constituents and support bases in education, health, production, commercialization, and tourism. Our interactions with Martín, as representative of the municipality, made it clear that their concern with the philosophy and practice of international aid is deep seated.

As both contemporary applied anthropology and the Zapatistas know, top-down giving that erodes dignity and fails to understand basic needs is unacceptable and largely unsuccessful. Control issues, we hope to clearly show, are basic to autonomy and central to the struggle for an alternative community development in Chiapas. As resistance communities, their municipalities, and the new regional development councils work to clarify viable and workable policy and programs, we hope to tell their story clearly, to walk with them toward a horizon of hard work and hope.

TELLING THE STORY

Uprising of Hope uses a literary technique that lets story merge into factual detail. In this way, the textual and textural background of historical and daily events becomes the preface to data usually included in the structure of conventional ethnography. We use vignettes, narrative, and verbatim testimony to introduce information about environment, social organization, religion, economics, politics, and the rhythm and cycle of life. The presentation of the data is not strictly chronological, nor is it a product of a single interview. Narrative is constructed by merging storytelling episodes and the voices telling the story. At times, an event described in one moment of ethnographic exchange is surrounded by details gathered about the same event at another time or from another source, especially when reconstructing history. We take a certain amount of authorial license in telling the ethnographic tale, but not without the consent and critique of those whose lives are the fabric of this book. The result is a text compiled by many, an ethnography where the ethnographers are sometimes authors and sometimes only scribes.

Part 1, "Arrivals," provides historical context by presenting the experiences of individuals arriving in the Rio Chayote valley between 1920 and 1998. Each narrative serves as the preface to a discussion of information critical to an understanding of Chiapas as detailed in the remainder of the book.

Antonio Sanchez, a young Tojolobal Maya, migrates from the canyon region of Chiapas to become a founder of the *ejido* and community of Cerro Verde. Antonio's experience leads to the description of the natural environment and is impetus for an analysis of land reform in Chiapas and Mexico, critical to an understanding of one of the stimuli for the later Zapatista rebellion. We also meet his wife, Dominga, a spirited precursor to Zapatista feminism. Part 1 is also preface to a presentation of the role of the Catholic Church in Chiapas under the auspices of Bishop Samuel Ruíz García. It also allows us to begin examination of the need for independent health and educational facilities in the region, services implemented later by the *municipio* of Tierra y Libertad.

Miguel Santiz, a spirited Tzotzil Maya, migrates from the highlands of Chiapas with a group of settlers. Miguel's experience provides a window into why migration takes place and how groups of settlers coexist, including the Guatemalan refugees who fled into the area in the late 1970s. It also begins presentation of the importance of Maya cosmology in contemporary life. In addition, it deepens the understanding of *selva*[7] adaptations and their dynamics, especially in terms of cash crops such as coffee.

Author Duncan Earle, a graduate student in anthropology at the State University of New York at Albany in 1979, has the questionable honor of being chosen to document the experience of Maya migrants to the jungle. Originally working with the organization Save the Children in Guatemala, events in that country force him to retreat to Chiapas. His arrival in Ojo de Agua provides the mechanism for a presentation of the history of the region in that era as well as a review of the violence in Guatemala. The interaction of Maya settlers and Guatemalan refugees in the region is an important part of understanding later events in the area.

Author Jeanne Simonelli, an anthropology professor at the State University of New York at Oneonta (and later Wake Forest University), arrives in Chiapas in 1997 with a group of students as part of a service-learning program, a trip that provides her entreé to Cerro Verde and Tulan. Her experience is the opening for a historical update, including the almost hysterical xenophobia of the Mexican government in the late 1990s, resulting in her own expulsion from the country in 1999.

These four chapters bring the reader into the ethnographic present, the subject of the rest of the book.

Part 2, "Seeking a Path," lays out the hopes, expectations, fears, and projects of three groups in the Rio Chayote region at the time of the rebellion: the Zapatista support communities as they enter into resistance and face complex confrontations with official Mexico, their progovernment neighbors negotiating long-standing rivalry and coexistence with the Zapatista rebellion, and the nongovernmental and civil society organizations active in the region during this era. It takes us through the height of the conflict as the communities build an autonomous municipality, NGOs introduce community development from above, non-Zapatista autonomy continues in Ojo de Aqua, many of the refugees go home, the *municipio* of Tierra y Libertad is "dismantled," women and men struggle to live out gender ideals, and Maya cosmology is the backdrop for contemporary dreams and decisions.

Part 3, "Defining the Dream," brings the reader into twenty-first-century Mexico. The PRI has lost power in both the nation and Chiapas. The newly elected government of Vicente Fox romances international capital in the form of the PPP, while the autonomous municipality works to help its communities toward self-sufficiency and access to information. Cerro Verde and Tulan try to maintain a viable rural economy in spite of the worst coffee prices ever, looking for avenues of production that will allow their children to remain at home. Migration becomes a dark measure of economic crisis, even in the jungle eden.

Part 4, "Horizons of Hope," brings us to the present and lays out guidelines for informed community development derived from work in the region. The ethnography is summarized not just in the author's analysis and conclusion but also in the words and pronouncements of community members in light of recent changes in Zapatista organization for development. The final field of discussion returns to the issue of building a viable, self-governing rural community in the context of globalization and the dire consequences of the failure of this metaproject for them and for us all. As Marcos said, obeying the call to speak for the *autónomos*, "Those who help one or various communities are helping not just to better the collective's material situation but a project much simpler but more encompassing: the construction of a new world, where many worlds fit in, where the handouts and pity for others are part of a science fiction novel, or of a forgettable and expendable past." The perseverance, patience and good humor of these jungle communities in the face of monumental global *topes* are a wake-up call for those who view the search for alternative development as futile. Their continued efforts are the uprising of hope.

NOTES

Portions of this text appeared previously in Earle and Simonelli (2000), Simonelli (2002), and Simonelli and Earle (2003a, 2003b).

1. For purposes of this text, community is defined as a loose alliance of households, united by common identity or goal, who have come together in order to facilitate a transformation in socioeconomic or political status.
2. Ejercito Zapatista de Liberación Nacional, or Zapatista Army of National Liberation.
3. Hernández Castillo (2001a) and Levya Solano (1998) provide the most ethnographic accounts of this region; Garza et al. (1994) have produced the only comprehensive testimony to the colonization experience in the region we describe.
4. Based in ethnicity but modified by politics and practices, including gender and age relations, indigenous notions of *usos y costumbres* have undergone a metamorphosis in the past two decades. For a look at the complexities surrounding this concept and the related ideas of autonomy, see, among others, De Leon (2001), Diaz-Polanco and Sánchez (2002), Rus et al. (2003), and Speed and Collier (2000). For discussions of gender, begin with Eber (2001), Hernández Castillo (2001a), Ortiz (2001), and Rosenbaum (1993).
5. Derived from the imagery of Emiliano Zapata, the name Aguascalientes was used to designate Zapatista regional governance headquarters until August 2003.
6. The Mesoamerican idea of milpa is commonly confused with the word used for a simple cornfield. In this text, milpa is a type of farming that includes many additional cultigens and semicultigens (tended wild plants). Milpas are designed to produce a varying food basket throughout the agricultural year.
7. In this text, the Spanish *selva* is used interchangeably with "jungle" and/or "rain forest."

ARRIVALS

CHAPTER 1

Antonio Sanchez Cruz:
The Road to the Edge of the Jungle

ANTONIO SANCHEZ CRUZ FELT THE SKY DARKEN long before he saw the angry charcoal cloud descend over the milpa. He was bending over the thick weeds that seemed to grow up almost overnight between the newly sprouted corn plants. He hacked them out with sure and steady swipes of his machete, and the sweat poured down the back of his white cotton tunic. Though it was barely January, the damp heat of a June wet season hung over the Rio Chayote valley. But suddenly, he was cold. He looked up into the darkening sky. There was a storm coming.

Antonio stood quickly and walked to the edge of the milpa to a place where he could see across to the tiny enclave on the slopes above the river. Thunder was rumbling down from the higher mountains, grumbling and growing louder with each successive round. The milpa was cloaked in shadow, and he saw the wind begin to snake through the high grass like the undulating body of a lethal *nauyaca*. Antonio heard the lightening sear through the tall trees standing at the edge of the next field; a short pause, and then there was a violent crack. He grabbed his machete and looked quickly for someplace to shelter. There would be no time to make it home.

The trunk of a huge mahogany lay along the boundary of the milpa. He had felled the tree fifteen years previous, in 1951, just months after his family and other landless campesinos claimed the territory they now farmed. Like others who would follow, they had left their village outside of the municipal seat at Las Margaritas, where they worked as day laborers on one of the many ranches owned by a handful of wealthy Chiapanecan families. There was no land for them in the ancestral Tojolobal settlements, and under the terms of the land reform following from the revolution of 1910, a group of unrelated individuals could inhabit unused or appropriated lands and start an *ejido*. Eventually, they could petition the government for legal title to parcels that would be held by the community.

The government opened this land to the south, seeking colonists to cut down the jungle, to migrate into the hot country, encouraging them to grow

Rio Chayote environment after colonization

coffee and plantains and, ultimately, cattle. How different the land was from when he first arrived here. The trees had been cut to make room, first for the milpas and then for grasslands to use for grazing.

Claiming more than 900 hectares, they called their new colony Orilla del Bosque—edge of the rain forest—and it truly was the jungle's edge. In the early days, ancient trees were a dense canopy, providing homes for the big monkeys that howled from one side of the river to the other. These *b'atz*, as they were called in Maya, were the same mythic monkeys that inhabited the old stories his grandmother had told him when he was a little boy and that he now told his own daughters. Though Antonio lived high above the river, up the other slope, he could still hear the *b'atz* screaming as they courted during the long night. Their cry was so ferocious that at times Antonio could not distinguish it from the cry of the *balames*, the sleek jaguars that lived in deep caves in the craggy rock faces and narrow ravines. In the early hours before dawn, the jaguar drank, in places where fresh water bubbled up from pure perennial springs. In the small lakes, *lagartos* swam with vigorous stealth, and in the forests javelina provided tasty meat. These days, Antonio missed that pristine wildness, where he was certain other characters from his *abuelita*'s Tojolobal tales still held forth during the dark nights, the trickster Juan Senton and the ghostly *somberon*. It was a powerful land.

The old mahogany was rotting now, and he sprinted quickly to it, taking shelter in the heart of the moist hollow trunk. He was just in time.

The sky grew darker than dusk, and he smelled the huge raindrops before he saw them, a sharp metallic scent giving way to a curtain of rain. Thunder crashed again, and this time the flash of the lightning was almost immediate, telling him that the storm was right above him. Antonio curled into a tight ball, moving away from the entrance to this timber cavern. Suddenly, the curtain of rain parted, and Antonio saw white balls, the size of beans but perfectly round, bouncing off the ground. Could this be ice? Yes, he was sure of it.

The wind was changing. It made an unnatural sound, roaring with ferocity not often heard in this land. It came like a whirling torment, a *remolino*, and he heard trees cracking and crashing in the distance. It was not so much the wind's ferocity that alarmed him as the timing. The winds usually came in March, just before the dry heat. But this was the end of December. Antonio was frightened, for himself and for his family, but there was nothing he could do for them. He would need to wait out the storm, hoping that they would be safe, sheltering in the pole and palm thatch house they lived in overlooking the river.

As fast as the wind came, it roared through and was gone. The rain lessened, and Antonio moved out of the tree trunk and into the slowly brightening afternoon. Looking around him, he saw that the tall weeds were flattened, and he was grateful that his corn was still close to the ground. It had not been damaged by the winds or by the strange white balls of ice. He picked up the woven net bag that he used to carry his tortillas, shouldered his machete, and followed the now muddy path until he reached the river.

It was strangely quiet near the river's edge. He looked above him, and the horizon seemed different, too. Where just this morning a thick cover of branches had reached almost across the narrowest points of the stream, he could now see the sky. There were trees missing, and in those that remained he searched for the movements of the howler monkeys, but they were nowhere to be found. They were hiding. Frightened by the wild winds. Lying still against the remaining branches. But it was too silent.

True, there *were* far fewer monkeys now than there had been when they arrived here at the edge of the jungle. Many of the big trees, the cedars and the mahogany, the pink-tinged rosewoods, had been cut. And now, the furious circular winds had upturned most of the younger ones, whose roots could not take sufficient hold in the stripped soil.

Antonio reached the hanging bridge across the Chayote, a narrow *hamaca* stretching across the river. He crossed quickly, stepping gingerly over new gaps produced when the storm winds snapped already brittle boards. The river was raging, and he was grateful that the men had replaced the simple *balsas*, the rafts they once used to get across. On the other side, he paused and sat on a rock, scanning the slope up toward the village of Orilla del Bosque, where his wife Dominga and their beautiful daughters waited for him. He stopped and took a deep breath and thought about his family. There were no sons. Two of his babies, boys, had been stillborn, too big to make it safely out of his diminutive wife's womb. So he had only daughters, but it didn't worry him. If they were anything like Dominga, they could hold their own against any man, Ladino or Maya, in the valley.

For five long years, he had waited for Dominga to become his wife. At the age of fourteen, she had been promised to another man, an older man, as was often the way in those times. When the time came for her to marry, Antonio and Dominga were already in love, they would meet in secret down near the water hole, and he would hide in the bushes and whisper to her from behind a blind of reeds.

Stealing a woman, eloping, was not an unknown practice, but in a place where you normally went to live with your wife's family after marriage, it could leave you out there alone, cut off from kin, land, and all social support. But Dominga was firm. She told her family, "I marry Antonio, or I don't marry at all. And you lose the labor of a good, strong son-in-law."

Still, her family refused to agree, all except her brother, who supported the clandestine couple, a foreshadowing of the female–male alliances that underlie Maya feminist strength and would be so important in their daughters in later years. Antonio could have gone to ask for her, formally, but he was a nobody, an orphan raised by his grandmother. There was no status in the match.

"Steal me, Antonio," she told him again and again. "It's the only way." Some days she made him so mad. He was frustrated and angry. He wouldn't come to the well for days. The years flew by.

Finally, one morning, he arrived at the well.

"Steal me, Antonio," she told him firmly. "It's got to be today. In broad daylight. The whip is hanging on my father's wall. If we fail . . ." Her brother had gathered a few things together, a start for them in a difficult land.

Antonio stepped out of the bushes behind the well, and together they went out to begin married life, a journey on a new path.

They'd been lucky so far. Lucky to have this *ejido* land, lucky to have healthy daughters. He stopped and rolled a cigarette from the dried leaves of wild tobacco and listened to the eerie silence once again. No. The *b'atz* were not hiding. He was sure of it. They were gone, driven deeper into the Chiapas jungle. Like the colonists who had cut their arboreal lairs, they were searching for someplace they could survive. Antonio sighed. The monkeys would not return. He would always remember this day, the day the howlers left the jungle's edge (Simonelli, field notebook, February 2002).[1]

The Mexican Revolution reached Chiapas belatedly, an afterthought in the national conflict brought to bear on a region sitting smugly in elite hands. At the turn of the twentieth century, large segments of the southern Lacandon were in the hands of U.S.- and Belgium-owned companies that exploited the vast rain forest, cutting mahogany and cedar (De Vos 2002). Other portions were claimed by landowners who set up cattle ranches, where Tojolobal day laborers turned jungle into grasslands. In other parts of the state, large coffee plantations dotted the coastal areas, while in the central Chiapas region that was the source of huge numbers of migrants, a group of Ladinos held title to large tracts of a fertile crescent of farmland in an area known as the *La Franca Fincero* (De Vos 2002). But the federal government held the bulk of the Lacandon, and it was these *tierras nacionales* that would later be opened to colonization.

When the revolution finally did arrive in Chiapas in 1914, these cadres of the privileged, who were referred to as *mapaches,* or "raccoons," quickly squashed it. Though the Constitution written in 1917 promised land reform, the Chiapas elites soon cut a deal with the commanding generals that guaranteed that the national redistribution of land would take place in the state in a way that benefited their interests. As opposed to limitations on private landholding in other parts of the country, the *mapaches* were allowed to retain or acquire up to 8,000 hectares per holding (Ross 1995, 69–70). They enforced this system using a mercenary police force, a practice that foreshadowed the paramilitary armies of the 1990s.

Antonio Sanchez Cruz was only one year old in 1927 when his grandmother's family migrated south from the canyons of Margaritas to search for work on cattle ranches in the far reaches of the Lacandon jungle. Like the others with whom he would eventually join to solicit the parcel of land along the banks of the Rio Chayote, Antonio's family left the arduous life of a landless worker to come to these alien lands. Raised entirely by his grandmother, he barely knew the rest of his immediate family, who had left the area to go to the coastal plantations near Tapachula, where work was more plentiful. They never returned. Years later, Antonio would travel to meet his brother for the first time.

Though he was in the vanguard of colonial groups who would begin to stream into the hot, low country bordering the Mexico–Guatemala frontier, he was by no means the first. In fact, his wife Dominga had been born in the *selva* and her family worked ranchlands that bordered the expanse that would become *ejido* Orilla del Bosque. Like Antonio, she was a Tojolobal Maya and still dressed in the white *huipiles* with wide, colorful flowered collars that were characteristic of the group. In the early days, Antonio also dressed in traditional clothes—white cotton three-quarter-length pants that made great sense on the narrow paths that became iced with thick mud during the rains that fell for much of the year. The downpours abated during six to eight weeks from March to May, the hot, dry spell the Maya called summer. But "winter" quickly followed—four months of heavy, violent thunderstorms that left the land saturated and the air oppressively hot and damp. During the rest of the year, gentle female rains, the "*chipy chipy*" drizzle, added up to yearly totals that exceeded three meters.

Lying between 300 and 1,500 meters in altitude, the Lacandon jungle encompasses over a dozen ecosystems and in those days held a diversity of species of flora and fauna. More than 39 species of fish, 25 of amphibians, 84 of reptiles, 340 of birds, and 163 of mammals inhabited various sections of the *selva*. The land above the course of the Rio Chayote, corresponding to the eastern edge of the municipality of Independencia and the southern tip of Margaritas, graded from subtropical to tropical, with altitude ranging from 900 to 1,200 meters.

Indeed, dropping down off the central highlands of Chiapas into the eastern Lacandon jungle is nowhere more dramatic than from the semiarid Mesa Tzuton, extending south from Las Margaritas and east from Trinitaria, through the tropical cloud forest region of the Montebellos Lakes, to the banks of the river. It is not just the 700-meter descent in six kilometers but also the total change in the physical environment, dramatized all the more by the fact that one is entering from a corner the largest tropical forest still standing in Mexico, with the Chiapas *Altos* behind and to the left and the towering Cuchumatanes of Guatemala looming to the right. The Chayote is the first significant water catchment system in the jungle to the east of Comitán, and the area contains most of the characteristics of the whole eastern Lacandon jungle.

Most obvious of these characteristics is topography. From the Chayote to the Usumacinta that divides Chiapas from Guatemala, all the mountain ranges run from northwest to southeast. They are all typically carst limestone outcroppings, very steep-sided with a high frequency of internal drainage systems. The Chayote and all its tributaries run on this northwest–southeast angle, interrupted by short northeast jogs through narrow canyons that cut through limestone ridges. While rarely are these ridges more than 500 meters higher than the relatively flat, basin drainages that sit between them, they can run 100 kilometers without major interruption, and their steep sides make travel across them very difficult.

The Chayote catchment covers an area of about 2,856 square kilometers, carrying about 6.2 billion cubic meters of water per year. Total rainfall per year, like most of the southern region, is over 3,000 centimeters, and it tends to have a shorter dry season than areas to the north, probably because of the proximity of the mountains. These mountain systems also cause the area to be cooler and more appropriate for crops such as coffee, even though they are fairly low. Antonio's land sat at about 1,100 meters.

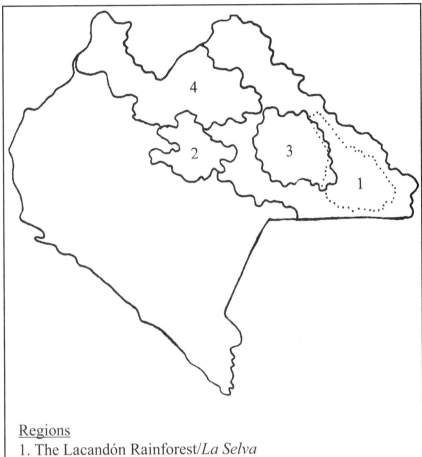

Regions
1. The Lacandón Rainforest/*La Selva*
(area inside the dotted line is the Monte Azules Bioreserve)
2. The Highlands/*Los Altos*
3. The Canyon Area/*Las Cañadas*
4. Northern Area/*El Norte*

Map of geographic regions of Chiapas

As in the rest of the Lacandon, the diverse plant species of the Chayote ecosystem could survive only as long as the tropical canopy remained intact. Exposed to sun and intense rainfall, the relatively thin soils would easily lose fertility, and it is only through loving exploitation of the land that humans and the jungle can coexist. Without responsible agricultural practices, settlement of the jungle was to become synonymous with destruction. While rational models of food and coffee production did exist in the mid-twentieth century, the prevailing cattle industry sacrificed future productivity for fast and immediate profits. It was against these forces and within this climate of land exploitation that *ejidatarios* such as Antonio struggled to subsist.

Through the decades of the 1930s and 1940s, Antonio and Dominga and their families worked the lands bordering the cattle ranches, in essence, squatters. All spoke Tojolobal, the true language, and kept the ancient customs of the Maya people, burning incense on special days and in sacred places to ensure bountiful land and a good harvest. By the mid-1940s, the first teacher arrived. Then came the radio.

"These things changed our mentality," Antonio remembers. "The people knew more before the school came. Soon they lost respect for their elders. We lost our language. Lost the culture." Decades later, he remembered the early years with a certain fondness, when the people were more polite and the children all had decent names, like Caralampio.

Many of those who began to migrate south in the 1930s and 1940s sought the land promised to Mexican campesinos under the terms of the Constitution of 1917, written to guarantee a new Mexico at the close of the chaotic years that followed the revolution. Under the terms of article 27, the poor and landless could petition for the use and ownership of idle, empty, and eventually expropriated lands. In theory, campesinos could claim these *tierras baldios*, or uncultivated lands, in one of three fashions. As *pequeños propietarios*, or smallholders, they could acquire parcels of not more than ten hectares that would be individually owned and titled. Indigenous groups were entitled to regain use rights to ancestral lands surrounding their villages in the form of *comunidades agrarias*. These lands were to be corporately held and administered under the form of governance deriving from indigenous use and custom. Finally, unrelated groups of campesinos could jointly petition the government for the donation of large parcels of land, called *ejidos*, to be held in common but worked in individually designated plots of about twenty hectares (about fifty acres).

Ejidos as political entities were an integral part of the Mexican land reform and an important piece of the agricultural development strategy of Mexico during most of the twentieth century. The key to this form of landholding was the fact that the parcels could not be legally sold, rented, or used as collateral because the community, not the individual, retained the basic property rights. The Spanish word *ejido* derived from the Latin *exit* and originally referred to the lands found at the boundaries of Spanish villages and used for pasture and other group activities, much like the English commons. Arriving in the Americas, the Spanish were perplexed by landholding practices with no direct correspondence to what they understood, and so they designated the lands as *ejidos*, a term that continued in use.

At its inception, the rationale for the *ejido* system was not simply the justice it offered the landless but also the claim that it would be a more productive use of the land and a more profitable land tenure policy for the nation. *Ejidos* were seen as having the potential to go beyond subsistence, producing goods that were needed for the national economy. Though it would be the mid-twentieth century before the practice would emerge in Chiapas, by the 1990s, over 50 percent of Mexican land was held in the form of *ejidos* (Brown 1997, 102; Esteva 1992, quoted in Nigh 1997, 209; Harvey 1994, 22).

Land reform finally did arrive in Chiapas in the late 1930s and continued in an on-again, off-again pattern for the next six decades. It moved at a snail's pace, with less than 2,000 hectares distributed and titled during the administration of Lázaro Cardenas. Between 1940 and 1949, land was made available in seventy-four municipalities, and in the 1950s the largest portion transferred was in the municipality of Margaritas (Reyes Ramos 1992, 81–87). There, as in other parts of the jungle, ranchers who allowed their workers to purchase marginal lands on the fringes of their holdings staved off true redistribution. Moreover, many of the parcels were the poorest agricultural land, steep slopes sitting above the broad valleys still held by the same elite families. These accommodation tactics kept actual appropriation from happening and created a zone of protection comprised of peasants who were indebted to the ranchers. Others acquired land to farm by trading labor for "rent," but eventually living conditions and demographic pressures moved campesinos to press for more land with which to maintain their families (Collier and Quartatiello 1994, 39–41). Las Cañadas typifies this situation.

Some of the marginal lands involved in redistribution had been taken from indigenous communities during the previous century, and their return as part of the land reform did not threaten elite landholding patterns. The decision to open the jungle to colonization provided further protection for their enterprises since it drew attention away from those holding the arable land that made up the Franca Fincero. For further protection, vast tracts of land, corresponding to the 773 *latifundias* existent in 1940, were divided into 9,000 separate holdings and exempted by law and certification from potential appropriation (Reyes Ramos 1992, 139–41; Rus 2004, 14). In spite of this, by 1975, over three-quarters of the state's territory was in the hands of the indigenous agrarian population. Absent from these figures, however, is the fact that the land was often marginal and was distributed in a fashion that replicated the elite system of patronage, reinforcing the traditional exploitative social structure. And, while the government urged colonists to go forth and produce, programs failed to consider the need to market that production.

Encouraging migration and the establishment of *ejidos* on the vast national lands to the east of the cities of Ocosingo and Comitán solved a series of immediate problems for the Mexican government. First, it relieved tremendous demographic pressure as population in the highlands and the high country of Margaritas grew. Second, it allowed the government to save face in terms of the promise of the Mexican Revolution and the guarantees included in article 27 of the Constitution. Finally, it worked to remedy Mexico's "underdevelopment" since the colonists would be encouraged to produce crops such as coffee and cattle for export, allowing the nation to integrate into the international market (Anaya Gallardo 1997, 7).

The lands of the Chayote drainage were included in the colonization program. Though not entirely in the municipality of Margaritas, whose extensive boundaries leapfrogged across the river and back again, the territory corresponded to two of the three official versions of the western limits of the Lacandon. In the final iteration, the Independencia portions of the zone fall outside the vast territory of La Lacandona that occupies the entire southeastern corner of the state. In spite of this, in a gargantuan Lacandon development plan proposed in 1971 (and resurrected in 2000 as Plan Puebla Panama), three dams and reservoirs were proposed along the course of the Chayote, beginning near Tulan and ending at Ojo de Agua (De Vos 2002, maps 13–15). The ramblings of the official boundaries of the zone during the decades following the onset of migration correspond to the development plans of various national administrations and their policies toward the use and sale of jungle lands. Agronomists making the same designations in 1978 argued for a boundary based on economic, social, ethnic, and historic characteristics in addition to climate, including the phenomena of colonization and migration. In a version drawing on this data, certain parts of the Chayote were officially designated as Lacandon, while others, just across the river, were not (De Vos 2002, 39–55). Officially, the lands of the new *ejido* Orilla del Bosque were both jungle and not jungle.

For the Tojolobal who made the trek from the fincas of Margaritas and the Tzotiles and Tzeltales who later left the highlands of Chiapas, the promise of *ejidal* land was akin to the Homestead Act, which stimulated westward expansion of nineteenth-century American pioneers. Though Antonio's and Dominga's families entered the region long before any official call to do so, they were poised and ready when land finally became available.

NOTE

1. Text derived from conversations with Antonio and other early settlers who remember the land and the "tornado" that passed through it. Recollections were stimulated by a similar storm in February 2002. Maya tales frequently are commentary on events in the present.

CHAPTER 2

Miguel Santiz:
A History of a Person

OVER TWENTY YEARS AGO, Duncan asked Don Miguel Santiz for an account of the founding of the Ojo de Agua *ejido*. He handed over a passable script from a twisted spiral notebook, with some creative variation in the use of consonants but still readable. It was a remarkable document, a history of a person, as he titled it, which read nearly as follows:

HISTORIA DE UN PERSONAL

"How I grew up; Inasmuch as I am an orphan, first losing my mother, then my father, what was left but to be an orphan? I stayed among many houses with the neighbors at the start, but they did not love me. Next I go off to live with my sister, a good distance away, but upon my arrival she is very angry all the time, caring nothing for me. My brother, now he wants me to stay with him, but his wife does not want me. Then one of my cousins gets in touch, and I go to live with him. Thanks be to God he wants my company, cares for me. He would get me things to wear, since I was suffering without clothes. And I became a caretaker of cows for a while, and got into doing some muleteering. We even went as far as Yajalon. I traveled well with him everywhere. So I am quite contented passing the time with him. As time passes, he starts taking me to the coast, in the Huixtla zone of Chiapas. So I get used to working there, at different times, and then it comes to mind I should find myself a wife, someone to make my food.

I go to school to study a bit, just a few words stay with me, but I have no idea what the letters say, nor could I say the smallest, simplest word in Castilian. Then, later on I came to know a certain Erasto Urbina, whose mestizo father was crossed with a little Chamula mother. Don Erasto was given good training by becoming an officer in the Federal Guard. And then he came to San Cristóbal Las Casas. There he began to bring together the indigenous people, so that they could receive their lands in the form of Ejidos (via INI).

And they begin to meet together all my indigenous companions, and they are able in this way to soon get their Ejidos. This was all done by Don Erasto, who loved me greatly and esteemed me greatly as if I were his own son, and only because of ignorance I didn't want to go live with him. In those days I was lost, into

Miguel, showing off his traditional garb; clothes still worn on occasion in 1979 but usually reserved for the cold country

bad things, but when I got to 27 or 28 years of age, and I began to talk with Don Erasto Urbina, pointing out that I myself don't have a parcel (of land) to work. And he told me there was "National" land up above Chiapa de Corzo. He told me, "Go and see if you like this land, make your meetings with your companions, the ones who want to find hot climates." And I went back to where I lived. I began to notify the people to come meet on a Sunday. And the people responded then, that this was very good, and others asked me if coffee grew there in Hot Country, if this was a good climate for coffee. So I went back and asked if the land was good for coffee. And he said that coffee doesn't grow there. I mentioned a different place, that he had talked about before, and pointed out this place does have a coffee climate. And when I returned once again to the community, I called a meeting to tell them what Don Erasto had talked with me about. Everyone placed themselves in agreement (to go to the coffee lands) and I began the Census. More the 100 individuals wanted to go work in the municipio de Las Margaritas and we made our agreement with Don Erasto. And from this beginning the head people of the National Indigenous Institute also came into this agreement, there in San Cristóbal Las Casas.

They (the INI, under Urbina) commissioned us to go find our new place. We went 6 of us including the leaders to see the National lands, where it was free. Well, we arrived in the jungle, but at that point I did not like it yet. But on the third time of going back and forth running errands, little by little, poco a poco I become accustomed to the climate. And I began to make the petitions and formal requests, and I brought the engineer to make the study, and then I began to make requests that the engineer move forward (our case) to give to us the provisional "title" (to the ejido). And as time passed I began to make the petitions for a Presidential resolution, in order to get definitive possession. The Ejido was then named Nuevo San Juan Chamula, municipio of Las Margaritas. Finally I finished all the issues that I have had pending with the Ejido. I made sure of everything, that nothing was left incomplete.

And after all this, the citizen president of the Republic arrives in the city of Comitán. I begin to petition for a road to the lakes of Montebello on the way towards Iscan (Ixcan), border with the republic of Guatemala. All of my petitions were accepted, with the blessings of God. I saw with my own eyes how I found ways to address all the need in my Ejido, in order to afterwards help all my companions and my brothers in other Ejidos of the indigenous races in the jungle. And this is how it is now. I go suffer for my companions and helping them with all their needs. I have suffered the walking and the hunger because before, all the people in these different places we went to didn't know us and they would not sell us tortillas, not even posol. Returning, we barely would reach our own Ejido.

Well, now we have our own school to educate our children, and we have our teachers to teach in all my communities, for the good of all this small group in the anexo of Nuevo San Juan Chamula in the municipio of Las Margaritas in the state of Chiapas.

On the other hand we need badly a road to come to this place, in order to be content, to get (more easily) all the products out of the Ejido. And another thing that is important is that they construct a wooden bridge that can hold up trucks to cross "over the river," onto this side. This would help bring food to the community. And another thing, we need a warehouse, like what they have with Conasupo, in order to sell corn and beans right here in the Ejido. So you see, we still have many needs.

In the history of my past I was raised with hunger, without family, or even a native teacher. I lived in a place that's cold and poor. Frosts are always falling in that place called Las Ollas, municipo of that same Chamula, district of San Cristóbal Las Casas. And with the blessing of God , I grew up—and now I speak a little with the bureaucrats, I know how to go to Mexico to get some help from the honorable president of the Republic, and my name is Don Miguel Santiz Castellanos, and I live in Nuevo San Juan Chamula, (writing this) so that I may be known, since I bring forth my example to be working for the good of serving in the community.

JANUARY 17, 1976

Miguel presented this paper to Duncan three years after he wrote it. He was forty when he began and seventy when he ends his edits of this basic tale, his foundational myth for the region. Much is expressed in this tale of struggle with hunger, adversity, and racism and also of perseverance and a certain egotism or at least some emergent sense of wanting to have his story be part of history. Someone marginal to his own people in the most profound way, no family and no land, he drifts through the adventures just suggested. He finds himself helping the people of his location and many other indigenous people seeking colonization as a way to have more land and a better life. The role of coffee in this parable determines their destiny, one hard to get used to in the jungle, and especially from Chiapas's coldest, highest region. Erasto Urbina plays the role of paternal culture broker, the one who managed to arrange for some national land to become available to them that is suitable for coffee. Missing from the tale is the role of the church, the struggles between *ejido* members, and the political battles Miguel had gotten into with the Chamula elites, especially a certain Tushum, who was president of Chamula around the time of all the efforts toward migration. I encouraged Miguel to tell me more, to go beyond his little paper:

I was born in Teopisca, but I lived for many years in La Ollas, there in Candelaria. We were all Chamulas living up there, but we came to feel not so good about the way they taxed us, from the town center, that damn Tuxum when he got in as Presidente Municipal, he was the one who started all the fighting and strife. They taxed everything, including widows, fruit trees, even a funeral—the dead were to pay with the living. Well we found out about how this was not a requirement of law because as it turns out Candelaria is not inside the boundaries of San Juan Chamula municipio, but in a corner of the municipio of San Cristóbal. This we found out from a priest, one who helped us defend ourselves when we did not wish to pay, along with many more hamlets to the north and northwest of us. It was like a revolt, you see they do not let you build any other chul na, holy church, but one, the house of Holy John, in Chamula center. The padre showed us the document that showed us we were out, and did not have to pay. We won it by the law. He was furious. Because I was an organizer, and I had the ear of Erasto Urbina.[1] Tuxum was very angry with me, and had me know I was threatened, a short life awaited me.

Don Erasto, he was like a father. Me, a poor orphan, who had to learn everything on his own. He took me in, treated me like his son, he would teach me Spanish and animate me to do things for my people. He was very good with me, with us, with all the true people, when he was a politico, and he used his position to work for our benefit. He even had a good plan with the government to get a big extension of land for us, so all who wanted land could go to the hot country and get some, come to where we live now. But he was not able to get it to happen, it was not possible. The government from Mexico wanted it, but the ones with the big fincas, where the coffee is, on the Soconuzco, on the coast, they were against it. That is how the state of Chiapas came to stop the project, when Don Erasto was the head of the Instituto Nacional Indigenista (INI). They say he even got threats, dark words sent to him. But they did not let Don Erasto's plan to go through, there was a blockage with those owners of fincas who feared the Chamulito would not show up to work the cafetales. We had all tried it out, two, three months working, sweating, it is a hard kind of work. And they pay you a misery, hardly worth the passage spent getting there unless you work like mad, unless you go like a rabbit. So they thought the move to Hot Country would rob them of their willing hands and fingers. So it went nowhere.

Then Don Erasto tells about some land, some place down in the Grijalva, this way from Pujiltik. Kindly Father, I ask Don Erasto, does this land of which you speak give coffee? We have worked this crop and we know of its value, can we make our fields of coffee there? Don Erasto says it is good corn land, for milpa, but no this land does not give coffee. So we said thanks anyway. We were waiting for some place where a little coffee would grow with our milpas. I wanted to leave from where I was, I was afraid of going to the teklum, where the Chamula cabildo and church are. Even in San Cristóbal, Tuxum has his people going everywhere, no place is really safe from him. Then my dear friend tells me there is coffee land, "national land" available, right where the big project was going to go. He could arrange it, he knew what had to be done to get it set up, at least a temporary while the families got settled, the land got measured out.

"Miguelito, do you want to go to the tierra nacional down in the Hot Country, the Lacandon? The roads and trails are few and poor, and it is very different from the climate of the highlands, the Altos. It will be tough. It will be hard. Do you want to go and see if this is the land for you?" This is what that great man Don Erasto asked, and we all agreed. Many neighbors in Candelaria and La Ollas decide to go, and we make a list, more than fifty households signed on.

But first we had to go and take a look. This first entering of the Hot Country was hard, so difficult that we almost gave up looking for our parcel before we got to it. We would get to a place, but it would be with an owner, and they would send us on. It was a fright even to sleep there the night, the jaguars roared and made you afraid to "busca un conejo"[2] in the darkness. The bugs were also ferocious, and people hardly could sleep there those first three nights. Then we returned to Cold Country.

My compadre went with me, Salvador Gomez, but he was shocked a little. He could have a parcel now if he had decided to stay in. But I wanted to go back, to give it a try. This was what we had waited for, and gracias a Dios and Don Erasto, we grabbed up this ejido. We'd not be denied. But Salvador, did not return to Hot Country, he went back to Chamula, ta sikil osil. It took me three tries.

The first year was a rough one, and before we got to the agrarian office in Tuxtla, where I was part of a commission sent by the group, we had a list of ejido members that was not the same as the first one. Half of the first ones quit Hot Country before they had enough money to send the delegation. The man in the office, the man in charge asked why it was there were scratched out names and others put in their place. Well, turns out there were some acquaintances from Baxekem, near Mitontik, on Chamula's north side, and they put themselves on the list as replacements. But the number was more or less the same. We paid him something for this change, then we were all enscribed as ejiditarios. We got the temporary; now we were a little official, there in the city of Tuxtla, there at the agrarian affairs office. Later we would get the engineer to make sure it was all legal and correct. Each one got forty hectares and a roomy house plot on the little urban lay-out. The school got a site and a land allotment to be worked for the school's interests and financial needs. Half the ejido was too mountainous to cultivate, so they got twice a typical claim's worth of land. You might say it's like having a monte ejido inside the ejido. We had it named inarable, to stay outside the land to be divided for the members.

I went on so many delegations, to the agrarian office in Tuxtla, and to Mexico, even. Just to get the definitivo, the one that is final, the paper that legitimates. Oh damn, how we spent money on the vueltas and tramites and bribes. But with the coffee money we finally got it settled. The engineer, he made the measurement, the final map, everything legitimate and straight, he got paid to make him happy. And everyone gave their part, the cooperation, to pay.

But it was not always coffee, no, at first it was just milpa, maize, and we planted way more than our needs. Well, good, but how much can you take and sell? The path was narrow, much mud. That is why they went to pigs, these ones could walk, take themselves to market, slow but not in the tumpline, not on your back. And they pay something in the market, whatever meat you bring to sell. Well, first it is a little beautiful, but then the pigs abound and get into everything. Worst of all was the treatment of new coffee plants. They would eat them up, oh God, the fights that would emerge from the persecution of plants. Well, we made a meeting, the leaders. I was the comisariado, the head. And we made it the law, the ending of the pigs, a prohibition. Some people were so furious, one family left with their herd, another killed them all in front of the comisariado building, pure waste.

Miguel's family harvests coffee

But that was the only avenue, the only way the tender plants of the bean of coffee were to live. This would be our sustenance. First only a few plants were put in the forest. Some planted more than others, especially ones with many sons planted many matitas. At first we did not invite our relations to work, there was not the pay. It was all by our hand, working the very big trees, the brush and the mud. It was only when the coffee was four years, five years or more that you saw the money, and another year and you start recruiting [labor], if there is enough planted. Some times a dozen families would come and go, with this cleaning, that weeding, the harvest. We had to feed them and give them somewhere to stay, so the women had a lot of work when they came. But it was what we lacked, especially with a high coffee price, more hands. Since we raised all the food we ate, attention had to be given to the milpa as well, so as not to have to buy corn. This takes the hand out of the cafetal. So we provided a little work in the fall and winter for those poor relations.

The Mexican government came with a program to help us with the coffee. Some things they were saying we do not believe, but we try a little. We also sell them our coffee on a two-part payment, with the remaining half coming later in the year. People liked it because they paid more than the coyotes of the region, sometimes almost twice. They did not like their suggestions about using fertilizer and less shade. They were tried, on small areas not to screw up a whole harvest. The fertilized plant gave more but it burned up after as little as twelve years, whereas the natural ones live to half my age.[3] We saw right away how it made it fleshy, and then later on dry, and how with the fertilizer of chemicals it always drew the roya, the illness of the leaf. The cutting down the trees and planting just the chalupa seemed too long and too much work, and besides, so many other nice trees would go, like the zapote with its sweet fruit, and the avocado, thin wild ones but still good. And where the ground gave in to form the places where water gathers, and coffee would only strangle, there the sugarcane is content to prosper. So we rejected what the tecnicos had to say, but we were polite like we had accepted it all. Some negotiated with the fertilizer for extra money to buy corn. But I had planted more than enough that year.

Then they left, they did not return, those sons of dogs, never paid the remnant that year, and INMECAFE[4] was dead. We were thrown to the mercy of the coyotes again, the same story of always. The word rolls like a ball that the jefe of the Coffee Instituto stole the money, went abroad, to France seems to me. The poor coffee farmer was left at halves. So it was harder to pay the Chamula kin after that, and when the place became full of refugees from Guatemala after 1982, hell there was so many in need of work, who would raise their own food and cook it, well it became a better deal to use them for labor for the harvest, for the weeding, the pruning. We got the Holy Bible in Tzotzil around this time, and set up the Dios Kop in our own little church, and I am the pastor. This is how we live now, in the annex of Nuevo San Juan.

Miguel Santiz left the Chamula homelands in 1960, the first of the Maya migrants to begin the trek to the wild and untamed Tierras Nacionales. Other colonists from the Maya highlands followed in the 1960s when the National Indigenous Institute (INI) and the Department of Agrarian Affairs and Colonization (DAAC) began a colonization program aimed at populating the southern portions of Margaritas. The Project to Relocate Excess Population from the Chiapas Highlands into Las Margaritas encouraged the movement of landless peasant groups and promised them technical counseling to learn to deal with the alien environment. Little by little, many of the Tojolobal sharecroppers and other Tzotzil and Tzeltal Mayas also learned of the existence of unused federal lands, and a steady migration into the area began (Hernández Castillo 2001a, 73; see also Earle 1984).

His story of the Chamula colony is echoed in the words of others speaking of the same era:

> When there was no longer grass for us to cut in order to make more cattle pasture and we could no longer endure the bad treatment by the patron, we began to hear that there was national land, and we could ask for ejido. This was how the people thought that they could have their piece of land, and leave the patrons. (testimony of Leonardo Mendez R, quoted in Legoretta Díaz 1998, 41)

As Miguel Santiz explains, finding and claiming land and making it a place that would support life was no easy task. Much of the technical assistance promised by the government was questionable if not ecologically destructive. The land titles were illusive.

At the same time that the government was encouraging the migration of indigenous and mestizo campesinos into the rain forest, they were also busy selling the northern part of the jungle to lumber companies. Mexican companies, bankrolled by American dollars, acquired 450,000 hectares of land between 1950 and 1960 (De Vos 2002). In the Lacandon jungle and the sparsely inhabited areas along the frontier, the Chiapas program of land redistribution was officially oriented toward the establishment of *ejidos* while at the same time seeking to create a breeding ground for a workforce dedicated to commercial agriculture. The collision of national agrarian policy and Chiapanecan patterns of indigenous exploitation could lead only to a series of agrarian conflicts in the following decades. In the final analysis, it was not so much that reform did not occur but rather the manner in which it occurred that left many disenfranchised and at the point of rebellion.

NOTES

1. Erasto Urbina became influential with the head of the National Indigenous Institute (INI) during the era of colonization.
2. Literally, to "look for a rabbit," meaning to go to the bathroom.
3. Miguel is about seventy-eight years old, telling his story.
4. IMNECAFE is the Mexican Coffee Institute, which bought coffee from producers as both a trading company and a source of credit.

CHAPTER 3

Duncan Earle:
Heading for Hell

A GLORIOUSLY COMPLICATED SUNSET retreated into the cool air of our compound in San Cristóbal de las Casas as we wrapped our mouths around the last series of Tzotzil Maya phrases our instructor and guide, Dr. Gary Gossen, had just taught us. We had been learning to do fieldwork for over eight months and were now supposed to have enough of the "True Language" to face our field sites. All that was lacking was to say *tameshebat* to the old Harvard Ranch, bastion of ethnography for the Chiapas veterans, and gird ourselves for the journeys to come.

Gary Gossen had a grant to study the diaspora of Tzotzil-speaking highland Chamula colonies, numbering some 100 within the state of Chiapas, he discovered. I was the relative veteran, having done previous fieldwork in Guatemala with the K'iche', and so I was to be sent to the hardest place Gary wanted to study, a Chamulas colony no one wanted to go to, least of all me. Gary had made plans to get me into this difficult community through his connections with highland relatives of the colonists. His compadre (ritual kin) had another compadre who was important down in the rain forest frontier, which the locals just called "hot country," a label both thermal and cosmological since the Tzotzil word was a variant of "hell." To get me placed in this jungle community, he would also take his advanced student Kasuyasu Ochiai, also a good Tzotzil speaker, and Kasuyasu's Colombian wife Inez. So the next day, I, the compadre, Gary, Kasuyasu, and Inez all got on the bus at dawn, heading for hell. It took all day to get there.

The last bus stop was still a ways from the little town of Ojo de Agua. I should have gotten a hint of our destination from the name, "Eye," meaning water hole but also meaning "watch out!" and a disease of the soul in Spanish slang. We were now walking in deep mud, following directions that always came out more optimistic and easy than things inevitably were. I had thought myself the pinnacle of readiness with my new high ankle boots, high so the snakes wouldn't bite me, I reasoned. The leather began the breaking in process on the soggy path, drawing attention to all the places where my feet did not yet fit their containers neatly. By the time we got to the swinging hammock bridge that crosses the raging Santo Domingo River, I was limping badly and feeling kind of stupid. The bridge was a challenge, one I rather fancied, but poor Inez almost went berserk. Clutching everyone indiscriminately, she got the bridge to gallop right in time with her gasps of panic. We almost lost our footing but managed to drag her flailing body to the other side intact. Some of the boards were missing, as they still are, and the dusk light was failing. I still don't like to share the bridge with anyone, after that first time flying about.

Shortly after the harrowing crossing, we were taken to the house of a certain compadre Miguel, the man we had come to see. We had come, in traditional Chamula ritual fashion, to beg for permission, for a favor, for a place for this ethnographer to live for the next nine months. I was certain the whole project was doomed as soon as I noted some of the signs of what might be called "reform" Catholicism scattered about the room we were received in. I knew the basic politics of the situation. How could we go about a traditional petition, complete with bottles of homebrew posh, the Maya rum, if the target was not a believer, a practitioner of the traditional Maya religion? I already knew this man hated the Chamula political and religious leadership and was something of an exiled political undesirable. That is why we brought a compadre of this man to help with the petitioning.

Duncan Earle contemplates the Ojo swinging bridge

I looked out at this sweltering darkened settlement. Rotting jungle planks gave way to crumbling cement blocks, roof thatch now almost all replaced with galvanized tin that makes talking or listening in the rain all but impossible. Cacophonous structures were separated by muddy streets filled with grass and little clusters of sad and bedraggled sheep and the odd horse. I looked up and out between clouds to the horizon, south and east, where the mountain range of Guatemala's Cuchumatanes peered back in cool, misty serenity. I was an exile from that country, the place I had come to love so deeply when I worked for Save the Children, the cool and mysterious highlands of the western part of Guatemala. Each day the political situation was getting worse, I knew, and slowly my presence there had become more and more of a problem for my friends, an opening for their enemies. I had to quit K'iche' and find new ground. So in the middle of my graduate studies, I was developing a new site, under a new professor in another country with a different Maya language; all these things I knew to be good for me, for my career, for my education. But I was miserable, forsaking the refreshing Hobbit-land highlands for this frontier swamp, full of malarial mosquitoes, chiggers, mites, ticks, and every kind of awful snake and critter. The last light surrendered into a drizzle as the rain pulled the curtain on my nostalgia and Guatemala faded to black. If they took me here, I could gaze on a lost love each and every day. Bitter consolation.

I was already itching as the first bottle of pox was presented. Our host scoffed at the gesture. I went into a silent panic. Was this but some flair of rhetoric in a traditional posturing of ritual reluctance, or was this powerful and successful community leader offended at the idea he was still under the dictates of a distant Chamula custom? I was too new at this to know which it was. I just strained to hear the Tzotzil best I could, as nominal and verb roots flashed by in the tumble of complicated parts of speech. It did not sound good. I heard the word "thief"; I could be one of those. Also, something about the unmarried females, something about a schoolteacher and drinking, and then they were saying something about—oh no—God and communists, let's see, *smajbil*—oh yes—fighting. He thinks I might be a guerrilla or something like that. My concentration ebbed and flowed as children came to stare and, as in slow motion, were shooed away by the women. Some food was served, and the loquacious flowering of formal couplets of polite supplication moved back and forth between Dr. Gossen and his compadre while the host stood his ground, countering each assurance and plea with reasoned doubt, the way a reluctant father of a young bride finds ways to make the petitions of a suitor's parents seem unreasonable. It looked hopeless, as one hour turned to two and then three and the darkness, the even rain, and the smell of wet wool and coffee shells chipped away at my concentration during this seemingly endless performance. Inez kept trying to find out if there was some other way back across the river.

Around one in the morning, Miguel reluctantly received the bottle in the traditional way. I was amazed. The compadre had a look like, "Just a matter of time" (as this is an old obligatory bond), and Gary beamed, having gambled well. Once the bottle was taken and the first round downed, the negotiations were on. Now all that was left was the cost for putting me up and the ritual drinking of the accepted offering, a kind of signing of the social contract. In drinking with his compadre as our sponsor and guarantor, Miguel had said yes to taking me in. By about five in the morning, the bottles were all drained and all the toasting and good words spent. Gary and the others said their good-byes and wished me luck. I was a wreck, head spinning in the candlelight, Tzotzil words like flies around my head, and hands shaking mine, saying, "Well Duncan, have a good time in the field," and then they were all gone.

I dragged my body to a corner and fell among the burlap coffee bags, happy I had passed the test.

Two hours later, the horn was blown, a sound like that of the giant caracol shell, inches from my ear it seemed, as I attempted to locate my sense portals and recall where I was. Finally, it dawned on me: Don Miguel was calling a meeting of the heads of household of the *ejido*. Then, as now, in Ojo or in Cerro Verde, it was not just the leader's decision, in the Maya tradition, nor is it just a majority that decides. I was over only the first hurdle. All the people at the meeting must come to a consensus. A new level of worry beset me now that I was alone, hung over, and without a clue what I was going to do if this did not work out. I managed a formal "thanks be to God for your hospitality" as we waited for the assembly to fill.

Soon the sound of wet rubber boots over hard feet came toward the house compound where I struggled to rouse myself. By the greatest effort I threw my body to vertical in the portico so that the nineteen men could see the case they were to shortly consider. Clutching the porch posts for stability, I strained to make my eyes work. Mist hugged the ground, and the group stared and fumbled with their machetes. They were outfitted for coffee work, stamping their feet a little as if to show impatience with anything keeping them from the fields, the place of their growing wealth. Don Miguel dislodged me from the house and brought me forth. I looked across the crowd; what a great game of poker this would make, I thought, swaying, standing next to Don Miguel.

Now came the same beauteous couplets, but this time out of my host's mouth, all the arguments laid against him by Dr. Gossen the night before, now turned on the group before him. All seemed to agree to this, except one. He took up Miguel's role of the night before, raising all the same doubts and concerns. Back and forth, back and forth, for hours they went, until finally the emboldened sun began to undo the coherence of the situation. The cool of morning was gone. Words were exchanged within the group for the first time.

Finally, with but one curt word, the last man gave in, some four hours after the horn had called them together, and he led the gathering away from Miguel's, toward the coffee and forest. Miguel went to get me a basket and a strap and with his two sons followed behind the group. I caught up with him and posed the question as we entered the great cathedral of the canopied jungle that gave shade to the coffee.

"Why did that man dislike me so? What has he against me that he does not want me here?" This made the whole family smile inwardly.

"Muyuk, it is not like that, young one," said Miguel. "It is me he does not like."

That evening at dusk, I bathed in the river, thinking about how we adopt our friends' enemies as the cost of our social affiliations and wondering if the foul-smelling medicated dog soap I was using would kill the 152 wood mites I counted that had burrowed into all my soft and moist parts from when I had been cleaning the *cafetal*. I had forgotten all about the blisters on my feet and about Inez. The distant mountains melted into the sky beyond the footbridge, and I resigned myself to my task, scratching.

In the months that followed, I learned the land from my Tzotzil hosts, learned to listen to it as I crossed through the jungle colonies on foot. I studied land use patterns and documented ecological change, chronicling the tug-of-war between the colonists and the other more ancient owners of these hills.

I am days out from my home community, summer of 1979. My map consists of vague accounts, and the people who gave them were contradictory, even the few I meet on the trail. This whole jungle has a network of these traces, foot trails through the dense foliage, but here all maps are living. The last guy, it was as if his eyes were laughing. He was probably sending me off the wrong way as a joke. It is getting late, it is outrageously hot, and I am not near a settlement but in the middle of the Lacandon. Settlements always have schools, buildings that are usually empty by night and have become informal billets for the travelers throughout this remote region that has no roads.

Maravillas Tenejapa was a great place to stay last night. People sold me good food, beans to wax poetic about, huge stringy chilies. There was a nice school, good beams for my hammock. But now, as the cicadas got deep into their evening screech, there was just more jungle trail. Then the smell arrived.

Smell is strange because it is a kind of contact with an animal. As I stand, something leaves this creature, a snake, and goes in my nose, as I am in his. It is a scent like chocolate, with a little cinnamon and myrrh. I jump back as fast as I can make my body go without any windup or digging in. "Just fly!" I scream at myself in silence, and somewhere my ears hear the leaves, and before me falls a very long, green viper, a *nauyaca*, making the sound of a full lawn hose slapping against humid ground and landing just where I had been standing. *Señal*, any Maya would say, this is a sign. Stop at the next high ground, anything semi-dry, with some field of vision. And hurry. The jungle in total darkness terrifies. I must hang my hammock now. Where did the colony of Nuevo Jerusalem go? I should have been there by now. Heat exhaustion begins to erode me. A small clearing near the trail just ahead will have to substitute for the *ejido* school. Shadows tie up my fingers in the rope.

Hammock up and swinging slightly, I can eat some pack food and bed down, pretend in my mind, with the netting over my slung bird's nest, that I am in the school in Nuevo Jerusalem. But I am apprehensive. I feel a little like a hanging slab of meat. I recall something my compadre Lucas back in Guatemala had said to me. Something about monkeys and how they know things intuitively, like a shaman, a Maya day keeper. I recalled Norman Lippman, a wild and brilliant gringo whom I knew in Guatemala in the 1970s and 1980s, who used to travel with a monkey. He had an encounter with some wild beast in the night, in the jungle, in a hammock, like I was now, feeling like salami hung in the lion's den, a lamb brought for slaughter. He said the monkey screamed bloody murder, and it made him do the same. In my own hammock, I can't sleep. Today is *B'atz* in the Maya calendar, the monkey day. Or is it *Balam Ix.*? My mind is swimming, swinging on the edge of consciousness.

I am like the last monkey. Yes, they all disappeared a few years back; some say it was the flu they got from the *vinik*, the colonists, or the cutting of the trees. Then there were the storms, the big wind. They were gone. The carnivore cats sorely miss their monkeys, I come to realize.

This line of thought is not helping. I excavate my flashlight, remove my clothbound notebook, pen on a string, try a few lines of poetry:

> You harvest the jaguar soul
> . . . in the clearings of resistance . . .
> You harvest the cat's roar
> in the middle of monkey screams
> where wood mites explore my pours
> mosquitos my protruding veins . . .
> You become the jaguar
> In those climbing moments
> Offer up a heart to the sky
> Offer up your heart to the earth . . .
> while we learn to disappear . . .
> somersault and transform into
> what ever animal we choose.
> Something to scare large cats?
> Something that escapes deadly snakes?
> Something impervious to mites, fleas, and ticks?

The whole thing is drifting toward my fears, fantasies, and mite bites. Another attempt at sleep, and after a time that seems an endless pause to listen, exhaustion wins the day. Then I am in a dream in which I am in the jungle, and a figure approaches, but I cannot see the face because of all the multicolored bright light beams coming out of where the face should be. The figure walks like a large monkey. He comes over and touches me with a kind of staff and a red ax, and in that moment I become aware of being awake, swinging subtly in the nest, and noting a smell, only this time it is distinctly like wet cat fur. Then the sound of breathing, that special animal breathing that also sniffs when it pants. Panic invades me, the thoughts spin with the poem in my accelerated mind, and like the monkey I start to scream, arching my back, bellowing like a madman. After a hysterical minute, all is again calm.

The great thing about being lost deep in the jungle is you do not have to worry at all about making noise. The yell is profoundly cathartic. What a visceral insight into the experiences of the first colonists, Miguel's first trip here, when it was all like this, and they were all salamis, I thought. From then on, I slept in schools.

Why do people make the choices they do? To come, to stay, to change the jaguar zone into neatly laid streets? Ojo de Agua was in contrast to the local Ladino community of Santa Elena and even more locally and strongly in conscious contrast to both the highland Chamula homeland and the larger, competing *ejido* faction on the other side of the ridge, a place now on the paved road. In the Anexo, people of meager resources made themselves king of their little hill, as did Miguel, without any patronage to saints or municipal tax collectors and their ilk. The ethic of apparent leveling to justify inequality was no longer necessary. Each *ejiditario* had a more or less equal chance, forty hectares and a family, and of course a few sheep. So here in Ojo, the gods of the ancestors withdrew into the wilds, like the monkeys had, into the caves, the mountains. Even the old cross they first erected when they came soon returned into the jungle, avidly received by a menagerie of bugs, rot, and microorganisms. No one wanted the traditional saint fiesta after a while, except Domingo, Miguel's brother-in-law. He still celebrated it every year, a modest spread, but he is the last. No, the rest of the settlers had turned to the representatives of a more rational Catholicism, their allies from the times of the tax wars in the highlands, the Marists on their *caxlan ca'etik*, literally foreign horses or motorcycles, and later the medically trained nuns. The nuns could also put you up in San Cristóbal if you had to go there. At the time, it seemed the course of the Annex to follow the shepherding of the distant diocese.

But the arrival of the Guatemalan refugees changed all that. When they came streaming across the border in 1982, 1983, and 1984, especially during the reign of President Rios Montt and the killing-fields part of that dark history of genocide and flight, the labor dynamics changed. The Chamulas, with coffee prices down and INMECAFE coming apart, were struggling to cover costs. They cut ties with kin in the highlands and hired the Guatemalans. More than that, they took them in like a kind of guest worker. The jobs their kin once expected to hold each season down in "hot country" now went to the Chapines, the Guatemalan *refugiados*. Unlike Santa Elena, where a refugee camp was set up in the cow pasture a ways away from their urban zone, the Chamulas took the families in, one, two, even three families to an *ejidatario*, and allowed them to settle in the town center on spare portions of *ejido* house lots. This arrangement was not altruistic, although it was sympathetic and based in identification with the plight of indigenous people marked for slaughter (see Earle 1988). The Chamula colonists were always quick to remark how it could have been them.

But such sentiments were clearly self-serving. It was an opportunity to finesse a dramatic situation of human need to alleviate the local labor shortage, with less overhead than using the highland relatives, because the Guatemalans could plant, harvest, and feed themselves corn with just some land lent out for milpa. They could even grow extra for their patrons, a kind of sharecropping. The understanding was that the *ejidatario* got first dibs on the Guatemalan labor at the low end of jungle daily rates.

Having the Guatemalans there in Ojo with us often put me back into deep Guatemala reveries, back to where I used to live in K'iche', the splash of faces, compadres and comadres, *ahijados* and *ahijadas*, the still living and the now gone. These were good people of dependable character and love of life, the ones who first gave me insight into the problematic of community development, showing to me how naive and ignorant so much of the efforts at assistance I had been a part of were. They had been my teachers and guides through the maze of complexities of rural Maya life; they had taught me by simply living and being and speaking openly, about the importance of the immaterial to the material, of culture to instrumental, physical aid, and of the importance of understanding social diversity and conflict to inform the way you go about starting local interventions and organizations.

I remember a still spry Don Lucas, my teacher, coaxed out of his divining room to go take a look at the model house the agency was building. It was just after the major earthquake of 1976, and the NGO world of the time had pounced on pretty Guatemala with all kinds of aid and programs. In some regions it had gotten partisan, with agencies claiming territory. Some towns got rebuilt by religious sects, so you could tell the religion by the building materials and the architecture. Once again, I had come into the picture as a young graduate student in anthropology, with both some actual archaeology and some ethnography under my belt. While doing some archaeological studies for my senior thesis, I had cultivated a small group of Maya archaeological aficionados that included a

Swedish diplomat. I had visited this man and his delightful spouse just before the quake in Guate City. But I was not taken on the first post-earthquake assessment team from the State University of New York at Albany, my school. I had to finish a semester first. From February to May, I stayed with the books but bolted as soon as the last class filed out of the term.

As soon as I could, I contacted my Swedish friend, and he told me there was a great dilemma and he wished my advice. The Scandinavian Save the Children agencies, especially Sweden, had money for a major presence, but the "good sites" had all been taken. None of the devastated towns were available for programs beyond their current commitments. The NGOs had sewn the place up. My suggestion was to go to the department of Quiche; the south had minor damage, but many houses were now cracked and at risk in the case of another strong tremor. For the ones who had lost their homes, I argued, the traumatic period was over, and they were rebuilding. The real need lay just beyond the devastation, where homes were still intact but damaged.

My logic was that they faced the greatest danger now, should there be renewed seismic activity, with their cracked walls. "Otro poquito, y viene la casa," people were quoted to say. The Save the Children alliance went for it, and I was hauled into the process of constructing an on-the-ground program for nine contiguous municipalities of the department, with 103 settlements and nine town centers, one of them the departmental capital of Santa Cruz del Quiche. An English program administrator was hired, and I was placed as his assistant with the idea I could serve in the role of anthropologist to help guide the direction of the program.

However, the primary activity of the program focused on housing as a material object, without taking into consideration its local cultural logics, its existence as an idea for those who live there. It was a thing, an expression of logical engineering that combined appropriate technology with easy-to-learn know-how, sure to not fall down in an earthquake of similar force to the one that killed 35,000 Guatemalans in the morning hours of February 4, 1976. They tested it on a flatbed with pneumatic bouncers to simulate precisely the earthquake conditions. This house was seismic perfection and would therefore provide security for the people, resulting in a higher quality of life and program success. This was how it was phrased, and this was what they believed.

The premise was totally out of touch with what a house meant for those who lived in them. Worse, the community development NGO personnel were unconcerned with this fact. When presented with data contrary to the rational model, the response was typically that they needed an education workshop to teach them the error in that way of thinking. It was an article of faith that the hurting natives would come around to their progressive view of the ideal house. This we would later call being in the developmental missionary position (Simonelli and Earle 2003a, 181–83).

At first, things seemed to go very well for our program. We found a good cadre of literate and bilingual K'iche' men and women through the Catholic Church, people very interested in the idea of rural community development and the formation of hamlet-level committees for reconstruction in keeping with a presidential decree that all communities in the earthquake zone should form such groups. Their abilities and enthusiasm gave a sense of success, and in some ways it began to become one simply by distributing subsidized building materials to poor communities. Many turned around and resold the tin and wire to buy corn, and so their kin ate better, much like we would see in future years with NGO projects in Chiapas. But that good was not the "intent" of the program; the Southern Quiche Reconstruction Program was supposed to change people's ideas about what constitutes adequate housing for their families, another version of social transformation. The goal was to get them to buy the message, make the house, and in this way ensure their betterment. It seemed so simple. It was so futile.

I remembered Lucas examining the model house with some care, with its neat portico, cutaway wall piece, and smart tin roof, while standing on a small hillock ten paces away, and after a pause out came the titter, a climbing whispery laugh peaking high and faint.

"Well Don Lucas, what do you think of this?" I waved my hand toward the new structure.

"Bonito," he chirped, with some enthusiasm.

"So you would like to have a house like this one?" Another titter.

"No, no es casa para mi," he laughed. It's not a house for me, hee hee.

Later I would get what was so funny.

"Why not, Don Lucas?"

"Pues, Don Duncan, they did not finish it, and it is abandoned, right here along the roadside, by the place where the four roads divide, the crossroads."

Oh yes, the crossroads, like in the Popol Vuh, where life meets death, and where the local spooks hang out at night. I had heard of this idea.

"And no one has put cross signs on the doors and windows to keep them out, as we always do when we must abandon our homes. It gives a fright, how it is. More because the way it sits, it looks. Don Duncan, perhaps we are odd to you but our houses look to the West where Our Holy Sir goes down into the saintly earth. Look around this valley, all homes sit the same. Except the graveyard, the prayer house for the dead, the oratorio, that one looks as this structure does, back to the east, back to death. Da susto. It gives a fright to have a house sit in such a way. They are now crossing themselves when they walk by, the people from these hamlets, and they walk faster, they do not tarry. Worse if night is on them. And no permiso, no one asked the Holy World for a license to build here."

Here is where I first saw how culture had to be woven into any community development approach. Here is where I saw its potential for being an obstacle but also for being a resource. We could have had the shaman do the ritual of permission for under two U.S. dollars, even though it would have made the *catequist* employees of the program cluck. For them, the traditionalist followers of shamans such as Don Lucas were spiritually misguided and wrong; that had also been in the otherwise liberating spiritual message. For more than a decade, the Catholic Church followers among the K'iche' had gained advantage, as so well documented by padre and anthropologist Ricardo Falla (2001), by their rejection of the traditions. But half the population, and the poorer half, still followed ancient ways and resented the outsiders who subsidized the abandonment of the ancestors. This model house was surrounded by them.

"Algo mas, Don Duncan. I don't know about everyone, but for me, those roofs of tin do not serve us well. First, they get hot in the day sun, chilly by night. Not like our tile from the fired clay. Then the poor corn, the maicito, up in the attic. The tin forms the drops of water from the dew onto our holy food. Oh, and who can hear our speech, when the rains come, with the roofs of tin. No sirve eso."

Now Lucas was on an ecological and linguistic roll. Houses had to fit into the ecosystem, just as facing west was also gaining passive solar heating in the portico after the daily rains recede, and afforded putting the back of the home to the prevailing winds that drive the rain. But he was pointing to their function as granaries, suggesting that a function essential to the home as a cultural and material structure is its storehouse role, where the corn is kept. The smoke from the fire below drives off the insects and deters the mice, making the house a good place to share with your corn. But not with a tin roof.

The program noted the storage function but recommended moving the corn to storage huts outside on the ground. This would have encouraged vermin and loss of seed, including the seed needed as viable for the next planting round. No one thought this all through because they could not see how the parts fit together and how space is a cultural text that must be read before attempting to tinker with it. And then there was the other meaning of seed, linked to the seed of men, which is to sit in its chair, the name for the attic, *tem*. To take the seed out of the *tem* has implications for masculinity.

The house, I learned, was also a temple, with an altar to the various entities above and below and to the ancestors, including the first owner of the house, no matter how long dead. There is a way that many traditional people see themselves as paying renters beholden to the first owner, who really still owns the house at the spiritual level. This rent is paid to the first owner at the house altar.

My mind bounced back to the material after imagining the strange idea of negotiating with the dead owner for house modifications. I saw how the tin roofing was a kind of Trojan horse because it was tied to a cost of metals that was volatile in global pricing and bought from abroad, unlike the locally made tiles. Tiles need replacement on an incremental basis, while tin sheets when rusted out represent a much larger outlay at a single time. Worse, the old way of making roofs by hand was quickly lost, and then there was no going back. Ease in building soon becomes a monopoly, and a new dependency is formed rewarding cash over labor, importation over domestic production.

Nobody copied the model in those 103 communities, although I couldn't say if it was material, social, or cultural problems that were more prominent in their minds when they ignored what the gringos came to suggest. I only know they were all important factors. I could see a few feeble attempts, perhaps by a housing promoter working for the program, or a *catequista* true believer, that crashed and burned when run by the spouse. Women, after all, may not own the house in a physical sense, but they are the managers, and Maya house symbolism tends toward the female, revealed in the name for wife, "house owner." Women have an essential role in K'iche' cultural survival in the space of family reproduction, which centers around the hearth and home. Not only would the women resist more forcefully the impacts of others from outside the culture than the more acculturating men, but they would express it in resistance to changes in the structure of the home. Surely their participation in the housing education campaign would have been useful. But they were not invited (no women were) under the assumption that as legal owners and the builders, men were in charge of housing modification. No wonder nobody but one evangelical pastor over in San Pedro ever took up even half the program's recommendations about house building alternatives. What a waste.

It became apparent that in the communities where both groups existed, we were working with only one faction, the one we had hired, the *catequistas*. When we would ask promoters why there were no traditionalists at the meetings they organized, they would say that they invited them, but they just won't come. They are silly and foolish. They do not come to the meetings of their religious enemies. We had stumbled into taking sides in a dispute that divided the people in two. We had helped the more advantaged group; it was more like us and easier to deal with, betting on the strong while alienating the weak. This would not have been so bad had this part of Guatemala not fallen into an abyss of local and state-sponsored political violence only a few years later. Many people who had participated in community development programs and projects in the western highlands were murdered in the early 1980s. We lost four. Some lost them all. It was not a good time to have been promoting divisions.

Many more fled the country, came here to Chiapas, as all hell broke loose in their remote communities when the army of Rios Montt went on a killing rampage in the northwest corner of their nation, in places such as the hamlet of San Francisco in the *paraje* of Nenton. They came and lived in Ojo de Agua, as refugees, as outsiders in a strange land. It was at this time Miguel and his clan moved to embrace a *templo* of Tzotzil Protestantism, leaving the Catholics behind since the Guatemalans were mostly Catholics. Few learned fluent Tzotzil, not even the Protestants.

"Everything we need is in the saintly Bible," Miguel announced.

It appeared to me to be a tiny society of Chamula orthodoxy in the face of new kinds of power asymmetry, with Miguel at the helm as always. The live-in labor could not be allowed to partake of the same faith as the landed class; this was no longer one congregation of the whole but rather a society of two castes, landed and foreign. Contrary to the Catholic approach, with the Protestant *secto* you designed your own church to fit neatly the social landscape and bounded it via the Tzotzil language. No one but Tzotzil speakers would feel at home in it. I had seen this in Guatemala, the circumscription of small "sub-communities" of fictive siblings, Hermanos, often caught up in conflict or competition with rival sects. Here there was hegemony, for even the Protestant Guatemalan refugees formed their own grouping to pray. It seemed to me as though the Chamulas employed their sect as a vehicle of class distinction, a process Weber talked about back in early Protestant Europe. They were now labor managers, a class apart in the social landscape, as well as de facto landlords. Coffee continued to pay a decent living since the costs of production had been depressed by a war across the border. The Guatemalans housed in the Anexo lived with work and the dignity it brought them, as contrasted with those in nearby Chayote camps who lived mostly off the UNHCR (United Nations High Commissioner for Refugees; ACNUR in Spanish) aid. The proximity brought with it the formation of mechanisms of differentiation and contrast. Miguel's reading ability served him mightily, as it had at the outset, to chart out the path of the *ejido*.

Miguel became the Pentecostal pastor, and his son Santos became the organist with the *aparato* and the amplifying equipment for which he was sound engineer. No sect is worthy before God without a decent amplifier and public address system, a *bocina*, or so seems to be the rule in these latitudes. They all knew the songs by heart. They had drawn a line around their community, the one from before all this change, when they were autonomous and mostly Catholic, except Miguel's first son. He had been an Adventist for many years, and the elder leader used to speak ill of his own blood for it. Later he would explain to me why their sect was superior to the Adventists: progress. I had returned once before, briefly, to see the seed of these changes, but that was before Zapatismo swept through the zone and Miguel had to take a stand amidst a new and unpredictable force for change.

CHAPTER 4

Jeanne Simonelli:
Invited to Abandon Mexico

"DID YOU SEE THE MOVIE *FORREST GUMP*?" asked Rene Pulido, the head of the Office of Immigration for the state of Chiapas. We were on a first-name basis. Rene's English was good, though he and I spent the bulk of the afternoon speaking in Spanish. He was soft-spoken man, Ladino, trim, contained, a good package for someone whose job included interrogating foreigners.

It was after five, on March 23, 1999, two days after the conclusion of the Zapatista-organized Consulta Nacional, a nationwide referendum on indigenous rights. I was sitting outside the whitewashed building housing the offices of the Instituto Nacional de Migración (INM), the tricolor Mexican flag waving before it, eating an ice cream sandwich and reading the poetry of Rosario Castellanos, back against the wall. The sun was hot on my face, and I devoured it, absorbed it, as if the penetrating rays could erase the events of the past forty-eight hours.

"Do you remember the T-shirt that Forrest was wearing, the slogan?" Rene continued.

A year had passed since the INM last ran wild, expelling foreigners from Mexico in a desperate search for outside agitators at the root of the Chiapas conflict. They were at it again, and my colleague Kate O'Donnell and I were a piece of it. We were about to be expelled from Mexico—asked to leave, told not to return, for watching an impromptu march related to the Consulta and now deemed to be "political." I shaded my eyes to look at Pulido, watching his face as he had watched mine, searching for involvement, conspiracy, and guilt, as I answered the same set of questions about the same set of events couched in countless different ways for more than three hours. His face was taut, sagging a little into tiredness. It was a long afternoon, five hours of talking and waiting and waiting and talking, and my gringa stomach felt sick.

Rene ran his hand across his chest to indicate an imaginary line of words on a T-shirt and smiled slightly.

"Shit happens," he said simply, recalling the movie. "And shit has happened to you."

I sighed, looking across to the mountain that hides the highland Maya village of Chamula; the mountain where five microwave transmitters are a crown above a sheltered grotto filled with countless Maya blue crosses piled one on one. Kate and I visited there two years ago, on our first journey to Chiapas together. As academics from two small colleges in the rural community of Oneonta, New York, we were doing preliminary legwork for student programs we planned to teach in Chiapas. On that same trip, we walked a narrow Maya path down into the pueblo of Chenaló, where the French priest who served there for thirty years was expelled in 1998 (Global Exchange 1999; Scherer and Lopez 2000, 22–26).

If we had to go, we would be in good company.

I sighed again, looking across to that trip, to two years of meticulous care in our Chiapas programs, two years keeping a low profile, distanced from any overt political involvement in the conflict, as we followed our own research interests. How do you define "political"? Why did we let down our guard?

Rene was following my gaze, staring off toward the mountains, maybe toward Mexico City, perhaps the playa, anywhere but interrogating foreigners in San Cristóbal. I wanted to think so.

Finally, I nodded in agreement. "Make this shit stop happening to me."

It was his turn to sigh. "You shouldn't be here," he began again, either really sincere or a good liar.

"Where? In Chiapas?"

"No, here in these offices."

This time the answer is a shrug. But though Kate and I knew we could leave, at least for right now, we were afraid that we had become a part of the piece of bad street theater that seemed to surround the Chiapas conflict, Orwell meets Fellini in San Cristóbal de las Casas. They were casting the production without auditions, and it was directed by consumed politicians. They looked to discredit the Zapatista movement, obscuring almost two decades of deteriorating living conditions and continued human rights abuses in Chiapas as the overall Mexican economy collapsed amidst a system of marginalization and repression dating back 500 years.

Looking at Rene's concerned frown, it was not clear what part he was playing in the production. Did he write the script? Did they fax it to him from Mexico City? Was it his crew of merry filmmakers and photographers, smiling and waving as they photographed foreigners, or were they professionals brought in from the big city? Whose signature should really appear in place of Rene's horizontal scribble on all the official documents? Should it be Labastida, his superior, the Secretário de Gobernación, Mexico's secretary of state and prospective PRI presidential candidate? Some other ruling party hopeful looking to gain headlines?

The whole thing seemed diabolical, but it was also damned funny. I'd just signed off on a statement of the Geneva Conventions, attesting to the fact that I was offered water, coffee, food, medical care, and sanitary facilities during the course of my interrogation. There was one violation; absolutely no toilet paper to be found in the bathrooms, only small squares of *La Jornada*, the liberal daily published in Mexico City. And what of the latent symbolism behind the little boy who ran around the office all afternoon dressed as a chicken? Was this a subtle reference to our fall semester fund-raising activities back in Oneonta, selling cookies to buy chickens for the *compañeras*?

I arrived in Chiapas first in 1989 for a short visit, delighted by the colonial city of San Cristóbal but oblivious to the social and political conflict percolating just below the surface. I didn't return until 1997, joining Kate to bring undergraduate students to learn there, as part of the Chiapas Project. I was a veteran of a decade of experiential teaching in anthropology; on-the-road programs in the American Southwest; fourteen months of research in Sonora, Mexico's northernmost state; and three books chronicling choice and struggle among people and communities faced by rapid change. Preliminary trips to Chiapas laid the groundwork for the project, allowing both of us to make program connections and begin to ask questions about the Maya struggle that linked back to our own past work.

In 1997, we taught a full-semester preparation course at our respective colleges in Oneonta. At the end of December, our combined student group left for Chiapas, just three weeks following the massacre of forty-five Mayas in the highland village of Acteal (see Hernández Castillo 2001b). The first year's program was a study in flexibility and caution and laid the groundwork for the fieldwork and student programs I would eventually undertake with my newfound colleague, Duncan Earle.

Though based in San Cristóbal de las Casas, the Chiapas Project's service-learning focus involved work with a women's health and economic NGO assisting Guatemalan refugees. DESMU (Desarrollo Mujeres, AC), an NGO funded by the United Nations, was located in Comitán and had a long history of projects in the Rio Chayote valley, close to the Guatemalan border. The group had its origin in the Centro de Investigación y Acción para la Mujer Latinaamericana (CIAM), founded in 1991. The two separated in 1995 to facilitate work in distinct geographical zones, but DESMU brought into its own mission CIAM's goals: to promote projects with refugee women to help overcome existing gender inequalities between men and women (Mama Maquin 1994, 16). In the mid-1990s, the NGO established projects in eight refugee *campamentos* in the *municipios* of Trinitaria and Independencia, including the Chayote valley.

Just after New Year's 1998, we set out with the students for a first trip to the field. We checked in to a hotel in Comitán where DESMU representatives spent three hours briefing us for what we would encounter in rural Chiapas. Our orientation taught us the difference between *refugiados*, refugee Guatemalans who fled death and violence in their own country during the 1980s, and *desplazados*, Mexicans and Mayas displaced by their own continuing war.

DESMU's projects were aimed at diminishing poverty using interventions incorporating the perspective of urban feminism, which focused on individualism at the expense of community. Their ongoing analysis eventually brought into question the entire foci of their work: to work only with refugees in an area where everyone was poor and struggling seemed unethical; to work only with women and children was divisive. As the conflict in Chiapas deepened after 1997, the idea of provisioning one group of communities at the expense of another seemed like a really bad plan (Earle and Simonelli 2000, 109–11).

DESMU was willing and anxious to take us to meet the groups involved in their projects. But we were a large group, and in order to keep a lower profile, we decided to split the students. Kate's group and a DESMU doctor went toward the border to visit health projects; my half headed into the mountains bordering the southeastern edge of the Lacandon jungle with Daniel, DESMU's agricultural extension agent. The next day we would switch.

We left Comitán in darkness, moving the sleepy students out of the hotel and into a battered microbus, and we headed east along the paved highway that paralleled the Mexico–Guatemala border. Just after sunrise, the left front end of the micro began a rhythmic banging. The driver nodded to his companion, and the man hung out the space where the door should have been, checking for the source of the noise. We banged on for a few more kilometers, and then the micro pulled into a *llanteria* at the intersection between the pavement and the gravel road into the mountains. I looked at Daniel.

"Llanta," he said simply. He had a sweet gentle smile and a sweet, gentle voice.

"Flat tire?"

"Sí."

"Shouldn't we get off?"

He shrugged. "If you want."

I wanted. I remembered a bus ride in Guatemala in the late 1980s where they'd stopped to fix broken springs and nobody got off, afraid to lose a seat or be seen by the murderous military. But this was a rented micro in Chiapas; there were plenty of seats, filled with dozing students, sleeping off a long evening in Comitán discos.

I jumped off the bus just as two men rolled a fully aired, bald tire off the roof, getting ready to replace the fully flat bald tire under the driver's side. Across the way from the *llanteria*, a white-haired, craggy-faced man was raking round, green stones on the surface of a basketball court. Curious, I walked over and the rocks turned out to be coffee beans, spread out to dry on the warm concrete. I was delighted. I'd never seen beans outside of Starbucks.

"Do they play basketball here?" I asked the old man.

He shook his head. "Puro café." Only coffee.

I wasn't surprised. The PRI is great about giving away slabs of cement just prior to elections. Communities are asked to propose development programs, but if you ask for anything with even a vague economic intent, even a place to dry beans, you won't get it. But everybody loves sports. I remembered this tactic from my years in Sonora a decade and a half before. Each season the pueblo would request PRI funds for some initiative: a women's leather co-op, a dairy barn, and, at the end of the list, a new plaza or basketball court. Each year the pueblo got cement—cement on the outskirts, cement in the center, cement by the old church, cement by the new church. When I left in 1984, there were five plazas in the town. Chiapas was no different.

I hunkered down in the beans, upstate New York style, and moved them around with a short stick. A few moments later, the old man joined me. I recognized the signs of impending conversation.

"I've never seen coffee growing," I told him.

He eyed me, curious. "What do you grow in your pueblo?"

"Rocks."

"Rocks?" He laughed. "Bad soil?"

"Hillsides," I told him. I waved my arm to include the steep slope where the rest of the road disappeared. Terraced milpas with drying corn plants ambled up the side of the mountain. "Like these, but we don't know how to work them."

"Where do you come from?"

"New York, but not the city. The mountains."

He nodded. "Very far, no? Did you walk?"

I processed his question, missed my cue. "Yes, very far. We came in an airplane."

The old man looked at me, sizing me up. I learned later that this was a cosmological question, not a travel query. Human beings can walk to their destinations over land. On the other hand, Underworld beings travel across the mythic sea or, by analogy, through the sky. The bus was an acceptable substitute for foot travel. But arriving by airplane left my human origins suspect.

I looked up to see Daniel standing behind me, smiling his gentle smile, listening to my cultural faux pas. I'd chosen to come with Daniel because I enjoyed looking at milpas and learning about harvests. Even though I'd written about women and childbearing choices in Sonora, I'd spent a good deal of time with them in the temporales, rain-fed fields away from the floodplain; the agricultural domain of women. And in New York, I'd told the story of failing dairy farms, dying under the weight of market justice. My interests had not changed.

The new bald tire was on the wheel, and we jumped back in. The bus made a metal on metal downshift as it pulled up the incline starting into the two-hour, nineteen-mile road. I sat with Daniel, watching small villages get smaller, the road cuts get steeper, and the people fewer.

"Tierra y Libertad," said Daniel, smiling once again. Land and liberty.

It was a nice sentiment. Land and liberty had been the cry of the original Zapatistas. With the revision of article 27 of the Mexican Constitution, bringing to a halt the fifty-year process of communal and small-farm land redistribution, it became a cry of the EZLN as well.

"Tierra y Libertad," Daniel said again. "Municipio in rebellion. The largest autonomous municipality in Chiapas." He waved his hand at the corn milpas

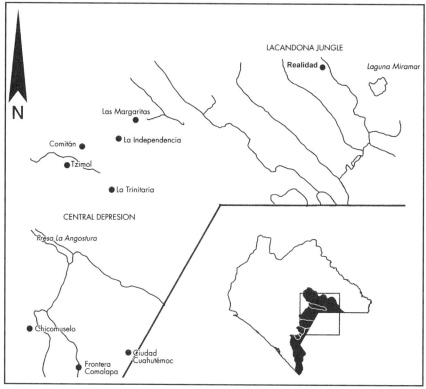

Map of the region, with insert showing the Tierra y Libertad autonomous municipality

outside the window, at the scattered Maya homesteads along the road. Daniel spoke no English; my Spanish was still limp. I was sure I'd heard him wrong. We were going to visit Guatemalans, refugees, in the camps where some of them had lived for almost fifteen years. No one said anything about rebels, rebellions, self-declared autonomous government, Zapatistas, nothing.

"Would you repeat that?" He did.

"Don't worry," Daniel reassured me. "The government knows you are here. Both of them, official and autonomous. It's okay that you are visiting the refugees with me, and then we'll stop at Miguel Hildalgo, a community of 'Mexican' campesinos." He smiled, a big *sonrisa*. He smiled a lot, and I would soon learn that they were smiles of many meanings.

This autonomous zone was where DESMU had been working since 1995, implementing their projects directed at empowering refugee women. The work ranged throughout the border region of Chiapas, and the women were offered small enterprises raising chickens, pigs, honeybees, and medicinal plants. The men sharecropped Ladino land, and the communities built tiny one-room schools and clinics.

When DESMU offered to take Kate and I and the students to visit these jungle communities, they were acutely aware of the pressing needs of the Tojolobal Maya population living in the region. As with Antonio Sanchez, many of them had been in the area for decades, moving down from locations farther into the mountains. Some had formal title to their *ejido* land. Others, such as the Comunidad de Miguel Hidalgo, were recent, attempting to acquire legal ownership of leased parcels. The Tojolobal groups held in common a critical read of Mexican government policy. They supported the Zapatistas but aligned themselves with Bishop Ruiz's catechists and so were against armed confrontation. Also held in common was total neglect in development projects, whether nationally or internationally funded. DESMU recognized this problem at about the same time the leadership of Tierra y Libertad began to envision the UN-funded NGOs as a means of bringing other outside aid into the area.

DESMU's decision to try and help Mexicans in resistance communities was at the root of Daniel's plan to take us to meet the people of Miguel Hidalgo. They hoped to create a solidarity link that might lead to international funding. That these were Zapatista support bases (*bases de apoyo*) was never mentioned outright and would remain unspoken for over two years. It was a good plan, and it worked because I believed it was possible and desirable for an anthropologist to remain politically neutral and to take students to the field with me to study anthropology and do community research.

During the 1990s, anthropologists working in Chiapas experienced a growing climate of hostility and suspicion regardless of the focus of their research. Whether working in advocacy roles with NGOs in communities, attempting to do other issues-based research, or leading student programs, getting official academic visas became more and more difficult. Though many of us typically conducted research on tourist visas, especially during the early phases, this was a gray area and left us subject to possible expulsion. The likelihood that field notes, computer disks, and lists of contacts would be demanded by the INM heightened. The only research or program acceptable to the PRI government was the classic ethnographic study of an essentialized Maya, an image of the indigenous that conservative voices in anthropology constructed during years of Chiapas fieldwork. Anything else was viewed as human rights related and therefore political.

It was amidst this increasing official frenzy that Kate and I found ourselves out at the INM in March 1999 gingerly trying to come up with an innocuous definition of "political." We prepared for our interviews, poring over our Spanish dictionaries, looking for neutral terms to describe the day. We made word lists. "March" and "rally" were discarded in favor of "parade" and "procession." We substituted "watch" for "observe" and "learn about" for "research." We linked our previous anthropological experiences to projects in Chiapas, mentally sanctioning past visits to women's weaving co-ops, justifying our very presence in the state, trying out all possible INM questions.

Anything even vaguely political was excised from the text. In the final script, archaeological sites, lakes, old haciendas, and waterfall hikes dominated our student travel itinerary. We were doing tourism in a big way. We produced a past expense summary, hinting at the $30,000 spent in two years during our Chiapas programs. If the Mexican government really wanted tourists in Chiapas, we were it.

Sadly, the truth was that the Mexican government didn't want tourists in Chiapas. As Bishop Samuel Ruíz told us in January 1999, you had to be a deaf-mute to be a tourist in Chiapas, had to travel from one acceptable tourist venue to another wearing blinders. Drench yourself in archaeology: Tonina, Palenque, Chincultic and Tenam, Yaxchilán, and Bonampak. This contradiction was a piece of the subtle intimidation, something that I had begun to comprehend. As visitors, we were in Mexico, our NAFTA trading partner, land of azure waters and mysterious and silent archaeological sites. But at the same time, we were in Guatemala, Salvador, Nicaragua, Myanmar, China, and Indonesia.

We knew, of course, that nobody was playing. We were being served a tiny sampling of the constant intimidation that structures the daily life of the people who live in Chiapas, another lesson. We had been cited for following a march related to the Consulta and participating in a prohibited political activity. Was the Consulta political? Was a related march political? Was watching it political? In a setting like this, every act is political. But I wanted to ask Rene the bigger question: why were these political events threatening to the

Mexican government? The answer was evident to anyone who had ever counted troops on the roads in and out of San Cristóbal or read reports of human rights abuses, low-intensity warfare, or small but constant body counts. Chiapas was under thinly veiled martial law, and for this day, the Mexican government chose to extend the conflict zone into San Cristóbal. They were desperately seeking foreign agitators on which to blame the conflict.

Kate and I had watched events surrounding the Consulta from the sidelines until we noticed that a march was beginning to move. A mass of people was exiting the plaza, moving like ants bound for sugar. The march had attracted all of the Zócalo regulars. Chicle boys with their boxes of gum; Chamula women carrying shawls, belts, and Zapatista dolls; a handful of foreigners; and shoeshine boys carrying their gear. We joined it at the rear. A few voices begin to yell in unison.

"Zapata Vive!"

Kate droped back to where I was walking. "If things get weird," she said, "you go left, I go right. We meet back at the hotel."

I nodded in agreement, disregarding the message in our planning, looking at the carnival atmosphere of the passing parade. The chant switched again and seemed familiar.

"El Pueblo Unido Jamás Será Vencido!"

I translated quickly into its 1960s equivalent: The community united can never be divided.

The voices were getting louder, coming together, fists in the air. A couple of kids from Washington State got in step beside me. They were studying in Puebla and thought they ought to take a week and tour Chiapas.

"What's going on here? What's happening?" they asked, totally clueless.

"It's the Consulta," I said.

"What's a Consulta?"

The chant changed again. We were moving toward the highway, picking up people.

"EE, Zeta, Ele, Ene! EE, Zeta, Ele, Ene!"

Kate was photographing. She had the color film, I had the black and white. There were cameras clicking everywhere, a real international Kodak moment.

Another rhythmic yell.

"Todos somos marcos. Todos Somos Marcos. Todos Somos MARCOS."

We were walking along the highway now.

"TODOS SOMOS MARCOS."

The place was crawling with cameramen, videos, and stills; the press was waiting. The Chicle boys backed away, protecting their gum, and the Chamula women kept a respectable distance.

Kate and I observed that a lot of the photographers were not photographing the march or the Mexican demonstrators. They were photographing the foreigners. In fact, a guy in a Cancún sweatshirt and a Nike hat was standing in the bed of a pickup with a handheld video, and he was focusing on us. We decided that it was time to leave. We started strolling back toward the Plaza but realized that the situation called for chocolate and sweet rolls. We ducked into a *panadería*, and Kate ordered one of everything.

We filled a bag with pastries and paid. Just as we were about to leave, a white truck made a screeching U-turn, pulling in front of the bakery. A uniformed man jumped out and walked toward us, not interested in *pan dulce*. He nodded, extended his hand, and said, "Sus papeles, por favor. Sus pasaportes."

The instant I saw the uniform and the file folder and the neat white papers with the fresh blue ink scribble signature belonging to Rene Pulido, I knew we were screwed. It was March again, and like a Tet offensive, the Mexican government was doing its spring cleanup of pesky foreign agitators, just as they had done one year before.

We left there with citations—orders to appear in forty-eight hours—filled out last name first, first name last. This initial iteration of names would appear on Sunday night national television, would be misspelled in the Monday local papers, and would finally be corrected a week later in the *New York Times*.

So it was that on March 23 I sat in a comfortable room in the IMN office, a long way from cells and rubber hoses and electric shocks. Even the expected Smith-Corona was replaced by a computer, with our detaining officer seated at the terminal. I noticed a portable tape recorder on the desk in front of me and a few used videotapes. Rene Pulido came in, shook hands, and positioned himself in the corner on the right side, where he could watch my face, watch my eyes, a special kind of watching. Rene concentrated also on my choice of words. Rene interrupted as I described the "parade."

"This is the most important part here. We must construct this section using words that cannot incriminate you."

He walked behind me. I looked back casually and noticed that he was cuing a handheld video camera. He put the camera down and came in front of the desk, took up his watching position, and waited. We spent the next fifteen minutes searching for words, much as Kate and I had done in our own preparations, the two men and I leaning over the computer conspiratorially.

"Back to the march," Rene guided.

"Parade," I corrected.

"They were . . . saying things . . . like . . . ?"

"El pueblo unido," I began, pausing.

The two men straightened, exchanged glances, then chanted, in unison, *fuerte*, like a couple of 1960s hippies, born too late.

"El Pueblo Unido Jamás Será Vencido!"

My turn to smile. I wondered, fleetingly, if the tape recorder was still running, catching their unbridled enthusiasm. We passed, finally, to the real question. Was the Consulta political?

¿Qué es political? I wasn't sure. What do you think is political? I told him I thought it was something democratic, trying to avoid nasty notions of politics, interference in the affairs of a sovereign nation. But, yes, if democracy was political, so was the Consulta. But we hadn't participated, hence no participation in anything political.

"We're almost done," Rene assured me. "Just a little longer."

"We don't have to watch the video?" I asked, finally.

Rene shook his head. "No, there's no point. And besides, there is no video. We don't do that kind of thing in Mexico."

We both laughed. He was oozing tired charm now. In another world, one where 70,000 troops didn't police and "stabilize" the population of one Mexican state, we might have been friends.

In the end, Rene told us he didn't think we'd have to change our travel plans. But it wasn't up to him. The decisions had been made in Mexico City before the citations took place. We only had to watch the screaming headlines in the papers, follow the inflammatory, inaccurate and misspelled "spin," to know how things would turn out:

"Outsiders Face Expulsion for Chiapas Meddling"

"Immigration Interrogates Ten Foreigners Who Participated in a Zapatista March"

"PROZAPATISTA FOREIGNERS INVITED TO LEAVE MEXICO"

"Rabasa Decries Tension In Chiapas: we will not allow the expulsion of a group of foreigners . . . who were involved with a Zapatista meeting . . . to aggravate the armed conflict in which the place dwells . . . though, without a doubt, these actions create a climate of tension in Chiapas . . . these strangers attack the Mexican laws."

"Mexico: Four More Americans Ousted: Two of them, Jeanne Marie Simonelli, a professor at the State University of New York at Oneonta, and Katherine O'Donnell of Hartwick College, also in Oneonta, denied that they had joined the march and said that they would try to reverse the orders."

On Wednesday, we returned to the INM offices at 8:00 P.M., upbeat, overconfident. We wound up signing copies of expulsion orders—forty-eight hours to leave, no return for two years—and Rene came in, looked us both in the eyes, and said, "I have a moral obligation to help you appeal this decision."

We spent the next half hour looking at immigration documents on how to file an appeal. Rene hesitated but made us copies; we asked about lawyers, but in the end everybody from everywhere had the same answer: Fray Bartolomé de las Casas Centro de Derechos Humanos.

The best show in town.

And Kate and I protested, one last time, that the Human Rights Center was controversial and that we didn't want to be involved in anything political.

On Thursday, we got in a cab and went down to the offices of the Frayba. I introduced us to the receptionist, shyly, that we'd just been expelled from Mexico, and she interrupted, made the "just a moment" sign, and walked to the back of the offices. Out came a tall, dark-haired, dark-eyed man. He took each of our hands and smiled, in gracious welcome: "Las Citatorias. Qué bueno. We've been waiting for you."

In the offices of the Fray Bartolome de las Casas Centro de Derechos Humanos, along with another young American also caught in the net, we filed our lengthy appeals. The Centro lawyers, smart, committed, inflamed with their work, sat at dueling computers composing the documents, legal arguments dancing between them, constitutional questions, fuel for government negotiations. The Diocesan lawyers, the bishop's staff, filed the case, joining ours with the expulsion of priests and nuns and human rights observers, and tacked it on to the up-front issues: the intimidation and repression and murder of Mayas and campesinos. They called it a human rights question, but for me it was a human obligation, an obligation to do what was, in the end, the only thing a middle-class American could really do for Chiapas, and that was to litigate. Let the Frayba lawyers take it to the courts.

The first stage of the appeal, a *recurso de revisión*, stopped the clock on the expulsions. By Friday, the *expulsados* became ex-*expulsados*, and we drank Dos Equis beer to celebrate. In the next four days, passing long hours at the Fray, we shook hands and chatted with the real story of Chiapas: Tzotzil vendors thrown out of the plaza, their wares confiscated; Las Abejas, "the bees," spirited survivors of the December 1997 massacre at Acteal.

We expected that our case would be stuck in the Mexican courts, facing conservative judges, that it would be dumped on the pile of contradictions alive in Chiapas, where 40 percent of the Mexican army remains in a place where nothing is wrong.

As the legal process continued, technically, we could not leave the country without permission, and we were forced to return every three months to keep the appeal alive, our part in keeping Chiapas visible in the international eye. We had attempted to remain neutral, but like most of civil society, we learned that neutrality was a luxury Chiapas could not afford. Back in the United States, my students were busy raising funds for projects as Daniel and DESMU hoped we would. Thousands of miles separated us, but the Chiapas low-intensity war was also a virtual war. Though travel into the Rio Chayote area became more difficult, we were just minutes apart via the Internet.

The hysteria that led the Mexican government to expel foreigners was just another version of the hysteria that led the military and security forces to attack communities in autonomous regions. As the story of Miguel Hidalgo (soon to become Tulan) will show, 1998 was one of the most difficult years for Tierra y Libertad and the Chayote communities.

Part 2

SEEKING A PATH

CHAPTER 5

Roads to Rebellion

We are conscious of how it has to be. We know that it has to be this way for us to win. Our ancestors have been marginalized. Our grandparents have been marginalized. We have been marginalized. We realize now that we are not the ones who will enjoy the fruits of our labor, of our resistance. We have seen how it is, many of us have lived a long life and the government has never helped us. We pleaded for them to help us, but our government never heard us when we asked for health care, for roads, for food for our children. They never gave us anything. And then we demanded these things, but we still never got them. (Cerro Verde, July 24, 2001)

THE LAND FROM WHICH ANTONIO SANCHEZ CRUZ and others would eventually create Orilla del Bosque was carved from a large ranch that became available as a result of the land reform of 1935. In 1951, the forty-six original *ejidatarios* began the process of petitioning for 906 hectares of idle land, *tierras baldías*, to be held in parcels of about 20 hectares each. According to Antonio, "We had been working the land for many years, but the people from the Church told us we needed a paper. We began the petition in 1951, and made our first trip to Tuxtla. In 1952, the engineer came for the first time, but without money you don't get the title. So we worked with the church; they gave us direction even then. It was a two day walk to Comitán, three when the mud was bad."

In 1955, they received their *definitivo*, final title to the parcel. Amplification added another 300 hectares and eight more *ejidatarios*.

In the canyons and jungles of Chiapas, this struggle to acquire and secure use rights to available national lands highlighted the need to understand the law and the ability to organize to use it. Confronting the ramifications of Chiapas's mutated land reform put the colonists into conflict with the ranchers and lumber companies who continued to hold the bulk of the land. A number of authors have described in extensive and excellent detail the birth and proliferation of peasant and civil society organizations that worked to organize the population of the Cañadas and *selva* from the 1960s to the present (see Harvey

1994; Legoretta Díaz 1998; and Rus, Hernández Castillo, and Mattiace 2003, 1–27).[1] While sharing the experience of confronting corrupt and co-opted national, state, and local powers, how that confrontation played out differed according to region, ethnicity, and religion. For Miguel Santiz and the *ejido* of Ojo de Agua, a shared identity figured highly in the shape that autonomy and resistance would ultimately take.

Among the groups that would play a large part in aiding the colonists of Orilla del Bosque in this process were the motorcycling Marist missionaries of the Roman Catholic Church. Beginning in the 1970s, alongside Marist brothers and nuns, families prayed together and began to organize, learning to believe in each other's capacity to right long-standing wrongs and change all that is unjust. Without sacraments, choirs, or priests to remind these tiny congregations of God's eternal presence, they worked on their own because "the word of God has no owner" (De Vos 2002, 238).

Or, as the catechists have stressed since they began facilitating community reflection sessions in the 1970s, "Listen to the Word of God . . . but also 'read the signs of the times'" (De Vos 2002, 39).

THE CATHOLIC CHURCH: "THE WORD OF GOD HAS NO OWNER"

The Roman Catholic Church has been a major facilitator in the expression of social conscience and in the struggle to find a lasting peace in Chiapas. The Church took shape under the tutelage of Bishop Samuel Ruíz García, who arrived in the diocese of San Cristóbal de las Casas in 1960 (Fazio 1994; Meyer 2000). Like other Latin American Catholic leaders of the time who gained inspiration from the Second Vatican Council (1962–1965) and the Latin American Bishops meeting in Medellín, Columbia (1968), Ruíz admits that he was born into belief, into the full flowering of faith, through the accompaniment of the poor and marginalized. This reflects a basic insight of liberation theology, which notes that the poor hold a privileged place in God's plan (Guiterrez 1997). According to Ruíz, their gift to us is that they allow us to companion them in their struggle (interview, January 25, 1999).

Though the change in the relationship between the Roman Catholic Church and the indigenous and mestizo campesinos of Chiapas is often credited to the coming of Don Samuel, it has its roots in the previous decade. As Presbyterian missionaries began to make inroads into indigenous communities, the Church realized that it was time to reconsider the model of evangelization derived from its priest-centered, hierarchical form. In 1952, Samuel's predecessor made possible the participation of the first indigenous catechists, including both men and women. Finally, in 1962, two diocesan schools were established in San Cristóbal to provide training for a large cadre of *catequistas* who learned not just to interpret the Bible but also a little carpentry, horticulture, tailoring, cooking, Spanish, math, and health and hygiene.

Though dynamic in form, the school's teaching methods and content failed to take into consideration the particular cultural practices of the Maya pueblos, and as a result these early catechists returned to their communities to work against the ancient beliefs and practices of their people. Evaluating their experience in 1968, these newly trained representatives of the Catholic Church criticized this and other limitations in their training, saying that "the Church and the Word of God have given us things to save our souls, but we don't know how to save our bodies" (De Vos 2002, 215–21; Kovic 2005).[2] Acting on this call to "embody the gospel" in the cultural and socioeconomic reality in which the indigenous lived, the Church and its missionary teams began a process of theological reflection based in the story of Exodus.

The use of Exodus as a springboard for reflection made great sense in the context of increasing displacement and out-migration occurring in the indigenous communities of Chiapas. Beginning particularly with the Tzeltal-speaking population, pastoral agents saw the opportunity to make comparison with the experience of the Jews. The indigenous were an elected people, set free from the slavery and injustice of the patrons. They had begun the road to the Promised Land of the *selva*, and this was the call to configure a new human experience, one that could transfigure the entire community of believers at the same time. In this light, many Chiapas clerics saw it as their opportunity to remedy the great missionary myopia of the sixteenth century, to wake up and become "conscient"[3] alongside the Maya congregations. Thus, the migration to the jungle became more than a move to a geographical location; it became a movement in social history and a setting for theological change.

Many of these new ideas were born in the Jesuit mission of Bachajón and the parish of Ocosingo, which was responsible for the majority of the Lacandon and whose pastoral team was intimately aware of the problems of living in the *selva*. In the early 1970s, the Ocosingo group held a meeting that invited the Tzeltal catechists to evaluate their work with the Church. Their key observation was that the people didn't speak, didn't participate, because the Church representatives acted too much as lecturers. According to the Tzeltales, the priests, brothers, and nuns needed to be facilitators rather than instructors.

A transition from instructor to facilitator among the priests and mestizo pastoral agents would have been of no consequence had it not been accompanied by a second transition, that of the metamorphosis of the Maya from objects to subjects of their lives in God and on earth. In the evolving theology, the Tzeltal were the elected, called to announce the new age, not just receive the message. Encapsulating this idea, a three-part catechism was produced from the ongoing reflections of the Tzeltal catechists in conjunction with the pastoral agents. This distinctly Maya version of the classic Catholic teaching text explained 1) the thoughts of God from the beginning, 2) how we live in oppression, and 3) faith, hope, and charity.

The second section of the catechism was revolutionary. It provided a concrete and unambiguous reflection on the situation of socioeconomic and cultural marginalization experienced by the indigenous, especially *selva* colonists. In this segment, and in the portion concerning hope, the gospel's spiritual concepts became politicized, localized, and democratized. Gradually, the insights developing among this group spread to much of the diocese of San Cristóbal, and the story of Exodus became a means of understanding and interpreting the ongoing experience of the Maya.

The process of reflection on a verse of scripture using concepts derived from the newly invigorated catechism encapsulated a divine direction from God concerning liberation and self-determination. In verses of the Bible, the Maya found passages that supported cultural autonomy:

> Our culture is like a spring, and from it we have drunk that which we have, that which we know, that which we are. It is here where we encountered God, because God speaks to us through the means of our own culture. . . . And we are united because we have the same hope, the same struggle to arrive at a better life. . . . The second commandment of God says this: Love your brother as you love yourself. God directs that we love ourselves, that we love our race, our community, our family. We don't disparage or forget our race. He who disparages his race disparages his mother, as well as the work of God. (De Vos 2002, 227)

Moreover, the Tzeltal colonists proceeded with the understanding that they were elected to struggle for the liberation of all: "We want to say that our hope and our responsibility is to acquire through our work the new land that God gives us. When the land with her seeds is for all men, it will be the Promised Land" (De Vos 2002, 221–31).

The Tzeltal emphasis on indigenous autonomy and liberation received wider exposure during the First Indigenous Congress, held in 1974, initiated by Chiapas governor Dr. Manuel Velasco Suarez, who sought the assistance of the Church and Bishop Samuel Ruíz. The Congress marked the first time that Chiapas Maya would be able to meet and speak out in a public conference. The bishop agreed to join Church with state on the condition that the meeting not be turned into a folkloric performance but that the indigenous would be allowed to give their true testimony in public after 500 years of silence. In preparation for the Congress, meetings were held in indigenous communities, reflecting on the themes of land, commerce, education, and health.

On October 13, over 1,230 delegates, totaling 587 Tzeltales, 330 Tzotziles, 152 Tojolobales, and 161 Ch'ols, gathered to consider the themes under discussion. A conclusion of the Congress was that the Maya must unite to be able to rise out of the abyss of oppression and exploitation (Kovic 2005).

Though the Congress was successful on many levels, it had not provided a forum for the indigenous to discuss the theme of cultural identity and their feelings toward the work of the Church. In response, in April 1975, Bishop Ruíz convened a meeting in the pueblo of Bachajón to hear and discuss the people's assessments of the Church's work. Stepping forward, Tzeltal catechist Domingo Gomez announced that, indeed, something important was lacking, namely, the opportunity for the people to hold in their hands the ingredients of the faith and to combine them as they saw fit. "Give us the Holy Spirit, and we will no longer blame you," he concluded (De Vos 2002, 215). Recognizing that the age-old structures of the Church and the hierarchical pastoral model engendered continuing dependency, Ruíz vowed to enter onto a road that would let the new Church grow from its indigenous roots and pass its direction on to the people.

At the same time that Samuel Ruíz and the pastoral workers of the diocese were realizing that the Catholic Church in Chiapas had to be an "*iglesia autoctona*," an autochthonous body of believers and practice resurrected from indigenous culture, it was also becoming painfully clear that migration to the Promised Land of the jungle was fast turning it into a wasteland. The long-term exploitation of land by lumber companies and ranches, in conjunction with aggressive agricultural practices, caused a rapid disappearance of vegetation.

As Miguel Santiz confirms, jungle migrants, especially those leaving the highlands after the call for colonization, did so without aid or instruction. As pioneers, they learned to survive in the land through trial and error. If their practices accelerated the process of destruction of the rain forest, it was in the context of trying to find a balance between respect for the natural resources and keeping the family alive. In his pastoral work in the newly settled territory, Brother Javier Vargas Mendoza, a Marist brother working with the Dominicans and past director of one of the catechist schools in San Cristóbal, spent fourteen years observing and documenting conditions in twenty colonies. Some of the production practices of the campesinos seemed to work, such as maintaining a canopy of trees over the cultigens, in order to preserve the jungle soil. Others were utter failures, such as the introduction of pigs, which were a quick fix when money was needed but competed ear for ear for the basic maize resources of the community and ate the young coffee plants as well. At the same time, Brother Javier was aware of the growing currents of dissatisfaction and discontent spreading through the jungle. Commenting on the hardships of the Tzeltal colonists, he cautioned that there is respect for the authorities, but at the same time lack of confidence, product of a long, negative experience of exploitation. This lack of confidence grows each time a functionary or commercial intermediary acts with deceit. From this, attitudes of ill will, stubbornness, passivity, hostility close off possibilities for dialog. They don't see valid efforts, using technical, economic, and legal resources that guarantee rational activity, in which they participate as managers and receive just benefits. True communication with them demands knowledge of the language, culture, values, interests and necessities. Their confidence is won not from words, but from deeds. (Javier Vargas, quoted in De Vos 2002, 174)

These deeds were not forthcoming. Then, as now, the government's call to go, colonize, and produce was unaccompanied by the injunction or mechanisms to market the coffee, plantains, and other potentially commercial items they cultivated. The arduous process of acquiring legal, definitive title to the land sometimes lasted over twenty-five years (Reyes Ramos 1992, 95–122). The absence of real technical advice; the lack of resources to act on sustainable, rational development practices that grew from the jungle experience; and continuing altercations between colonists and with elite landowners all became ingredients in the stew of discontent. Ultimately, the Mexican government's capricious solution to the Lacandon problem—the declaration that the 500 Lacandon-speaking Maya were the legitimate descendants and rightful owners of 600,000 hectares of the rain forest—was both cause and effect of the increasing unrest. From the perspective of the authorities, the Lacandones were utterly apolitical and thus easily manageable. They would be far easier to deal with than the other campesinos who had begun organizing.

What the Lacandon Maya did bring to the situation was their long-tested method of milpa cultivation, one that worked within the jungle context (Nations and Nigh 1980; Nigh 2001). Like anyone who has spent careful time observing and participating in *selva* production, by 1975 Javier Vargas came to similar conclusions about models of sustainable agriculture. Optimum use of the jungle involved a locally rational division between traditional milpa and potentially commercial cultigens, household garden, pasture, and forest reserve, dispersed in a way that replicated the natural jungle. Like the Zapatistas who followed, Vargas realized that the creation of successful demonstration farms would be the only real method of making hard-pressed campesinos change practices. Leftist agricultural engineers from the Mexican technical university at Chapingo proposed similar concepts. Twenty-five years later, other academics would finally reach similar conclusions concerning ecologically sound practices.

In contrast to jungle colonies to the east, where families of culturally intact Maya sought and settled colonies together, Orilla del Bosque was a conglomerate. Like Antonio, some of its founding members (*originarios*) were Tojolobal day laborers from the immediate area whose family members spoke little or no Tojolobal. In the official census of the INI, they were second-generation Maya who had made a "successful" transition to the national Mexican identity. Others were Chiapas mestizos unable or uninterested in tracing their indigenous ancestry. Still others came from neighboring states such as Vera Cruz, product of the call for colonists issued nationally in the 1960s. In truth, this portion of the Rio Chayote was the margin of the margin, its settlers a forgotten brew of people inhabiting lands peripheral to the Lacandon experience, as delineated by the administrative and ecological criteria of the era.[4] Not part of the Catholic Maya missions working to refine the indigenous Church, it was 1980 before social circumstances would converge to bring pastoral teams into the shrinking jungle, armed with Exodus and the catechist model.

As in other *ejidos* along the river's course, many Orilla members had recently converted to Protestantism, and *ejido* leadership, a rotating elected office, was becoming dominated by Presbyterians. At the same time, refugees from the Guatemalan war were streaming across the border, finding their way through the looming Cuchamatanes Mountains, pursued by the Guatemalan military. As in Ojo de Agua farther south, they sought shelter in and among the *ejidos* and ranches of the Chayote. In response, pastoral teams from the diocese Zona Sur joined international and nongovernmental agencies offering aid to the refugees, many of whom were nominally Catholic. Using motorcycles to get from one remote location to another, the Marist mission responded to a multifaceted call to a region where rising population, deteriorating environmental conditions, and politicoreligious division were about to collide.

The particular circumstances of the *selva* migration, the social awakening of the Church, and the need to organize for strength led to a serendipitous alliance between radical catechist campesinos, Maoist agronomists, and incipient unions in the Cañadas and *selva* of Ocosingo and Margaritas. Though the Church and its pastoral teams would struggle with differences on the road through the jungle and to an autochthonous Church, it was this branch of liberated theology that would be carried to the *ejido* Orilla del Bosque. Beginning with regularity in the late 1970s, pastoral teams directed by Marists from Comitán, including Javier Vargas, would carry the Word of God and Sustainable Agriculture to the communities of colonists along the Rio Chayote, including Cerro Verde, the *ejido*'s new annex.

CERRO VERDE: DEFINING RESISTANCE

In 1980, a new road was cut and graded along the course of the Rio Chayote, replacing the rough jungle track. It intersected with the paved "highway" moving slowly along the Mexico–Guatemala frontier, encouraging colonization, commerce, and evangelization. With the promise of improved access that the

Mural in La Realidad of Marcos, Zapata, and sustainable agriculture, all of which are components of resistance

graded side road would provide, several members of the *ejido* Orilla del Bosque elected to create Cerro Verde, an annex and population center closer to the river and along the new route. To the campesinos, the road held the possibility of markets and easier access to the city of Comitán, where they might be able to sell the few commercial goods they produced, including the coffee they began cultivating during the early 1970s. This easy access also foreshadowed other social changes.

In the heart of the jungle, independent peasant organizations were forming; agroecological and production cooperatives became the social forces dealing with land reform, labor, commercialization, and credit. Sometimes allied, sometimes in competition, these groups established communication between distant locales and gave the campesinos a united voice (Collier and Quaratiello 1994, 69–81). Though facing the same issues plaguing campesinos families in other parts of Chiapas, the eclectic composition of the Cerro Verde *ejido*—indigenous, mestizos, and immigrants from other states—worked against unity rather than for it.

When Marist Brother Javier Vargas sought out the families of the newly established *ejido* annex at Cerro Verde, Antonio Sanchez Cruz was already a grandfather.

"We knew very little about organizing," remembers Luz, Antonio's eldest daughter. As the child of one of the *ejido*'s *originarios*, she and her new husband Rodrigo, one of Antonio's senior sons-in-law, became *ejido* members with their own land:

> We began organizing in Orilla del Bosque in the 1970s. After the move, in the 1980s we voted more liberally. In 1989, everyone voted PRD.[5] Everyone was Catholic. Then the evangelical pastors began to arrive, first the Presbyterians, then the Pentecostals. The ejido began to divide based on religion and then they switched parties to the PRI, to get the government aid. (Cerro Verde, July 24, 2001; interview July 30, 2000; FBCDH PLA 00011)

Javier Vargas also remembers those days:

> Luz and Rodrigo were a young couple when I first met them. They had one daughter only, Ana, who had a difficult childhood, and they sought medical care with the nuns in Comitán. Like the other young adults, they were uneducated, without shoes, even, trying to survive on what their milpas produced, and anxious to learn production techniques that might increase their yields, and give them something to sell. We began working with some of the members, and they learned to read with the Bible. Even though there was a primary school at that time in Rio Blanco, complete, with a teacher, it was an hour's walk away, and the young people, the heart of the community were already grown. So we taught a few, and they taught each other. In this way they learned to speak, to feel capaz, capable to interpret both the Word of God, and the world around them.
>
> The communities were in charge of the process. They formed committees and some became catechists. It was dynamic, they had such wisdom, and the reflection and learning gave life to this. Their faith began to live in their daily life. The young women and men, with their new families, began collective work, especially in health and education, providing for themselves what the government failed to provide. Where there were no medicines, they began herbal gardens, set up a community pharmacy, learned to be health promotoras as they learned to make the environment they lived in healthier. All of this was born from the Word of God. It was a great horizon of hope. (interview with Javier Vargas, August 5, 2002)

Recalling those early days, community member and catechist Davíd Hernández Gomez agreed:

> Through the Church we learned to organize, to listen with care, to form committees. The men and women in this community work well together, they complement each other. It was the same need to organize that we realized, so as men and women, we became united to help each other. Since we are one family and one people doing the same job, all our jobs we do here as collective . . .

we do organized work. . . . The women created their own systems of support and informal organization, which were facilitated by the Church and the cate-quistas. (interview, July 2000)

But according to Brother Javier, "There was a great deal happening in the early 1990s, violence, changes in agrarian law, organizing. The Church had helped to open the road, but there were other paths, and so the separation between groups began."

We heard the details of this story of the separation between groups for the first time in July 1999, an oral history that helped us continue to document the saga of this frontier region. In the months following Jeanne's first naive encounter with this group of "Mexicans," the story had been peeled back with a calculated but nonchalant grace that reflected a slow growth of trust in the midst of justified suspicion.

The men retired to a closed room to plot out a seven-point presentation that would take us from the 1980s into the current era.[6] As we waited, Duncan was out under the dining ramada, whittling a piece of coffee wood, drinking sweet coffee with Don Antonio. The old man's reminiscences meandered through time, collapsing some events and keeping others current, much the way that tales are told in everyday conversation. The revolution that pre-dated his birth merged with the era of land distribution, the breakup of one of the largest ranches in the area, and the establishment of Orilla del Bosque.

Duncan elicited Tojolobal vocabulary from the depths of Antonio's memory as Jeanne bounced Luz's daughter around the outskirts of the ramada.

Luz took the baby and slipped her back into her rebozo as the other women arrived to cook the feast that would accompany our afternoon meeting. In the distance, a gray rumbling began in the sky, a mechanical sound that was not thunder. We all looked up beyond the rooftops, as a dark blue two-engined plane began a low circle over the compound. Not a tiny prop, like the tourists use to cut across the southwestern tip of the jungle on the way to the Montes Azules Reserve or the archaeological sites on the Usamacinta River, but a military transport belonging to the State Security Forces. Seguridad Pública. The blue meanies.

"Should I go put mud on the license plates?" Duncan asked, indicating our rented VW bug. The plane pulled up and away, circling back over a few minutes later. According to sources, these planes were outfitted with sophisticated tracking devices, gifts from the Americans for use in curbing the drug trade. At the start of the uprising, they had been quickly pressed into service to track Zapatistas (Nash 2001, 137). We laughed together and moved out to take a photo of the plane, knowing that in spite of my tenuous immigration status, it was far better to show that we had nothing to hide.

Davíd opened the door to Luz and Rodrigo's tiny plank house and called to Duncan and me. I put down the bottle of Nan 2 formula I was preparing for Luz to give to her youngest baby and followed the two men into the room. A circle of chairs was set in front of an old bureau holding an aged black-and-white television. When there was electricity, its one channel kept the community appraised of the international news. They were better informed than most of the people I knew, and we had discussions concerning everything from floods and fires in the United States to past massacres in Kosovo.

We took our seats in the circle amidst a gathering of all the men of the community. These men were the patriarchs, founders of the *ejido*. They were the youth nurtured by the Church, now grown to grandfathers, and baptized as elders by both age and experience. These were their sons, raised up in the struggle, socialized from birth to meet, reflect, discuss, and share the decision-making process. It was second nature now, but for their fathers it had been an evolution. Davíd remembered the community's dilemma.

"Yes, it was the Church that helped us to wake up, to know that we needed to know more, and we were grateful," he began, as I listened and Duncan took notes. "We had worked with the Church in a number of projects, health and education. Rodrigo worked with ISMAM,[7] going to Motozintla and Tapachula, to learn to grow better coffee and to find avenues to market it. But finally, we were pensive, seeking for a path."

It was that preoccupation that would lead them into the mountains in 1994 in search of the Zapatistas.

"This is how our work began, then, knowing what the Church taught us, to respect our heritage and identity as indigenous, to trust in our dear god. But we heard that there were others further into the jungle who could teach us more. We talked among ourselves and asked 'En donde estan trabajando estos hermanos?' Where were these brothers working, and where could we find them?

"Three of us went off, looking to find the EZLN. We walked up into the mountains, to La Revancha, but we were not known to the people we found there.

"'Who are you people? We do not know you,' we were told. The first time we went, we weren't trusted. They sent us away.

"We came back to Cerro Verde, and we waited. We met among ourselves, and we talked. But we wanted to know how to enter into resistance, so we walked back into the mountains. This time, well, we were received, at least. They gave us some ideas to take back with us to the others.

"Again we waited, and we talked. And then we returned to them a third time. Finally. They took our names, and they gave us much better information. We liked it, yes, and because of our faith, we heard it. We heard it well.

"When we came back this time to Cerro Verde, we began speaking to raise awareness, to many who were frightened. For fear, others thought to leave the community completely, but that was kept under control. We knew that we could stay and work underground, informally. About twenty families, twenty-five families, were with us. Then, one year later, we made a declaration in the village and the *ejido* that we were in resistance" (interview, July 30, 2000).

Zapatista refusal to meet with Cerro Verde representatives in their initial forays into the mountains is in sharp contrast to the image of a middle-class Marxist army seeking out and entrapping hapless Indians in a futile armed struggle, as presented in mainstream accounts of the rebellion (Oppenheimer 1996). The group's story supported the Zapatistas' own version of their arrival in Chiapas, of chilly rain-soaked months waiting for the Maya to seek them out. Arriving in 1983, they took refuge deep in the mountains, at times taking shelter in caves like those beyond the village of Guadalupe Tepeyac. According to some accounts, their only contact with the villagers was as medical volunteers, promoting vaccination campaigns throughout the Cañadas (Ross 1995, 279). Gradually, the people of nearby indigenous villages came to seek them out, eventually appropriating the struggle, melding it into a Maya model of rebellion. This version of the Zapatista creation myth was credible to us because it replicated our own experience in getting to know the Chayote communities. Little by little, visit after visit, trust was established, and decisions to share information were made.

The taking of municipal headquarters in six Chiapas cities on January 1, 1994, by armed members of the EZLN was followed by twelve days of active war. For those marginalized indigenous and campesinos who lived in areas bordering the Zapatista strongholds but who were not directly involved in the armed confrontation, it was a signal of hope and impending change. The Church was split by theological debate, and the campesino unions had failed to come to an adequate political solution (Legoretta Díaz 1998). For the families of Cerro Verde who ultimately made the decision to enter into resistance, it was a sign that there was another way to confront the endless poverty and hunger, that they were not powerless. The Zapatistas had taken up the armed struggle, and without doing so themselves, the families could become part of a united front and provide a base of support. Their assistance to the movement began in the form of peaceful civil resistance to government policies and programs, those age-old pork-barrel handouts that served to foster division and envy, one PRI program after another that served to create dependency and make a sham of democratic practice by buying votes in exchange for aid.

"We made a formal declaration in front of the *ejido* committee that we were in resistance. We did this even though the *ejido* said that they would throw out Zapatistas. It surprised some of the others that there were those in resistance. In the assembly, we made a declaration of resistance, and we made an agreement with the *ejido* that there were some things that we would not participate in. We said that we would cooperate in all activities that had to do with agriculture, that had to do with the fields and the trails, but not health or education. An *ejido* is about agriculture after all, and we would not use our labor to promote other government projects supported by PRI money. Our declaration, the *acta*, was respected at first, but we had not documented it. It was just verbal. In 1994 (at the time of the January 1 uprising), we were not integrated with the Zapatistas. But after 1994, we became integrated with the Organization. That's when the persecutions of our community began."

Davíd paused in the story, and the men seemed to heave a corporate sigh. These individual topes in the formation of their work as a resistance community were raw wounds, and each remembrance was an opportunity to reflect on the decisions that had been made.

We glanced at each other. When we made our first trip together, we were still acting on Jeanne's astronomical naïveté concerning the political leanings of the community. We were interested in how NGOs such as DESMU worked with the Mexican campesinos, as they had been described to us. Not-so-subtle signs soon clarified some of Cerro Verde's politics. Wandering the enclave was a political dog pack. The alpha male was Cleenton, a russet-colored mutt of golden retriever ancestry, whose birth coincided with the signing of the NAFTA treaty. His look-alike son was named Zedillo, after the Mexican president. And finally there was Albores. A roly-poly pup, he resembled his rotund namesake, the interim governor of Chiapas who would order the second invasion of the Lacandon in 1998. Even the latrine had political referents. Hidden deep in a grove of orange trees and coffee plants, it was named after Zedillo and invited you to make a deposit in the mouth of the PRI party. Regardless of these hints, in an early article about the group, Jeanne wrote that "though the families with whom we worked were not flagrant, armed rebels or professed Zapatistas, they were openly in resistance. They were rebelling against inadequate or non-existent services and blocked access to the markets and education that might make a difference in their lives" (Simonelli 2002, 48). Now, we were slowly learning the extent of Cerro Verde's involvement with their organization.

Jeanne's ignorance of exactly who and what Cerro Verde and Tulan were politically was a blessing in disguise during the interrogation process surrounding her expulsion. Since she knew nothing about their Zapatista involvement, there was no way to be caught in a lie. And in the final analysis, that we entered into the situation from the perspective of community development and not as part of an ongoing search for the one true Marcos helped gain the trust of the community. Duncan could speak about the degradation of the natural environment and the development of the coffee economy from firsthand experience, providing mutual points of reference and conversation that went back over twenty years and did not hinge on pure politics. With each visit, we learned a little more.

THE FIRST INVASION OF THE LACANDON

"In 1995, the army came." It was Rodrigo's turn to narrate the story. "It was February 9. The names of many of our followers had been given in a list to the Seguridad Publica. Some in the ejido ignored the accord, and the denuncias began."

The February invasion of the Lacandon jungle marked the end of the cease-fire that had been in effect since January 1994, one of the worst years in recent history for the Mexican nation as a whole. President Carlos Salinas Gortari, in his sixth and final year of presidency at the time of the uprising, was not succeeded by his handpicked heir, who was assassinated in March 1994. Ernesto Zedillo was chosen to follow Salinas, in a decades-old practice of naming the PRI candidate, who was affirmed through irregular electoral practices. Taking office on December 1, 1994, Zedillo inherited an economy in crisis and an indigenous rebellion. Following the collapse of the peso that began on December 19, 1994, over U.S.$10 billion in foreign capital was withdrawn from the country by investors questioning the nation's stability. Indeed, a memo that was quoted in the February 17, 1995, *Washington Post* and attributed to the Chase Manhattan Bank stated that "the [Mexican] government will need to eliminate the Zapatistas to demonstrate their effective control of the national territory and of security policy" (Oppenheimer 1996, 244). On February 8, the peso hit an all-time low. The voice of international capital was strident: invade the jungle, eliminate the Zapatista leadership, or lose financing.

On February 9, acting on information provided by a purported Zapatista defector that identified Subcomandante Marcos as a middle-class Marxist Mexican named Rafael Guillen, the government issued a warrant for his arrest and that of other "terrorists." Among those sought for political crimes was Jorge Santiago Santiago, director of DESMI,[8] a Church-backed NGO that promoted agroecological models of community development, sustainable agriculture, and self-sufficiency. In response to just such ongoing "treasonous" acts, over 30,000 troops streamed into the Lacandon.

"We were all in one house, when the army came and surrounded us."

Those who came together in the house in Cerro Verde on February 9 to pray, plan, and shelter their children from the ensuing wave of destruction of homes and crops did not include the subcomandante. They did include women and men, teenagers, and grandparents who had been schooled in the Church's notions of ecology and sustainability and, since their declaration of resistance in the *ejido* assembly, worked collectively with other Zapatista support communities in the interests of health, education, and production. This was the *trabajo* that the community so cherished, especially the women, who took on new and expanded roles in all aspects of their daily lives. Attending workshops, learning and teaching health and hygiene, and designing a primary school curriculum that was responsive to the history and needs of their own children were the terrorist acts of these rebel communities.

As we sat listening to the men's version of the story, we thought of our separate conversations with the women. "I love my work with the women," Luz once commented, as we drank thick, dark café in the tiny communal kitchen.

Even the protective *cuarenta*, the forty-day period of seclusion after the birth of a baby, became an unwelcome interruption in the new and improved division of labor guaranteed by the Zapatista Women's Bill of Rights and embraced by the women and men of the community, the amazing and functional Zapatista feminism we had seen in action during our visits.

"In the small pueblos we have different areas of work—health care, education, representatives for the Church," added her sister Alma, Davíd's wife. "And we share Catechism with the children, and share our work with the children. This is what we have at one level of the group. Some of our women do health care. Since 1995 we became integrated with the others in health care. We became capacitated to help our own families. This came about by necessity. We looked for people to help us become capable."

These meetings to plan strategy, the increasing number of training workshops, and follow-up reflection sessions brought other resistance groups to the Cerro Verde compound. And these gatherings only heightened suspicion among the PRIista factions of the community.

According to Alma, "We began to suffer, to run. We began to run because the military occupied the town. There were police, Federal troops, and people were being asked to watch us. It was partly because we were in resistance, and partly because we are Catholic and there are a lot of evangelical church groups here. The village is very divided, and it has gotten worse since the struggle began in 1994. Everyone in the village was Catholic before the struggle. The sects divide the people; the evangelicals receive food and money from the government."

Now, Rodrigo's continuing narrative affirmed this telling. "The army began to have a 'social service' presence in the village. Those who didn't come for social service, well, it was clear that they were the resistance. We decided then that it was time for us to become more integrated, to have a more united response. So then it was that we began an effort to have an autonomous municipality."

The first invasion of the Lacandon jungle had combined destruction and overt violence against rebel communities with the construction of a fortress of intimidation, the hallmarks of low-intensity warfare.[9] Though it is possible that the spring 1995 initiative may have been timed to immediate political and military objectives, subsequent spring incursions were not accidental. Designed to divide men from women and disrupt the normal flow of daily life, there was no timing so dangerous as during the critical annual planting cycle. Interrupt any phase—clearing, burning, planting—and six months later families were without corn and beans, without food. That winter, they would be forced to sell coffee to the first coyote that passed through, needing money to buy food and seed. And then the army would arrive, handing out beans, rice, and corn.

With the permanent arrival of the military in the Rio Chayote valley, the little graded road cut in the 1980s chugged on through to the north to connect with the road to the Zapatista strongholds. "After 1994, that's when the government started to fix the roads, so they could get in. They did it for the benefit of the military, and so they could continue to watch us."

Between disruption caused by daily patrols of the military and the state security forces and the increasing demands of cooperative work, Cerro Verde's economic trajectory took a downturn. Though the entire *ejido* applied for and received organic designation from a Brazilian certifying agency for much of its coffee, the continuing war made it impossible to keep parcels of land certified. Daily life was shaped by a complex mixture of avoiding government offensive actions, known as "preventative counterinsurgency," completing collective obligations, and making deliberate choices concerning the definition of well-being and future prosperity.

In December 1995, thirty-eight geographical regions in all corners of the Chiapas conflict zone took development into their own hands by forming autonomías. Thirty-two survived the Lacandon invasion, building governments and programs with varying success. Cerro Verde became part of Tierra y Libertad, the largest and most sophisticated. A fair amount of the planning took place in the compound that surrounded the little house that Luz and Rodrigo shared with their children.

"And we refused to go over to the side of the government, to eat government food, because it is tainted. We needed our own strength, and we kept strong by working together. This became our trabajo. And that's when we knew we had to look for our own authorities, to coordinate us, to organize us, and to help us to educate ourselves. Our enemies made us strong."

This seemed to be the case. Government actions to crush Zapatista resistance backfired, as oppression strengthened their resolve. The government response was a dark teacher, a working model of how not to win over the people.

Rodrigo paused to wipe away the sweat that was gathering on his face. The little room was closed room and dark, the air was dense and still. Suddenly, the door flew open. His niece Marisa came bouncing in, weighted down by Davíd's gurgling baby. Davíd smiled at her, looking out through the bottle-thick lenses of prison-issue glasses.

"Then the repression really began," Rodrigo added.

NOTES

1. It is not our intention to write a comprehensive history of this process or of the experience of the Church but instead to set the sociopolitical stage for what was to follow in the communities we are accompanying.

2. The bulk of the discussion of the role of the Church through the mid-1970s derives from this excellent social history.

3. In Spanish, the term used for this awakening is to "*tomar consciencia*," a phrase with no direct translation in English.

4. Hernández Castillo (2001a, 3–4) comes to a similar conclusion concerning Mam settlers who established a colony east of the Chayote. Officially "mestizo," these colonists used shared identity as Jehovah's Witnesses as an opportunity for cohesion and organization.

5. Partido de la Revolución Democrática (party of the Democratic Revolution).

6. The first two points, formation of the work and declaration of rebellion, are covered in this section. For the remainder, see chapter 8.

7. ISMAM (Indígenas de la Sierra Madre de Motozintla) is an organization that works with coffee production and commercialization in the Sierra de Motozintla, a distant but active portion of Tierra y Libertad.

8. DESMI is Desarrollo Económico Social de los Mexicanos Indígenas, AC, not the same as DESMU.

9. Low-intensity warfare is characterized by low but constant body counts, maximum disruption in the daily lives of the people, and the strategic use of partisan development aid. For descriptions of how low-intensity warfare manifests in Chiapas, see Ortiz (2001, esp. 141–92); see also Olivera Bustamente (2001, 103–17).

CHAPTER 6

Construction, Destruction, and Reconstruction

FAILED NEGOTIATION: BUILDING THE ORGANIZATION, 1995–1998

"AFTER 1995, WE BECAME INTEGRATED together, especially for health care. We became capacitated to help our families. This came about by necessity, as we looked for people to help us learn. We went to them to teach us hygiene, concerning health issues, how to protect ourselves from disease. We learned about Western medicines and about herbal and medicinal plants and trees. The health promoters learned acupuncture, massage, how to administer plant remedies. We looked for people in civil society to teach us these things because we saw the necessity for health care. And we share our burdens, our responsibilities, but we also share our happiness. Everyone here does their own specific jobs, so everyone has their own role in the community, the collective, the Organization."

The first invasion of the Lacandon in February 1995 prefaced long months of alternating hope and desperation. With the initial cease-fire officially broken and the new Zedillo government under orders to stabilize Chiapas, a massive militarization program began. By June 1996, there were forty-four military installations in Chiapas, thirty more than at the time of the invasion (Nash 2001, 189; from Global Exchange 1998). By 1997, estimates of troop numbers varied, ranging from low-end figures of 40,000 to upper estimates of 70,000, roughly 40 percent of the whole Mexican army. The low-intensity war continued, a program of preventative counterinsurgency designed to eliminate "problems" before they could even begin to occur. Soldiers masquerading as social servants monitored the insurgent threat of autonomous and independent schools and rural clinics. In the highlands, the Cañadas, and the area surrounding the Zapatista centers of Realidad and Guadalupe Tepeyac, peace camps sprouted, staffed by international observers whose aim was to keep the quiet war from escalating into renewed armed conflict. But in the Rio Chayote, the Zapatista bases were on their own, relying on the eyes and ears of NGOs like DESMU to keep overt violence at a minimum. As the militarization of the area continued, this became an active piece of the NGOs' work.

On the official level, dialogue began and ended and failed to bear lasting fruit. Zapatistas had rejected the original government proposals in June 1994 but accepted the mediation of the CONAI (Comisión Nacional de Intermediación [National Commission of Mediation]) under the direction of Samuel Ruíz. They weathered the first Lacandon invasion and agreed to return to negotiation and dialogue after the February 1995 arrest warrants that had been issued for purported and actual leaders were suspended. Months of discussion began between the Zapatistas, CONAI, and the government-created COCOPA (Comisión de Concordia y Pacificación [Commission for Agreement and Pacification]) in the highland village of San Andrés Larrainzar, now San Andrés Sacam Ch'en de los Pobres. In the same months, a series of local, state, and national meetings led to the birth of the CNI in Mexico City, as work on four areas of discussion—Indigenous Rights and Culture, Democracy and Justice, Welfare and Development, and Women's Rights—continued in San Andrés. Of the four foci, only the first would yield any kind of agreement. On February 16, 1996, the San Andrés Accords on Indigenous Rights and Culture was signed by the EZLN and the Mexican government. But the government failed to show up for the next round of dialogue, and after consultation with its support bases, the Zapatistas suspended negotiations.

A key portion of the San Andrés Accords focused on the demand that indigenous autonomy be recognized. The Zapatista presence helped vitalize that demand, but the struggle for formal recognition of cultural autonomy predated the uprising: "it represented years of collective development by pluriethnic indigenous groups that coalesced in the monumental conventions of indigenous people and their supporters that began with the quincentennial [1992] celebration of five hundred years of resistance" (Nash 2001, 199). The Accords recognized the right of indigenous peoples to communal autonomy and self-determination in areas ranging from development and language to women's rights, education, and health practices (see CIACH, AC 2001). In the daily, lived form, autonomy also included a move to recover traditional indigenous agriculture, promote organic production, control production and marketing, and eliminate commercial middlemen. Forms of democratic governance involving widespread participation by all members of the community in political process were a culturally acceptable replacement for electoral democracy (Hernández Castillo 2001a, 219).

In the jungle, the Zapatistas continued their own work of forming and strengthening autonomous municipalities and hosted the First Intercontinental Encounter For Humanity and Against Neoliberalism, known as the Intergalactic Encounter. Emerging from the muddy remains of this jungle gala, the EZLN set five conditions for the resumption of talks. These were as follows: 1) liberation of all the presumed-Zapatista political prisoners as well as those members of the Zapatista support base detained in the north of Chiapas; 2) designation of a government negotiating team with decision-making capacity, the political will to negotiate, and respect for the Zapatista delegation; 3) installation of the Implementation and Verification Commission as well as the implementation of the Accords signed on the issue of indigenous rights and culture; 4) serious and concrete proposals from the government for the talks on democracy and justice and a commitment from the government delegation to reach agreements on this theme; and 5) an end to the climate of persecution and military harassment against the indigenous communities of Chiapas as well as the disappearance of the *guardias blancas*, or a law that gives them institutional recognition and uniforms so that they cannot operate with impunity.

Ignoring the stipulations, COCOPA proposed a constitutional amendment on indigenous rights, based on the San Andrés Accords. After lengthy consultation with its bases, the Zapatistas accepted the amendment, but the Zedillo government reneged. They put forward an entirely different and unacceptable proposal, a version of which would ultimately be signed into constitutional law in 2001. By 1997, the peace process was at a standstill, and the countryside was heavily militarized and patrolled. The official federal army and state security forces were augmented by a series of armed paramilitary groups, descendants of the revolutionary-era mapaches.

Through all the months of deliberation, concordance, and betrayal on the bureaucratic level, the families of the newly formed autonomous municipality of Tierra y Libertad living in the Rio Chayote worked to construct the world being negotiated for them. They divided up the work, forming committees and choosing committee leaders to serve initial three-year terms. Working in the areas of education, health, production, safety, and external affairs, women, men, and children over age twelve took on responsibility for cooperative tasks on the community and municipal levels. In their work, they sought help from the women and men working for DESMU.

THE *ENGANCHO*

"The government is optimistic, without grounding. In the last four years, life has gotten worse in Chiapas. . . . They build a fortification of intimidation around the people; intensifying the divisions within the community to create the impression that it is the people that are fighting each other. There is injustice, with impunity, in the midst of poverty and starvation. . . . Yet we have darkness with light inside, and that light is the hope" (interview, Samuel Ruíz, January 13, 1999).

As 1997 drew to a close, life was getting steadily worse for campesino communities throughout Chiapas. In the Highlands, forty-five people lay dead in the tiny hamlet of Acteal because growing unrest and violence had been ignored. In the Rio Chayote valley, PRIistas vied with Guatemalan refugees and Zapatista supporters for fewer and fewer resources. The army patrolled with disturbing regularity. It was clear to those working for DESMU that injustice in the midst of poverty and starvation, as described by Bishop Samuel Ruíz, was unacceptable. The Zapatistas agreed.

For several years, observers in the Zapatista communities watched NGO representatives as they crisscrossed the zone in their refugee aid work, sometimes walking for days from the last paved road. The Zapatista leaders of the newly organized autonomous municipality of Tierra y Libertad kept track of their movements and projects and took notice of the funds and resources flowing into neighboring enclaves. In late 1996, they began negotiations with staff members of five border-region NGOs, asking to be included in the projects in some creative way.

Inspired by these preliminary conversations with the *autónomo* leadership and no longer ethically able to work only with refugees, DESMU directors sought and acquired funding from a Swiss foundation to begin a beekeeping enterprise with the women of the Zapatista support community of Miguel Hidalgo. The Mexican women met with DESMU-UN–funded refugee counterparts already involved in honey production in order to learn how to handle bees. Though this kind of creative and efficient use of funds and regional resources, crosscutting special interests, is exactly what grassroots development needed, it violated the NGO's official charge as a refugee aid organization. Though the choice would return to haunt the NGO's leadership, DESMU continued to seek backing for small projects for eight Zapatista support communities in Tierra y Libertad, moving quietly off the politically neutral fence that refugee work had allowed them to straddle. When Daniel took the Chiapas Project into the Rio Chayote valley on that early morning in January 1998, they were inviting us to move into the fray with them.

Jeanne (1998–1999): With its flat tire fixed, the rented micro carrying the students of the Hartwick-Oneonta Chiapas Project inched its way up a narrowing dirt roadway overlooking the teal blue waters of the Rio Chayote. We drove on another hour; the road got thinner. We passed the Telesecondaria, a big satellite dish bringing high school classes into a valley people seldom leave. The road ended. We all got out and walked.

Escorted by Daniel and DESMU codirector Claudia, we went first to visit a remote refugee community called Nuevo Israel, where Guatemalan families sharecropped borrowed land belonging to a long-time Ladino rancher. We had a Polaroid camera with us, seemed like a good idea at the time, and the students took scores of pictures—pictures of women with babies, pictures of babies with grandfathers, pictures of grandfathers with daughters, pictures of daughters with gringo students, pictures of gringos with babies—and we left them all behind. When we departed, Daniel was out ahead, and as I hurried down to join him, I had a slight twinge of conscience. Suppose the photos turned up later, on some rampaging army day, when both the official and the autonomous governments didn't know it had been okay for us to be there? What were the implications of celluloid gringo faces in Guatemalan refugee camps? That question was answered almost immediately.

At the bottom of the slope, Daniel stood talking with a tall man in cowboy hat and button-down shirt. He had a high-powered rifle tucked under his arm, and the sound of Spanish was heated, Daniel nodding his head. Still smiling, he called me over.

"Juanita, this is the patron. This is his land. He wants to know why you are here."

I looked hard at Daniel. He said softly, "I can't help you here."

Daniel sat down, Claudia beside him, in the hot *selva* sun in front of the patron, in front of a line of day laborers sharpening machetes in a wide arc around the landowner. I looked at the man's face and saw PRI, saw *mapache*, engrained history, saw paramilitary, saw in living color one side of the Chiapas conflict. I clicked into a tourist litany mode, naming points of interest: Palenque, Tonina, Lagos de Montebello.

The man cut me off, no bullshit here.

"You must understand," he said. "I have no problem with you visiting the refugees. I have no problem with DESMU trying to help the people I allow to remain on my land. But I have a big problem with gringos who come here wanting to help the campesinos, looking for Zapatistas and Subcomandante Marcos. I see Americans, in this time of conflict, and I cannot assume that you are here to just look at Guatemalan chickens."

All this in rapid Spanish, the students lined up behind me, Daniel and Claudia sitting on the ground, the sun beating down on my neck, the men sharpening machetes. The bad news was we were going to get hacked to pieces, Acteal style. The good news was the machetes would be sharp. Well, folks, you wanted to see the real Chiapas.

We stood in standoff mode, going round and round with fruitless discussion for almost an hour. Finally, the patron leaned the rifle against a tree and turned away from us; dismissal. Daniel stood and led the group down the path to the bubbling river. We took out lunch, and the patron rode down on horseback and watched us until we left. He watched, and there was no place to go, nowhere we could walk, no way to go to the bathroom. Fortification of intimidation. This was a minor version of the encircling tactics that were part of Chiapas's low-intensity war. They kept children from going to school, men from going to the milpa, women from going to the river to wash, gringas from going to the bathroom. We were learning fast.

Back to the micro, Daniel giggled, his smile turned nervous.

"There's a Comunidad down the road called Miguel Hidalgo. Mexicanos. Tojolobal Maya. DESMU got tired of them asking why we only help the refugees. They asked aren't we poor; aren't we hungry? Are there too few of us being slaughtered? We found some money, and the women decided to accept a beekeeping project. They're expecting us."

The afternoon was aging. It was almost three; we were due back in Comitán for dinner with Kate and the other students, a three-hour ride. I'm not sure what's just happened, but DESMU made the arrangements; how long could it take?

The micro pulled up in front of a big, seemingly deserted building. I recognized the structure immediately as an abandoned mill. I lived next door to one in Sonora in the early 1980s; it fell into disuse when it became too expensive for the pueblo to grow and mill the wheat they needed to survive. There were rumors that this was taking place with corn in Chiapas, a by-product of the NAFTA treaty.

We walked to the side porch of the mill, where a basket of fresh-picked oranges was sitting outside the door. I looked up, and a short man with baked, wrinkled skin and sweat dripping from under a rolled red bandanna told us each to take one. We did, gladly, something to settle out the uneasy lunch.

Then people came from everywhere. *Compañeras y compañeros*, brushing away fresh milpa dirt, moving into a vast empty storage chamber built to hold tons of maize. And from everywhere, every hidden side room, closet, and storage shed, benches appeared, and as fast as you could say "Cesar Chavez," the place turned into a meeting hall.

A quick aside here. We were not stupid or frivolous or incautious. We had not neglected liability and safety issues; we were sure of our organizations, and DESMU was concerned for our well-being. We said we wanted to see Chiapas, and this day Chiapas was showing herself to us dressed in all her *vestidos, huipiles, camisas*, shimmering fashion-show changes, as she whirled on a runway of uncertain slope.

We arranged ourselves on the benches, eight of us, thirty of them; and this time Claudia smiled, the same refrain: it's up to you, Juanita. My Spanish was getting better by the minute; by the time the sun set behind the Lagos de Montbellos, I would be tripping over conjugated verbs matching up with the tenses I was trying to talk about. I looked across the room, looked at long-haired Maya women wearing well-worn polyester dresses, men in mended sandals. This was not the tourist litany; these people would not be impressed by Cancun and Chichen Itza. I was about to open my mouth when the small man with the bandanna asked, "Who do you represent?"

Bloody hell, that was a new one. I didn't represent anybody, hadn't been sent by anybody. I represented attempts to get students out of the classroom and into something bigger than the Oakdale Mall. I represented attempts to make sense out of dying farms, migrant labor, collapsed oil-field economy, women with too many children, Navajos living on cable television, conversations with friends about retirement income, kids looking for reasons not to get pregnant, so I said, "We don't represent anyone. We're just a bunch of students." Everyone took a deep breath, audible sigh, and he said, "We don't represent anyone, either. We're independent."

I looked directly across; there was a man stirring, orange shirt setting off *moreno* skin, untamed beard, full hair. He introduced himself as Francisco. Next to him was his wife Carmen, a soft woman, dark gentle eyes avidly searching each of ours. She placed her hand over her husband's as he opened his mouth to speak.

"We're independent," he reiterated, a refrain that we would hear over and over again in the next six years. Then he said softly but with immeasurable force, "Chiapas is bleeding; this is a storm that rages around us and Chiapas is forgotten; we are Mexicans who are forgotten, hijos de la chingada; our children bleed with our land."

Indeed, the community of Miguel Hidalgo represented a last chance for independent survival for these forgotten of Chiapas. A mismatched band of poor and landless, driven by the promise of Exodus and the reality of daily exploitation on someone else's finca, they came together under the guidance of Francisco, a young catechist, and Carmen, his *curandera* wife. Unlike the families of Orilla del Bosque and Cerro Verde, who had migrated into the *selva* years before, the people of Miguel Hidalgo were relative newcomers. But Francisco and Carmen were not newcomers to liberation theology. In the Tojolobal communities of Margaritas, they were visited early by diocesan priests, seeking to organize the campesinos to know and live the Word of God.

Francisco and Carmen met in their catechist classes. He had already found his voice, his *trabajo*, his insight. God would lead him and whoever chose to follow to a place where they could become self-sufficient, working for the collective good, in the sight of Our Lord and the Dioses of the other world. Carmen, too, had recognized her calling. Drawn to be a midwife, she worked without pay so that she could get the training she would need to attend to women during their pregnancies, ultimately adding primary care medicine and dentistry to that mix.

Francisco and Carmen fell in love early. Deciding to live together near Francisco's parents, Carmen told her now common-law husband that she had work to do. She would not be kept *cerrado*—shut into the life of a campesina woman, turned into a childbearing machine, under the direction of someone else's family. This was not a problem for Francisco, but his family would not abide it. He could control his woman, or he could leave. Francisco and Carmen chose the latter solution.

There is a common theme running through their story, a story of Maya feminism much like that of Dominga and of Dominga's Zapatista daughters. Each time a gendered impasse is met along the road to rebellion, an uncle or brother appears, the male counterpart of the feminine, a living symbol of the complementarity of Maya women's lives. Francisco and Carmen left his family compound, where he harbored the memories of his own mother's abusive life, and with the help of an uncle, they set up a new household, eventually marrying. Seeing no hope for land in the up-mountain Tojolobal communities, they gathered together this group of like-minded followers and eventually rented a piece of land on the upper Chayote River. They dedicated Miguel Hidalgo to the glory of God and the Zapatista movement, and it was in that collective setting that we were meeting that late winter day.

I opened my mouth to respond to Francisco's poetic pronouncement, but suddenly I was back in my own formative adolescence. Why do people make the choices that they do? All I could see was the image of Che and Fidel rolling into Havana. I was eleven years old, and it was New Year's Eve 1959, and Mom and Dad were down the street dancing and drinking, and I was home alone glued to the radio. Batista was running, and Che was singing, and who can really explain why one's later life commitments begin, a middle-class kid with a socialist heart. Now, four decades later, this man was telling me that he has been waiting for fifty-five years for a piece of stinking land. It's too late for him but not for the children, and what can we do to help? Can we help them learn what else to plant, figure out how to purchase the land that they are now renting, accompany their children in their struggle to have access to education and medical care, give them a glimpse of the dreams that my students toss away in fitful affluent slumber, understand their children's dreams of self-sufficiency through collective work?

And I wanted to tell him . . . them . . . the women who would be the beekeepers, that I was just another objective anthropologist and I couldn't do shit.

Instead we rose to the occasion, just as DESMU's workers Daniel, Claudia, Ariana, and the Autónomo hoped we would do. We had voices. We had e-mail. We had access. We have opportunity. We would go home and take their words, words like seeds, to plant in the fertile ground of young American consciousness. Words to grow into support, both financial and in spirit. Two hours more and it was awfully late, and Kate was back waiting in Comitán, freaking. We all walked out, benches melted back into closets, and the man in orange said, "We have prepared some water for you to share with us."

And Daniel whispered, "Don't."

"Miguel Hidalgo" community harvest honey prior to the breakup of Tierra y Libertad, spring 1998

Don't. Don't? Don't share water with *compañeras* after a long, heartfelt, and probably risky meeting biting on the bitter fruit of Tojolabal neglect? Don't. Don't? It was getting dark, and I was thinking about amoebas and they were thinking about ceremony and blessings, and I told him, "We're a bunch of gringos with really weak stomachs." And we passed up the sweet orange water, my second cultural faux pas of that January day.

As we returned to the rattletrap micro, a few of the Comunidad women grabbed rebozos and bags and joined us, taking advantage of the free transportation to the nearest market, almost three hours away. They needed to buy the materials to make beekeeping costumes, and they chatted gaily about the prospect of keeping bees, about visiting with refugee women already making honey, about learning how to handle the hives and plans to bring the bees to the flowers from both cooperatives.

I was thinking about their story, of how they came together from settlements all through the Tojolobal country, in order to form a community and farm on a piece of rented land, working towards self-sufficiency, of their unambiguous request for specific community development aid.

"The men in the orange shirt, who facilitated the discussion . . . what was his name?" I asked Micaela, one of the women.

She looked at me with curiosity and shook her head. "I don't know," she said. "I'm not sure who you mean."

Years later, we would laugh about it. "He was my own father, but I told you I didn't know his name. We didn't know you. Just because you came with Daniel and Claudia, how could we be sure?"

TIERRA Y LIBERTAD: THE SECOND INVASION OF THE LACANDON JUNGLE

"When the government saw that we could educate ourselves, when we had been in the Consejo for four years, they came in and arrested our leaders."

The *chipy chipy* rains of the winter wet season nurtured the waxy white blossoms of orange trees and coffee plants, calling out to the bees to come and drink. By the spring of 1998, the beekeeping operation in Miguel Hidalgo was flourishing. The women had twenty hives initially; by late April, they had more than thirty, a nongovernmental development project that looked like it might work. In their handmade regalia, they talked to their bees, urging them to make honey in the jungle hives. Downriver, knowledge of medicinal plants resurrected from the memories of the elders, first by the church, aided by DESMU projects, blossomed into a full-blown pharmacy in Rio Jade. Close by, *curanderas* turned dentists, like Carmen, operated a small dental practice using skills learned in workshops before and after 1994. In Cerro Verde, the education committee stated their philosophy of learning: to educate the children in an integrated manner, that they learn that problems are resolved through dialogue between the teacher (promotor de educacion), parents, and children, and to learn to participate and make their own the educational project so that one day they can also be teachers of autonomous education (Calderon 1998). And at municipal headquarters in Santa Elena, moved out of Luz and Rodrigo's enclave in order to safeguard the children, municipal administrators issued birth and death certificates and made marriages official. A small jail held those under suspicion of violating official regulations until adjudication could take place. A tiny *central de abastos* stocked the dry goods only available hours away in Comitán.

Though the Rio Chayote was technically off the beaten Zapatista track, for the Mexican government these attempts at autonomy, in production, education, and health, were a serious threat. Though the population of an autonomous region might include outright Zapatistas, sympathizers, communities in resistance but not in rebellion, and progovernment groups of all degrees, the declaration and practice of autonomy placed the area and all those living and working in it in the *zona de conflicta*, or "red zone." Such was the case with the Rio Chayote region. The designation of this large region of southern Chiapas as the autonomous *municipio* of Tierra y Libertad removed the entire area from the realm of neutrality in the eyes of the Mexican government.

President Zedillo and his second in command, the *secretario de gobernación*, were deeply concerned. Though the government made official noises concerning direct dialogue with Zapatistas and about reconciliation and amnesty, the hidden agenda was remunicipalization, or the substitution of new government designated municipalities for those organized and run by the Zapatistas. Roberto Albores Guillen, appointed as interim governor of Chiapas, replacing the interim governor before him, was given the order to dismantle three of the most offending autonomous entities, among these, Tierra y Libertad (Burgete Cal y Mayor 2002, 14–15). In April and May 1998 Albores launched a massive military campaign aimed at crippling all attempts at autonomy in the state. In the case of Tierra y Libertad, the purported initiating event stemmed from the right of the autonomous council to adjudicate in their own territory based on *usos y costumbres* (Speed and Collier 2000).

In all likelihood, the Tierra y Libertad invasion was planned long before it occurred since it took place on May 1, a holiday in Mexico, just as the other municipal destructions had taken place during the festivities of Holy Week. These were days when they were most likely to find people at home, grouped together, not off in individual milpas, where they would have been difficult to round up or could have taken advantage of intimate knowledge of the jungle terrain in order to escape.

In late April, members of one of the Rio Chayote support bases accused two brothers, Guatemalan refugees, of illegally taking wood from community land. The brothers were summoned to appear before the autonomous council of Tierra y Libertad to answer the charges but failed to show. As was normal procedure, the president of the council and two justice ministers of the autonomous council signed an order for their detention. One of the brothers was apprehended and placed in custody in the municipal jail. He denied his guilt and refused to pay reparations, a normal solution for this type of problem. Since the brothers were Guatemaltecos, the *consejo* notified ACNUR, asking them to help negotiate a settlement. According to ACNUR, this was a fairly normal procedure and, in fact, a desirable one because it helped to facilitate dialogue leading to the solution of disputes in the region. After a week, one brother replaced the other in the jail, and on the third day of his detention, as the authorities awaited the arrival of a representative from ACNUR, more than 1,200 Mexican army and state security forces, assisted by agents of the INM, and two truckloads of female police, began a daylong raid against the Zapatistas, both men and women.

According to the Albores government, ACNUR had invited them in to intervene to recapture the two "kidnapped" Guatemalans, who were being held in violation of their civil and human rights. But according to ACNUR, the *secretario de gobernación* had ordered them not to go to meet with the *autónomo* since that would be "a recognition of the Council's authority." And the council maintained that they had not kidnapped anyone but were acting on the authority given them as elected officials of the autonomous municipality, charged with enforcing the law while respecting *usos y costumbres*.

"We were accused of kidnapping those we accused of theft. We didn't kidnap anyone. We detained two Guatemaltecos for an illegal act. Did that justify sending 1,500 people to destroy our homes, schools, and clinics? They arrested seventy-three people. Fifty-three were beaten and taken to Cerro Hueco. Six of us remained for more than a year and a half," said Cerro Verde's Davíd, one of the six *consejo* authorities. "They wanted all six of us, but they could only get four. So they took two others instead, one of them an old man." Martín, the *municipio*'s first head, escaped.

While news reports appearing in the first few days of May reported the detention of at least forty-seven Zapatistas and concentrated on the violence taking place on one day at the municipal center in the hamlet of Santa Elena, the story told by the Chayote communities is a different tale. The Rio Jade pharmacy and dental practice, the Cerro Verde school, and the Miguel Hidalgo beehives all fell to the destructive force of the invading military. When supporters finally arrived at the municipal headquarters in Santa Elena with a truck to try to save the official archives and the storehouse of supplies, the army had already seized the papers and the dry goods. The men who were arrested were not all grouped in one convenient municipal headquarters but were sought out and detained in their homes as they relaxed on a holiday, by authorities acting on concise and accurate information. With their husbands and fathers in Cerro Hueco, the women of the support communities were quick to denounce the incursions:

> The women of the Comunidad de Miguel Hidalgo, autonomous municipio of Tierra y Libertad, wish to denounce the governor of Chiapas and the Mexican Army and the Security forces. The 3rd of May we abandoned our community, our homes, and our works because of the repression of the army, done during the day and the night, to the joy of the PRIistas. . . . We know that in our community, they are going to make their barracks, and if the place remains free, they are going to burn our homes. . . . At this date, we are suffering from hunger, desperation, and the children are sick . . . we don't have money because we can't work, because we had to abandon our lands. . . . They have destroyed our fields, taken our animals, our chickens, and anything we left in our houses. . . .
>
> As women, we ask, why do the rich wish to be richer, and the poor have nothing? . . . We ask the government to recall their soldiers, who we see armed, going from house to house, demanding food . . . this army is our defense, but now we see them violating human rights. . . . Governor Roberto Albores says that he will work for peace in Chiapas, but he supports the course of war; for us, the poor, we are always left to one side. This is how the government wants to construct a Mexico of equality. . . . For the government, it wouldn't be difficult to comply with the San Andrés Accords, because they have a lot of money that they get from our productivity and through our suffering.
>
> We are placed firmly in the struggle, with confidence in the civil networks and public press, which will explain to the whole world our sufferings as the poor. (e-mail, received June 12, 1998, 10:08)

While the women who composed this letter could describe in detail the destruction of their homes and fields, they could not predict the ultimate effect on their children, who witnessed the violence, too young to speak out against it. These, the littlest Zapatistas, could only relive in nightmares the coming of the army, afraid to sleep, as loved fathers and uncles languished in prison for eighteen months.

The men of Miguel Hidalgo were released from Cerro Hueco one week following the invasion. Returning to the abandoned mill, they found that the women had scattered into the hills and that their landlord was revoking their land lease, creating just the disruption that the breakup was calculated to cause. The community fractured, reestablishing itself, albeit smaller, on another piece of land. This time they called themselves Tulan.

During 1998, with DESMU as intermediary, we kept in touch by e-mail. My students and I had agreed to accompany the community in its struggle, to return to the United States to try to raise small amounts of money to used in projects that would contribute to its developing autonomy. At the same time, my research interests were also beginning to coalesce and would take more concrete form as the months passed and Duncan and I began to work together, documenting the development process in these same communities.

In retrospect, 1998 is remembered as one of the worst years of the struggle by the Zapatista communities and their civil society supporters. Maintaining its campaign of xenophobia, Mexican immigration tossed out human rights observers who ventured into these red zones, including a gross of Italians who protested the dissolution of the autonomous municipios. All level of presence in the state was questioned: tourist travel off the beaten track, development work with communities and organizations, and research as anthropologists interested in social interactions. The government reaction to foreigners was just a small version of the larger conflict faced by Chiapanecans every day, an ambiguous state lying between war and not war. Many more campesinos were sent to prison at this time, leaving several of the Mexican women with whom DESMU had been working as political "widows."

By September 1998, DESMU workers were truly off the political fence, especially Ariana and Claudia. They openly aided the families from Mexican communities and on weekends packed the women and children into their little red pickup and made the five-hour drive to Tuxtla Guiterrez to visit relatives in Cerro Hueco. Inside the prison, political prisoners from all over the state had the opportunity to meet, reflect, plan, and refine their attempts at autonomous government. As Davíd noted, "In Cerro Hueco, together with others from other regions, we really learned how to govern. We formed ourselves into a shadow government and made plans for how we would reconstitute the municipality when we were all released. So our work was never discontinued. It just went underground."

In early 1999, some DESMU members began to operate overtly in the area of human rights, using their credentials and recognition as refugee workers to move freely through an area that remained heavily militarized. The appeal of my March 1999 expulsion began its slow crawl through the Mexican legal system. In a Felliniesque turn of events, Kate and I were now not allowed to leave Mexico while the case was in the courts. Receiving special dispensation so that we could go to the United States to work, we traveled under a visa identifying us as Mexican nationals living abroad. But we were obligated to return to Mexico every three months to keep the case active and renew these visas. Traveling with a sheaf of legal documents in place of a tourist card, in June it seemed safe enough to return to the Rio Chayote with Gabriela, DESMU's director.

In addition to charting the progress of DESMU projects, Gabriela was involved with tracking troop and paramilitary movements through the area. I hadn't expected the NGO to mix development with politics in such an overt fashion. I was learning slowly that these "Mexican" communities were pro-Zapatista, so my apprehension functioned on two levels. First, the communities had no reason to trust me. In some cases, we had never met before. Second, I was still persona non grata in official Chiapas circles and could be a danger to them. We also met with both refugee and Tojolobal-Mexican communities as she attempted to begin new health related initiatives.

The process of integration of the 12,000 Guatemalan refugees who remained in Chiapas was progressing rapidly. In fact, the communities were no longer referred to as refugees and instead where now called immigrant communities. They had made the decision to stay, and with that decision came all the benefits and responsibilities of Mexican citizenship. Without the extra support of international agencies, they were about to slip into the dismal poverty of their established Mexican neighbors.

We drove out through the mountains, leaving the paved road to begin the slow trek toward the Rio Chayote. On the way, we passed only two patrols: army and security forces in close succession. But there were no checkpoints, and I breathed a sigh of relief. As always at this time of the year, it had rained in the night, but the day dawned dry. As we chatted and drove, we watched the sun begin to burn through the mists. It promised to be a decent day.

Our official destination was a meeting in a new immigrant community on the other side of the Rio. The Chayote is a raging watercourse during the rainy season, wide and brown, and carrying with it trees and other debris coming down from the *selva*. The *hamaca* across the Chayote was swaying lazily, and Gabriela was, unfortunately, looking down at the rushing water below her, a sure prescription for vertigo.

"But you have to look straight ahead. If you look down, you'll feel the movement of the bridge too much," I said.

She stood debating the crossing when three women arrived. They were wearing worn "jellies" on their feet and carried huge bundles of corn from tumplines across their foreheads. They mounted the bridge and, one by one, strolled to the other side.

Embarrassed, Gabriela tried again.

"You have to look straight ahead," said an old man, barefoot, carrying a sack containing 200 coffee plants. He too, crossed flawlessly.

We finally gathered ourselves together to make the crossing, walking up the hill to the tiny Guatemalan community.

Since I was with a DESMU representative, I assumed the meeting would be with the female *compañeras* of the community. When we arrived, a young man picked up a large white conch and excused himself, walking a distance before sending out a deep, long, and mournful summons on the shell.

The community of fifty families was spread up the sides of the hill. They were actually two communities who had come together, Mam and Kanjobal speakers who joined fortunes and with international aid were able to purchase enough land to grow corn and coffee. With the community in a stable location, DESMU and other organizations had decided that the group needed to build a permanent health clinic. This meeting was to discuss the progress of this project with what I expected would be the women of the community. The conch sounded again, and slowly the community began to arrive—barefoot and jellied children and tanned men in hiking shorts and open shirts. I looked around for the women, but they were nowhere in sight.

Gabriela began talking, in her deceptively soft voice, making introductions and asking the men to introduce themselves. There were five of them gathered, each with an official title covering some sector of the community's functioning. They were exceedingly well organized, exceedingly well spoken, but they were all men.

"Are you a Mexican or from some other country?" asked one, looking at me curiously. Perhaps he was remembering the gross of Italian observers who had passed through the region prior to being expelled the year before.

"From the United States," I said.

He nodded. "We've never met anyone from the United States. Nice of you to come all this way to visit us."

He sounded sincere, and I smiled and shook his hand and the callused hands of all the others.

DESMU was working with a midwife training program and had been trying to bring immigrant and Mexican women together to learn the skills that would help them follow other women throughout their pregnancy. They would work with the *promotoras* (health aides), and it was hoped that some of these services would be centered in the new clinic.

"We are curious about DESMU. Before we are willing to accept any projects, we need to understand better what your organization's philosophy is. Then we can bring the proposition to meeting of the entire community, and they can vote as to whether they want to be part. And we want to know more about how this famous Health Center will benefit us. This is a very busy time for us, and if we are going to spend time constructing this building, then we have to stop planting. This is the period for new plantings, and we've bought hundreds of young trees and coffee plants. And, besides, the women are really busy, off in the other area trying to find firewood, because there is very little here."

Gabriela was busily taking notes. "Bueno," she said, beginning. "Let me answer some of your questions."

She went on to describe the philosophy of a women's organization to a group of men, to talk about reproductive health, about domestic violence, about the different genders needing their own space and their own time to work out some of the problems and stresses that come with trying to survive. It was a presentation couched in urban mestiza feminism. She added a small discussion of maternal mortality and the need for well-trained midwives and ended with a brief discussion of the problem of AIDS.

I sat quietly, listening intently and watching the men's faces.

"All this is good," answered the head of the committee for health. "But we are also wondering how the clinic will be organized. Is it just for our community, or will it be for anyone who helps to build it? And if others come who didn't help build it, will we be able to charge for the services and the medicines. And, about this, where will the medicines come from?"

They were all interesting questions. Once again, DESMU's plan had been to use the clinic as a means of integrating the two populations, to extend the resources available to the Guatemalans to their poorer Mexican neighbors, as they had with Miguel Hidalgo's bees. Including the Mexican campesinos in the building of the clinic allowed them entrée into its use, even if the funding was earmarked for refugee/immigrant projects.

Gabriela continued her descriptions of how the clinic would run, stressing the need for midwife and health aid training for the women of this community. Building was scheduled to begin on the clinic in the next week, and the design called for a structure made entirely of cement blocks. Thinking of our experience crossing the river, I was immediately struck by how arduous it would be to carry the blocks across the swinging *hamaca* and up the mud slopes during the rainy season. I also was plagued by one of those fleeting ethnocentric questions: why build so far from the road?

We closed up the meeting with the men's promise to consult with the entire community, including the women, and have an answer for DESMU the following Monday. As we stood ready to recross the river, Gabriela looked at the bridge and voiced some of the same doubts.

"It was a great error of judgment to plan the building at this time of the year," she said. "But it was a technical decision, made by the engineers. It will make everything much harder." The question of location was less of an issue. The community was by no means the farthest away on that side of the river. The clinic could also serve those who had to come down out of the mountains for help. The community had the land, the foundations had the resources. "I guess we should have done more planning with the communities," she added.

We mulled over this dilemma as we made an easier passage back across the Rio and walked to the truck to continue on to Tulan, the Zapatista community once known as Miguel Hidalgo.

CONSTRUCTING TULAN

Dodging ocher mud holes, we continued up the road, moving two wheels into the high grass to avoid getting stuck. We passed the then-abandoned mill where the January 1998 student group met with the entire Miguel Hidalgo community, a people full of hope and energy at the start of a new venture.

We stopped in front of three newly built houses, rough milled plank structures, rústicos, as the Ladinos called them. Gabriela waved to a family gathered in front of the most distant of the houses. A young man came over to greet us.

"No esta aquí Doña Carmen?" she asked him.

I reflected once again on the negative construction of questions at certain junctures in the conversation. Was it the image of limited good, an expectation that the situation would not be positive, so you entered into the conversation through a doorway of negation? Doña Carmen isn't here?

"She's here. She's coming," the man answered.

Gabriela smiled, and together we walked toward the other house. The yard, too, was recent, dug into the orange earth, an attempt to level a space for both house and farmyard. A few chickens pecked along the edges near where some of the beekeeping equipment was hung on an enclosing fence.

Arriving, Doña Carmen led us into the house. She looked around as she did, shaking her head sadly. "I am sorry for the condition of my house," she said. "Do not think badly of us."

Gabriela and I sat down quickly on a simple bench, murmuring "don't worries" as we did. I looked around the ten-by-twelve-foot building. The house was dominated by a double bed and a hand-carved wardrobe. A chair stood next to the bed, next to the door, dividing off a small kitchen area. A huge blue polyurethane honey barrel filled the other side of the room, and beyond it was a basket overflowing with liter bottles of the amber liquid. Two babies, close in age, were engrossed in crawl races on the bed, shepherded by a beautiful young woman in a full-length apricot dress. I was drawn to the color, the same muted shade as the gown worn by the Virgin Mary in one of the side altars at the colonial church of Santo Domingo in San Cristóbal. Like the Santa Madre, Micaela radiated a saintly light that seemed to illuminate all that was going on around her. I remembered her as one of the young women who was with us on the micro back to Comitán in January 1998.

A small man came in, dressed in a worn sweater and polyester pants, a man grown smaller with the passing months: Francisco, who had spoken so long and so passionately to us in the old mill. He was hunched with an air of defeat, and I think I stared openly into his shadowed eyes, excluding all else. I never noticed Micaela leave the room. She returned with two cups of hot honey tea.

I took one gladly, thirsty, but also glad of the opportunity to finally drink with this family, to share their water. It was a tea made only of heated water

Drawing of Tulan, as seen by Alejandro

with honey, but I had refused their hospitality last time. I was sure they remembered, but probably not. There had been far more serious injuries in their lives in the past eighteen months.

Gabriela asked how things were. Francisco sighed, his eyes remaining masked. He launched into a long telling of the coming of the army during the breakup of Tierra y Libertad, of the beatings of the men and women, of their removal to jail, of the breakup of their community, as many fled into the hills. He told the story in surface words, a whiny singsong designed to appeal to potential financial supporters, a stock plea for aid between seemingly unbreachable social classes. Doña Carmen told her story in the same voice, and I could sense Gabriela's uneasiness. She had heard this kind of telling before.

Gabriela took advantage of a pause. "Juanita would have come back last May and this January with other students, but with all the checkpoints, it's been difficult. She has had difficulties here with immigration."

I looked up, surprised to hear her bringing this up. She began to say more, then turned to me.

"You tell them," she said.

It was my turn to recite my tired litany, told as often as theirs was, perhaps with the same whine.

"I was expelled from Mexico in March for political activities."

As I talked, Francisco's eyes cleared, and he sat up, losing the pose of defeat.

"I didn't do anything." I spread my hands and shrugged.

Francisco laughed. He didn't seem convinced. Somehow, the fact that I was sitting in his house on an unpaved road three hours from Comitán was evidence enough. He moved forward on his chair, acknowledging that having a common enemy made for a certain social symmetry between us. It was like the moment in the mill when we had all agreed that we didn't represent anyone. Francisco resumed his tale, but this time it was as a fighter, a member of the quiet support army who were the constant eyes and ears of the rebellion on the routes into the selva, the road to Realidad.

"They don't want you to see anything. They don't want you to talk to anyone. They don't want you to tell anything. They wouldn't want you to be here."

The more he talked, the more certain I was of that.

"The last patrol came through here a few days ago. Four hummers of army, followed by a company of security forces. But worse, there have been armed groups of Guardia Blanca, the white guard paramilitaries. They are from the ranchos around here, and we know them. But some we had never seen before, and that is more of a risk."

He described the passage of the Guardia through the fields and near the houses, and I concentrated on his Spanish. His voice had become animated, and he looked suddenly younger. Still the hostess, Micaela placed a small ear of steamed white corn in my hand. It was the time for green corn, *elotes*, and I attacked the ear with gusto, letting the juices drip down my chin. Gabriela was devouring her ear as well, and as we ate, Francisco opened his arms to his grandbaby, and she crawled into them, laughing. Francisco's smile was as big as she was; it spread into his eyes and into his whole body. For a moment, it forgot hunger and desperation and paramilitary activity and barrels of honey without markets. For a moment, a timeless moment in a long struggle, it knew only love and hope.

The baby was constant motion and crawled out of his arms and back onto the bed. It couldn't be easy for them. A few makeshift cloth diapers, washed out daily in water hauled from the river, hung out to dry on the fence, mildewing in the humid damp of the long months of rain. Francisco patted Carmen on the knee and resumed talking.

"The army is tired. The men seemed to have lost interest in this conflict. With the rains, they just want to be back in their cuarteles, back with their families. The government no longer has their hearts and their minds. The killing is no longer in their hearts."

I looked over and noticed that Gabriela was taking notes. "How big are the patrols?" she asked Francisco.

"They've gotten much smaller. At the time of the Consulta, there were twenty-five trucks at a time. Now we see perhaps four or five. Of this, we are grateful. Maybe it's a good sign."

I shared his hope but was not as optimistic, thinking of recent newspaper accounts. "There's been a lot of movement of troops into the selva in the last two weeks. It could be that they are all in place there." I went on to describe the reports of thousands moved into the interior pueblos at the governor's request. "But perhaps they are all staying home because of the rain. It seems that way with the checkpoints."

Gabriela agreed. Both she and Francisco noted that these, too, had diminished after the spring sweeps. There was no longer a rainbow of forces at these roadblocks. We laughed about the *arco iris* of uniforms, checkpoints of all colors, green, blue, black, white, perhaps even yellow and purple.

Gabriela opened a file folder and extracted a four-page typed form filled with questions about violence, occupation, destruction, and the movement of forces through the area. It was part of the Frayba Human Rights Office's effort to gather information from the more distant areas. We had not discussed this part of our day's work in this valley. My eyes widened to saucer size.

We talked about a very recent army incursion in a community about fifteen minutes away, about the impunity with which the forces traveled, about the fact that even at that short distance, the information often didn't get out to other communities. If it didn't travel that far, how would it reach the outside world?

"Aren't there peace camps in the region?" I asked, referring to the settlements of foreigner watchers shepherded by the Frayba in the Altos and in the Cañadas.

"No," Francisco answered. "These are only much further in. We have no observers here, except those friends like Gabriela, Ariana, Claudia and DESMU. And now we have you. You will continue to tell this story in your country. And you will come back."

I shuddered. I wanted to return to this region, to the hardworking, hard-pressed, fragmented community of Tulan. My careful constructions of apolitical edu-tourism were crumbling in the wake of advocacy.

In spite of the breakup of the community, Francisco and the other three remaining families now had thirty-four hives. A second disaster had occurred when a crop duster destroyed the bees, but they had been replaced by the company doing the dusting, a miracle in itself. The crop-dusting issue was one that plagued me on another level, as I thought of the human implications of airborne spread of chemicals that could annihilate thirty hives of bees in one pass. Gabriela and I talked about this later. It was not an isolated or random incident. The chemicals also destroyed any chance of having a coffee crop declared organic. But the new bees were prospering, and the community was producing far more honey than they could ever hope to market under current conditions. This marketing issue was one that also occupied my thoughts.

Old-fashioned anthropology involved ethnographic research, a process of gathering information through participant observation. We came, we stayed, we got involved in daily activities, and we watched. In the early days, we produced descriptive studies of how communities functioned. In recent decades, we came to the communities seeking answers to specific cultural questions. In the applied branch of the field, we also sought solutions to the problems that our questions explored. I had been trying to form a coherent research question for my own work in Chiapas and to find the place where the question, the problem, and the people all came together in one locale. I had been drawn to the Rio Chayote region since the first visit while at the same time struggling with philosophical and practical questions of how you do development with a human face.

The issue of marketing the production was a part of this dilemma. The communities of the region were extraordinarily successful at the production end of the process. But though organized collectively for production, in one way or another, the communities had to interface with a brutally capitalist economy. They had to find a means to get their goods to consumers, and the products had to be consistent in quality. At present, DESMU was buying most of the honey produced in Tulan. They were the ones searching out the markets. Roads, transportation, and commercial connections were all factors that entered into this equation. Could they arrive at a form of capitalism with socialist goals?

As we talked, these social-scientific questions began to swirl in my mind, but I was also plagued by another anthropological dilemma, this one ethical. How did a gringa anthropologist plunk herself down in the middle of a group of people struggling for survival and deal with money issues? My heart and my affluence allowed me to solve the problem of buying the land they were on in one payment. My daughter, like others her age, could spend in one month the amount of money it would take to pay off their note.

I knew that the students could find donations to help, holding a few more bake sales, as ultimately happened. But what of the things that would arise while I was living in their community? I thought about offering them the same amount of money per week as it would cost for food and housing during a homestay in San Cristóbal, negotiating this before attempting to stay there in December, as I was planning to do. Finally, there were also safety issues. If I were working with Carmen in midwifery, sharing health care skills, I was less likely to attract attention to myself that was of a political nature. The simple presence of military and paramilitaries in the area, the community's increasingly apparent Zapatista sympathies, and my status as an unaccompanied woman were all potential problems.

I decided then and there that this was really no place to do fieldwork alone. The usual problems of intellectual isolation and loneliness were compounded by the possibility of making a bad decision in a dangerous situation. It was time to resume conversations with Duncan Earle, who knew the region and was working with the same community development issues. Years later, we would learn that the Zapatistas were grappling with similar international development dilemmas as they constructed a fiscal policy in their dealings with the outside world. Serendipity, if there is such a thing, would ultimately bring us all together in one place.

These thoughts passed through my mind like a hummingbird hovering in front of a *bugambilia* blossom, then dissipated. In the room, Gabriela was taking a bag of new toothbrushes out of her pack, supplies for Doña Carmen in her *dentista* role.

It was getting late, and I realized that Gabriela had scheduled a series of stops at other Mexican communities to talk about military movements. So much for maintaining the aura of neutrality. Micaela was busy fishing around in the basket of honey bottles and brought me a liter.

"This is a gift from me to you," she said. She was younger than my own daughter, and at that moment I wished that I could see her have the opportunities that American teenagers wasted during their own affluent adolescent angst. Then I wished my daughter could have the opportunities that building a self-sufficient life provided for Micaela. I accepted her gift as graciously as possible, saying that we would see each other again. As I paid for an additional four liters of honey, Francisco stated it as a certainty.

"You will come back," he said again, as though he were talking about an addiction.

CHAPTER 7

Millennium Dreams

IN DECEMBER 1999, the millennium was splayed out before us, the American Y2K hysteria reaching a crescendo that crossed the border and traveled into Mexico. It should have been a sign of what was in the wind, the terror of *terrorismo*, the fear of fear, easily dwarfing Mexico's own xenophobia. Albores, in his final year as PRI governor, led the cry of alarm in Chiapas. On a shadowy night on the anniversary of the rebellion, when the technological world was scheduled to end, the Zapatistas would surely stage a reprise. Another 5,000 new troops moved into Chiapas, flying into Comitán to begin the slow rumble into the jungle and canyons.

Jeanne too arrived back in Chiapas just before the turn of the millennium, file folder of *tramites* and other official documents granting mandatory reentry to the *expulsada*. It was be her first solitary field stay in the Chayote communities, a return to Tulan, to a place where the threatened millenium shutdown would be just another part of a cultural blackout that had already lasted 500 years. But the Y2K fervor had indirectly penetrated into some of the remote communities as fear of travel forced tourism down even further and many Maya families lost the little bit of income that might have been generated by the presence of visitors.

CROSSING OVER

Jeanne (December 1999): It was raining, light winter rain again, as I waited for Ariana Avila in the boisterous Comitán zocalo, remembering so many past trips here accompanied by students and friends. Here, we'd fought burrowing jungle mites with layers of Vicks Vapo Rub. Here, too, I received news of my mother's death in 1998, alongside word that the Tierra y Libertad *autónomo* had also died. Duncan would arrive just before the new year, but I was alone for this preliminary trip, looking forward to staying with Doña Carmen at the new enclave upriver from the abandoned mill where it all started for me.

Ariana brought other news.

"I think it's not a good idea for you to go to Tulan, Juanita," she said, as we headed out of the city in the DESMU pickup. "They are too isolated up there, and the paramilitaries are far too active. The army is moving; so is Seguridad. Better to stay at Cerro Verde. They're part of a village. You'll be much more protected."

I was saddened by the change of plans since I looked forward to learning herbal medicine and a little midwifery with Carmen. But Ariana knew best. The presence of a gringa in an isolated Mexican community would only draw unneeded attention to the group, as had our Chiapas Project student visit to the same region two years before.

I'd met the Cerro Verde women once, briefly, with Gabriela. They were a larger group than Tulan, with lots of children, so we stopped at the Comitán supermarket and purchased some rice and beans and other staples to contribute to the community larder. Ariana also advised me to bring a few cans of Nan 1, a popular type of formula for infants. There was a new baby in Cerro Verde who couldn't nurse and needed the milk.

On our way to the jungle, we stopped briefly at the Lagos de Montebello and watched the long green lines of Zedillo's troops slink along the highway, forming a caravan twenty trucks long. We arrived in Cerro Verde by midday, and Ariana dropped me off among the women like a stray kitten seeking a home. I wondered what a community felt when saddled with its first anthropologist. Among these second-generation Mayas, there was no formal ritual process of reception as had greeted Duncan in Ojo de Agua in 1979. So Rodrigo and Luz welcomed me, and I never saw the meetings that took place later that night, after I went to sleep, sharing a tiny room with a then-unmarried Camila and her toddler daughter Cari. Unlike Ojo, where Duncan's fate was decided by lengthy debate involving only the men, the Cerro Verde gathering included women and men and even the older children.

When I arrived, Luz was in the kitchen bottle-feeding a tiny baby, barely two months old. I remembered Luz vaguely from the afternoon with Gabriela and recognized Alma, the health *promotora* with whom Gabriela had worked. I took out the Nan 1 and pushed it across the table, trying to get a better look at the infant's face.

"What's the baby's name?" I asked.

"Natalia," she said.

Natalia. Birth. Christmas. A name celebrating a special coming, given to a baby whose very life was a piece of the identity of the place, a *milagro* in time and space that ultimately cemented my own relationship with the community. Like the infant Moses set adrift on the river, or the unborn Jesus in need of a womb, Natalia had been found by a few of the boys one late October morning on the banks of the Chayote, only a few hours old. They quickly sought their Abuelita Dominga, a traditional midwife and grandma. Because the newborn was lying covered with birth blood and tiny red ants, Dominga cleaned her

Jeanne with baby Natalia, December 1999

quickly, cut the cord, and brought her back to the enclave. As always, there was room at this inn, and though at first it was uncertain which of her daughters would raise the infant, the gift went to Luz, aged forty-two, mother of six, and planning no more children.

When I arrived at Cerro Verde for that first anthropological stay, I was fifty-two, mother of two grown daughters, and bemoaning my lack of grandchildren. I fell easily into the role of surrogate caregiver, evolving rapidly into the Abuelita Gringa. Natalia became a well-loved symbol of the community's solidarity, a miracle befitting scripture, center of attention, and queen of the village. Her life represented the merging of stories and traditions, a biblical "virgin birth" of sorts, laid on the banks of a Maya river, where human blood and supernatural ants added a taste of the Popul Vuh, the Maya creation history, and made a multimetaphorical statement.

They had adopted Natalia, taken her in. Why not also take in a stray anthropologist?

Luz was newly freed from her *cuarenta*, the forty days of semi-isolation surrounding a baby's birth. She moved Natalia on to her back and disappeared into the tiny kitchen. Cups of coffee appeared on the table in the open-air dining room, a plate of black beans. Slowly, all the women stopped by, gracious but curious.

Overhead, clouds were just beginning to drift in. The sun had been bright all morning, the women told me, giving the kind of heat needed to dry the coffee that was now spread out across the cement patio in the middle of the enclave. A small plank house was at its top, the kitchen dining area along one edge. Bordering the other two sides were hedges of peach and red *bugambilia*, protecting small plantings of herbs: basil and mint, fennel, and rosemary.

There were small children everywhere, caretaking each other, and they too wandered over to look in wonder at Juanita, the stranger, who almost spoke Spanish. Each took a turn moving the coffee around on the patio, and with frank curiosity I took the opportunity to ask about how it was grown.

Coffee grows like high bush blueberries but is usually red and looks a lot like cranberries. Because the beans ripen separately, they must be picked by hand, harvesting the ripe ones and leaving the yellow to ripen at another time. Like picking blueberries, the branches are selectively stripped into a basket tied around the picker's waist, and when the basket is filled, it is dumped into a sack and taken back to the community.

Next, the fruit is shucked and the pulp removed with a cleaning apparatus, some hand cranked, others attached to gasoline motors. In Cerro Verde in late 1999, there was still a motorized *despulpador*, and there were still a few extra pesos to hire a Guatemalan family to help with the picking.

With the red hulls gone, the beans, now slippery and brown, must be washed, and this means a trip to the river, down the hill, hauling the beans to a place where the aqua water is not too deep or too fast. Then the drying process begins: days of sun and a constant turning motion that reminded me of shoveling snow. Once dried and bagged, the coffee can be sold, but only in its crude state, *pergamino*, since a tiny thin skin still remains. I marveled at the amount of work, learning that there were still three more steps before it could become my morning pick-me-up. The removal of the thin skin produced *oro*, and it was only this gold that could be commercially toasted and then ground.

Marta, Luz's young daughter, grabbed my hand. "Come on. I'll show you."

The women breathed a sigh of relief as a passel of children led the gringa into the bushes to see coffee growing. An hour later, they led me to the banks of the Rio Chayote.

"Aren't you going to bathe?" asked five-year-old Miguelito.

Gingerly, I stripped off some of my clothing and waded out into the chilly water. Slowly, the children were joined by the women, carrying the laundry, and the men, dirty from the day's work in the *cafetal* and ready to wash.

Later, Luz handed me Natalia and a bottle and darted after a spindly hen. We ate *caldo de pollo* that night, as I began to learn how to eat chicken broth with only a corn tortilla as a utensil. It had been a relatively dry year, and the one cement water tank near to the enclave was dry. Before the last of the cloud-covered daylight could disappear, we took stripped plastic ollas and went to the river to get water to wash the seemingly endless mound of dishes. Returning, Luz met me at the door of the kitchen, handed me a late-night cup of sweet coffee, and ushered me inside. Her husband Rodrigo was seated there, with brother-in-law David, his short-cropped hair and thick glasses, telling a story of their own. David stood and gave me his seat, then glanced at the others and shut the kitchen door. Now it was time to talk.

"We are poor campesinos," Rodrigo began, leading into what would become an almost ritual greeting. "We are isolated here, and it is not often that we get people from the outside to come to visit us. So we are pleased to have you here and want to know more about what you want to know about us."

Poor Mexican campesinos. Not Maya, not Zapatista. At this moment, his appeal was not based in ethnicity or in politics but rather in class. They were marginalized agriculturalists who, they stressed, were in resistance to government programs. Nothing more.

I was glad of this open-ended and ambiguous description of their place in the political world. I explained that I was an anthropologist interested in community development and the ways in which they assessed the projects brought to them by NGOs such as DESMU. I was not on the trail of the true rebellion, looking for shortcuts to Realidad and Guadalupe Tepeyac. That would be a surefire way to get thrown out of the country forever this time.

At the time, I didn't know about the negotiations between DESMU and the now dismantled *autónomo*. The NGO's commitment to look for international support for programs in what we later learned were Zapatista support communities was why I had been brought here. We were being led like liberal lambs to a willing slaughter, slabs of meat to be hung up beside the Zapatista hammocks, guided into a step-by-step commitment to accompany these communities on their development trail. But it would be many months building trust before Luz would begin speaking openly to us about "our Organization."

Rodrigo sighed and looked through the smoky haze that wafted from the open cook fire, filling the tiny kitchen.

"Surely, surely," he said. "I have to believe, that somewhere there is a foundation that wants to help a grupita like ours realize our dreams to be able to support ourselves on this land. Surely."

He looked at me questioningly. A short silence ensued.

David spoke next, explaining that he had just recently returned to Cerro Verde after an eighteen-month stay in Cerro Hueco prison. He mentioned Tierra y Libertad but provided no other detail. That he had been arrested when they dismantled the *municipio* should have told me enough.

I countered with the *expulsada* story, knowing that we were quietly laying out our credentials, without need for further comment or elaboration. I launched into my ritual reply, crafted in the initial encounter with Tulan, when that group was known as Miguel Hidalgo. I described my dreams of building a better world. I told them what we could try to do, what we could never do, who we were, as academics and students.

David smiled. The answer was sufficient for him, enough to begin preparing a willing offering for eventual sacrifice. The fish was on the line. How much would it take to land us?

Rodrigo was a little skeptical. "Give up these ideas of change on a global level," he said. "Start here, start with one tiny group, one river valley. I believe this can be done."

We parted company, and Luz took me to where I was to sleep on the hard bed opposite Cari and Camila. Cari was there, sound asleep. Camila returned much later, after watching the late-night *noticias* on a tiny black-and-white TV connected to the group's one dubious electrical line, after meeting with all the others to make a decision about the visiting gringa.

I awoke early and suddenly. The sound of morning was the soft slap of bare feet, skin tough, like a *plátano*. They stopped outside the doorless doorway to the tiny house, and a voice called loudly, "It's clear out!"

In the next room, Rodrigo rose, slow like light beginning in the east, beginning high over the *cafetales*.

"It's clear out? 'Tabueno!" he responded, pleased.

Another day without rain, without fog, another day to cut the coffee sheltered in the thinning forests above the aqua waters of the river. As it tumbled on toward Guatemala, the Chayote was a river to wash the coffee in, a river for bathing tired bodies, a river that was the well, the sweet water source, and the repository of the black.

"Camila!"

The call was the second cry of morning.

"Camilita!" Rodrigo called again, a father needing breakfast.

Across the cluttered room, where I dozed in dawn slumber, Camila stirred on her wooden pallet. Her daughter would waken later, frightened to find her gone, to find only the curious stranger. Camila pulled on a turquoise sweater, smoothed her hair, and went to boil the coffee. They used the dark, damaged coffee, the beans too wet to sell even to coyotes, the scavenger merchants who had already begun to come to the door with sad tales of poor markets. Armed with a roll of well-worn pesos, they came to pick at the thin flesh of those surviving on a diet of hope and too many tiny dreams.

"Camila, the dishes are dirty again!" Luz called out from the kitchen.

How could they be? I remembered washing them, the last minute before going to bed. The meeting must have gone long into the night, fueled by infinite cups of coffee and the few remaining refried beans. I sat up too and put on a polar fleece sweatshirt. Camila admired it and asked how much it cost. She bridged the space between us with shy questions about clothing and living in a place so far away the image was obscured. All she could see was the gross of tortillas still to be pressed.

"Camila!"

The morning was more silent than the night had been, without the steady swish of the ancient generator, the midnight lullaby of the machine that cleaned the coffee beans. Hulling was not work for the Guatemalans. They picked the ripe fruit, a family of four who were also waking up, sleeping in hammocks draped over the rough beams of the dining space, getting ready to head back to the *cafetal*.

Rodrigo leaned close to Camila, and she stopped working the corn masa and rubbed his shoulders. The air smelled sweet with fermentation, the odor of the rotting hulls lying near the pulping machine, near to the latrine on the other side of the house. The scent was sweet and tart, like honey and vinegar, like the hope and anger captured in Rodrigo's aching arms, taut with muscles, soft with love.

Last night, an hour-long rain wet the drying area, but the coffee was safe, returned to peach-colored plastic *bolsas*. As the men and older boys grabbed their bags and bottles of pozole, to walk out to the *cafetales*, the younger children began to empty the bags and spread the beans once again, exposing them to the sun.

We cleaned up from the breakfast, more dishes, and Marta and I went down to the tiny autonomous school. She was proud of the ten-by-twelve room and read easily from the colored drawings taped to the boards. We were joined by the others under the age of twelve, not yet ready to go to the *cafetales* but with enough of their own daily tasks to finish close to the enclave. The school day would begin later, in the long afternoon, a rhythm keyed to changing agricultural patterns as the seasons passed.

The children leaned easily across one of the tables that served as a desk, reading aloud, a side-by-side story in Spanish and in Tojolobal, a picture book I'd brought with me. They were hungry for learning from books and from visitors and from those like Ana and Alma, who taught in the tiny building. They didn't attend the government school up on the hill, where all too often the teachers brought in from the other side of Mexico did not show up or when they did could be heard condemning the *pinché indios*, stupid and dirty, and let's get another beer. Cerro Verde built their own school, this tiny building, a school that rebelled against forgotten language, a place where the light leaked in through uneven boards but where the walls were lined with paintings and pictures and words that weighed heavy, a child's view of erratic conflict.

The coffee had a full day's drying, but it looked like we were due again for night rain. The evening thunder rumbled into the valley, heard far off, like tanks lumbering slowly. It was almost Christmas. A string of lights stretched

Cerro Verde children in their old school

around a huge begonia, a jungle-size version of the houseplant I knew from temperate climes. Though there was now a small Catholic chapel at the top of the hill in the heart of the pueblo of Cerro Verde, it was not their turn to have a priest for the holidays. But two of the nuns from Comitán were here to visit, so a festive evening lay ahead, practicing the Christmas posada.

We scrambled up the path slick with mud, climbing higher still, past houses standing empty, coffee covered with plastic. I sat with the others in the cement-block building on hand-hewn benches while we practiced songs and the nuns explained each person's role in the traditional pre-Christmas pageant. Two of the children were selected to play Mary and Joseph. Camila's turquoise sweater became Mary's characteristic veil, buttoned over her head. The boy was draped in a shawl, with another fastened around his waist and with a red and yellow Zapatista bandana tied around his head, a lovely metaphor. It was December 22, and I shuddered a bit, not just from the penetrating damp chill but from the memory of what had occurred two years ago this day in the village of Acteal, in a church a lot like this one. I was alone here, and it was hard not to be frightened. The rain was now dancing on the aluminum roof, blowing easily into windowless windows. I imagined the sounds of booted feet, cloaked in the smell of death, like those they must have heard in Acteal.

The nuns, their smiles sweet as molasses, finished the story of Jesus, how he came 2,000 years ago to change a world that was torn by injustice and inequity. And wasn't it great? And here we were two millennia later still living in a world of poverty and repression, and he was coming again. I wondered how the people could be expected to have hope in the second coming when the first coming seemed to have changed nothing. But that was my problem. It was 1999, and I had yet to learn the strength of Zapatista faith and hope.

We finished practicing the posada songs we would sing after snaking down the mud-slick paths to the scattered houses lining the side of the hill. I watched people watching me. Who was the gringa staying down at Rodrigo's compound? Would she offer a McDonald's selection of development projects like the other NGOs?

We filed out of the church into the damp darkness, to sing our way into shelter for the holy couple, stopping at doorways, asking for a room. I followed at the end of a long line. At the front, someone held a single flashlight, dying Energizers lighting the trail. The ground was slippery, the leaves and vines and coffee plants hung into the path. As I approached one particular bottleneck, I could see a shadow shape in the bushes, dim light reflecting off thick glasses.

A branch popped down in front of me, blocking my way.

"Es un retén," David sang out. A *retén*. The ubiquitous checkpoint that turns up in unexpected places, guarded by men in a rainbow of uniform colors. A checkpoint. A boundary. We stood face to face, David's hand holding the branch in front of me, the line of singers passing out of sight and into the darkness. A checkpoint. Did I want to involve myself with a community in resistance? Did they want to open their story to public scrutiny?

I looked at David and tried to read his eyes. A checkpoint. They had no reason to trust me. I had no reason to trust them. The code of anthropological ethics flashed before me, objectivity and social science, research designs, publications, AAA presentations, the genuine risks of working in a conflict zone. *Un retén*. To cross it was like signing an *acuerdo*, an agreement between Cerro Verde and the anthropologists that we try to understand this conflict together, a give-and-take that would stretch each of our definitions of appropriate behavior. I wondered what I would have to leave at the checkpoint to pass through. Joseph and Mary were singing softly in the distance, asking for shelter. David raised the branch briefly, dropping it behind me as I crossed over, and slid down the path toward the music.

Morning came quickly in the tiny room I shared with Cari and her mother. "Camila!"

We rolled out of bed, feet touched the pressed-dirt floor. A gross of tortillas, and the dishes were dirty again.

FIELD PARTNERS AND FIELD PARTNERSHIPS

Back in San Cristóbal, Duncan arrived safely, just before the new year. A huge artificial Christmas tree decorated exclusively in Coca-Cola emblems dwarfed the black cross in front of the cathedral in the Plaza de la Paz. The tree was perhaps a portent of the political changes that would take place six months later in Mexico, as the PRI lost the presidency to Fox, a Coca-Cola executive. At midnight, fireworks exploded, strangers hugged strangers, but the Zapatistas never arrived. The world did not end.

We left the city early, on a quiet postmillennium Sunday, traveling through a world that was still with us, a surprise to the Evangelicos. Duncan was returning to Ojo de Agua, to the scene of his studies, to the study of the scenes that filled the community's years. Ten years had passed since his last visit, while his life wandered, as is the case for anthropologists and academics. But Ojo remained a fixed photo for him, still-paused in memory.

We crossed the rebuilt bridge from the village of Santa Elena, where autonomy brought disaster to those such as David, the autonomous administrators trying to legislate the ecologically sound existence that the settlers in Ojo had once lived. Strange, the placement of our two sets of research interests, lives and events taking place barely kilometers apart. As we walked up to the gate, Jeanne stepped back to become the biographer as the family welcomed Duncan. Children had become women, women, the mothers of children. There was not a second's hesitation, as they called his Maya name in greeting.

"Lucas!"

Lucas. Like it was yesterday, like it was as it is, the rolling flow of time that knows only absence and presence.

REVISITS AND REVISIONS

Duncan (January 2000): The road was so much better now. What an ironic turn of events that the lowland jungle roads would get better, thanks to the military, while the highlands got worse, more so with the growing outbreaks of *topes*. It made my first return to Ojo de Agua, now known as the Anexo or annex of the original Chamula colony, so very strange. I was reentering the jungle lands on the same road but at three times the velocity or more, like fast-forward video footage of where I used to trudge through mud on foot in the steamy sun. As with my first arrival, it used to take all day to go each way. Now, on the highway, the distant Tzeltal colonies of Maravillas Tenejapa and Nuevo Jerusalem were less than an hour from Ojo. The three-day walk to the middle Jatate River drainage was now under three hours. The change was staggering.

It was only a few short hours from Comitán by VW Bug, and I was back to Ojo, that corner of the region's oldest indigenous *ejido*, sitting calmly on the far shore of the river, the one that drains the edge of the highlands off into the Lacandon. The fence was the same—some dark, twisted-grain wood that swings exactly as it did in 1979 the first time I was here. And beyond, the little *potrero*, where the animals grazed and a small foot trail leads upriver to the base of the swinging bridge. There has always been a bridge there, since the start of the *ejido*, as far as anyone can remember. This bridge seemed to be of a notably recent remodeling, always a good sign with the *hamacas*. One of the very important collective activities carried out by labor organized by the *ejido* leaders a generation ago was the maintaining of bridges. For a time, they even charged a crossing fee but only for through traffic. Locals were free to come and go. That was before the main road got militarized.

To get out to Ojo, once the only population center on this part of the Santo Domingo, you crossed through Santa Elena, as we now did. The hamlet was hushed, except at the school, where kids yelled out their lessons in an ancient chant of rote. The trail was the same, but the buildings were many more, prosperous homes and gardens, with lots of little *tiendas* on the street corners. Something about the place seemed tense. I could tell by the relief masked in the faces of people passing on the path when I spoke—relief to see who I was, speaking their language so well.

This was the gateway to the testing ground for my initiation into Chiapas fieldwork. And the only way to get there used to be by crossing the bridge, before the road was made from the new vehicle bridge five kilometers downriver. No one crossed the ridge from the Anexo to the main colony on foot any more, unless they were local. Now Ojo was off the beaten track while still close by Santa Elena, where you got off the bus.

Even more than the last time, a dozen years ago, when I passed through the gate into the pasture, I felt relief in getting out of Santa Elena, traumatized, militarized, and battered Santa Elena, once the great hope of the Tierra y Libertad autonomous municipality, until the soldiers of Zedillo put their boots to the neck of the municipal center, the *cabecera*, Cerro Verde's story. I was thinking this, recalling memory, living my own migration back here, the smells and sounds reverberating in the green shade telling me why I came, to again try to figure out why people make the choices they do and to grasp what the consequences of those decisions are, when the structures of community change.

The first shock was the physical environment. The monkeys were already gone when I first came, but what of the javelinas or the jaguars who once sniffed my sleeping form? The skins for sale on Calle Guadalupe in San Cristóbal told me how the cats were doing, adjusting to all the new traffic. The political environment had also changed. In the 1980s, the Guatemalan Kaibiles, a military named for a Maya jaguar–warrior figure, came down to their borderline and exterminated a thirty-mile-wide swath of life to create a "national security perimeter." Now we had the other side, the Mexican army at work in the fields of policing, politics, and profit. Rare hardwoods were being bled away, by night and day, with the okay of the security forces, when before it was strictly night smuggling on a small scale. Now it was massive, the stuff that makes conservationists roar after viewing satellite photographs. No wonder the army was not willing to go home. Not in fifteen minutes, not fifteen months, and we will see about fifteen years. The jackals cannot be cajoled into leaving the fresh kill. Crossing through Santa Elena, I remember this. When the military came to break up the *autónomo* and all the Zapatista heads of household were safely locked away, the army went upriver, outside of Orilla del Bosque, Cerro Verde's parent *ejido*, and stripped the remaining forest.

Clear-cutting is a sin in the traditional Maya religion. It is sure to offend the owners of the mountains when they have hacked down God's milpa, as my compadre Lucas in Guatemala would have said. That is an expensive *permiso*, many, many candles, pounds of copal. But no one is burning the offerings, only burning the fields before the planting; they are only offering more of what they take. It will end badly, he would have said, looking at this millennial Lacandon. All the owners of the places, of the plants, of the animals, even the springs and cave owners, will rebel. The jaguars will emerge from their sacred corrals, from where they moved freely between worlds at this the Navel of the Earth and snatch people up and devour them in service to the Most Holy Earth and the Heart of Sky, Oh God. Lucas always had a sense of drama. In Ojo, the elders still remember all this potential, know that the jaguar cave is just above the village, open and waiting, only they don't talk about it out loud.

When I went into the field in Ojo over a generation ago, I was immediately aware of the delicate nature of the ecological situation because already large tracts of land had been cleared in some of the closest land to the highlands, mostly for pasture. They can be seen now on the road down from the Montebello lakes, looking barren like the green hills of Ireland. In the struggle for autonomy by the Zapatista communities that find themselves in this unique ecological region, there is another fight besides ones with the government, the army, the paramilitaries, and the coyotes. This is the struggle to create a more sustainable and healthy environment.

In the Zapatista communities, every time we walk into the fields we see experimentation with new types of natural controls of pests, natural fertilizers, alternatives to burning, and other actions that show recognition of the problems of adequate stewardship. This is not a new issue, although the older *ejiditarios* recall how very wasteful people used to be of the forests. In Ojo, there have been rules for a quarter century about coordinating burnings and staying out of the inarable sector, and while there have been violations, in general their land is more intact than up the river. But awareness and plans for change are deeply entrenched in the *autónomos*. This speaks to a profoundly important global issue: how do we "save the rain forest"?

The models used by many in the West follow the pattern of our national parks, but for most of the less developed world, this model is hard to enforce.

An alternative model, more likely to succeed at providing a modicum of protection under conditions of high population pressure, is occupation by a population committed to conservation and sustainable ecological integration. Such people are the only ones positioned to provide real security to fragile lands, and to be effective they must both believe in what they are doing and know how to manage it sustainably. As is clear in the case of the Montes Azules preserve, which has come to pit recent communities with environmentalists and the government, no one wants to talk about this alternative, yet all other political paths are likely to turn either violent or destructive.[1] The only hope for these delicate lungs of the planet is settlement by live-in conservationist peasants. I am afraid that for many regions, nothing else will work. For all the other political players with power, the jungle is just a plum to be picked, a hunk of meat to roast, a casualty in the making of an ever more desperate desire of aging capital for available value.

We began finally to climb up the approach and to cross the bridge. I let go of all my musings in the pasture so as to put all my concentration into examining the boards that spanned the thick wires to be sure they were all there. Three were missing. The gaps were nicely distributed in the arc of the lazily galloping *pont*. Not enough space to lose a drunk through, but the work had seen better days. No one was taking any fees any more. The field was spotted with sheep and bled into foliage holding homes at the edge of fence lines, emerging streets creeping away into the hillside. There was a moment of eternal pause with a shushing rush of water below, jade lawn boundaries.

We crossed the bridge and started toward the cropped sheep pasture.

Two boys were jumping from the sturdy Mimosas into the shaded aqua water. In the shadow of one of these slight trees, a youth was standing, scraping one new boot against the other. He looked like a local Chamula, but I could see was dressed like a northern rancher, what they call a "*chero*" from the Spanish "*ran-chero*" up on the border where I live: the hat, the big belt buckle, the country-and-western shirt, the clean jeans, with a cuff to frame fine leather boots. The fruits of his labor, I could see, and recent. You can spot a migrant who has returned even in a crowd these days.

"Ya estas aquí, Lucas," he said.

He's informal, too casual for Chamulas, but normal for the North, like a mestizo. Who was this forward rake? Then I recognized him, Felix, the last of Miguel's vast family, Chevela's final male, the utterly angelic child who appeared in so many of my ethnographic photographs from back in 1979 and 1983. I see in the flash of memory how he stood naked to his knees in the river, hands clasped in delight. Beyond him the older girls bathed diligently or washed clothes. The sun was golden, the scene the sheer beauty of remembrance.

"Eres tu Luuucas."

It *is* you, Lucas?" One of the boys scrambled down from a branch, went off up hill puffing, calling ahead, "Mero Lucas." The true Lucas. The other scampered behind.

Miguel was, of course, in the *cafetal*, but Chevela, the wife who replaced the woman who wouldn't leave the cold country in the 1950s, quickly brought coffee. The women were all here, all grown, and someone went to fetch Miguel. It was late afternoon, and an old man shouldn't be out in the *cafetal*.

"Lucas!"

Lucas. Like it was yesterday, like it was as it is, the rolling flow of time that knows only absence and presence.

Jeanne watched as they surrounded him, asked the awkward questions first. Where has your life gone, and we wondered when we would be reassured that what we remembered was reflected in the cave of your heart. Miguel returned, smiled, his face lighting up like a lamp springing to life, his gravel voice unsurprised.

"Lucas. Ya llegaste." You arrived. Switching between the languages of their two lives, we are whisked away to worship, to sing, to praise the Protestant God, who followed after the Catholic, shadowing the old beliefs. Then Duncan held court, the men filled with questions; the bawdy and the suggestive and the replay of months compressed into moments, the comings and goings of the separated selves.

Miguel closed his eyes, skin taut over his high cheeks. We were sitting at the table, where the food was spread. The meal was the welcome, with the women at the edges. The men talked of harvests and chainsaws and how many were left, how many took the new highway and moved to Pacayal, a place that was once accessible only over the mountain.

I moved back and forth between Tzotzil and Spanish as Miguel narrated a saga of declining economic prospects, linked to the failing coffee economy. Even beans were scarce. Looking around, the little village seemed prosperous. Miguel's sons and daughters lived in a two-story house across from the original compound. There was even an old pickup in the driveway.

So what of my model of the "dual economy"—a balance between subsistence and cash crops that flourished in good times and hunkered down in bad patches so to never have the kind of problems that now seemed in evidence? To be sure, no one was starving. The land gave much corn, some beans, and other products to be eaten. But the quarter century of prosperity was now hard for them to leave to simply retreat back to the milpa patterns for survival, to the ways of the past. Cash flowing out of coffee and into the community had been its lifeblood, as it was for the Guatemalans they employed. No other crops were ever developed to diversify things, even though they were aware of the need to do so years ago. They had toyed with cardamom, but the government prohibited it because they had no national market, and they assumed that such plants were destined for clandestine export to Guatemala. This is ironic now, as the zone receives drugs smuggled in from Guatemala, but then there was no notion of free trade. It was national markets or none. Now with free trade, barriers swept away to expose the vulnerable campesino to the vagaries of the galloping global market, coffee value sank to the level reflecting supply, and Vietnam had become the most recent spoiler, another story of shortsighted global manipulation. Had they gone to total coffee production, like some had in Santa Elena, it would have been far worse, no doubt, since you cannot eat coffee. But it seemed that the rising expectations and increased consumerism brought on by their decades of relative wealth made them still vulnerable to the loss of their cash crop.

A generation earlier this was a rough-hewn paradise, a place where the environmental, economic, and social balances and interactions seemed to guarantee infinite stability and sustainability. Now it seemed, as Miguel waxed biblical about the apocalypse, that this was just another "*engaño*," another trick not entirely unlike the one that had been used in the West, where the jungle was killed by convincing *ejiditarios* to go in and cut it down, only to be driven off later into virgin lands by cattle interests (see De Vos 2002; Nations and Nigh 1980; Ortiz 2001, 23–60). While coffee was king, then, it was useful to have all these peasant producers who were forced to sell to the coyotes while the nation used the export for foreign exchange. Now as the realities of NAFTA brought this gamble to a close, it was time to make some other plans.

Miguel mused about his options, to stay, to go. They had a place in Independencia, a larger town, off the road to Comitán.

"We went there in '94, '95, you know, after the rebels came and settled themselves in Santa Elena. Some of the young people here said they wanted to join the Zapatistas, and we said, fine, you go, it's your decision. And when you come back, we'll hang you." He smiled and took another tortilla. "They stayed," he added.

The government came looking for them in Independencia, saying that they had to go back to Ojo and reoccupy their houses, or the EZLN would loot them, and there was nothing the army could do to protect the town. Land occupations had been a reality of the uprising, but it was equally likely that some representative of officialdom had known about military plans for the area, the invasion in 1996 and again in 1998. Looting was a certainty, but more than likely it would have been by military or paramilitary forces, as occurred upriver.

So women talked of making goods for the tourist market in San Cristóbal, young men talked of migrating to the mythical *norte* where they paid in *"dough-lars,"* and old men, like Manuel, mused about moving to some city. One of his young daughters was already gone to the highlands to work as a maid in a San Cristóbal home, reversing the migration stream of twenty-five years previous, when highland relatives sought work down here in Ojo.

Now, this *ejido* had no sense of unity, no collective vision to pool their resources, their ideas, their energy. It was every household for itself. What I had not taken into account in my pronouncements of paradise was what the Chamulas lost when they fell out of the care of San Juan, the santo of the distant highlands. It had been the unifying totemic god of their homeland brethren, but they fell away from it and from the Catholic world and its communion. As Weber would have predicted, with no encompassing social contract, social capital is overthrown by personal capital. Protestantism and individualism had turned Ojo into a place where isolated women dwelled in two-story houses and were alone in their kitchens at 6:00 A.M., their crying babies competing with the blaring electrified sounds of Tzotzil Jesus music.

Miguel sighed.

"They say that Marcos and the Marists with their motorcycles are living together in a big cave behind Guadalupe Tepeyac," he told me, a question in his statement.

I shrugged. Where else would the rebels and Catholics go, except to a cave, where they could commune easily with the Lords of Xibalba? Surely their souls had been captured by the owner of that part of the *selva*. I had no answer for the aging, wondering patriarch. We would leave for Tulan and Cerro Verde in the morning. Perhaps the *compas* could confirm Miguel's Zapatista rumor for us.

NOTE

1. The Montes Azules Reserve covers 817,918.81 acres and is located within the Lacandon *selva*, itself comprised of 1,235,526.90 acres of the second most biodiverse region in Latin America. At the start of the twentieth century, the Lacandon had almost 4,942,107.60 acres and only 20,000 inhabitants. Today the forest has been reduced to almost one-fourth of its size and has an estimated 350,000 inhabitants. The 1971 presidential decree granted a large portion to the Lacandon Maya. Since then, legal and illegal incursions by timber companies and peasants trying to make a living have destroyed two-thirds of what was left in 1971. In 1978, the Mexican government declared the remaining acres an "off-limits" natural sanctuary. Today, Montes Azules contains forty-two population centers, thirty-one recently created by displaced campesinos escaping political and religious persecution and poverty. Some experts calculate that this humid tropical reserve will disappear in twenty years, and Montes Azules remains an active and volatile situation.

CHAPTER 8

Analyzing Community Development with the Help of the Community

THE YAMAHA KEYBOARD

"At the end of these years the story of the development of DESMU's projects has been a list of good guesses and errors, an intense reflection concerning our work with indigenous women, as designed and implemented by mestiza women" (Duran Duran 2001, 2).

The VW Bug bounced along the rutted dirt road, up past the village of Rio Jade, and along the aqua banks of the Chayote. The river was in its crystal blue stage and would remain that way through the all-too-few weeks of the hot season. Then the rains would turn it first to jade and then to roiling opaque moss. Since we had a car and we were not planning to stay the night, it seemed safe enough to make a visit to Tulan after leaving Ojo de Agua on our way to Cerro Verde. We wanted to meet with the group and its bearded and charismatic leader and see just what the Tulaneros thought about the community development projects they'd participated in or witnessed in recent years. This was, after all, the focus of our research, the reason we were in the Chayote Valley together, comparing outside development efforts in Mexican resistance communities with Ojo de Agua's self-development.

The road along the river was newly graded, the product of the arrival of Albores's 5,000 new millennium troops. Somewhere up ahead, this dirt and gravel byway intersected with another, finally arriving at Tepeyac and Realidad. We were on the road to Reality.

We turned into the tiny drive leading around the few rustic buildings that made up Tulan. There was at least one structure more than during Jeanne's last visit with Gabriela, as the Tulaneros added individual houses for growing extended households to the original community node. Two of the young men emerged cautiously from within the milpa, trying to identify the new arrivals. The appearance of a vehicle was out of the ordinary, and while we were awaited, we were not expected. Moreover, the Tulaneros had never met Duncan. They were excessively cautious and justifiably wary of strangers. Recognizing Jeanne, one of the young men ran to fetch Francisco.

He emerged from the milpa growing thick behind the compound and came toward us, slowly.

"Well, Juanita," he called. "It's about time." His soft voice was laced with humor, and he looked to Duncan, waiting for an introduction to this pale-skinned stranger. To set him at ease, we emphasized Duncan's long years of connection to the region, his familiarity with the Rio Chayote, even though he had lived downriver in Ojo.

Francisco was limping, his guarded footsteps masking his strength and force. He called to his wife Carmen, and she emerged from within the clinic building opposite the kitchen. Even before the greetings were finished, there was water boiling on the raised, open kitchen fire as Carmen slipped away quietly. Another free-range chicken was about to become soup.

We stood in the center of the enclave, chatting, visible to anyone passing on the road. One of the older boys came in quickly from another direction. He said something to Francisco, then looked at the car.

"Lucas, can you move the car around back?" Francisco asked quietly.

Obeying, Duncan went to move the VW. As he did, a reverberating rumble came from downriver, growing louder with each moment.

"Doña Juanita," said Alfredo, Franciso's son-in-law. "Why don't we wait inside?"

The car door slammed, and Duncan joined us as we went into one of the unfinished buildings. From the door, we could still see the road, and now a mud-green line of humvees and troop trucks crept into view. The Albores 5,000 were on the move, and the Tulaneros hoped that they would not find any reason to pause down by the garden gate.

Alfredo smiled, a nervous smile, and ducked purposefully through a curtained doorway into an adjoining room. With the military coming, we might have expected him to return with some piece of paraphernalia of an armed uprising, if not a gun, perhaps a set of binoculars to get a closer look at what the trucks were carrying. The curtain parted as he came back into the room, arms laden with a strange rectangular box of black plastic. He placed it on the floor in front of us and said, "Disculpe, but perhaps you can help me to read some of this. You see, it's in English."

We glanced at each other and took a closer look at the box. It was not a gun or camera or any kind of recording device. It had nothing to do with the army or monitoring troop movements. It was an electric keyboard, a big Yamaha, outfitted to play original music or to autoplay a set of prerecorded songs.

Duncan did a cursory check of the apparatus. "You got batteries for this thing?" he asked.

Alfredo disappeared into the other room, emerging with a box of D-cell Energizers. He inserted them into the keyboard, turned it on, and then indicated a line of words along one end of the front.

"What, for instance, is this?" He pressed a button on the top, and a familiar tune began to play, conjuring up memories of a silent and snowy Christmas, 'round yon virgin, heavenly peace.

That one was easy. Duncan explained that it was a Christmas song, the American version of "Noche de Paz."

"Ah," said Alfredo. "And this?"

The keyboard had an array of show tunes, old standards, folk ballads, spirituals. Alfredo pressed a button. "Darktown ladies sing this song, doo-dah, doo-dah." We laughed nervously.

"Well, this one comes from our history, when the blacks were slaves," Jeanne began. Alfredo's eyes widened. American History 101 was in order.

Alfredo was clearly beginning to relax, forgetting the company of troops that had now come to a halt just a little way down the road.

"Can you sing it?" he asked.

Duncan made a quick assessment of the relative value of singing a rather offensive ditty while skulking inside a Zapatista house, waiting for the army to pass. He cleared his throat and began.

The humvees were moving again, now almost in front of the compound. Alfredo seemed unperturbed. "This one?" he asked, hitting the button on another tune. This one took us to the Mississippi delta, plaintively telling the story of a lost life. Duncan summarized the tale. Alfredo's eyes were filled with expectation.

"I used to sing this when I was young, playing the guitar in the 60s," Jeanne said. She took a deep breath and belted out the first verse of "House of the Rising Sun." Duncan came in, harmonizing on the chorus. We were getting into the spirit.

Thirty minutes and numerous show tunes later, the army was gone, the chicken was soup, and Alfredo and the others were visibly relaxed. Mentally, Jeanne added a new item to the "to do" list of ethnographic field preparation. Make sure you know something to sing. We settled in at the kitchen table with the entire group, with soup, tortillas, and chilies making a filling repast. Duncan reached into his bowl and pulled out a dark, wiry leg.

"This one of those DESMU chickens?" he asked nonchalantly, referring to one of the NGO's McDevelopment projects. Francisco put down his tortillas and leaned back from the bench against the kitchen wall. He let out a deep guffaw. Carmen went to the stove and brought brimming mugs of coffee sweetened with the honey from their now restored hives. She looked at her husband.

"Let me tell you something about those NGOs," she began.

"Don't get me wrong, it's not that we don't appreciate the help, the projects that especially DESMU has tried to bring to us. But, you know, we are way out here, and how often do they come? Once every one, two weeks? If a grant comes to them, in our name, we have to wait for them to give us the money, little by little, like we were children, like we wouldn't be able to set it aside, save it until it was needed. So take the bees, for instance. Comes a day when there is a big wind, or maybe the paramilitary, and the cajas get destroyed. We need to rebuild them. Now. Before all the bees are dispersed. But we can't. We have to wait for Ariana or Daniel or Gabriela to show up, to dole out the money. What do they think? Learning to be accountable, learning to control the money is part of learning to do development."

Carmen was on a roll. Francisco was nodding in agreement.

"Juanita, you know the money the students sent to help buy this land?" he asked.

Jeanne paused. Sometimes she forgot that the Tulanero compound was also a beneficiary of Chiapas Project cookie sales.

"That was a grant, right? Not a loan?"

She nodded.

"Then why does the NGO keep trying to make us pay it back? They are not always all honest."

Carmen sighed. "It's not just that. Working with the bees is not easy. The money came to the women, a women's cooperative. We took it, of course. But we can't do all the work ourselves, just the women. We never have. We are a community. We need to work together, especially when there are groups of people working against us. Why do they want to divide us so?"

Carmen's perplexity at the structure of NGO development projects designed for women only was one we would hear again later that day in Cerro Verde. Projects designed for women seemed theoretically sound since they empowered women by giving them their own economic assets. But as Francisco and Carmen were fond of saying, you can't talk about the validity of theory until you have put it in practice. And here, the practice didn't support the theory.

While feminist organizations working in Chiapas criticize the Zapatista platform concerning women's rights as having little or no impact, women in communities such as Tulan provide their own critique of feminist-based objectives in development projects. This is not to say that feminist analyses don't bring broader understanding of why previous models of women/men in development are inadequate. But though projects promoting social transformation through economic empowerment for women have helped Maya and Maya campesina women gain greater voice and power within their communities, the divisive nature of some of these projects has been seen by these same women as undermining collective goals. They stress the importance of the idea of complementarity in their lives and in the projects proposed by internationally funded NGOs.[1]

The concept of *complementaridad*, complementary opposition and dualism, reflects opposed elements that together make a whole and is a key to Maya cosmovision. In fact, the elusive primary deity of Mesoamerica is a dual god, the primary unity being made up of two opposed and interdependent entities. Indeed, as Gary Gossen (1996) notes, ancestors, deities, and ritual personages are given a "bisexual honorific title" translated as "fathers-mothers" (316). This dualism concept is manifested all through the culture, all though the ages. The holy prayer is always in couplets, always said twice. Shrines have double places to make offerings in, and the offerings are made twice. A balancing of dual and opposed elements is woven throughout the religion, the worldview, and the social order, and appears in poetry and mythic sagas like the Popol Vuh. The idea is a bit like the yin/yang concept, but it manifests itself in very many cultural locations and acts.

On the other hand, while this may be implicit in the sacred world of highland Mayas, many Maya households don't always bear out their ideal gender complementarity in daily life (Eber 1999, 68). Indeed, uneven distribution of the division of labor, differential access to literacy, increasing domestic violence, and arranged marriages remain part of the contemporary Maya world.

Bearing this contradiction in mind, as women like Carmen gained a voice in conjunction with the Zapatista movement, they have articulated the need to respect cultural tradition. At the same time, they work to change those customs that may not respect women and their roles within the family. Within this difficult setting of mixed cultural values, Carmen and Francisco, like Cerro Verde's elder couple Antonio and Dominga, were assisted in their personal struggles by at least one other influential family member who held a deep respect for complementary gender relations.

Relying on complementarity is visibly logical among highland Mayas, whose ceremonial life unfolds around them in daily sacred detail. But these displaced, acculturated Mayas had no such reinforcement. With only the elder members of the community as cradle Tojolobal speakers, they had no linguistic reason to force relations into merged dualistic categories. And yet the Maya cosmovision was implicit in their lives, reflected in a kinship system that merged roles and responsibilities, and in their lived reality, one in which complementarity in gender relations still made the greatest sense. Given this background, it was logical, practical, and philosophically correct when the Tulan women, while willing and able to perform many of the beekeeping tasks, invited the men to take over some of the work. Slowly, the women's project, at the women's insistence, became a community endeavor and a tremendous production success.

DESMU: ORGANIZATIONAL REFLECTIONS

As the years and projects rolled on, it was not just the Tulaneros who realized that to focus on women only, at a time when divisiveness was bad development, was also downright dangerous. Some NGO members were also beginning to really listen to what the women were saying to them. One of these was Claudia Duran Duran, a past director of DESMU who died unexpectedly on June 18, 2001. Her death at the age of thirty-seven was a tragedy not just for her family and friends but also for the communities with whom she worked. In her final year guiding the NGO, as the organization struggled, downsized, and searched for funding, Claudia had begun to grow her theoretical insight concerning the role of DESMU in particular and NGOs in general by looking at the practical implications of their work. Her development as an emerging applied social scientist was evident in the paper she presented at the annual meeting of the Society for Applied Anthropology in Merida, Mexico, just one month before she died.[2] Her analysis of DESMU's mistakes illustrates a set of metaphors that encapsulate shortcomings in the relationship between NGOs, communities, and donor agencies.

DONORS AND THEIR MISSIONS

Funding organizations define their areas of interest and concern in formal mission statements that also encapsulate their ideologies of aid. They seek out situations that allow them to fulfill that mission: generic domains of need or fields of opportunity that seem to call out for intervention. This expresses a subtle type of paternalism that says that a mission of intervention can be efficacious in the first place, a belief that they can and should use that aid to promote change.

As intermediaries or ombudsmen, NGOs such as DESMU solicit resources and implement programs that derive from the interface of the NGO's own mission and the donor's stated intent. The ideas and plans of larger funding agencies and donors are translated into actual programs in diverse cultural and geographical settings regardless of the particular conditions of each specific place and point in time.

As a woman-focused NGO, DESMU was selected to implement programs of the United Nations High Commission for Refugees because of a perceived goodness of fit between the stated missions of the two groups. UNHCR's mission statement says that "UNHCR pays particular attention to the needs of children and seeks to promote equal rights of women and girls" (UNHCR 2001, 2). In like manner, DESMU's work was always presented through the perspective of gender, looking to find a way to make the relations between men and women more equitable. With these goals in mind, the funds the NGO received were earmarked for specific types of programs, and there was little wiggle room in terms of project design. As Duran Duran commented, "The design of the projects was subject to the vision not just of the implementers but also, in a greater part, of the financiers. In our case, this was the UNHCR. Planning excluded those who were recipients of the programs, for which we received serious criticism from the women and communities."

DESMU's projects were aimed at diminishing poverty through activities targeting women and children. In most cases, interventions were devised using the perspective of urban feminism, which focused on individualism at the expense of the community. Yet those working for DESMU soon realized that there were serious differences between the notions of gender held by both the donor and the implementing NGO and that of groups with whom they worked. According to Duran Duran, "these [ideas] developed from an analysis of socioeconomic and cultural conditions radically different from those that develop in an indigenous, rural environment" (2001, 2).

Realizing that the financial agents were trying to impose work schemes that did not correspond to the "Maya cosmovision," DESMU eventually found mechanisms to divert designated funds into projects that were a better fit with the cultural and political logic of the region. Needless to say, they quickly ran into problems with their donors (see Earle and Simonelli 2000).

DESMU's initial years of work, carried out according to its own mission and that of UNHRC, became the field analysis that should have taken place prior to any work at all with and in the communities. Duran concluded that finding methods to alleviate poverty under the difficult conditions of the Chiapas conflict required an analysis of the social and political barriers to alternative development (Duran Duran 2001, 5). Yet there are few funding agencies willing to finance this type of microlevel study of a particular group of people responding to a specific set of circumstances that, in general, fit the mission of the organization. A belief in *proyectismo* (projectism), or the project as object, excludes the possibility of developing from below. It leaves communities stuck in a missionary position where assuming the validity of the mission silences the voices of the people.

Still, there are few funding agencies that do not at least pay lip service to the notion that communities should be involved in decisions concerning the nature of donor/NGO-sponsored projects. According to the UNHCR mission statement, "UNHCR is committed to the principle of participation by consulting refugees on decisions that affect their lives" (UNHCR, 2001, part 2). Often, this type of semiconsultation is manifested in a fast-food model of community involvement in its own development decisions. For DESMU, the model involved a process of action–reflection–action. They offered women's groups a limited menu of possible projects, a choice between a selection of small-scale productive activities, including hens, horticulture, bees, or rabbits (action). The women retired to discuss these possibilities (reflection). Later, they would "decide to accept" one of the proffered activities (action). Thus, the illusion that grassroots decision making led to the acceptance of a project was preserved for all.

Since a donor's overall mission gives rise to particular areas of aid, NGOs often struggle to come up with projects that correspond to foundation assessments of what are seen as the poverties of local life. According to DESMU, all their productive projects were intended to respond to set objectives, both social and economic. Thus, mission-determined project limitations or McDevelopment limited the form a project might take and ultimately short-circuited any realistic and practical ideas the community might have concerning the alleviation of their own poverty. NGO projects in the Chayote region were directed at the production of commodities for local consumption, particularly products to improve the immediate nutrition of women and children. Community groups, on the other hand, were more interested in converting these activities into something that might be commercialized, with long-term benefit for all. For them, social transformation without economic outcome was useless. Economic outcome with culturally inappropriate social transformation was also unacceptable. But in spite of the contradictions, group after group chose to eat from DESMU's fast-food menu of projects. As we learned from DESMU's experience, communities will agree to participate in NGO projects even if they are determined to be useless by all the stakeholders if the NGO is seen to control access to other valued resources, including information and outside contacts.

Beyond all else, DESMU, like other NGOs, had a continuing interest in its own longevity as an organization. In such cases, continued funding is usually contingent on the ability to claim success in project development and implementation, which provides the ultimate justification for sustaining the program's infrastructure. Successes are presented to the donor in an annual report, a positive portrayal of the results of the previous year's work and an index of "sustainabullity."[3] In short, the organization that has the best line of bull concerning program success is most likely to sustain the organization.

DESMU was born out of a split with a sister NGO and brought into its own mission that group's goals: to promote projects with refugee women to help overcome existing gender inequalities between men and women (Mama Maquin 1994, 16). Yet DESMU's years of fieldwork eventually brought into question both of those foci. To work only with refugees in an area where everyone was poor and struggling seemed unethical. To work only with women and children was divisive. As we have seen, as the conflict in Chiapas deepened after 1997, the idea of provisioning one group of communities at the expense of another seemed like a really bad plan. Moreover, while their annual reports described the widespread acceptance of DESMU projects, in actuality the hens had been eaten, and the home gardens were covered with weeds (DESMU 1998).

Emerging from the NGO's own reflection was a series of conclusions and solutions. These included changing the paternalistic and protective attitude toward the communities, supporting communities' efforts at designing their own programs, making programs inclusive rather than exclusive on all levels, and limiting the duration of involvement of the NGO in a particular project or community (Duran Duran 2001, 6). And all this added up to one problematic conclusion: to continue to receive funding meant to write reports that included the obfuscation of the actual results.

Paralleling DESMU's reanalysis of its own shortcomings, project beneficiaries such as Tulan and Cerro Verde also provided a critique of the pitfalls of sustainability. They saw themselves as pawns in a process by which NGO staff wrote reports ensuring their own continued employment at the expense of viable community projects. On yet another level, the competition between NGOs for limited funding also meant that sharing information about project success or failure with each other was also out of the question. NGOs working in the same circumscribed geographical region sometimes replicated each other's failed projects since to make this information public might undermine their efforts to sustain funding.

In 1999, as the last Guatemalans returned to their country or became Mexican citizens, the NGO's life cycle as a provider of aid to refugees was coming to an end. Nevertheless, DESMU could have continued to be a viable avenue for women-focused projects. Instead, the group attempted to change its organizational focus to projects that respected the Maya cosmovision and ideas of complementarity. This adjustment came too late to save the organization from the community critique we were now hearing in Tulan, but at the same time it was too innovative to be acceptable to the funding organizations. Work in politically divided villages, and within these, with families as a whole rather than women and children, was not "politically correct." The stance became the kiss of death for the NGO. Years later, one of the Guatemalans who was a recipient of the seemingly endless supply of UN–NGO projects would provide a spontaneous and scathing confirmation of all that Claudia and DESMU were realizing as the new millennium began.

DESMU's analysis and conclusions also paralleled those arrived at by Duncan in his comparative study of Ojo de Agua and Guatemalan development completed twenty years before. Comparing our assessments of authorized community development with that reached by Claudia, the Zapatistas, and now settled Guatemalan Mexicans, a set of development guidelines was emerging, a living model of how to help without creating more hurt.

Community-authored development or "authorized" community development (ACD) is the practice (and documentation) of actions and plans that have been checked against the record of failure and success and have the enthusiastic support and engagement of the people involved. This authority to design alternative social landscapes cannot come from the authorship of donors or designers. It is given authority by the intersection of the voices of the residents and includes structured generalities based on the assessed experiences of the past. And if we agree that all voices carry some authority and are prejudiced by it, then authorization must come from multiple sources, a kind of checks and balances in the construction of an ACD.

ACD provides that the conditions of community development be contingent on giving agency to the people who these changes will affect. It also means that the authors who report on the development enterprise must have their efforts "authorized" by sharing them with the participants and reporting on their reactions, interpretations, and assessments, a process of interactive consultation.

Within a series of proposed ACD guidelines, a set of dos and don'ts was emerging, a checklist of what are major domains of concern that can make or break development efforts in low-resource areas and among underempowered people. Summarized, these included but were not limited to how the interventions do or do not do the following:

- Enhance social solidarity and community harmony
- Work within the power environment or "political landscape"
- Stress diversification in productive activities as a step toward economic independence and interdependence
- Strive toward ecological balance and sustaining the natural environment
- Work and communicate within the "cultural logic" and worldview of communities
- Identify all social groups affected by the intervention
- Avoid dependency relationships by limiting the time frame of the program

- Promote reciprocity and symmetry in relationships with the community
- Make the organizational mission explicit and understandable
- Reflect jointly planned, executed, evaluated, and reported projects

For Tulan, reconfiguring the honey project to reflect their own worldview and priorities was something that they could do with little difficulty. But there was another, more serious problem derived from NGO shortsightedness and atomistic *proyectismo* that could not be so easily solved. This was the issue of marketing, and on one level or another it was the heart and soul of many campesino difficulties.

It was getting late, long January shadows beginning to descend over the upper Chayote valley. We finished another cup of honey sweet coffee, and Duncan slipped out of the kitchen returning with four empty one-liter bottles.

"Got any honey to sell? We'd like to buy some."

Carmen groaned. Yes, they had honey. Too much honey. Huge plastic barrels full, small sixty-five-pound gasoline cans full, plenty of honey. We could buy all we wanted, but the problem was that it was all crystallized.

"We are grateful, happy to have the bee project. Before the municipio was dismantled we had great plans to work with the refugees in Comalapa, to bring our bees to them, and theirs to us to take advantage of the cyclical emergence of the flowers. It was a good project, innovative, working together to get even more out of the foundation's money than they ever dreamed. But they forgot one thing, so anxious to see the project completed. They forgot about marketing. We can produce 600 kilos of honey a harvest. But we have no way to sell it."

In 1999, DESMU bought and sold most of the Tulan harvest. This year, with the NGO struggling and the military active along the road, there had been no marketing plan. The honey was solid, turned to sugar, as pure honey does if it has not been pasteurized or watered down. Not only couldn't they market the *miel*, but they couldn't even get it out of the barrels and into the bottles.

Francisco carried a twenty-liter tambo into the kitchen and put it close to the fire trying to get the honey to pour. By the time the bottles were filled, the long January shadows had turned to nightfall. We loaded the honey into the car and said good-bye to Carmen and Francisco. There would be almost two more years of loving work on the Tulan land before we all met again.

NOTES

1. In her ethnography of San Pedro Chenalo, Christine Eber (1999) describes the place of complementary dualism in Maya daily life. "Pedranos say that men and women are indispensable to one another. Without jnup/jchi'il (my complementation, companion, or spouse), one cannot be a true man or woman" (67). She goes on to describe the

ideal type of Tzotzil Maya household relationship, derived from the notion of gender complementarity.

2. In March 2001, community members, NGO staff, and anthropologists working in Chiapas participated in a session titled "Workshop and Conversation: Building a Network of Cooperation for Chiapas" at the annual meeting of the Society for Applied Anthropology, Merida, Mexico.

3. Our thanks to Walter "Chip" Morris, whose many effective and cynical years working in development in Chiapas led him to coin the term "sustainabullity."

CHAPTER 9

The Expulsion: Legalizing Autonomy in Cerro Verde

On the path where unharvested coffee rots,
I appear as if from some other world
laden with bundles, my tentative smile
reflecting your face, fraught with concern—
just a short visit this time.

A cautioning nod from you
brackets a flood of words—
we can't talk much
in places where Marta can hear
don't want her to fear;
to be afraid that the men
who came for her uncle
are the same ones
who imagine masked apparitions;
self-appointed vigilantes
who patrol the night
who pass in the dark hours;
and the dogs bark, justified.

Marta sleeps better
since her uncle returned
from the distant prison
filled with autonomous administrators
and self-taught artists.
She doesn't know that
twenty-five years
of labor and sweat
on these lands
that were ours at the outset
might end; could end
in this valley,

where hibiscus honey turns crystal
for want of a just market
for want of a market without coyotes
to scavenge the entrails of our existence.

We haven't told Marta
that the accords we crafted with care
in a village of outcasts
once known for tolerance
could well be forgotten
when the heavy words of intimidation
encircle and imprison
our neighbors of conscience.
We don't speak loudly near Marta
just as we closed the kitchen door
on our past conversations with you—
and the comal hearth smoke
cut acrid into your heart.

We waited for you this week
waited with our carnival feast
a thin soup of bitter greens
thinking that we would be
the Lenten sacrifice
that the pueblo offered up
our hopes, the palms burned to ash
as they turn us out of our homes
with foreheads blackened by accusation.
We waited for you this week
in the still hours before dawn.
Just a short visit this time.
Better you don't pass the night
blanketed here in our solitary fear
lying with us on the horizon
of our smoldering dreams. (Simonelli, March 25, 2000)

THE 3:00 P.M. MICRO DROPPED JEANNE at the entrance to Cerro Verde just before Easter 2000. Hefting her backpack and laden with gifts for her grandbaby Natalia, she moved slowly through the heat and dust, down the hill to the Cerro enclave. It was summer in Chiapas, the six-week period of sun and warmth in the time slot we call spring. Luz was in her kitchen holding Natalia, the place strangely silent. As we talked, seven-year-old Marta leaned into her lap, watching her mother's taut face. The child's hair was ragged and unkempt, her eyes ringed with raccoon-like circles.

"Juanita, we can't talk in front of Marta," Luz said. "I can't have my children crying in fear, up all night, unable to rest, because of this conflict." She sent Marta off on an errand and closed the kitchen door.

"Luz, what's wrong? Where's Rodrigo? Where is everyone?"

She sighed. "The ejido leadership changed hands on February 1st. The new comisariado ejidal is from the PRIista side of the conflict. He is coercing the assembly."

An assembly governed the *ejido*, with periodic changes in official leadership. "Coercing the assembly to do what?" Jeanne asked. "Where is Rodrigo?"

"They voted to expel us, the families in resistance, from our lands and homes, in spite of the fact that my father and his brother helped found the place fifty years ago. They said that our refusal to contribute labor to government funded schools and health clinics meant that we were not fulfilling our ejido obligations. They told us that we must either participate in all projects or pay a yearly "tax" of $15,000 pesos ($1,600 U.S.). Give up autonomy and resistance, or get out."

This type of intimidation and expulsion, based on political and religious animosities, creates a huge population of displaced persons in Chiapas. Often, political divisions replicate religious difference, including divisions between Catholics and Protestant evangelicals or even between traditional Mayas and reform Catholics. In this case, the PRIistas threatening Cerro Verde were also Protestants (see Kovic 2005).

"We have lived in peace in this divided pueblo since 1994," Luz continued. "We must come to some kind of accord." That relative calm had prevailed in spite of the fact that part of the village of Cerro Verde was PRI and the rest pro-Zapatista was a small miracle. "Rodrigo went to San Cristóbal to consult with lawyers at the human rights center. I don't think you should stay this time, for your own safety."

I unpacked a few cans of Nan 2, the formula Natalia needed. Luz loved the baby, but taking on a new child remained an additional expense. Still, she offered me hospitality and asked if I wanted something to eat. I took Natalia from her, and she returned with two plates of *acelga*, boiled bitter greens, and a hard-cooked egg.

It was a short and unsettling visit, unexpected after our stay there the previous January. Fresh from our discussions of development with the Tulaneros, we'd arrived in darkness in Cerro Verde and once again introduced Duncan to the group. He was an immediate hit with all ages, exchanging Tzotzil-inspired Maya with Don Antonio; keeping up an easy banter with Luz, Alma, Dominga, and the other women; and winning over the kids by reading a series of bawdy Tojolobal tales. We'd been introduced for the first time to the dogs, Cleenton, Zedillo, and Albores, and spent long hours discussing development with groups and subgroups: women, men, children, and teens.

"If, in this world of hopes and dreams, you could fund any small project, what would it be?" we'd asked each bunch, separately and then together.

Jeanne knew of a small church foundation back in Oneonta that funded international projects. The deadline for proposals was the following week, but with the magic of the Internet, she could submit a request to them on time.

"A bakery," the women said. "A place to make yeast-raised, sweet bread." There was no bakery in Cerro Verde, and they estimated that they could recoup their investment and make a surplus if they were able to do the project. The men agreed that it was a good idea, something that the women should undertake. The children thought longingly of warm, sweet, yeasty rolls.

We'd made a comparison of the drawbacks and advantages of various types of ovens. Propane was hard to come by but environmentally less destructive than cutting the rapidly diminishing supply of firewood. But gas required continuing monetary inputs and the purchase of a stove. With a wood-fired beehive oven, the men could construct it, and they could use their labor, a resource they had in excess, to cut fuel. They dictated the proposal, Jeanne took notes, and we sent it off the following week.

By March, we knew that the proposal would be funded. But that news would mean nothing if they were evicted from their lands, expelled from the *ejido*. Jeanne told Luz the news anyway, hugged Natalia, and returned quickly to San Cristóbal. The next morning, just as she was preparing to return to the United States, a story appeared in the Chiapas daily *Cuarto Poder*: "Prozapatista families could be expelled," read the headlines. Telling the story briefly, the newspaper identified Rodrigo as indigenous and described the March 20 deadline for the ten affected Cerro Verde families to pay or go (Herrera 2000).

Rodrigo's identification as indigenous was curious. How many times had the group bemoaned the passing of their Mayaness, claiming that with the loss of the Tojolobal language they had also lost other culturally based customs and practices? When we first met, the community made the choice to appeal to us on the basis of economic identification. They were simply poor campesinos, trying to eke out a living on the margin of the margins. Now they were choosing to seek support based on ethnicity, a strategic assessment at a specific moment in history. In reality they were Maya and campesino, and time would show that they were not so far from their roots as they first maintained (Earle 1992; Hernández Castillo 2001a).

With the help of the Frayba lawyers, Rodrigo issued a formal statement in front of the Subprocuraduria de Justicia Indígena, denouncing the actions of their longtime *ejido* brethren. Peace observers from Spain returned with Rodrigo to Cerro Verde to gather the community's story as it related to the ongoing attempt to displace them. The presence of outsider observers would avert the violence that Luz so feared.

Though the change in *ejido* leadership was the immediate stimulus of this round of political and economic extortion, there was far more at stake here than met the eye. The group's autonomous clinics and schools, though destroyed in 1998, were up and running again, and they worked. The Zapatista organization provided practical support for the community, as Cerro Verde sent young people to Realidad to be trained. When they returned, they taught in whatever space was available, and the reality was that the children of Cerro Verde could read and write, while many of the *ejido*/government-schooled kids could not. This easily recognizable difference stimulated envy, *envidias*, and was one of the unmentioned factors in the *ejido* dispute. A second was the struggle for land itself.

Encapsulated in the alternative practices and programs found in Zapatista communities are models of land tenure and land use that take advantage of labor patterns and human–land relationships that are the heart and soul of autonomy. Given the importance of land, it is no wonder that one of the most powerful stimuli for the armed rebellion that occurred in Chiapas was the 1992 modification of article 27 of the Mexican Constitution. This change allowed for the private sale of communally held *ejido* land that had been granted constitutionally in 1916. For the first time, the *ejido* could be sold, borrowed against, or commercialized (Collier and Quartatiello 1994, 84–85).

The amendments to article 27 passed by a PRI-controlled congress made it clear that there was no more land to distribute to Mexico's landless and, more critically, changed the nature of land tenure. Up to that time, campesinos holding land use rights deriving from the land reform of the 1930s could pass that land on to a nominated successor, or, if none were available, the land would return to the communal body for distribution to a landless individual. The land could not be rented or sold (Ley Agraria 2002, 9–36).

In reality, there were a number of ways in which *ejido* land was being transferred outside of article 27 stipulations, and some observers claim that the amendments to the article regularized those processes already taking place (Gledhill 2002). Critiques of original article 27 restrictions also noted that because farmers did not hold definitive title to their lands, they could not obtain financing for improvements by using the land as collateral. The changes made it possible for campesinos to obtain title and use that land as desired (Ley Agraria 2002, 39–44).

To handle the process of entitling land, a new federal office, called the Procuraduria Agraria, was created. Among other tasks, the office was to oversee the certification of individual rights as set out in 1993 in PROCEDE (Programa de Certificación de Derechos Ejidales y Titulación de Solares Urbanes). As described by a PROCEDE spokesperson, PROCEDE is "an instrument of agrarian justice that regularizes and certifies the right to ejido and comunidad property" (Fuentes Muñoz 2002, 2).

There are three steps involved in the process of obtaining outright title to *ejido* lands. First, *ejidatarios* must undergo certification of individual rights to determine that they are legally part of the *ejido*. Once this has occurred, there must be a majority vote in the *ejido* assembly. This means that if only a few *ejidatarios* seek private property rights, they can't continue with the process. In March 2000, the Cerro Verde *ejido* was in the throes of considering whether to "PROCEDerse," a newly coined reflexive verb form describing the privitization process. Needless to say, the Zapatista contingent, including two of the surviving *ejido* founders, were unlikely to vote in favor of the program. For the *ejido* leadership, a neat solution to this and other related problems was to force them out entirely.

The weeks that followed the threat of expulsion for the Cerro Verde community were tense and frightening. Representing DESMU, Ariana Avila did massage workshops with the women, behind-the-scenes stress reduction sessions designed to keep Zapatista tempers from flaring. Once again, we were kept apprised of events via e-mail, but it wasn't until the following July that we would learn the full details from Davíd and the others. Once again, we gathered behind closed doors to hear the tale.

DOCUMENTING AUTONOMY

"You know how it is here," Davíd began. The Municipio is in resistance; but half the ejido is PRI. We've lived together here for thirty years and we have one thing in common. We are all screwed. We are all poor. Look at us. Mayas who don't speak our language. Look at them, Mexicans who are really Mayas. Our children die of the same diseases. We are the true forgotten of Chiapas. You know how in 1994, after much thought, we went looking for our path, we entered into resistance. The ejido had said that they would expel Zapatistas, but we said that our resistance was nonviolent. We would do all the work of the ejido that related to agriculture and trails, but no other government projects. The ejido agreed to honor this arrangement, but we didn't document it.

"Here is where we probably made our mistake. But it was respected by all, until February 6th, when we were summoned to a meeting. We didn't know what to expect. The strategy was to make us join the PRI, to make us accept the quick fix handouts of the government." He named a couple of the more recent incarnations, PRONOSOL, PROCAMPO.

"PRO PORQUE?" he mused.

"In other communities near us, they have been successful in expelling families. It goes on all over the state, like in Nicolas Ruiz and Venustiano Carranza. With the past Comisariado Ejidal, he just did nothing when he was approached by the army, Seguridad Publica, the PRIista representatives, wanting us out. This really got the hotheads of the ejido angry. So when the new head was elected, a Protestant, he immediately presented the demand."

Rodrigo continued the story: "The new executive committee called us to a meeting and told us that we must contribute to cooperative labor on schools and clinics and roads. We said that the ejido was about agriculture and that was all that we were required to do. They presented us with a document signed by all the PRI ejido members. The leaders said participate or pay or go. Join the PRI. We said, 'How would you like it if we tried to make you join our Organization?'

"Some of the others got really insulting. We tried to do things calmly. We continued to go and do our work on fields and trails. The Comisariado even tried to keep us from playing fútbol with the Cerro Verde team. This made us really angry. We got them to give us a fifteen-day postponement to discuss what to do. I went to San Cristóbal to the Frayba to get guidance."

"The Frayba helped us to prepare a response to the ejido's acta. They sent observers to stay in the community. We issued our formal denuncia," Davíd added.

A second summons brought them to yet another meeting, a full gathering of the *ejido* assembly, not just the leadership, like the last time.

"Only four of us went. We didn't know if they would kill us."

But this time there was a federal *ejidal* judge there, from the Procuraduria Ejidal.

"Everyone knew what we had done for years, and what had been done to us, about the army and security forces. But the leaderships' statements were filled with all manner of lies and exaggerations. They demanded that the municipal police carry us off.

"The judge said let them speak! He listened to our story, and then to the charges of the commission," Rodrigo continued. "The PRIistas thought that they had a good reason to put before the government to expel us, that we didn't contribute to labor on schools, health and other official projects. The judge asked us why we didn't take PROCAMPO money or support the schools. And we said we had our own, and weren't interested in others.

"Then he asked the Assembly if it was true that we didn't do our required work and no one agreed, even though they had signed a paper a month before. They had worked beside us for years. In the end, they couldn't lie. The ejido leaders were shocked. They lost control of the assembly.

"The judge, the PRI judge, ruled in our favor. He said that in an ejido, only issues related to agronomy required our participation, cleaning paths, repairing roads, attending meetings, contributing to the costs of sending representatives to the city on ejidal business. After this pronouncement, we presented a document stating our willingness to keep working, and the judge said all was in order."

"I accept this Acta," the judge said. "This is not the proposal of rebels."

"But to save political face he asked us to pay a 'reintegration' fee of 50 percent of the original amount. The amount was negotiated with the ejido assembly. Seven thousand pesos. He gave us three weeks to decide."

Rodrigo leaned back in his chair and sighed. "We didn't want to pay. We left the meeting, and we talked about how it would be seen as being legitimately expelled, admitting that we were wrong. But in the end, we knew also that if we did pay, the acta would be *cerrado*—closed—we would have a written document giving us the right to have an autonomous organization. It was the same agreement we had had with the *ejido* since 1994 but not on paper. So we decided to go right back and sign the agreement. To close it. Legally. To pay the 7,000 pesos. And do it right away, before anything could be changed."

The men's faces grew somber.

"Of course, they never expected us to agree. To come up with the money."

"How did you feel when you agreed to compromise?" Jeanne asked Rodrigo. We could see his attitude shift with his body, like a faint breeze ushering in four centuries of conditioned response. Yet the decision was not a sellout to past patterns of exploitation and interaction but a strategic decision, a coping strategy. The human species survived by picking its battles. Rodrigo knew it. Old Antonio knew it. The women knew it. We knew it. It was not capitulation. It was a step toward reconciliation. And it brought them a level of legality in autonomy like none other in the state. The *ejidal* judge had formally, legally, and in writing recognized the Zapatista right to autonomy. All it took was an act of peaceful reconciliation, a few outside observers, and 700 U.S. dollars. This last was our part of the story.

In early April, an e-mail had arrived from Ariana at DESMU. She outlined the predicament of the *compas* in Cerro Verde and asked how the "cookies for chickens" fund-raising was going, the *galletas por gallinas* drive. Was there any way that we could come up with the bucks?

Our students had been selling cookies nonstop for the past six months, running a close second to the Girl Scouts.

"Yes," Jeanne replied, thinking about the ethical implications of turning into the International Bank of Anthropology. "Ariana, it can be arranged. But tell the folks that it is not a donation or a gift. It is an advance on the oral history of the community, from the time of their arrival in the jungle to the present."

She relayed the message. The community met quickly and agreed to tell their story, and the money was transferred.

The women also had their view of the conflict in the *ejido*.

"What did you think of the whole experience with the ejido assembly?" Duncan asked them later that day.

The women shifted in their seats.

"No one asked us. No one told us anything. We didn't know if they would come back from that last meeting. If it was a trap. What do they think, that this isn't about our lives, our children? These are family issues. We talk, the women. It's our cooperative."

Duncan with Marta on a visit to Ojo de Agua

She was referring to the corn-grinding mill, held jointly by the women, on the piece of land near the community's cooperative store, the place where, according to January's plans, the bakery would be built. Luz, Alma, and the other women were remarkable people, Dominga's daughters, living examples of Maya feminism, where complementarity is the key. Sometimes the men needed reminding.

We thought about all this later that afternoon, during a community meeting, where we announced the acceptance of the January grant proposal and watched the community make the next step to realizing their dream. We'd arrived with the money, and Jeanne was happy to get it out of her pocket and turn over full control to a Cerro Verde committee comprised of two women and two men. The very act of turning over the money had startled the community, which was used to paternalistic NGO control that doled out project funds like a teenager's weekly allowance.

"What do we do now?" they had asked, taking the zip-lock bag filled with cash.

"It's not our problem," we said, happy to be relieved of the burden of keeping a substantial number of pesos secure.

The community spent months reflecting over the most effective and efficient way to deploy their funds. Ultimately, they rejected the original proposal, the bakery co-op to be run by the women, in the interest of investing in ways to make their coffee crop more marketable. Traded bread for coffee; limited markets for multiple markets. Presenting their findings to us, the women defended the decision.

"Coffee is not just a men's thing, Juanita," said Luz, as if she could hear the criticisms of our San Cristóbal feminist friends drifting in on the *selva* wind. "Coffee is something of the entire family. And we have already invested twenty years in its production. The bread would be something new, taking our energies."

Bread for coffee. Limits for options. Luz braced herself, as if expecting a fight.

"Fine," we said. "It's your project."

With each consecutive visit, the project moved slowly toward realization. They purchased a coffee dryer and roaster and bought the lumber to build a small structure to house it. They were, after all, a community in resistance, working to encounter globalism on its own terms, not just counter it with rhetoric, slogans, and epithets. They told us about each step shyly, as though still expecting the Patrón to emerge from somewhere within our rented Volkswagen Beetle.

Ironically, the continuing overt conflict between the Zapatistas and the government forces, the suspended dialogue and army buildups, made space for a covert war between communities such as Cerro Verde and the existing structure that marginalized and exploited them. The visible conflict diverted attention from quiet attempts to make change on the level of immediate survival, be it in negotiation over land rights or through autonomous development projects.

All over Chiapas, land-related disputes had ended in armed confrontation and expulsion, but Cerro Verde was determined to solve their problems peacefully. More important, the group recognized the importance of written documentation, and theirs was the first case in Chiapas that had ended with a signed act of *autonomía*. Whether the *ejidal* judge representing the government realized the implications of the agreement for the larger issue of legitimate autonomy is unclear. In the same way that Jeanne's expulsion and its subsequent resolution under constitutional law forced the government to reevaluate and change its policy toward foreigners in Chiapas, the Cerro Verde *ejido* altercation resulted in an unexpected triumph in one area of the struggle for indigenous autonomy. They hoped that their coffee project would help them reach another.

CHAPTER 10

Informed Permission and Invigorated Autonomy

IT WAS A CLEAR, DRY, RAINY SEASON DAY IN JULY as we began to descend into the edges of the Lacandón rain forest, returning to Chiapas this summer with eleven students. It was the first Wake Forest University/University of Texas–El Paso Maya Summer Program, and we planned to spend several days working with the people of Cerro Verde.

The road into the jungle had become a familiar trail, now nicely asphalted for better military access, and as we traveled on it, we passed through an army checkpoint bristling with eager officers and their anxious enlisted followers. A sign stated that it was a place of "control," and an officer explained that they were "controlling foreigners on this road."

"Are the foreigners out of control?" Duncan asked in heavily accented Spanish, reeking of naive New York tourism on La Ruta Maya.

The officer thought about it for a moment and looked puzzled enough to simply wave us through with only a cursory glance at Duncan's passport. The forces of the state were still trying to gain control, to monitor traffic, to reestablish their dominance in this once-forgotten edge of Mexico, but they were no longer sure why.

Our thoughts turned to the huge Zapatista mobilization that had occurred three months before in the spring of 2001. That journey brought thousands of rebels onto the roads, headed for national center stage in the Mexican capital, and had as its leitmotif the question of autonomy. The march occurred just months after Vicente Fox defeated the candidate of the PRI, becoming the first opposition president of Mexico in seventy-one years. Soon after, the Mexican Senate took the previously negotiated San Andrés Accords and removed language it felt was threatening, once again reiterating the state's fears about granting recognition of local autonomy.

"Mommy, who are these people?" asked Camila's four-year-old daughter Cari, as she looked at a photo of the Mexico City zocalo, packed with Zapatistas and their supporters.

"Son nuestra gente," answered Camila proudly. They are our people.

And now, as we traveled toward Cerro Verde once again, it was representatives of that same multitude and of a newly reconstituted autonomous municipality with whom we would have to negotiate the future of our relationship to the people who awaited us.

NEGOTIATING COOPERATION

Our encounter with autonomy began even before leaving the United States. The 2001 field program was to be five weeks long and had been in the planning stages since the winter. Cerro Verde had agreed to host a visit, the students were selected, and they were refining their own research interests, which dovetailed with our ongoing work. Prior to leaving we each spent days locked in contentious exchange with our respective institutional review boards (IRBs). We attempted to point out that it was unethical and unsafe for our so-called subjects to sign individual informed consent documents. They would welcome us, if they chose to welcome us. The impulse to consent or reject would be of their design.

As we struggled to arrive at an agreement with the IRBs concerning the informed consent process for both our work and our student's projects, an e-mail arrived from Ariana Avila in Chiapas. She was relaying a message from the Cerro Verde community, as she had since her early days with DESMU. We marveled at the dimensions of virtual fieldwork as she conveyed the concerns of the community's members.

The e-mail was confusing. There was a problem with the *municipio*, something we needed to talk about as soon as we returned to Chiapas. When she spoke of the *municipio*, we automatically thought about the PRI-dominated leadership of the *municipio* of La Independencia, where Cerro Verde is located. Had that municipal government begun to harass and intimidate the group, as had the *ejido* the previous year? With Luz's sister's husband an elected PRI official of the municipal government, anything was possible. Arriving in Chiapas, we were relieved to learn that the problem was not with the PRIistas but instead with the leadership of the autonomous municipality of Tierra y Libertad.

"What autonomous leadership?" we asked Ariana.

Hadn't the *autónomo* been disbanded in 1998, it leaders jailed and held in Cerro Hueco as political prisoners for over eighteen months? Though we had heard the story of how the leadership had regrouped and learned invaluable skills while housed together as guests of the government, in our visits to Cerro Verde there had been no discussion of a reconstituted government outside the prison. Our initial interactions were with the communities alone as we developed research interests in conjunction with their development needs and aspirations. Perhaps we had been on a "need to know" basis.

"Yes, compañeros, there is a Consejo Autónomo," Ariana told us. "And they have some questions for you, issues that affect your right to be in the community and their desire to remain autonomous."

Relieved that it was not the old officialdom causing problems, we were excited to see what this other political entity had to ask us. What, in fact, were their concerns? Behind this was the larger question: what is it about questions of autonomy that place that demand ahead of any other, including resources and, in some instances, peace itself?

The following day, we made our way out to the edge of the jungle, armed with Ariana's cryptic message about the concerns of the ethereal autonomous leaders. We needed to get clarification before our students arrived.

At both of our universities, service learning was a growing initiative, and we had always included this aspect of learning in our ethnographic field programs. This summer's student visit related to their desire to help provision the community's autonomous school. In addition, we also brought a small sum of money, the result of countless more cookie sales and other fund-raising events, that we expected to use to construct the actual building. As we approached the pueblo, we wondered about our plans and our position vis-à-vis the community and the municipality. The greenery got greener, and the road got rougher. The answer was complex.

"Hermanamiento," said Davíd, ex-member of the ex-government. "We have to go together to the Enlace Civil in San Cristóbal to file official papers if we all hope to continue to work together." He paused. "And if you want to be able to bring the students here," he added.

Now we were truly confused. The Enlace Civil was many of the many civil society organizations that had developed in San Cristóbal to handle the new forms of organization, protest, and appeal that appeared in the wake of the Zapatista rebellion.

We looked at Davíd as if not understanding. *Hermanamiento*. Sister city. How could a university be sister city to an illegal administrative entity? Davíd took our perplexity as criticism.

"We're really sorry," he said. "All this inconvenience. Una molestia."

"Not a problem," we assured him.

The whole thing was truly intriguing, our anthropological selves delighted at the turn of events. We would meet on Friday in San Cristóbal, go together to the Enlace, and file the papers. We would dazzle them with our understanding of how a shadow government could have a foreign policy and an embassy to handle the official clearances to boot. It would all make perfect sense.

For the people of Cerro Verde, the five-hour trip from the *selva* to San Cristóbal is a combination of pickup rides and combis that must begin before first light. On Friday, Jeanne spent the morning cooking a pot of beef and vegetables, a chance to repay hospitality that added up to a lot of free-range chickens slaughtered in our behalf. Ariana arrived first, with Arturo, another of her friends, one of the many university leftists from the capital who had flocked to Chiapas to help out with the intellectual side of the rebellion. It was he who had challenged the military at the sacked *municipio* headquarters in Santa Elena in 1998, arriving with a borrowed pickup to salvage what was left of the archives and other supplies.

The doorbell rang, and it was Rodrigo, alone as representative of Cerro Verde, dressed in his city best and looking apprehensive and tired. Jeanne ushered him into the parlor, where Duncan and one of the students waited with Ariana and Arturo.

A round of niceties, and we got down to business.

"The Consejo," began Rodrigo. "The Consejo wonders why they haven't seen your papers before this. They need to know what you propose. What you expect to give to and get from the Hermanamiento."

"Rodrigo," Duncan began. "This is the first we've heard about the existence of a Consejo. Or the notion of Hermanamiento. What do you need?"

"Disculpe," began Rodrigo, apologetic, as Davíd had been. "Don't you have any official letters? Something stating your purpose? And lists of the students? With names and addresses. And e-mails. And passport numbers?"

We looked at each other. Of course, we had official papers. There was the letter from the dean of continuing education at Wake Forest, describing the program in terms of its academic content, making a great point to use the politically innocuous term "cultural exchange." We thought of the big, raised seal of the university, embedded into the gold and black letterhead stationary, a document prepared in case the official government questioned our intent. And yes, we had lists of students, a precaution designed to avert hour-long stops at military checkpoints while semiliterate soldiers wrote down the details of our visas and passports. We had come prepared, but we hadn't counted on having to present that information to the other government.

We nodded affirmatively and reached into the folder of official documents. These included not just our current credentials but also the resolution issued by the Mexican Immigration Institute overturning Jeanne's short-lived expulsion from the country. We hadn't realized how much mileage we would get out of all of them. Rodrigo took the raised-seal letter.

"Disculpe la molestia," he said apologetically as he accepted it. He read it quickly and turned to Ariana, pleased.

"Eso," he told her. "And we need something defining your intent to continue to work with Cerro Verde. And to be considerate of the needs of the entire municipio of Tierra y Libertad. But don't mention the money we already received for the bakery/coffee project. We don't want to complicate things."

Out came our trusty minicomputer. A veteran of many years communicating with bureaucrats, Duncan could construct a significantly wordy, overly polite, deferential, and obtuse letter suitable for any type of interaction with Mexican officialdom, legal or illegal.

Had we known more about the responsibilities of Zapatista support communities to the larger organization, thought out the implications of their slogan "For each of us nothing, for all of us everything," Rodrigo's little injunction about the coffee project would have set off all sorts of bells and whistles. But we were still learning the depths of their relationship to the larger ELZN and, by default, our own increasing connection.

"Aren't the autónomos illegal?" we asked Rodrigo, out of curiosity.

"Pues, sí!" he answered. "Yes, they're illegal. But they're legitimate."

At that, Jeanne signaled to the student, and together they went back into the kitchen to finish preparing the meal. He was a Chicano activist and needed to experience what it meant to be a contemporary, female applied anthropologist. First you meet with the community in resistance, and then you make dinner.

Duncan typed up the letter, Rodrigo checked it for content, and Ariana added the finishing touches. The midday meal was on the table, as Jeanne ran out to make multiple photocopies of all the documents before the shops closed for afternoon *comida*. It was pouring, a rainy season San Cristóbal downpour that turned the streets into rivers. Back at the house, we packaged dry copies of all the documentation into a Wake Forest envelope. Rodrigo would take them to the still-unnamed representatives of the *autónomo*, somewhere back in the selva.

"Disculpe la molestia, Juanita . . ." Rodrigo began again.

We traded glances. Clearly, we weren't done yet.

"I have to take these back to the Consejo, and they'll check them over, and then we still have to go together to the Enlace, with their letter, in order to register the relationship. So I'll be back on Monday."

We groaned. Not so much for us. We were staying in San Cristóbal. But Rodrigo would have to spend another ten hours going back and forth to Cerro Verde to get all this squared away. Clearly, he didn't think it was a bother. As a representative of his "*grupita*," it was important that all this be done correctly in the eyes of the illusive Consejo. The process was beginning to look a little like the complex requirements for obtaining an FM-3 visa from Mexican immigration in order to do field research (see SLAA/Chiapas 2000). Didn't the autonomous government have just as much right to demand credentials from us as foreigners visiting and working with their communities? Perhaps we should call their papers an "FM-free" in honor of their intended separate but equal governmental status. Secretly, we were thrilled at the prospect of continuing with this procedure, of having the opportunity to be part of the process of civil society trying to construct foreign policy.

"It's not a bother," Duncan told Rodrigo. "We find the whole thing fascinating. And we'll work with you to do what we need to do. Hasta Lunes!" he said. We mentally rearranged the student schedule and wondered how either Wake Forest or the University of Texas–El Paso would feel about our prospective relationship.

Monday was our last program day in San Cristóbal, and we had a list of errands and purchases guaranteed to take the entire morning. We were leaving on a seven-day *recorrido* around the entire perimeter of the state, eventually arriving at Cerro Verde. Some of it was pure tourism, other parts involved service in another remote community noted for its poverty and paramilitaries.

Rodrigo was late, and our schedule was packed. By the time he arrived, the skies had opened again. Carrying packages of hammock rope, mosquito netting, and Dramamine, we waded over to offices of the Enlace Civil.

Sophia wasn't there. As "consul general" of the Enlace, she was away from the *autónomo* embassy and would not be back until after we left town. We groaned in unison. Wasn't there anyone else we could talk to? An appointment was made to talk to the vice consul at 5:00. I wrung out the bottom of my full-length skirt, and we agreed to meet Rodrigo back here again at five. We had a performance of the men's theater group Sna Tz'ibajon to attend, followed by a Maya-style blessing for the well-being of the group and our travels, and finally a formal dinner at Museo Na Bolom. It's not a bother, we reassured Rodrigo, heading back out into the deluge.

We returned at 5:00. No Rodrigo. While we waited, we talked amiably with the Enlace's representative. About our intentions. About their operation. She was sympathetic but doubted that we could get the proper paperwork done before our 8:00 A.M. departure. For all practical purposes, it appeared that they had replicated the bureaucracy of the government they were trying to avoid. We were going nowhere, so Duncan pulled out our credentials. He said something casually in Tzotzil Maya, and then added the phrase "*expulsada.*" I reached into my folder for my expulsion papers, and before long, everyone was smiling.

It was 6:00 P.M. in San Cristóbal when Rodrigo arrived. 6:00 P.M. in the city, *tiempo oficial, tiempo de Fox.* It was 5:00 P.M. anywhere in resistance, and that included Cerro Verde, where Rodrigo set his watch. *Tiempo de Dios, tiempo interior.* In Chiapas, even the time is autonomous. We talked a bit and then passed him on to the Enlace. We looked legitimate. All that remained was for Rodrigo to vouch for us. A mad dash for dinner, and yet another return, 8:30 P.M., *tiempo oficial.* This time, there were smiles all around. We were handed a signed, stamped form, describing our group and our purpose. It allowed us to travel freely to Cerro Verde, in the autonomous municipality of Tierra y Libertad. We thought about our institutional review boards and all the counterproductive discussion we'd had. We had just been granted informed permission by the "subjects" of our research.

TENEMOS QUE HABLAR: WE HAVE TO TALK!

We left San Cristóbal on time, our travel and research visa safely tucked away amidst innocuous documents as far away from official eyes as possible. These were strange times in Chiapas. Whatever was taking place on the official level, with the exception of one military checkpoint, the main roads were eerily quiet, the army convoys off doing social services or watching the World Cup on black-and-white television. Though functionaries of the state of Chiapas maintained that they no longer interfered with the business of the illegal but legitimate *autónomos*, we still wanted to keep a low profile as we traveled around the state on our way to Cerro Verde.

> We left in the afternoon for Cerro Verde, a scenic drive that delivered us to a community strategically placed on the road to Realidad. . . . I was not prepared for the way that they opened their hearts and home to us. . . . We were given a presentation by the school children . . . riddles, poems and songs, opening with the Zapatista hymn. The children's creativity was a remarkable reflection of the effectiveness of the community's teaching methods. After dinner, we were treated to guitar music, and then dancing. (field notes, Jodie Owens, July 23, 2001)

Jeanne and Isa at a checkpoint

Our reception in Cerro Verde was anything but subdued. We were welcomed with resistance *corridos*, a children's march, a slapstick performance of an original satire, riddles, and "*bombas*," followed by an attentive rendition of the Zapatista hymn. It was well into the evening when the classic, Zapatista-style dance, until the wee hours under the misty moonlight, began. It was past midnight when the festivities welcoming the Maya Program to Cerro Verde began to wind down. Our final dance was a rousing two-step with the aging patriarch and matriarch of the community. We waltzed our respective partners back to the sidelines and joined the students, near our indoor–outdoor sleeping quarters. They were exhausted but enthusiastic, anticipating tomorrow's service activities. They had not yet realized that the dancing and singing were a big part of those activities. Now they were about to learn firsthand what the Zapatistas meant by service. The evening was just beginning.

As we watched the movement of the people who welcomed us, we could catch a glimpse of their organization as a group. But what really showed us the difference in how these rebel communities get organized and seek to manage their own affairs were the many meetings. Thus, the real learning began when we moved to another section of the Cerro Verde enclave, summoned to a meeting with Martín Arevelo, the elusive leader of the Consejo Autónomo.

The space was set out a little like a rural courtroom, with Martín seated in front. We were in the first row facing him, with the students arrayed behind us. In El Paso, Earle had worked with his bilingual students, coaching them in techniques of simultaneous translation. As we began introductions and discussions, two things were clear. First, a primary service of the El Paso students would be as language intermediaries, serving both the community and us during our interactions. Second, the purpose of this particular program was to define future relationships with the Zapatista communities, to refine a model of service that served their needs and pushed at the limits of our definitions. Consequently, the first meeting was largely a probing conversation between Martín, as *municipio* leader, and us, a series of introductions to mutual expectations. As we spoke, we could hear the low murmur of translation from behind us. When one of the students tired, the job was passed flawlessly to the next.

On a more somber note, we were later scrutinized by a member of the autonomous council . . . who seemed to be interested primarily in what our intentions are and what kind of a relationship we intend to have with the community. The conversation with him, Dr. E and Dr. S was like a dance, flowing and gliding back and forth—barely touching, but maintaining intense eye contact. . . . There was a fierce protectiveness that seemed to radiate from him, but apparently we passed the litmus test enough to be allowed to stay. Still, I'm not sure he was satisfied with the results of this "little experiment." It's hard to fault him though, for being cautious in this land of betrayal, repression, and exploitation. (field notes, Jodie Owens, July 23, 2001)

"What is your commitment to pursue the relationship that we have started here?" Martín asked us. "Are you ever coming back? What is the process of learning that you have begun with us? What is hermanamiento?"

Finally, the students were asked to spend the next day reflecting on their commitment to the Zapatista communities, to be ready to define service in the context of Zapatista need.

Meetings became our pivotal activity. As the first encounter broke up, we saw Luz and Rodrigo hovering anxiously in the darkness. It was becoming clear that the two entities, the community and the municipality, were negotiating with each other as well as with us. They sought to determine where the limits of autonomy of a group should lie and what kind of obligations need arise between the entities involved. We were seen as representatives of potential assistance for development, whether direct or from a sister city relationship, as they were proposing. What was taking place in the meetings was the fine-tuning of the daily details of autonomy, how it is "operationalized" as a concept in the face of the need for communication, compromise, and consensus. We were privy to a community development process in which the community struggled even with their most proximate political allies for the right to negotiate their lives on their own. We suspected that the coffee project fell somewhere in these negotiations.

We joined Luz and Rodrigo, comparing our individual perceptions of the meeting with the Consejo, agreeing that the discussions went well. Luz seemed really tired. Natalia was sound asleep on her back, lulled by the late-night deliberations.

"It's not easy at times here," she said. "We have to make sure we are doing things right on all levels. On the level of the pueblo . . . the community; on the level of the Consejo . . . the municipality; and on the level of the comandancia . . . the Zapatista leadership. We spend a lot of time talking."

This was evident during our stay. At times, when the men and the women were having their individual discussions, the children also gathered to talk about the same issues. To discuss, to reach consensus, is part of the socialization process, learned in the larger classroom of daily experience.

Their meetings, their desire to consult and dialogue, were key to how they worked so well together. They were a conscious community, a community that had arrived at tentative self-governance though this process of consultation with all adults and many of the youths. It was a balancing act between larger *ejido* obligations still acceptable to those in resistance and past obligations to the official government that were not acceptable, particularly in the areas of education and health, as had occurred the previous year. As we were gradually learning, these were forms and obligations they were developing for themselves, with the help of the Zapatistas, who provided training, skills, and adjudication, giving them the raw materials for autonomy.

One of the chief concerns of this new representative of the autonomous municipality, as he explained it, was that NGOs and others use their contacts with communities to raise funds that don't get to the community in the end, in essence exploiting the rebels to run an organization and pay outsiders. This was not an unfounded concern since it has been noted that at times 70 to 80 percent of international aid turns into salary, overhead, and benefits for those who generate it.

"We need to monitor resources that don't get to the people who need them, but are resources which are raised in their name. We need to know who is doing what, and where."

This sounded so familiar. Who controls community development, after all, when NGOs deploy their projects? We had talked about this with Carmen and Francisco in Tulan. For the municipality, it was a form of foreign policy.

"We also want to make certain that the truly remote communities are not neglected," Martín told us.

This also sounded familiar. Favoritism, divisionism, was bad development. For the municipality, it was also a form of domestic and fiscal policy.

So here was the irony. In order to gain freedom and autonomy from the control of others from the outside, it seems these communities of Maya rebels must cultivate being communicative and cooperative within their own group and with the *municipio*. To succeed, they must give up some autonomy and some actual resources in the process. Our visit was helping the municipality probe at a model of where and how outside support should fit into these programs.

"So you see," Martín continued. "The communities are not completely free to accept money and service from you. Some of these resources must flow to the organization as a whole."

As "donors," we had no problem with this idea and said so. "Have you thought about taking a portion, say 10 percent, of all donated monies to use in a municipal development discretionary fund?"

Martín laughed. "So you think that if a hundred pencils arrive in a community, we should take ten for the municipio? How would you administer such a thing? A development tax."

"It's something to think about," we said, offhandedly.

We were becoming sensitized to the concerns of our previously unidentified development partners. But, arguing for our friends, we tried to point out how the locally based development success happening in Cerro Verde and

Tulan as a result of our ongoing relationships could benefit the other levels by providing an effective model for prospective donors to see.

As we met and talked, it was becoming clear that Cerro Verde's position on community development and development partners encapsulates a "seventh generation" foresight similar to that held by native North Americans.

"We resist, we organize, not because we know it will be better for us, but because maybe our children and our grandchildren won't have to live like we do," Luz told us as we debriefed following another midnight encounter.

This position leads to incredible patience, the ability to acknowledge that moving out of marginalization means accepting that change through community development will take place slowly. It requires strategic planning and the fortitude to hoard precious development resources, especially in times of extreme scarcity.

"Even if we eat only beans one day, and we eat nothing at all the next, at least we all eat together or go hungry together," Luz said. She yawned and shifted the baby onto her back.

"Poco a poco. Así es," said Rodrigo, as he and Luz started into the humid darkness toward the house they shared with their children and grandchildren. Little by little. So it is.

What makes for a challenge in applied anthropological and NGO work is how to manage an aid organization on the one hand and allow the helped group to maintain and increase autonomy and control over their lives on the other. Even when people are unsure how they might safely improve their life situation, they want to have some control over the process of other people's efforts to help.

"So we will keep working and resisting . . . until God sees fit to free us."

MEETING THE PROCESS: INFORMING CONSENT

Two days later, it was drizzling in Cerro Verde, the dense mists of the late rainy season dripping off the edges of a lamina roof. The orange glow of a single lightbulb cut through the night, attached to a ragged cord spliced into the electric line that supplied the entire enclave. In the open-air ramada, a colorful array of notebooks, crayons, pens, pencils, and other school supplies were laid out on a rough wooden table, surrounded by the children and adults of Cerro Verde and the anthropologists and students of the Maya Program. We presented the supplies and bid farewell to sixteen-year-old Ramón, off to complete a six-month teacher's training program in the Zapatista stronghold of Realidad. As we did, we realized that we were about to enter into yet another round of late-night dialogue concerning the shape of community development in Cerro Verde and the autonomous municipality of which it is part.

"We gotta talk," Rodrigo said again, a statement and a plea and a mantra. No one left out of the process, nothing is tabled. Meetings are the hidden transcripts of the fight for autonomy, the place where autonomy and cooperation merge. No wonder the military set up a control station in the jungle. The state was losing ground to self-development, to local control, to more autonomous alternatives. Nowhere was this more poignantly demonstrated than in the meetings cycle, where living was renegotiated on an ongoing basis.

In meetings with the children and teachers at the tiny autonomous school, they explained their philosophy of education, in which teachers, students, and parents assisted each child as she moved at her own pace through levels of learning. Children can read, write, do math, and have a good grasp of the history of the world and their relationship to it. They read and write poetry and enjoy music and art. It is a compassionate and effective system. Teachers are raised up from their own communities and, most important, return from training to share their skills.

In learning how to teach, Ramón spent twenty days away in classes in Realidad, mastering each of the four study areas: languages, mathematics, history, and the natural environment. Then he returned to Cerro Verde for ten days of practicum, applying his newly acquired skills in the tiny classroom. Armed with questions, problems, and successes, each practicum was followed by the opportunity to reflect on and revisit the experience back in Realidad. And each year, those who had completed the courses returned for further workshops, all taught by volunteer educators from throughout Chiapas and other parts of Mexico. This time, Ramón had come back to the community with two other young teachers whose own villages were too far away for frequent returns. They stayed with Luz and Rodrigo and taught alongside Ramón, completing their own practicum. As it turned out, our donations to the community food fund were making it possible for this Zapatista support base to support others with no access to outside aid.

These encounters with the educational system, coupled with the meetings, were part of the community's carefully crafted plan, part of a cultural translation process that guided us to seeing the wisdom of disencumbering the educational funds we brought, of providing the opportunity for them to exercise autonomy in using the money. Our quick-fix project of rebuilding the school was replaced with the long-range goal of funding education and training. It was another part of a continuing process of consultation and reflection in the construction and evolution of aid initiatives. In the end, our school funds became an investment in human infrastructure, not just for Cerro Verde but also for the municipality as a whole. As such, this arrangement was beneficial to Cerro Verde as it sought to define and fulfill its obligations to the larger polity.

Demanding greater local control seems a reasonable position for a rebel group representing indigenous and peasant issues. It is a compromise between the impossibility of total autonomy (secession) and the intolerability of government ineptitude and corruption. The very manner in which leadership operates in the Zapatista struggle, "to lead by obeying," suggests serious suspicion of the legitimacy of authority, especially in the way it must consult with its constituents over most decisions and in its general use of consensus to reach decisions. Autonomy means some escape from the authoritarian actions of a centralized institution, sustainability achieved through having control over the development trajectory.

As we learned in our lengthy negotiation with the Cerro Verde community and the autonomous leadership of Tierra y Libertad, this type of development planning is not amenable to a quick-and-dirty model of involvement.

These days of consultation with the community and the *autónomo*, as they began to refine their foreign, fiscal, and domestic policy, did not end with our decision to release control over previously designated funds. As anthropologists, we were involved in research, a somewhat different focus from the solidarity brigades and development agents the Zapatistas were used to encountering. As such, a product of our dialogue would always be the formal sharing of our work and words through presentations and writing. Thus, a portion of the informed permission that we received from Martín included additional directions concerning research and publications. We would continue to meet prior and during every visit. We would also send copies of our proposed publications for review.

"We have no desire to censor," said the representative of the Zapatista Autonomous Review Board. "But you need to be sure you are getting the details right. You are no longer witnesses to the process of developing autonomy here in Chiapas. You are part of the process."

We left that night's midnight encounter with the community and the *consejero* and returned to tell the results to our students. We had shared their reflections and concerns about what an *hermanamiento* meant in terms of responsibilities and relationships, including our growing perplexity about how a diverse group of individuals might aid a huge number of villages in territory as vast as Tierra y Libertad. It was an evolving relationship that would take years to hone out as the Zapatistas addressed these same questions on an organizational level.

In the meantime, we looked forward to future meetings with our institutional review boards back in the United States. They needn't worry. In Cerro Verde and in other Chiapas villages, we found that, once again, communities don't need our paternalistic protection. They may still be working out the details of autonomy, cooperation, and collaboration, but they know what pitfalls they are protecting themselves from. In fact, they are concerned that we understand the implications of becoming part of their social and political experiment. A score of meetings later, we consented to be part that evolving process. We gave them our informed consent. We had entered into a relationship between ourselves, our students, and the Zapatista communities that was reminiscent of *compradrazgo*-like ritual obligations. We were godparents, cosiblings to a working dream. The *hermanamientos* model was fluid, the nature of sponsorship always in flux.

During our tentative negotiations with Martín in the summer of 2001, we were unaware of the level and depth of reflection taking place among the Zapatista support communities and with their autonomous municipal representatives and the larger Organization. The spring march to Mexico City was a betrayal of the dream of indigenous autonomy by the Fox government. Marcos, as spokesperson for the Zapatistas, entered into a lengthy and pensive silence. But internally, the people had begun a long and serious conversation.

Meanwhile, in Cerro Verde, love was in the air, as Martín and Camila became a couple and married, merging their families. Cari gained an older sister as thirteen-year-old Linda, one of Martín's children, came to live in the community. Rodrigo ruminated over the implications of having the Organization resident in the village, becoming father-in-law to the *municipio*. The coffee roaster sat unused on Antonio's front patio. Oversight was imminent and permanent.

On the day of our departure from Cerro Verde, as we prepared to move the program down to Ojo de Agua for a comparative look at the development paradigm, Old Antonio stuck his head into the inside–outside sleeping compound, as was his habit. He loved to talk, relive his story, sit and pore over maps, and ask questions about the world outside Chiapas. He was dressed for the milpa, net bag over his arm, bottle of luncheon pozole. Something was on his mind, and Duncan invited him in, and the two sat in the midst of mounds of luggage, head to head. Finally, Duncan approached the group.

"Antonio has a milpa, up across the river, overlooking Cerro Verde. It needs to be weeded, cleaned out . . . corn and pineapple, some chayotes intercropped. He's been busy all this week, first with the preparations for our visit, making sure there was enough wood, building the ramada to keep us out of the rain, then helping to teach us. The milpa's been neglected. We've got a few hours yet, and this is something we can do. Service, with your hands, the way you want it. If you're not in the mood for a hike, the rest of you can stay and work with the children a little more. "How far is it, Antonio?" he asked.

Antonio put down his machete. "Pues, for nosotros . . . half an hour, actually. For you." He shrugged.

About eight of us decided to go. As if by magic, as many machetes appeared and after a quick workshop in how to carry a blade and not cut off any limbs, we started off into the jungle. Six of us made it to the top, breathing heavy, trying to keep up with seventy-five-year-old Antonio and his sons and grandsons.

We spiraled up and up and up, over and down, sliding backward at times on slick mud trails. Rodrigo's dog, Lobo, kept coming back to check on us, as did one of the younger men. As we walked into a thick copse of trees, there was a small, rugged building off in the brush. Jeanne gave it a curious look, and the young man smiled and said quietly, "At times we have to hide, to disappear into the mountains. '96, '98, '99. Who knows when?"

We arrived at the milpa, sweating and sticky, and got fast lessons on how to cut weeds. As always, we were curious as to why the weeds were never pulled, but it became clear that they played a critical ecological function in trapping moisture and topsoil near to the corn, coffee, and other plants, as long as they didn't grow too high to strangle them.

We worked silently for an hour or two, scattered through the milpa, then preparations began for a camp lunch. Rodrigo unearthed a battered pail from under some bushes and filled it from trapped water in a shallow cave. Antonio built a fire and over it a tripod to hold the pot. Aurelio brought green corn and a few chayotes and put them in the pot to boil. Sugarcane and *plátanos* we gathered and cleaned for desert. We slowly wandered back from our respective work plots, now filthy as well as sweaty. As Jeanne walked toward the little fire, Aurelio broke into a broad grin.

"Dona Juanita, tu regreses a campesina," he called, an implicitly Marxist pronouncement. You return to being a campesina. Return to the beginnings we all share, to that collective world where we will all someday, in God's good time, be able to dwell.

It was the best lunch of any Chiapas visit.

We started down the hill and returned to Cerro Verde, exhausted, satiated, tranquil with the work and the walk. It was good-bye time, and we loaded the luggage into our vehicle. A second one had been commandeered to take us all down the hill to the intersection with the main road off to Santa Elena and, beyond it, Ojo de Agua.

Jeanne jumped into the cab of the big white truck and turned to the young boy sitting next to her behind the wheel.

"Are you coming with us to the turnoff?" she asked, looking around for the driver.

The boy smiled. "I'm driving," he said, placing a few more pillows on the seat so that he could see over the wheel.

He was eleven years old. The truck belonged to his father and used to be driven by his brother. But the older youth had gone to Virginia to work in the chicken-packing plants. On the night before he left, he taught his little brother, *el chamaco*, to drive.

The boy was an excellent driver and brought us safely down the mountain. In the back of the truck, the students practiced Pentecostal hymns. There was a major military checkpoint at Santa Elena, and nothing closed down the questions faster than a rousing chorus of "Jesus, Mi Salvador." Growing wearier and wearier of their long vigil protecting the jungle from rebels and foreign agitators, the last thing the army wanted was to be saved.

OJO DE AQUA: THE (REVISED) HISTORY OF AN EJIDO

Duncan went ahead with the little red truck filled with our bags, looking like a proper pastor on the way to spend a few days with a group of *evangelicos* down the road. He alerted the soldiers to the our small band of missionaries, who would be arriving in groups on public transportation, mouthed a final "Dios es amor," and headed into Ojo de Agua on the new, paved road. Some five kilometers long, it reached the main road right by where it crossed the Chayote and brought vehicles into Ojo.

The rest of the group passed easily through the *retenes*, departing the combis at Santa Elena. Our troop of bedraggled students, five days out from a real bath, made their way through the pueblo, buying out the entire supply of Agua Pura from the tiny *tiendas* that dotted the town's streets. There was still no large store here, though it was an ideal place, halfway between Comitán and Marqués de Comilla, that overcut corner of Chiapas colliding with Guatemala. The *autónomo* had their own Central at one time, a large general store, but it was destroyed and looted when the army came in 1998. From what we had just learned from Martín, it was in the process of being rebuilt. But this afternoon, we purchased a bottle here, a bottle there, and packets of cookies, the jungle version of hitting a convenience store off the interstate.

We crossed into the pasture that leads down to the Chayote, preparing to enter Ojo on the infamous swinging bridge. Duncan was up ahead, and he waited, camera in hand, to catch the looks of disbelief or pleasure on the faces of our traveling band. Like the last visit, there were three or four boards missing, but not so many that we could lose a slippery gringo to the embrace of the raging Rio.

There were, as always, women and children in the river, bathing and doing laundry at a few level places cemented over to provide steady footage while you did the wash. Many of the students looked to the water longingly, dreaming of a cool bath and the prospect of cleanish underwear. This seemed like a good idea, a way to wile away the long jungle afternoon, where time didn't quite stand still but proceeded according to different laws of nature.

We herded the students up to Miguel's compound, unloaded the mountain of luggage, and did a fast reconnaissance of the floor and hammock space allotted to us. It was in the new house, a two-story, built by Miguel during the coffee years, a series of lovely rooms, with a backyard kitchen but no latrine. We made general introductions and then sent the students off to bathe. Duncan stayed behind, a twinkle in his eye, his Tzotzil flying quickly, as he made program arrangements with the *ejido*'s remaining elders.

PASTOR AS POWER

Duncan (July 2001): There were only three men of the nineteen original *ejido* founders left, three men who remembered the long trek down to the hot country, the reasons why they left the Highlands, and what it had been like in the early years. Hearing the history of the *ejido* from the *originarios* was important for our students, but I knew that if we were to get anything like a complete story, we would have to get the men together. Not because I was unaware of the history of the *anexo* or even sought some missing chapter. But so much had changed since my fieldwork of a generation ago, and it seemed to me a retelling of the past would be an oblique but telling inquiry into the present. No one was disappointed.

With students in tow, we left Miguel's house at one end of the "urban zone," where house plots were allotted, arranged along a grid pattern. These used to be just "lawnscapes," part of the communal land of the settlement used for grazing of sheep and the packhorses that brought in the corn from the remote milpas, but now this lane was a graveled road. I could see other changes. The distant ridge had suffered some burning, although things seemed largely intact, environmentally speaking. The houses were bigger, more cement work, more tin. The recent Evangelical church was a huge addition, just across the street from Miguel on his son's plot. Santos played the organ and also gave sermons, all, of course, in Tzotzil, and clearly sought the mantle of his pastor father when he passed.

To be pastor was a logical continuation of Miguel's moral authority over Ojo, following his earlier roles as head (*comisariado*) of the *ejido* and founder as well as go-between for government interaction in the process of gaining permanent title. His life was always a struggle for legitimacy as a leader, using his good understanding of Spanish and of outsiders, thanks in part to Erasto Urbina, to gain a position of superiority. But times had changed; he was not sought out for filling out endless *tramites* any more or enlisted in commissions to lobby the authorities. The newer center of Nuevo San Juan, called Pacayal after the small edible palms that were found there, had long ago passed Ojo by, being on the now much improved main road to the jungle interior and Marques de Comillas. But it seemed that through the window of Protestantism,

Miguel and his sons could have the helm of their tiny empire, which as the price of coffee fell and fell must have been a source of solace as paradise began to falter, fade.

So it was not that surprising that when we arrived at the other side of the settlement to bring together Miguel; his father-in-law, Mingo; and his eldest son by a prior marriage, Shalik, history had changed. We met at old Mingo's house, at the end of the street, on his back patio. The students took seats on benches, the *profesores* were toward the front, the young men hung out near the kitchen door, and the three elders held court in front of the group. The women were crowded into the kitchen, leaning forward through the open half door to catch the gist of the conversation.

The three old men had once been rival representatives of the three religious tendencies of the region: Catholic, Protestant, and Traditionalist. Miguel had been trained by the *catequistas*, Shalik was a Seventh-Day Adventist, and old Mingo kept a santo and the old ways alive. I recalled how Miguel would rail against his son's Adventista path, wishing he could outlaw Protestant sects. Now he led a rival one. And as he began to make account of the past, the quarter century of Catholicism, with the Marists on Cashlan Ca' (motorcycles) and the *hermanas* from San Cristóbal who taught hygiene and nutrition, vanished into air. It was as if they went right from the old traditions of erecting the big crosses straight to the Protestant period, eliding the Catholicism that was now the enemy. Miguel had suggested earlier that the danger of Fox and the PANistas was that they had plans to prohibit Protestantism and pass Mexico into the hands of the pope. I can't remember the exact context of that conversation, but it had included some lively discussion of Martin Luther and the ninety-five theses.

I had expected some editing in this telling of the Ojo tale, but what we heard was truly history conceived from the present. Mingo, himself never entirely happy with the activist Catholics because of their opposition to the old ways, was the only one to mention the *hermanas*.

I translated the turn taking while the crowd of kin and neighbors listened to the telling. Not only was the revisionist tale a postmodern commentary on power relations in the community, but so was the order of speech. First the elders talked, then the older young men, then the professors. Afterward, I invited the students to ask questions, and in a mood of equity unfamiliar in Ojo, I asked that the women take their turn. They were silent, still hanging out the kitchen door. To get the conversation going, Jeanne tried a surefire icebreaker, asking about midwifery and birthing positions.

"In our country," she began, "women give birth like this." She threw herself back on the bench and spread her legs wide in best delivery room style. The women giggled, and the door opened. One of the men tried to describe a Maya birth, but the women had their opening.

"This is what we do," explained Pasquala, old Mingo's wife. She threw her arms around the waist of the nearest standing male and squatted. Everyone laughed. Now the women took advantage of this opening to bring up a current pressing problem. Many of the town's women had taken up embroidery to raise scarce cash, but the problem was that they were poorly paid for their work, handing the blouses over to an intermediary who made most of the profits at their expense, paying them fourteen pesos for a week's work.

The women explained, "Without coffee money, we need to find other ways to make some income." But they made almost nothing because of the price paid by the buyer. They were not talking with us to resurrect the past, glorious and dead, but to meet the crisis of the present, where the coffee work did not pay for itself and some other strategy for making income had to be sought. These voices, usually silenced by the more public males, were breaking forth in their desperation, born of a shift from cash abundance to scarcity. And they had other plans to capture our ear, an insidious divide-and-listen strategy.

The meeting ended at about five, and since it was Saturday, there was to be a long prayer meeting at Miguel's church. We were invited and planned to attend. But the women had other ideas. As we talked about the economic problems facing Ojo, Pasquala opened the kitchen door to invite us in, and several of the others began to arrive with bags of embroidered blouses. The ubiquitous pot of *caldo de pollo* appeared from over the cook fire. We were seated and fed, a captive audience, and good manners as well as genuine interest made it impossible to slip out to go to church. It was a traditionalist coup. But eventually we excused ourselves, promising to meet with the women the next day at Miguel's to discuss how they might get around the coyote who took such advantage of them. We caught the end of Miguel's service.

Later, as I wandered over the grassy backstreets and an occasional woman slinked up to me, wanting to know if I would buy a blouse, peering around to see that no one else saw them, another reality crept into mind. The women are sneaking around, one by one, competitors for the scarce money of the Mero Lucas and La Xunka.

The following day, we gathered in the house compound of Miguel and Veronica. The clouds darkened as they do on hot afternoons. A dozen or more women huddled in a cluster while we dressed up the students in the embroidered shirts and blouses. It was an impromptu "fashion show" so that they could see what gringo/a bodies looked like in their work. Isa, one of the tallest of our group, struggled with strangely sized armholes, necklines, and sleeves, a source of great entertainment. I explained the notion of targeting your product to the shape and tastes of the consumer, so as to be competitive with the hugely overproducing San Cristóbal tourist market. The women paid close attention, asking about small stylistic changes that might improve the chance of sales. Later, Isa contemplated the situation:

> I see clear examples of problems within a Protestant, discordant community. When we were in Ojo de Agua there was some unrest over our being there. The problem was that the community thought that we were "overly" paying the family with whom we were staying, therefore creating an unfair economic opportunity for only this one family. Really, when the discord settled, and the payment was decided upon, it was Rosa's mother, Veronica, who bore the burden. She had to cook for thirteen additional people, twice a day, and got paid very little for her extraordinary efforts. In fact, she was always so busy cooking, cleaning, or herding their sheep and chickens that I never got an opportunity to speak with her. Every responsibility fell to her while we were there, and I am sure when we left it continued to be that way. This is simply the effect of a nuclear family in this environment where they have no running water, modern machines, or technology and all of the work is placed on one woman. I am not implying that they need to accommodate themselves to the "industrial and civilized" world by becoming more technologically advanced, rather I am critiquing the Westernizing that has already taken place. In contrast, just by living for a short time in Cerro Verde, I was able to see how very different the women were able to live their lives because of the different levels of demands they faced and the network of support in which they were surrounded.
>
> Protestantism has also helped create the individuality that is present in the community. This every-woman-for-herself attitude is the effect of a society that rewards personal, economic gain with power. Logically, under those circumstances, if people desire their own profits, they are less likely to unify themselves for any purpose. For example, in Ojo de Agua, we often heard a baby crying while dinner was being cooked. A woman can either cook or watch her child; she needs another person to do both. However, in Cerro Verde, the babies were always watched because there was a collective space where women cooked, conversed, and watched each other's children.
>
> There may be countless other results of the conversion to Protestantism in terms of women. However, the main issues at this point are to understand the problems that the new religion has created for the women and how to help the community come together. This crucial point of actually helping the community unify itself, especially the women, became a goal during our stay at Ojo de Agua. (field report, Elizabeth "Isa" Story, August 2001)

While the meeting continued, the sky became progressively darker, blue-black, and lightning flashed in the distance. As the big drops began to pelt the patio, we all clustered closely together under the porch overhang. A massive clap of thunder and simultaneous flash was a cosmic commentary on the event, a serious *señal*. There was a deluge coming. The women were looking for new options, the sons were continuing to migrate to the United States, and the government spokespeople broached the topic of a hydroelectric dam. Later, Miguel would once again represent his people, attending meetings in Santa Elena that left him to wonder if his land would be lakefront property or underwater. He worried about his future, alone, an aging Maya capitalist unable to depend on his sons. On our next visit, he would tell us that the government had a plan to remove inundated people to Campeche, a strategy used before to relocate many Guatemalan refugees.

"What is Campeche like?" he asked me. "I am too old to start over, in some new and different land. If the flooding comes . . . that is the end for me." But if this Noah was too old to prepare his ark, other change was in the air.

Part 3

DEFINING THE DREAM

CHAPTER 11

Alternative Constructions

JEANNE (SPRING 2002): A LONG RAGGED BLACK ROPE of electrical wire snaked across the Cerro Verde indoor–outdoor eating area, ending in a set of alligator clips, connected to nothing. It dangled above the area's three-quarter wall, where a large stuffed horse pranced on into imaginary mountains, a Chamula Maya woolen steed bearing two masked Zapatistas, identified as Marcos and Ramona. Running along next to the wire was another length, equally ragged, this one connected with fraying twists of electrical tape, ending in a single sixty-watt lightbulb.

It was an electrical inspector's worst nightmare, but the line brought power into the Cerro Verde enclave, feeding about six bulbs, a portable radio, and a barely booming boom box. Alternating, an aged refrigerator and/or black-and-white television also drew on the single electrical source. We stood below the bulb and watched it flicker, following both lines to their final destinations. Luz followed our gaze.

"This," she pronounced, pointing to the wire that went nowhere, "is the official line. And this, the one that lights the bulb, is the unofficial line, the 'linea revelde.'"[1]

We nodded. Just like keeping time in the summer months, there was the party line and the Zapatista line, an alternative way of doing things responsive to the practical and ideological thinking of the community. Electricity was no exception. In fact, the issue of paying for electrical power had been a part of the resistance package for Cerro Verde for the past nine years. Their refusal to pay the Federal Electrical Commission's (CFE's) asking prices for electricity generated in the state of Chiapas was not an exclusively Zapatista gripe but one that crosscut political lines and had the potential to draw people together.

As the Fox government moved forward with plans to privatize the electrical industry, protests were building among all segments of the population, not just the Zapatistas. Campesino groups sought preferential rates for the state of Chiapas since the state produces the bulk of the electricity used in Mexico. In the southern frontier area, mixed bodies of campesinos met with some success in their negotiations with the CFE. Municipal and resistance leaders, with certain caveats, viewed these fledgling attempts to form a nonpartisan resistance movement as positive. It was a start.

The cost of running a few lightbulbs and the occasional appliance in the jungle was (and is) exceptional. While people in urban San Cristóbal paid fifteen pesos every two months for minimum usage, in the jungle a basic bimonthly bill could be upward of 300 pesos. Because rural electrical usage was unmetered, the CFE could arbitrarily declare the amount it thought a home used. Cerro Verde had ceased paying the official bill in 1994. Sometimes the lights were on, and sometimes they were off. Most recently, the group had used a frequently invoked tactic, running a line into somebody else's official service.

"And the line in rebellion, where does it go?" we asked Luz. "Do you have the approval of the other household?"

"Pues, si," answered Luz. "They're PRIistas, but they've always been friendly to us. And actually they pay the same amount, no matter how much electric they use."

So the spliced Cerro Verde electrical line spliced into somebody else's line, where switchless lightbulbs also dangled precariously, brightening the often starless jungle nights. But it was an arbitrary arrangement, and a myriad of small insults or envies to the source household could result in the electricity going off again. It was just such a period when we arrived with a selection of electrical carpentry tools for use in the soon-to-be-established Cerro Verde carpentry shop.

It had been a particularly long run in the dark, almost a month this time, and the men were in throes of negotiation with representatives of the *ejido*. It was not that they minded paying for the electricity they were using, it was just that they minded paying so damned much and paying it directly to the *pinche gobierno*. There was a meeting scheduled for the following day, and they hoped that some agreement could be reached before we left so that a power tools safety workshop could take place. But, *ni modo*, if not, we'd find some other sympathetic PRIista household where we could plug in.

Earlier that morning, we met with the kids in the newly completed autonomous school. The children were seated at the few chairs and desks that survived from the original rudimentary plank building. There would be desks for all once the power tools safety workshop took place, a product of the community decision six months previous that they would rather have tools and make their own furniture than money to buy tables and chairs at the market in Comitán.

As always, meeting with the kids was an education for us, and today we were talking about electricity. Jeanne asked the children how their lives were altered

Duncan demonstrates power tool safety in Cerro Verde

when they "had to do without" electricity. Ramón smiled, a teacher's patient smile.

"But Doña Juanita, why do we need electricity?"

In spite of anthropological objectivity and valueless judgments, the way in which we live is so ingrained in us that at times it is difficult to fully see the shape of someone else's dream. Images of lights, computers, air conditioning, heat, cooking, and water cascaded into the forefront.

Gently, Ramón described all their accommodations to these needs: candles, conversation, ventilation, and the daily rhythm of work, the cook fire, and tanks for water collection.

"The radio?"

Alejandro pointed to his horse munching on grass in front of the school, a jungle version of the Pony Express.

"We're not accustomed to it," Ramón added. And they weren't, and they didn't plan to be, regardless of how deficient an outsider might describe their material situation.

We remembered his answer in mid-August 2003, when somebody's official electrical line somewhere in the great northeastern U.S. power grid went awry. Within the next hour, fifty million homes were without electricity. New York City came to a standstill, as the repercussions of not having electricity took a toll on ground and air transportation, elevators, food storage, and phone service, among other necessities of American life. The city began to shut down. Millions of New Yorkers, in reasonably high spirits, began the long walk home to the Burbs. When, three days later, the power was finally restored, one grateful New Yorker told a reporter for National Public Radio, "We ought to make a national holiday in honor of electricity."

Earlier that year, North Carolina Electric was also shut down, this time by an ice storm. With temperatures in the twenties, Jeanne huddled in front of a single fireplace, burning candles and lamp oil, cooking potatoes in the coals, and bemoaning the absence of a camp stove on which to make coffee. It was beginning to look a lot like Cerro Verde. Then, as in the great northeastern blackout, Ramón's words resounded.

"But Doña Juanita, why do we need electricity?"

The lights were back on in the Northeast and North Carolina within a few days. Cerro Verde entered into a second month without juice, so Duncan prepared to pack up the power saw and followed the men down a path to a connected PRIista compound. Men, boys, and a few girls and women from both political camps huddled around him indiscriminately as he went through the safety guidelines and demonstrated how each tool worked, how to work in pairs for safety, and ways in which certain tools and attachments could imitate more complex machinery to make strong furniture joints. Then he watched the teams of two go through the same moves. By dusk, they had built a chair that Duncan tried out and had an order for a table from a non-Zapatista family. Fast learners.

As we waited, Luz's sister Barbara arrived with her husband Alonso. They were a curious couple, encapsulating all the divisions present in the Cerro

Verde pueblo. Barbara was a PRDista, had never been a Zapatista. Her husband was a PRIista who came to village through marriage, had none of his own *ejido* lands, and had acquired them through just one of the under-the-table land transactions that PROCEDE claimed to be regularizing. In addition, he was the elected municipal representative to the PRI and had to seek release from his *ejido* tasks for the period of his political service. That period was coming to an end, and he wanted to throw a big bash for the entire *ejido* for supporting him in his work. Thus, they had arrived with a proposition. They would need mole for 1,500 people, and did the Zapatista contingent want to do the cooking? They were coming first to Luz because she was family. We sat, listening in interest, another marvel of Cerro Verde political accommodation. Luz said she would present the proposal to the other women. Barbara and Alonso invited us to the party. Duncan would be gone, returned to the United States. But my daughter Rachel and her friend Ryan were arriving in a few days. It would be a good opportunity to introduce them to the Cerro community.

We arrived on the micro, the express from Comitán, cracked windshield standing up well under the weight of bundle after bundle of groceries and dry goods. The roof was loaded, as were the aisles, as those who run the tiny *tiendas* in the Chayote pueblos went to Comitán to bring back goods to sell at inflated prices. It, at best, was a two-and-a-half-hour trip. Young Dominga got on at the Comitán open-air market, the Central de Abastos, and Rachel, Ryan, and I had a friend with us on our first attempt to get to Cerro on public transportation.

We got off the bus and went right to the house of Barbara and Alonso. The entire community was there, a kitchen full of women cooking, the smoke thick from the open fires, tubs full of freshly butchered cow waiting to become tomorrow's dinner. Luz turned and greeted us, wiping her hands at her sides and reaching out in an *abrazo* greeting. She was wearing a red bandana with EZLN emblazoned in black letters. Still in resistance.

Ryan was led off by the men, Alonso's side of the family—PRIistas who were sitting around a open cooking fire on the other side of the road, drinking. Another division here, of course. Most Zapatistas don't drink. But Ryan, being the good (and innocent) young student of anthropology, took what was offered and taught English to guys whose Spanish was so slurred that they became the caricature of the Mexican drunk.

Cooking continued, carrots and onions, tomatillos, *jitomates*, and chile ancho adobada for the mole. As the sun began to drop, we made our way down the hill, past the co-op store, past the old *escuelita*, past the new one under construction to my corner of the compound. We brought hammocks this time, far better than the floor. We got set up for the night, and I wandered over toward the bathroom with the toilet. On the way back, Camila greeted me and asked if I'd like coffee (of course), and I entered the kitchen to find Martín seated at the table.

We were on amiable terms, left over from a productive encounter at the last visit, and we talked about looking for grants and what was happening in the San Cristóbal NGOs I'd visited since arriving. The development NGOs were repositories of valuable information, but it was rarely shared among them and certainly didn't make it to the resistance organizations. I told him about an NGO leader who said that those in resistance didn't want to attend the workshops and meetings that the NGOs sponsored, in part because some of these were funded by money from the Mexican government or the World Bank, both variants of the Mal Gobierno. We discussed looking for some funds to set up a neutral location where there could be a few workshops, bringing together some of the autonomous municipalities so that accumulated information might be shared.

"Don't you folks talk to each other?" I asked Martín.

He shrugged. "As of yet, no. We don't know what's going on in the Highlands, for instance."

We talked about getting a proposal for an *autónomo* Central de Abastos out to some foundations, and he suggested giving me a disk with one of their proposals on it so that I could rework it more easily. So far, so good.

"So, then waddaya think about this fiesta tomorrow?" I asked. "It could be interesting, no?"

"Interesting? No," says Martín. "It's not our party. This is a party given by a politico to celebrate his politics, and we, as we are in resistance, won't celebrate with him. Luz agreed to do the cooking, because family is tighter than politics, but they won't be going."

"Ah. Well," I said. "Lucas and I were talking and we wondered if it was an attempt to try to reintegrate the community into the larger fabric of the ejido. Or perhaps an attempt to, as we say in English, co-opt them, by putting them in an awkward position."

"The word is the same in Spanish," said Martín. "And it is not an attempt by either side at co-optation. It is just a political party that family is involved in, but we won't go."

"Well, then, as visitors, we respect your decision and we won't go either." Sigh.

Martín smiled. "How long will you be here? I want to get you together with the rest of the Consejo. Do you want to meet them?"

"As you wish," I told him, delighted. "Only I'm not sure of my Spanish."

"Don't worry," Martín said. "I understand you perfectly."

From up on the hill in the area surrounding the PRIista government school, music pulsed, *norteña* rhythms of a live band at the fiesta that we came to attend. Yet here we sat with Rodrigo and Luz, Natalia, and the others who remained behind. Another face of resistance was not to attend the party you have just spent two days cooking for, the fiesta we catered but wouldn't set foot in. The children listened to the music and looked wistfully up the hill. Others have gone: young Dominga and her children, accompanying old Antonio and Tata Dominga. Even Marta snuck in for *un ratito*, as did Ana's husband Aurelio, returning with a huge pot of the beef mole that we prepared yesterday.

Now, the loudspeaker up on the hill continued to send speeches out over the many levels of Cerro, up and down the once-forested hills overlooking the azure Rio Chayote. Alonso thanked all for coming and for their support, and especially the family, his wife's fine family, for providing all the food. All were invited to eat and dance as he reminded them of the bounty of the past three years. I could not help but wonder how many lamina roofs it took to keep the peace in a place where no one was doing more than surviving. How many extensions to the school and repairs to the bridge must you trade to secure the votes needed to stay in office and ensure that your wife's family and their friends still feel pressure from all sides?

So as the kids looked sadly into the distance, Marta confided that it was all *muy alegre*, but the men were drunk, *bolos*, and at times ugly. Rodrigo and I chatted, and Luz put her feet up on the bench so that the tortured rope veins in her legs didn't knot up after standing up for eighteen hours, cooking.

Old Antonio came home, just as the music ended and the night fell. We looked up into the dark Chiapas sky, where the grin of a Cheshire cat moon was surrounded by stars, *Kanal* in Tojolobal. Antonio commented that we didn't come to the party, and I said that since Rodrigo didn't go, we also stayed behind. Antonio sighed and said, yes, they have their cargo, and they are keeping it. But he was the father, and since the parents of his son-in-law were there, he and Dominga had to go to support their daughter. And though it was late, we all went back to the tiny kitchen where the *foco* in resistance still lit the room, the official *foco* was still disconnected, and the two remained separated by the Chamula doll of Marcos and Ramona ready to gallop off into the night.

A few days later, an agreement was reached in the *ejido* assembly about the electricity. Cerro Verde would pay the required fifteen pesos for the electric, but not to the government. They would pay it into an *ejidal* fund, and the *ejido* officials would pay it to the CFE, a little like laundering the money or running a line. Once again, they had carved out a third space where compromise was not capitulation, a space within the deep silence that appeared to be settling over Zapatista Chiapas.

PLAN PUEBLA PANAMÁ

In the months following the election of Vicente Fox, peace blanketed Chiapas. Not the peace that comes of mutual agreement and signed accords between two contesting parties but a peace derived from a calculated process of ignoring the EZLN and its supporters while at the same time altering nothing. As the new year began, President Fox declared that in Chiapas, all was tranquil, *in santa paz* (Expreso Chiapas 2002). A few of the military bases changed locations to comply with Zapatista demands. Overt surveillance of Zapatista communities decreased. As we experienced traveling to Cerro Verde and Tulan, some of the army checkpoints seemed to disappear, and foreigners could move back and forth without fear of expulsion from the country. But in the final analysis, the conditions of life for the rural populations, both Zapatista and non-Zapatista, were little changed as the Fox government tried to move forward a massive development scheme known as Plan Puebla Panamá (PPP) (Bellinghausen 2002).

Early one evening in the first year of the Fox presidency, the women of Cerro Verde gathered in their tiny *capilla* to consider the words of the gospel. The sounds echoed off the rough beams of the little chapel in a way that made the reading difficult to understand. It was after dark, 7:00 P.M., God's time, which was an hour earlier than the official daylight savings time the Maya campesinos refuse to acknowledge. A dim glow came from three fast-burning candles, and the young woman reading the scripture had to move back and forth quickly to keep the page in the flickering light. The electricity had been off for over two weeks this time.

Davíd, a catechist, led the service. The little town sees a priest twice a year, if luck is with them and they have no deacon. So it was that the only person in the community prepared to interpret the reading was Davíd, catechist, activist, father, farmer, and ex–political prisoner.

"Unless you believe in Jesu Cristo," intoned Davíd, "you will not enter into the kingdom of heaven." Clear enough.

"Unless you believe in Jesu Cristo, you will not enter God's kingdom here on earth."

"Unless you believe in Jesu Cristo, we'll all wind up victims of Plan Puebla Panamá, and a huge dam will be built, and all our land will be underwater."

The change in direction happened so fast that it was easy to miss the transition from the realm of the soul to that of the earthly struggle. This was catechist Catholicism, liberation theology at its most basic. Without sacraments, choirs, or priests to remind these tiny congregations of God's eternal presence, they do the best they can. They work together, organize, and believe in each other's capacity to right long-standing wrongs and change that which is unjust. This is what they mean by reflection.

With the price of coffee at an all-time low, campesinos families are taking a hard look at their options for survival. Consequently, every social gathering from religious services to community meetings to primary school classes includes serious sociopolitical questions for reflection, and the voices of all, women, men, and children, are valued in crafting solutions. In Cerro Verde, the community gathered to discuss the specifics of the plan, to view the maps of transportation corridors, and to discuss rumors of a massive reservoir to be built just down the road, its waters reaching as far as Ojo de Agua. Working from copies of official government documents, they studied the proposals.

On the surface, PPP has the appearance of a program of responsible, integrated regional development. As stated in the official PPP documents compiled by the Mexican government, PPP seeks to promote and consolidate development in southern and southeastern Mexico by means of the implementation of public policy and programs and projects of public and private investment, in an accelerated and coordinated manner, oriented, among other things, at education and health of the population, the expansion of an integrated development of basic infrastructure, the promotion of productive activities, the modernization and strengthening of local institutions, and the expansion of the technological base of the region.

PPP seeks to contribute to sustained and sustainable economic growth that preserves the environment and natural resources of the region, coordinated and summarized by the governments of the Central American countries, in a climate respectful of survival and seeking accord and consensus (México Presidencia 2001).

Critics of the plan note that the businesses that respond to the call for participation in PPP will experience a development epoch free of fiscal regulations, characterized by extremely low labor costs, these justified by the excuse that they will provide a steady source of income for those who can no longer survive off the land. According to Carlos Fazio, "Mexico, as a client state continues ceding strategic sectors of her economy and will offer the most lucrative opportunities to US capital" (2000, 1). Other analyses highlight the fact that regardless of PPP plans to invest in human and social development, the percentage of investment dedicated to this area is only a fraction of the total projected investment in the plan. In 2002, for instance, over 82 percent was dedicated to communications and transport (Villamar 2002). In short, most benefits of the plan are aimed at investors and commerce from the top.

Though news of the plan seemed to surface rapidly with the election of Vicente Fox, it appeared that the new president simply resurrected the schemes of his predecessor Zedillo as well as an even older project concerning the Isthmus of Tehauntepec (Barreda 2001; Fazio 2001). In the case of Chiapas, plans for the construction of dams and reservoirs date back to the colonization epoch of the early 1970s (see De Vos 2002, map 15). A comprehensive study of development needs for the southern states of Mexico was published in the same month Fox was elected and prior to his inauguration (Davila, Kessel, and Levy 2000). Part of the transition process between the *sexenios* of Zedillo and Fox consisted of a briefing by the World Bank, summarized in a book-length document titled *Mexico: A Comprehensive Development Agenda for the New Era* (Guigle, Lafourcade, and Nguyen 2001) As is often the case in times of political and economic change, the simultaneous elections of George W. Bush and Vicente Fox allowed well-developed plans to proceed with accelerated impetus.

The goals of PPP were summarized in a PowerPoint presentation that appeared on the website of the International Development Bank and was prepared for Japanese consumption. The first objective seemed benign: "to realize the potential of the human and ecological richness of the region within the scope of sustainable development that respects cultural diversity," while the second spoke of the need to "define strategic investments and policy decisions that foment the integration process on a physical, economic, and social level" (International Development Bank 2001). Similar enticements for investment appeared in an announcement for Expo-Inversión 2002, a business fair in Mérida sponsored by the Mexican government and Banamext (the Banamex–Citibank hybrid) (Expo-Inversión 2002). For some observers, the plan was not a strategy to end endemic poverty; rather, it directed critical public funds into projects that would induce private investment (Pickard 2002, 1).

The initial PPP documents were optimistic, speaking frequently about ideas for sustainable development and preservation of biodiversity as part of the investment and construction strategy. But the continuing protest against the plan forced a second round of official writing, reflecting belated concern about the need to consult with communities. The International Development Bank's Program for Information, Consultation and Participation was targeted at gaining "the acceptance of [PPP] activities on the part of the participating populations," noting that mollifying the communities could reduce costs (International Development Bank 2002).

Beginning in the summer of 2001, anti-PPP meetings took place all over Chiapas. These community meetings were derived from international forums in Mexico and Central America that brought together representatives of national and international civil society to discuss PPP and plan strategies for opposition. The meetings produced a series of concrete proposals for action. These included continued dissemination of information through regional and local forums, widespread mobilization of local resistance, active monitoring of government actions with related research and critique, the formation of alliances in all affected nations (including the United States), and, most important, the construction of alternatives for development.

PLANNING ALTERNATIVE DEVELOPMENT

The majority of the alternative development plans being proposed by civil society derive from recognition that the way out of poverty does not involve a complete overhaul of systems of production in indigenous areas. Like the analyses of Netting (1993), Scott (1999), and Bodley (1999), they focus on investing in the fortification of existing agricultural and production systems, providing the tools to build on long-tested strengths without destroying the fabric of indigenous life. This is a conscious choice for an evolutionary, incremental change that does not create powerfully disruptive shocks in the lives of people close to the survival line.

Making rural life viable in the long run involves the ability of producers to diversify and be flexible, to survive in spite of what happens in the market. With prices to coffee growers at an all-time low, the rationality of relying on a monocrop, whether produced by hundreds of independent campesinos or mass-produced on a plantation, as the Mexican government suggests, is questionable. Rather than sell land or seek wage labor, civil society consultants are encouraging rural households to diversify their agricultural production, maintain adequate milpas, and acquire additional skills. They are also making efforts to promote the kind of regional self-sufficiency sought by the Zapatistas.

Disengaging from an economy governed solely by the market is viewed as a means of rehumanizing economic relationships and is a key constituent of solidarity economics. Campesinos are being asked to eschew a model of economics in which relationships and the value of exchanges are determined far from the farm gate and are compensated with money alone. They embrace a self-sufficiency in which the substance of the exchange and the relationships it engenders are as valuable as the exchange of goods and services. The contrasting models of neoliberal economics and solidarity economics have been discussed and presented in international meetings all over Central America and bear a striking resemblance to the theoretical distinctions between formal and substantive economics as debated in anthropology in the early 1970s (see Schneider 1974, 1–21). It also reminds us of Marx's original concern with what happens when social relations are undermined by capitalism and the division of labor into unitary and exclusive roles.

Development of regional mechanisms of exchange, derived from an enhanced knowledge of one's own region, is a primary proposal of those who advocate solidarity economics and social agriculture in Chiapas. Whether it is possible, feasible, or desirable to be completely self-sufficient economically is another issue, the subject of intense reflection in regional Zapatista meetings.

Maintaining local control over the ability to meet the needs of the household or community is key to the ability to live autonomy on a day-to-day basis. Some resistance communities have been more successful than others in doing so, in part because, like Cerro Verde, they have been able to tap into international aid. Others, like Tulan, operate closer to economic collectives, leveling family differences with pooled resources and pooled labor dedicated to linked, coordinated, productive activities. The primary educational and health programs, staffed by community members like Ramón, survive and flourish. At all levels, the work of training and teaching is collective responsibility. Everyone takes a turn. In the area of economy, valuing the exchange relationship and the social organization of production comes as second nature.

"In my community, we met to discuss how we could be self-sufficient, and not at the mercy of the coffee buyers," said a young Chol Maya from a resistance community in the Chiapas municipality of Huitiupán.

"What do we need to live? We need food: we can grow it. We need clothes: our grandmas can make them. We need education: we already have our own autonomous schools, teaching our own values and history. We need houses: well, we can look for other means to build them, like adobe."

In the final analysis, autonomy is more than subsistence. To gain more control within the global economy, one must strategically participate, but on terms where dependency is minimal and where the global market has high levels of demand for the products one produces (Earle and Simonelli 2000; see also Scott 1999). This involvement in turn draws international capital that circulates locally and nationally, serving to help the development of the whole country without resorting to foreign financing, investment, or ownership. Self-sufficiency becomes societal sufficiency. It is the promise of bottom-up economic reform.

A canyon lies between the logic of PPP and these alternative proposals since the latter stress the importance of fostering investment in a viable rural economy. In the International Development Bank–Japan proposal cited previously, southern Mexico and Central America are described as regions being "held back by extreme poverty." This description is reminiscent of unilineal models of cultural evolution, implying that because of their current social organization, communities are being held back from participating in a singular road to progress. In PPP, no amount of culturally and environmentally sensitive buzzwords can mask the unwavering dedication to a singular, one-world model of development, a model guided in godlike fashion by the all-powerful entity known as "the market."

The alternative and autonomous development proposals derived from community forums recognize a set of roads to well-being that are the antithesis of PPP. Encapsulated in their plans are models of land tenure and land use that take advantage of labor patterns and human–land relationships that are the heart and soul of autonomy.

The modification of article 27 under the regime of Salinas de Gortari and the development of PROCEDE under Zedillo were critical antecedents to PPP. Yet initially, the plan made no project recommendations concerning agricultural production. With over one-half of all of Mexico's campesinos living in the southern states, a proposal generated in the Mérida meeting finally added a platform on agricultural development projects (Declaración Gobierno 2002).

Failure to include agriculture in the original PPP may reflect an implicit assumption that the rural regions would be irrevocably changed as plantation production and industrial development resulted from capitalist transformation. This is encapsulated in the official document base of PPP published by the office of the president of Mexico in 2001, which notes:

> The restrictions from Article 27 of the constitution effective until 1994 over the possession or leasing of great expanses of land effected in a special way the South-southeast region. This region has conditions suitable for perennial products (coffee, banana, sugar, African palm, and lumber among others) whose cultivation is more efficient in plantations of wide expanse and that require considerable financial resources. *Securing property rights of these lands is essential for the producers of these cultigens.* (México Presidencia 2001, 3[20]; emphasis added)

The notion that efficiency is related to the ability to mass-produce goods is a critical pillar of capitalist production and the ideological justification for displacing other methods. In contrast, the alternative development proposals derived from anti-PPP forums hinge on a very different perspective on efficiency. As the Zapatista organization continued its long period of official silence, there was a new sound coming from the communities, the sound of deep reflection and economic reorganization.

AUTONOMY AND THE "SANTA PAZ"

Once again, the aged microbus was already packed when it pulled up in front of the Comitán market. Ariana Aviala and I pushed our bundles further under the backseat to make room for another load of passengers and passed up five-peso chicken sandwiches being sold in the aisle. Looking out through cracks in the rear window, I saw Rodrigo waiting with two tables and four chairs, ready to board the bus for the trip to Cerro Verde. The furniture was hoisted onto the roof of the bus, and Rodrigo scrambled up the metal ladder behind it to make sure it was secure. He climbed back down, noticed us, and smiled broadly in greeting. Rodrigo was effervescent. The tables and chairs were for the newly completed autonomous school. The plan was to paint the building on Sunday and inaugurate it officially on Monday. We had been working for over two years to raise the funds for little building, and now it was done.

As applied anthropologists and now activists by default, we were becoming more and more involved with development projects in the communities that were the heart of our research. I was in Chiapas this year for a period of eight months, for the first time without Duncan, my fieldwork partner. I was dedicating my time and resources to what I knew how to do best—using the Internet to research sources of funding for community development in the areas of production, education, and health. Alternative development, development without *dinero*. Ariana would also work with me, using her years of experience since 1994 to track down the existing repositories of information needed by the determined communities of the *autónomo*.

In the communities, hope hung in the balance. It was a time for profound consideration of what had taken place since 1994. Without the concrete image of the corrupt, repressive, militarized PRI government on both the national and the state level to struggle against, the communities were like the jungle awakening after a long drought. No one was sure what to expect or how exactly to proceed. All that was certain was that the new government hadn't complied with the demands of the Zapatistas, especially recognition of the San Andrés Accords, and so they remained in resistance. They explained their position: "Cumplir es complir." To comply is to comply.

The central spirit of both the San Andrés Accords and the Ley Indígena as proposed to the Mexican Congress is indigenous autonomy, not just in Chiapas but in all of the country. Autonomy refers to the right to organize, govern, and adjudicate on the community and municipal level in a way that derives from traditions and customs of an indigenous or campesino group (see De Leon 2001). Included in this is the right to free determination in all facets of daily life. Though not recognized juridically, the pueblos have long exercised the right to autonomy (*Yorail Maya* 2001a).

While recognizing culture, democracy, justice, and women's rights, an important piece of the Zapatista demands and the demands of the *autónomos* extends to autonomy in development and, deriving from this, the autonomy to use their own perceptions of well-being as a measure of prosperity. Indigenous groups in Mexico as a whole cite Convenio 169 of the International Labor Organization, a treaty signed by the president of Mexico in 1991, with the approval of the Senate, as the legitimizing document concerning autonomy (see Nigh 2001, 239). As defined in articles 7 and 15, the treaty states that in the case of development plans, the interested pueblos have the right to decide for themselves their own priorities and have the right to control economic, social, and cultural development (Alianza Civica 2002, 7). Recognizing sovereignty concerning the disposition and use of natural and biological resources would allow indigenous groups to make their own decisions about long-term development. In contrast, in PPP, transnational interests supersede these concerns on the basis of the state's presumption of greater authority and knowledge of rational development.

In 2001, the Ley Indígena, the Indigenous Law proposed to the government, was acutely modified by the Congress and ratified by only seventeen of twenty-nine Mexican states. These modifications weakened notions of indigenous autonomy and made the law impotent. While the ratified Indigenous Law recognizes the right to autonomy in thought, it does not recognize indigenous territory as apart from national lands. While the law recognizes the use of resources in a collective form, it does not allow for the collective management of those resources since the only type of ownership recognized is individual. While the San Andrés Accords stated that local laws and customary traditions must be recognized in the management of collectively held resources, the law as ratified changed the word "must" to "can," thereby changing an obligation for total recognition of autonomy in development to an option. In short, the law permits autonomy but doesn't allow it to work. Twelve Mexican states, representing the bulk of the indigenous population of Mexico, refused to ratify the Indigenous Law (Luna 2001; *Yorail Maya* 2001b). It was returned to the Supreme Court, which ruled in August 2002 that the diluted version would stand. Without the constitutional right to autonomy in the practice of development, the legal road to prosperity, as defined by communities and the legitimate autonomous municipalities, was cut. According to civil society spokespersons, the decision meant that state and national governments were acting to criminalize legitimate modes of expression of civil organization. This only strengthened Zapatista resolve. Once again, government action backfired.

As the peace spread along the surface of Chiapas like an alien gel, the months of being ignored turned resistance into endurance and endurance into work. With the relative quiet and the absence of overt conflict, international attention turned to other more pressing sociopolitical emergencies in other parts of the world. Zapatista communities and municipalities working to maintain their autonomy were faced with the practical realities of constructing a viable world without much outside support and in the window of neglect standing open while the government bedded down with international money with the goal of extracting valuable energy resources and setting up a maquila model of industrial production. The challenge of the *autónomos* was to help its members find viable markets and market alternatives before they sold their communally held land, crossed the northern deserts to the United States, and deserted the countryside for regionally located factories providing

Cerro Verde as seen by Marisa

steady minimal income. Thus, the challenge of peace was even more critical than the challenge of conflict. The *autónomo* leadership understood this. Marcos was silent, but they were working on a solution.

The micro rattled on along the edge of the Santo Domingo River, a miracle of public transportation unheard of in rural America. We arrived safely, hopped over sacks of sugar and dried corn, and walked down the path toward Cerro.

The school structure was completely enclosed. Four shuttered windows and a double door spoke of added expertise in the construction. Martín, the newly married-in son-in-law and then president of the Consejo, brought new skills to the community. In addition, the Cerro kitchen was also enclosed, just in front of Martín's house and the *municipio* office, complete with its computer and printer, operated on diverted electricity. The new kitchen also provided us with a place to hang our hammocks in privacy. The new school held promise of a dormitory to house visiting groups of students.

That first evening, the family was invited to a birthday party to be held for one of Luz's young relatives, turning seventeen. The host family was Charismatic Catholic, yet another brand of religion in the overall Cerro village. Though we calculated our arrival to come well after the religious part of the celebration was under way, this underestimated the fervor and extent of this particular Palabra de Dios. Readings, homilies, exhortations, and a cacophony of group prayer encompassed us. A quartet of *guitarron* players led hymns. The children slept sitting up; Martín slipped off into the night, and we were finally invited to greet the birthday girl. Then all sat down to eat a fiesta meal of tamales and sweet coffee, a plate of six banana leaf–wrapped tamales for each of us. They were delicious and more food than any of us could eat, so we began surreptitiously slipping them into pockets. In the end, plastic bags were produced, and the remainder of the meal was carried home to those who'd came up with a reasonable excuse for not attending.

It was after nine, and the rains had come. Torrential downpours were spaced by low-hanging and palpable mists. The paths were slick, the night dark. We said farewell and started home, a long line of well-wishers picking carefully through the undergrowth toward the road. The men carried the babies, swaddled in protective blankets, a thin wall against the next round of *gripa*. Back in the Cerro kitchen, we compared impressions of the meeting, agreeing that it was indeed a blessing that God had only one word that night, or we would never have left. The rescued tamales were distributed to those who hadn't eaten. It was well after ten when Rodrigo told me that Martín was leaving on the 5:00 A.M. micro. Did I want to talk with him a bit? Of course. There was always time for a meeting.

We settled into the cooking part of the kitchen. In spite of the new building, people still preferred to gather next to the open *comal* fire, providing a little warmth in the damp night. Martín was finishing his dinner. I refused a late coffee, imagining a dark, midnight run in the mud to the latrine.

"Are there things we want to talk about?" asked Martín, after the usual greetings.

I nodded emphatically. Pinned into the pocket of my blue jeans was a Ziploc bag containing 9,000 pesos, the *municipio*'s cut of the recent round of foundation and university donations, the first return on our commitment to *hermanamiento*. Martín took the bag and promised an appropriate receipt. I explained what I had been up to for the last two weeks, looking for possible grants and seeking appropriate foundations.

"We in the Municipio," started Martín. "This is what we have been thinking. We've been relatively successful with the autonomous schools on the level of primary skills. We teach reading and writing and mathematics, environment, and history. What we are also thinking though is that it is time for us to move to the next level."

We'd talked about this last summer when learning about how the schools were being run and the teachers trained with the help of the Zapatistas. At that time, they'd sketched out the possible shape of the postprimary educational system, noting that when the time came, this would be developed. The time seemed to have arrived.

"We want to be able to start a level of vocational training. In part, in the areas of education, and health, and veterinary, which already exist to some extent.

But it needs to be expanded to have courses in other areas of technical and vocational skill. Electric and construction, marketing and administration. This is what we would like to do next. So on the one hand we have a need for projects, and on the other, a need for services. Are foundations willing to fund both?"

"It depends," I told him. "Sometimes it must happen that you search out specific donors for specific things. Sometimes they support a small project, and when that is successfully completed, will support another. And often, you have to get small pieces of money from different sources. Once one gives, often the others follow, because they have more confidence in the group."

We talked a little about the work that Kinal Anzetik, a San Cristóbal NGO, had done in helping set up training programs, and I suggested that we obtain some of their materials so that they are not starting from scratch, reinventing the wheel. I think I said "reinventing the tire."

Martín explained that it would be a boarding school of sorts. Students would come and stay while they received their training. In my mind, that added up to the need for food, shelter, and transportation with the same related problems of money that the Realidad primary school teacher-training program had. But there could be creative solutions. The construction program builds the school and the dorms; the agronomy program plants the food gardens. Community members take turns at maintenance.

"Do you have the place for this vocational program?" I asked.

Martín shook his head. "No. We don't quite know where to begin. Whether to first get money to finance the site. Or to look for funds to train the trainers."

I thought about more attendant related problems. Where was there neutral ground where a large group of Zaps could come together for vocational training without creating problems?

Still, Martín was asking for help. We were, in subtle ways, becoming development consultants. *Consultar obediciendo.* The Zapatista development model.

"I think the first step is planning," I answered, as clearly as I could. This, in a sense, was what my first grants were all about. Donors want tangible projects, but without the planning stage, it's like building a house without a foundation.

"The other thing we would like to do is to develop a regional cooperative for the women to run. And here they would need training in administration," Martín said.

"This is something the women want?" I asked, wondering if it was a plan hatched by a group of males thinking about what women might want. He assured me that the request came from the women, and I told him how the women of the Jolom weaving cooperative in San Cristóbal had moved from their primary educations through the Secundaría and were now in the Prepa, little by little, slowly, how they had learned accounting and were working out the difficulties of trying to keep track of products and finances in a lively international enterprise. Perhaps a meeting with them to share some of their successes and failures?

The grants cycle was next on the discussion list. More time to wait. But these were people of enduring patience, and they understood the meaning of "step by step." Finally, we moved on to the third facet of the plan, the venerable need to find avenues for marketing goods, beginning on the regional level, moving to the national, moving finally to the international. Encompassed in this was the need to be formally organized and recognized, under law, as a cooperative.

For over ten years, being in resistance has meant not participating in government-sponsored "pork barrel" aid programs or political patronage programs or acknowledging the government's right to regulate, record, and monitor births, deaths, marriages, and commercial transactions. But in the lull created by the impasse in government–Zapatista dialogue, autonomous municipal leaders in diverse parts of the state began taking a hard look at what strategic compromises they might make to enhance their economic position without sacrificing the ideals and logic that have guided their struggle.

A basic requirement of participation in commercial sales of campesino-produced goods, ranging from coffee to *artesanías*, is to have a *carácter jurídico*, a legal face that allows a group to register a trademark, seek commercial partners, and apply for financing. The preliminary requirement for this is that cooperatives must form an AC (civil association or cooperative) using legal means, providing names and credentials for a governing body plus a listing of all the associates who form the cooperative. Without this, export is impossible. More important, campesino groups cannot seek certification by either Mexican or international bodies that monitor marketing of goods under the trademark of *Comercio Justo* (Fair Trade). Formal recognition under Mexican laws is also needed to begin the process of having coffee certified as organic. The entire procedure is costly in terms of both actual monetary expenditures and social and political values. But both Fair Trade and Organic production represent a niche that increases marketing possibilities for producers. It is, however, one that is being rapidly co-opted by agrobusinesses using a plantation model (FORO 2002).

When faced with these basic requirements for being part of international business, the initial response of community members and the municipal leadership was negative. Shaking his head, Martín lamented that they couldn't form legally as a cooperative or register a trademark because that involved interactions with the still *mal gobierno*, regardless of what political party was in power. I smiled, getting over my shyness for a moment.

"Perhaps, then, this is something you need to gather and reflect on. I can bring you the information on how to do this. You need to decide how much involvement is acceptable to you."

Martín considered the proposition. "Fair enough," he said, promising to finally get some stuff for me on disk so that I could work with their proposals. We bid a cordial good night, while he went off into his home/office to write and print a formal letter of receipt and thanks. Returning to the bedroom/kitchen, I joined Ariana, deep in conversation with Rodrigo and Luz. Rodrigo looked at me in question.

"Everything okay?" he asked. He was still concerned about community–*consejo* relations, and that Martín and I develop a congenial working relationship. I gave him the equivalent of a thumbs-up. Martín returned with the letter, formal and eloquent and complete with the stamp of the *municipio*, a ski-masked bust of Emiliano Zapata. I read it in the glow of the unofficial lightbulb, illuminating the paper with an orange misty radiance. Around midnight, the rain began again on the lamina roof, and with little grace I slipped into the cocoon of my hammock and was sound asleep.

Somewhere near dawn, Carmen shuffled into the kitchen. She started the fire and warmed tortillas and a few of the leftover tamales. She and Martín talked quietly as he ate a quick breakfast and went off in search of the early micro on some unnamed task for the *autónomo*. I gave my hammock a quick push to start the gentle rocking motion and was lulled back to sleep.

Daylight brought concerted morning sounds. The dogs barked at Linda, Martín's thirteen-year-old, as she moved sleepily into the kitchen from the house she shared with her father, stepmom Carmen, and half sister Cari. Linda was another product of the Zapatista uprising, the aftermath of a personal breakup where one partner remained committed to the movement and the other left. At first, Martín tried leaving Linda with the grandparents so that he could carry out his own work. But they were PRIistas, and he was afraid that she would be unduly influenced by their political beliefs and practices. And Linda did not want to give up the work she had begun with the women of the movement. When Martín began to court Carmen, Linda slipped quietly into the family, becoming yet another beloved *hija* among the cadre of *hijas* and *hijos*, accepting Luz and Rodrigo as Mami and Papi. Later, she would leave to follow her own path into the Movement.

In Cerro, Sunday was truly a day of rest. The people rise slowly; eat beans, tortillas, and egg drop soup in the usual shifts; and attend only to those tasks that are close to the house. It was still raining, so even the remaining coffee couldn't be uncovered for drying. We gathered in the cooking area and chatted easily, drinking the sweet dark coffee that boiled in a soup pot in the warm ash at the side of the fire.

Luz was pregnant. At forty-six, it had come as a great surprise since she had welcomed what seemed to be the first tentative warnings of menopause. She was riddled by guilt as much by her sense of foolishness after nine years of family planning, a decision she and Rodrigo came to together to have no more children. With the arrival of Natalia two years ago, the little miracle, she was thrilled, and she and her informally adopted baby were an inseparable pair. A series of medical tests in Comitán yielded the unhappy news that she was indeed expecting, a condition complicated by serious varicose veins and high blood pressure. She faced the prospect of a C-section delivery in mid-May.

Luz's guilt stemmed as much from messing up on her commitment to family planning as from her self-loathing for not wanting the baby. On the one hand, she saw her condition as a disgrace before the community, and on the other, she felt her own intense feelings were inhuman and against God and her own spirit.

"I'm resigned to it now," she told us. "Marta asked yesterday if I was pregnant. She touched my stomach, searching for the pulse of life in the baby. I had to tell her."

Marta was her youngest natural child, eleven years old, another story of childhood in the long and convoluted litany of the effects of war on communities in resistance.

Ariana rubbed Luz's arm. "No, Doña Luzi. It isn't a question of resignation here. It is about accepting. And there is no disgrace. Everyone here is only concerned that you take care of your health. And think of this as an opening, a window, where the women can have frank talks with their daughters about reproductive health."

Luz wiped away a few tears. "They say I have to rest for three months before and three months after the baby is born. I won't be able to do my work with the women, my share of our cooperative jobs. I love what I do with the women. I just don't want this."

I looked across the smoky kitchen at Luz, without appropriate words of comfort. A few seconds later, the moment was lost as Alejandro, her thirteen-year-old son, came running in, explaining that he was off to finish work on the fishpond he was constructing with another of his buddies.

Several years ago, some NGO arrived in the area peddling a *pisicultura* project. The object was to interest the communities into raising freshwater fish in pools on the banks of the nearby Chayote River. By 1998, all that remained of the idea was an oral history of yet another development failure. But here, five years later, the teenagers had discovered the idea for themselves and were hot at work making a pond where the water could flow in and out. They were purchasing two-inch baby *talapia* for a peso a piece from some enterprising fish salesman. As Alejandro scooted off dressed in his Sunday worst, our talk turned to protecting the baby fish from the ample appetites of hungry San Martins, waterfowl that could easily decimate the new project.

The story was reminiscent of how the Zinacantecos up in the Altos became flower moguls. They too had rejected a foreigner's proffered project that involved building poly houses to capitalize on the skills of their green-thumbed members. He left the area, dejected by his failure. Not long after, with the help of a local priest, the community returned to the idea on their own. It became an unprecedented success.

After breakfast, the enclave was relatively quiet. Marta, like Alejandro, was busy with her own production project. She raised ducks with astounding success, a tribute to her skill with animals. Someday, we all hoped, she would attend the veterinary training program the *municipio* hoped to build.

Rain turned to mist, and the lingering moisture made painting the school's exterior impossible. The inauguration would go on tomorrow anyway since all planned to be present for it. The women would gather in the afternoon to festoon the building with crepe paper hangings. In the meantime, many of them headed up the hill to the tiny Catholic church for a meeting to hear another version of the word of God.

Cerro's religious background remained a critical underpinning to its resistance, and they remained practicing Catholics. In spite of the upheaval being perpetrated on the structures of the San Cristóbal diocese by its new, Vatican-directed bishop, Felipe Arizmendi, the seeds of liberation theology were sown in the communities. They had been left to fend for themselves, seeing a visiting nun perhaps once a month. The sacraments reached them twice a year. They carried on with Bible readings interpreted in the face of struggle and conflict by their trained catechists. The church was truly autochthonous. But it seemed easy to understand the growth of other religious sects in the area. These were not dependent for an important part of their ritual on the availability of ordained clergy. Like the charismatics we'd visited the night before, they raised them up from their communities and endured the results.

The sun cut through the lingering mists, a finger of blue appearing high above the orange trees. Since the school painting project was still postponed, Ariana and I decided to take this opportunity to visit upriver in Tulan. It would be my first visit there in two years. A final late-afternoon micro would pass through sometime soon, so we packed our sleeping bags and walked up to wait at the side of the road.

The meeting in the church was over. Members of the seven remaining communities in resistance had walked for hours to get there, leaving distant enclaves at 7:00 in the morning. Now, they began to disperse, and we were delighted to meet Micaela, Carmen and Francisco's daughter, and two of her children as they waited for the same micro back to Tulan. I remembered her face from that first visit to the Rio Chayote in January 1998, remembered her later in her peach-colored dress as she gave me a gift of a bottle of honey. Then we talked about resistance. Now we discussed commercialization.

The little coffee orchard in front of Tulan's wood-frame buildings looked vibrant and healthy. The plants were a deep loden green and shiny and bore their first few fruits of this season. At the side of the property, a plot of medicinal plants was fenced against wandering pigs, and cane plants towered over the rest of a milpa that began just behind the buildings.

The enclave was still a hospital. Doña Carmen is a product of multiple Zapatista training programs—a midwife, doctor, and dentist whose tiny clinic held the remains of the larger one destroyed by the army in 1998. She collected medicinal plants, cared for patients who walked in from villages a day's hike away, and contributed what she could to the dental health of those in resistance. The rescued dental office from the Tierra y Libertad clinic gathered dust in one corner of the building; baskets of molds for making false teeth remained next to a gas-generated drill, no longer in service.

We found Francisco in the kitchen, decobbing three types of corn into a basket to make masa for future tortillas. His shoes were off, and he greeted us with surprise. It had been a difficult winter for his health. Rheumatism and arthritis plagued his knees and legs. His story was becoming familiar. It was the aftermath of resistance, which took its toll on the health of those who kept the faith. The children were unvaccinated against normal childhood diseases; those who had entered the struggle in their youth were awakening to the aches and pains of middle age, multiplied by years of poor nutrition, lousy living conditions, and little access to formal medicine when it was truly needed.

The Tulaneros were still beekeepers. Honey still ran like an amber river from the hives. They harvested and bottled liter after liter, storing it in the kitchen and in the hospital, waiting for prospective buyers. There was still no marketing plan, no NGO that had taken the step from production projects to commercialization. Perhaps there was an implicit assumption that these Marxist rebels would eschew anything that vaguely smacked of capitalism, profit, and free-market exchange. The NGOs somehow didn't consider the possibility of capitalism with socialist goals, production and marketing that used the reality of commerce to obtain the commodities and money needed to support the rebel vision of life.

And so, of course, our conversation turned to commercialization: the futures market in honey. They were about to begin to harvest this year's crop. The February–March batch was a dark syrup, *miel de café*, a product of the bee's romance with the pearly white starflowers of the coffee plant. The second would be almost clear, as the rest of the jungle burst into flower, the coffee fruited, and the bees switched their affections to bougainvillea, wild mint, and orange blossoms. Though we bemoaned the out-of-season rains that left behind a field of sloppy mud, it was good for the coffee, good for the bees.

I had not seen the family since my first long-term stay in the area when my intention had been to stay with them and learn medicine and beekeeping from Doña Carmen. But the paramilitary activity in the region was too high, and the isolated outpost of Tulan was unsafe for foreign presence. Thus, I had moved downriver and began my association with the larger and more protected community of Cerro Verde. But student efforts in the past had brought some support to Tulan, and they remembered this with fondness but also with a measure of suspicion. Memory is long in places where foreigners come only once or twice a year. As we learned in our long talks with Francisco, the old suspicions don't fade easily. Sometimes they never die.

Francisco had legitimate concerns. The newly reconstituted Consejo Autónomo of Tierra y Libertad and its umbrella clearinghouse of the Enlace Civil in San Cristóbal needed to be apprised of our intent to visit and to work with the community. We assured him that I was known to the *Enlace* and had, in fact, spoken with the *presidente municipal* of the *autónomo* just the night before, that we were well acquainted and had established a relationship of some trust by listening to the *municipio*'s concerns and returning with a small grant for the larger body's integrated development fund. In the end, it was a good visit.

Dawn was at least three roosters away when we flagged down the commuter micro traveling back downriver. I thought about my conversations with Francisco as the micro bounced down the road, the shock absorbers a vague memory of years gone by. Francisco was concerned that we follow Zapatista rules. At the same time, he repeated the group's original mantra: we are independent. We left Tulan with an agreement to seek out markets on the international and national levels for both honey and coffee, to bring information about the legal process surrounding the registry of marketable goods.

As we rode down the muddy, rutted road through the upper Chayote, the micro came to life as passengers sang out sleepy greetings to compadres from other villages and turned the aged bus into a business office on wheels.

We stopped for a few minutes while a passenger in front signed a check for someone who boarded at a darkened storehouse. Further on, we loaded up a few *bultos* of coffee. The seller dictated the price, entrusting the transaction to the bus driver, yet another intermediary on the road to commercialization of coffee.

Commercialization. Within a week, Chiapas governor Pablo Salazar would journey to Washington to meet first with President Bush and then with the World Bank. And yet I doubted whether any investment arrangement would ever benefit the resistance communities such as Tulan and Cerro. Indeed, it was unlikely that any of the poor campesinos in the Chayote region would be primary beneficiaries of commercial arrangements.

Cerro was still sleeping when we crossed the coffee-drying patio in front of the main house. We startled Cleenton, the scraggly russet dog who had survived his presidential namesake's tenure in office. A round of barking and crowing guaranteed that no one would sleep much longer. As we tiptoed over to our hammocks to grab a few winks, Linda stumbled sleepily into the kitchen to start the fire and begin the day's cooking. Though it was already 6:00 A.M., Cerro Verde was "sleeping in."

"Buenos Dias!" called Luz called later, through the open Dutch door leading into the combined dining and bedroom. "There's sun."

There was sun, indeed, a welcome change form the bone-chilling mist and rain of the past two days. The whole community was up and about, and I rolled out of the hammock, pulled on some clothes, and gathered up a pile of dirty dishes from the night before. Clean dishes were critical to the next round of meals, and this morning involved preparations for the lunch that would follow the school's inauguration. Several chickens had already been killed, plucked, and cleaned and were waiting to become *caldo*. Since Cerro had recently experienced an epidemic chicken disease that killed all but three hens, it was likely that these had been purchased from someone else in the village.

The kids were all in high spirits and ran to join Ramón in one of the buildings at the other end of the enclave. They huddled together, doors tightly shut, so that no one would get advance notice of the show they were preparing to put on after the official ceremonies. At ten sharp, we moved to the mudflats just below the enclave for the ribbon-cutting ceremony of the Escuela Autónoma Miguel Hidalgo.

All of the community, adults and children, were gathered in front of the school. Rodrigo asked us to clear the doorway, and I looked up to see the *viejitos*, the elders of Cerro, coming down the hill. Doña Dominga was in front, and she carried a smoking incense burner, the copal scent filling in the spaces between the orange trees and the clear blue sky. It had been more than fifty years since she last wore a *huipil*, but to be Maya is to be Maya. She held the offering before her, her thin face contemplative and quiet. Someone strummed a guitar, a few words were spoken, and the ribbon was cut. The double doors opened wide, revealing the gaily festooned interior of the new school.

We sat on benches and chairs facing the front of the school, where two blackboards hung on the walls. I admired Martín's carpentry and the really fine job someone did on the concrete floor. What a change from the plank-sided, dirt-floored shelter where rain seeped in between the boards and through the space where the roof never quite met the walls. The old building was already down, the space set aside for some future construction. Progress.

Jeanne in front of newly built Cerro Verde school

Dominga put the *incensario* on the floor in front of table. I recognized it as one that Duncan left for them and thought about how pleased he would have been to have seen it. The table was set with a series of gifts, ears of corn, tortillas, holy water, flowers, and candles—sacred offerings with a long history but transfigured here into those items available both in the memory of the old folks and in the local environment. Had there been a priest or even a deacon, they would have begun with a mass. Even Davíd, the eloquent catechist, was away from the community, completing three months of work in Mexico City. So another of the elders provided blessings and homily. As was the custom in both secular and sacred meetings, all were invited to speak. My father had died three months before, and I mentioned for the first time that instead of flowers, friends and relatives donated money for the Cerro education project. Eventually, the school would bear his photo and be dedicated to him.

Somewhere around the "Our Father," Luz's PRD sister Barbara and Alonso, her PRIista husband, entered. This was interesting and in fact even touching. In spite of the fact that Rodrigo and Luz had not attended his party, he was here. Family is thicker than politics, yes. But also it could well be an attempt at reconciliation. We took the holy water and the flowers, and I carried the water as we blessed the new building and all that would take place there.

After the blessings, the music began, and everyone stood for the Zapatista hymn. I watched Alonso's face, set like stone, as the community stood at attention. Afterward, when we were all asked to comment again, he spoke of his joy at their joy and mentioned that he had another appointment and would not be able to stay through the entire festivities. In the end, Ariana and I left before he did.

The program was much like we experienced during our summer visit. Bombas—*mis padres quedan muy macho, andan en el camino del Comandante Tacho*, riddles, the entire repertoire of EZLN commemorative corridos, other songs, and, of course, a few satires. The story of El Burro, a seemingly politically neutral slapstick, brought down the house. We sat in the sun around the coffee patio, laughing and chatting; Natalia sat on my lap; we were all smiling. *Poco a poco. Caldo de pollo* for forty people later, Ariana and I caught the 3:00 P.M. combi back to Comitán.

"PORQUE SOMOS EN RESISTENCIA": SEEKING ACCEPTABLE SOLUTIONS

March arrived, spring-break time in the United States. Arriving for a short stay was Lauren Carruth, a Wake Forest student who had decided to take on some of the responsibility of organizing a service-learning program to be held the following January, comprised once again of Wake Forest University and University of Texas–El Paso (UTEP) students. So, loaded down with school supplies, food, hammocks, and packs, we took a rented combi out of San Cristóbal on yet another soggy, chilly dry season morning bound for the Chayote. With Duncan back in Texas, Rachel took on the role of proxy for the UTEP portion of our *hermanamiento*. Drawing on the first line of the Zapatista hymn, which encourages the world to look to the horizon, we named the program El Horizonte.

On the road between Comitán and Playa, there was new troop action, rumored to be because of recent violence in Guatemala, but this did not explain the twenty-seven truckloads of army we saw heading that way. Other rumors said that the time had come to get those pesky thirty-odd communities out of the Reserva Montes Azules so that the oil that they were purportedly sitting on could be easily extracted as part of the PPP. The movement of troops was nothing unusual since their numbers hadn't diminished. The previous spring, amidst considerable hype about complying with Zapatista demands to close critical army bases, we came upon a convoy in the process of trading locations. Within the truckload of soldiers carrying automatic weapons was a huge Coca-Cola machine in transit. Coming up to get a closer look, we noticed that one of the men was sitting on a large cardboard carton. If the labels were to be believed, the box held a complete Barbie house. The implications of this have never been clear, but it did not inspire confidence.

In spite of the increased military action, our happy band arrived at Cerro without incident. This contingent included our students and, much to my delight, two venerable representatives of the elders, anthropologist June Nash and her husband Frank Reynolds, recently retired from the University of Chicago. We were three generations of anthropologists attempting to define a new model of field research along with our community colleagues.

We occupied the new school, freshly painted in the EZ's symbolic colors, café, red, and black. There was to have been white as well, but that can of paint didn't make it off the micro two trips back.

The community was pleased to see us, but there was also a pervasive air of sadness. A funeral was being held among relatives a few kilometers away at a tiny community high above the river. Two young men working in agriculture in Virginia as part of the valley's undocumented migrant contingent had been killed in an automobile accident. It was not hard to imagine the chain of events. Getting someone to identify and claim the bodies, making contact with the families, and arranging logistically and financially for the bodies to make a final journey to the Chayote took almost three weeks.

Everyone was understandably subdued in Playa. The parental generation, already opposed to immigration, saw this as confirmation of their worst fears.

"They leave for the North," said Alma sadly. "And then the next time you see them they are dead."

Certainly, this event only reinforced the desire to make the local economy work so that young people wouldn't be tempted to leave their wives, children, and parents behind to wonder if their loved one would ever return. This, we knew, was what was happening downriver in Ojo de Agua, with ruinous results.

Luz punctuated her own fear and opposition to immigration during a lively kitchen discussion between Martín, Camila, and myself. Martín, on behalf of the *municipio*, had asked that we do some English lessons as part of the upcoming service trip. Luz was opposed.

"Why do we need English, living here?" she asked. "It will only make them want to leave more."

But Martín explained that a selective knowledge of the language was important in order to access the market, to sell goods with proper labels, to negotiate with prospective buyers. In addition to his first language, Tzeltal, acquired Tzotzil, and Spanish, Martín had an extensive vocabulary in French and English, self-taught by reading English- and French-language materials. Admitting finally that the *municipio* computer was housed in the "*palacio municipal*" next door, I promised to bring back some interactive English-as-a-second-language CDs for him. We did a linguistics minilesson on the spot, looking at the way that Spanish syntax couples with English words on the border.

The continuing amiability between Martín and I built on increasing trust in the fact that even with my often faulty Spanish, they were learning what they needed to know from my networking in San Cristóbal. When we arrived back in Playa, it had been arranged that the rest of the *Consejo* would gather to meet and talk with me. On the regional level, reorganization was already taking place. Martín had become head of a group of heads of the four *autónomos* connected to the Aguascalientes of Realidad.

If you remember, when we last left the resistance communities of Tierra y Libertad, they were sadly shaking their heads and commenting that they couldn't form legally as a cooperative or register a trademark "*porque estamos en resistancia.*" My response had been that it was their problem and that perhaps a reflection or two might yield a solution. I was, therefore, more or less amazed when Martín announced that during a *Consejo* meeting, they had done just that and had decided that it was time to investigate the legal route. But that opened up a number of other areas of question. Wouldn't it cost money to file as a cooperative and to seek certification?

To their surprise and mine, I had already gotten the figures for the process and, in fact, had answers to many of their new questions. The remaining queries could be easily answered. Prior to the visit, I'd prepared a list of areas for my own reflection with them. It was really a treat when it turned out that these were the same ones they'd been considering as part of both short- and long-term planning. We spent some time considering the following questions together:

1. What are our existing resources, those that we have already been able to sell? How can we improve the sale of these products for the coming harvest so that we are receiving a price somewhere between "*jodido y justo?*"
2. What are other products that we grow for subsistence but have never commercialized?
3. Do we grow enough of either of these to market our goods by ourselves on the community or the municipal level?
4. What are possible ways to turn a subsistence resource into a market resource? Can we consider the dried fruits and vegetable market, using existing low-tech processing?
5. What do we need to know about what we do, about our land and our potential industry, to make our labor yield more return in the long run?

I left the meeting with more questions to pursue. We also agreed to follow up on a possible grant for an exchange between those involved in alternative schools in the United States and those in Chiapas. Unexpected as it was, being consultants for the *autónomos* was not at all a bad position to be in.

The students held their own meetings, trying to set up the January service program. This prospect was a go from the Cerro side, with the kids asking that we work with some projects with plants, in essence getting the school to have its own little market garden. There was something refreshing about a group of kids who were asking to eat vegetables! Now that I knew how commerce worked in this zone, with the arrival of such staples as potatoes, onions, and carrots coming only once a week, it seemed that there were niches yet to be filled, at least for the short run. Luz also mentioned that the banks of the river are loaded with campers from the city during Holy Week. Since the *compañeros* are the closest to the river, they could reap seasonal windfall profits by marketing certain treats to the visitors.

June and Frank brought a basketball and hoop for the school, and a short game took place, captured by us on video. Through all of this, the women were noticeably absent. They, it turned out, were up in the kitchen discussing the possibility of making small embroidered cloths to sell in San Cristóbal de las Casas and the states, featuring the Escuela Autónomo Miguel Hidalgo and happy masked children learning to read. They agreed that this would be a good idea, cleared it with the *municipio*, and would begin shortly.

Meanwhile, building on last summer's discussions of what to pursue next in education, the *municipio* identified four areas: *contabilidad, tipografía, construcción*, and *electricidad*. By the latter, they meant repair of small appliances, which seemed like a great area for young women because it was something they could do at home, requiring only a few tools. My kingdom for one decent development grant. There was a little office down in the basement of the World Bank where a Wake Forest alumna was hard

The Cerro Verde autonomous school, Escuela Antonoma Miguel Hidalgo

at work on community development projects. Perhaps they might be interested.

We took a short trip to Ojo de Agua to visit as well. The big news down there was that the women continued their revolt. Two of Manuel's daughters took off by combi to attend an International Women's Day march in Las Margaritas. And Isa's friend Rosa, Miguel's older daughter, was leaving for a first domestic position in Comitán at the end of this month. We brought a bunch of U.S. blouse patterns with us so that the Ojo women could experiment with different styles using the same embroidery and manta cloth as we'd discussed during the thunderstorm fashion show in the summer of 2001.

Marta came with us since she loved to go places and meet people whose lives were different but similar. More than that, she loved to see what animals they were raising. She longed for a lamb to add to the battalion of ducks she shepherded around the Cerro compound, her own little *empresa*, contributing to the upkeep of the whole group. We had a small moment of indecision as Marta contemplated the Ojo de Agua swinging bridge, but in the end she walked bravely across. We went back to Playa with a nopal cactus, a PRIista plant for the Cerro Verde garden, one of those quiet, everyday acts of exchange that might one day be the seeds of lasting reconciliation.

Reconciliation, like development, can't be imposed from above, but the Fox government seemed to have missed this point. Representatives of the PAN danced through the state sponsoring *mesas de reconciliación* in an attempt to declare peace, another manifestation of a well-orchestrated effort to annul the entire conflict. Wars are declared. Peace is negotiated between opposing forces who come to an agreement concerning the shape that cessation of conflict should take. Yet the current government and the post-Ruiz church preferred to act as though the past eight years and the decades leading up to them never happened. Neither the Zapatistas nor their adversaries were willing to acknowledge the current top-down peace declaration as their own. Even Paz y Justicia, the Zona Norte paramilitary organization, began to sound curiously like their counterparts in the autonomous *municipios*, announcing that the government didn't speak for their membership at the reconciliation table. The Zapatistas still refused to say anything, and if Marcos never issued another communiqué, both the state and the national government would breathe a collective sigh of relief. So would the official Church.

In Cerro Verde, another kind of reconciliation took place a few weeks later, with the birth of Luz's baby boy. He had healthy lungs and a hearty appetite, and Luz happily reconciled herself to being a new mother. As we sat together chatting one evening, she heard a baby crying and mused, "Now whose baby is that crying?" The realization that it was hers came quickly, and she laughed, once again infused with the kind of love that is part of the miracle of birth.

Another small miracle was that the baby was born on my birthday, so he was named Juanito Antonio.

Around us, the nights were long and clear and dry, but the hot season was coming to an end. Soon the summer rains would arrive, ending the Zapatista spring of hard work and reverberating silence.

NOTE

1. In Mexican Spanish, the *b* and the *v* are sometimes interchangeable, providing multilayered meanings to words or phrases. Thus, *revelde* might mean "rebel," but it might also mean "revealed." In like manner, *linea* combined with one of these variations also has multiple meanings. We leave to the reader to select the appropriate one.

CHAPTER 12

Whirling Silence

JEANNE (JUNE 2002): THE 1:00 P.M., God, Maya, Campo, Resistencia time departure from Comitán (that would be 2:00 P.M., official, *gobierno, verano,* daylight savings time) was right on schedule, with very few passengers, and only three or four sacks of sugar. But the micro filled to almost capacity at the Rio Chayote turnoff. The summer rains were here again, the long months of steamy heat. It was also campaign time for the official municipal elections, and some governmental agency, political party, or candidate was in the process of paving the road. This involved one large piece of heavy machinery and a crew of at least twenty men, most from Cerro Verde and points north. More government pork-barrel, electoral sweets. The repairs consisted of filling the combi-sized potholes and digging drainage ditches on either side of the road to catch the waters of the *aguaceros.* Perhaps with the next election it would also get paved. The rains had become nightly torments, complete with thunder and lightning and electrical outages not related to normal deficiencies in the functioning of the regional electrical system.

We picked up the returning road workers just above the village of San Clemente. Replete with their pozole bottles and shoulder bags, they boarded the bus, stopping only to leave their machetes at the door. Whether this last was to avert conflict with the ever-present drunk at the back of the bus or to ensure that no one got inadvertently hacked up should the micro be unable to regain stability during one of the not-infrequent two-wheel turns was not clear.

I arrived in the heavy, late afternoon. Two of the littlest girls came running down the road with arms open, yelling, "Abuelita! abuelita!" Marta's duck pond was still dry, though the once-cracked soil was now soupy mud, and the next weeks would refill it. All was pretty tranquil in El Cerro, so I greeted Luz and took Natalia down to the river where Marta, Cari, Linda, Camila, and Martín were washing their clothes and their sweaty bodies. Linda was caught between giving me a proper greeting and keeping her breasts covered, so she crossed her arms in front of her chest and gave me a no-handed hug. I waded in to help with the laundry and then returned to the house as the next storm began to rumble down from the mountains.

We gathered around the low table in the tiny kitchen, chatting amiably and listening to the rain. Once again, I silently thanked the Zapatistas for not drinking. Doing fieldwork alone in a Mexican community could be really hard when alcohol was involved, especially for women. Here, I felt safe, comfortable, protected. I shared a few pieces of literature from the most recent workshop I attended while in the city as the thunder cracked and the single lightbulb sputtered and died. We bid farewell to the electricity and dug out our flashlights.

The issue of the electrical power has served to provide a continued forum for cross-political discussion during both national workshops and rural meetings. Thus, as Plan Puebla Panamá (PPP) and dam issues presented the possibility of real challenges for the area, there was a nascent move to begin organizing. But Martín again provided an amused critique of the limitations of the average campesino in the area of organizing. They had yet to learn to become a part of the process of reflection, discussion, and decision making. They were not ready to craft solutions, only to validate the solutions found for them. This in many ways resembled the government's own practices in which a custom that exists for a while is then legislated into law, as with the modification of article 27. *Ah bueno*, people are illegally selling their lands? Let's make it legal. *Ah bueno*, people are refusing to pay more than fifteen pesos a month for electricity? Let's organize to say we won't pay more than fifteen pesos.

There was another international conference, this one concerning cultural and biological diversity, planned for the end of June in Quetzaltenango (Xela), Guatemala. I offered to pay transportation and food for a *municipio* representative to attend this anti-PPP gathering, but Martín shook his head.

"You go Doña Juanita," he said. "Bring back the information." It was getting to be routine.

On a regional level, the *autónomos* were really concerned about the issue of *transgénicos*. The leadership of the newly organized regional municipal organization was considering banning genetically engineered plants from the four *municipios* it represented. This promised to be another potential touchy autonomy battle, like the one that got Tierra y Libertad dismantled in the first place. In 1998, it was less the challenge of the alternative education and health system than the parallel system of justice and laws that brought in the troops. In that case, it had to do with the right to take lumber off *municipio* land. Trying to control the planting of crops was not much different. But the Organization wanted to get the point across to campesinos about the potential contamination effects of genetically engineered seed. We talked about

"Green Revolution" failures. It was new to Martín, but he really liked the name.

Martín and Camila left early the next morning for parts unknown, something to do with *madera*, or maybe it was Madero. At the same time, crisis was building in the next set of houses as young Dominga, one of Luz's sisters, complained of lower-right quadrant pains going down into her leg. Ana came by to do a diagnosis, suspected appendicitis, and sent her to the clinic at Santa Elena, accompanied by one of the other women. This provided a guide for me to the triage of resistance. When loss of life was possible, then resistance became tolerance of government-funded facilities. We were not optimistic. We'd heard stories of the services provided in Santa Elena from Miguel in Ojo. They hadn't given any real help to him during his heart problems.

Young Dominga was promptly sent to Comitán. A loudspeaker summons later, Rodrigo took a phone call and was off to the city to oversee at the hospital, where they inquired as to whether they were Zapatistas since they came from Santa Elena. By midnight, they'd done a complete hysterectomy, having found an ovarian mass. Rodrigo returned the following day, replaced at the hospital by the Don Antonio and Doña Dominga, the *viejitos*. I didn't push the issue of whether the operation was actually needed or whether sterilization was just a good way to keep Zapatistas from reproducing their autonomous selves.

Doña Dominga is a true campesina. The day before she'd trundled off dressed in her best apron and bandanna to sell ripe bananas hours away at Cardenas. In exchange, she bought *maíz* at Hidalgo. Hidalgo *maíz*, she explained to me, grew abundantly because they used a lot of fertilizer and insecticides. In contrast, her husband's corn was stunted, sparse. But organic production was another of their cargos. *Así es.*

By the end of the day, we were down several mother figures and the traveling team of *consejos* still hadn't returned. Cari cried forlornly from inside their empty house; Luz was with Juanito, the new baby, and Linda had gone to the river to get water. I decided that as the only bosom left in town, it was time to pass through the hallowed portals of municipal headquarters to comfort her. She sat dejectedly, sobbing on her bed in a plank bedroom papered with back issues of *Cuarto Poder*. I patted her on the back, reassuring her that her mom always came back. On the bedside table were all the accoutrements of rural communication, printouts of correspondence from deep in the jungle. I resisted the temptation to read any of it, not wanting to violate a growing trust.

Martín and Camila's frequent absences confirmed that something was afoot. With the rains, the river made its transition from azure to jade and finally to deep moss, the same color as the trucks and uniforms of the military, who were moving again on the road above the compound. One day, they

Jeanne, Natalia, and Antonio read Jeanne's book, Too Wet to Plow

camped for an hour or so in the football field near the house as the jungle heat built up, like a heavy foot pressing us down into a deep sleep. We sat in the shade waiting while Alma went to count troops and trucks. Overhead, a plane flew by, headed off toward Realidad, then another. A little later, one circled around and flew back, this time at a lower altitude.

Cari's fears disappeared for the day, but later that night she fell into a fit of apprehension concerning whether her mom had to cross the river on a *hamaca* and could potentially drown. Marta, now a veteran of the Ojo swinging bridge, assured her that it was completely safe. That evening was a long, gentle one. With Rodrigo and Martín both gone, we women pulled a bench out of the kitchen and gathered in front of Luz's house embroidering Escuela Autónoma textiles. Between squinting at the needles as we tried to pass the multicolored threads through the eye and checking each other's colors and stitches, we took turns quieting little Juanito, who was growing really well. Santa Paz.

I've learned that the phrase "Santa Paz" is a colloquialism, meaning "tranquillity." But there is actually nothing really tranquil taking place. It occurred to me reading the papers and listening to conversations of visitors to the Tierra y Libertad *palacio municipal,* which was also my bedroom, that in the long E-zeta silence, what was an initial unrealized objective of the rebellion may have quietly come about. There are rumblings and grumblings of protest from all over the country, not just from the indigenous states of the south. To some extent this reflects growing distrust and distaste for the article 27 children— PROGRESA, PROCAMPO, PROCEDE, and now PROFIANZA, government programs designed to buy off unrest. But it also may be a sounding board for what kind of resistance PPP will get. By "declaring" peace in Chiapas and showing potential rebels in other states just how little the government is willing to change, they may have set the stage for much more widespread conflict, another policy backfire.

In March, in the state of Michoacan, a confrontation resulting from agrarian issues turned violent as tensions burst through the "apparent calm." Three people were detained. The community responded by coming together to put pressure on the federal agency responsible for PROCEDE. Nearby, a disagreement between indigenous farmers and the army left three dead on each side. Though the government claimed that the event was related to drug trafficking, the community denied it. Michoacan was anything but tranquil.

Similarly, in the state of Oaxaca, a massacre on April 4, 2002, took the lives of twenty-seven people in the village of Agua Fría. Arising from an unresolved conflict over land use rights, observers warned of similar potential for violence in the Montes Azules protected area of Chiapas. Montes Azules remained home to around thirty communities. Some of these had been displaced by the war in Chiapas and fled into the reserve seeking refuge; others pre-dated the overt conflict. Under the pretext of protecting the resources of the zone, the government stated publicly that it planned to forcibly remove the groups from inside the boundaries of the reserve. Disguised in language concerning conservation of natural resources was the battle for control and extraction of strategic commodities, including water for hydroelectric power, oil, and uranium.

In June, outside the Mexican capital, the *ejiditarios* of Atenco held the military at bay with raised machetes in the place where the government planned to seize the land for a new international airport. The Fox government relented, and the *ejido* claimed victory. Coincidentally, the triumph took place on the day that Juan Diego was canonized as Mexico's first indigenous saint. In Chiapas, they called it his first miracle. And up in the north, campesinos blocked border bridges, in growing protests against the North American Free Trade Agreement (NAFTA), ALCA,[1] and other children of "free trade." In the Chiapas countryside, daily flare-ups were the early warning signs of impatience. Unresolved struggles over agrarian rights in the *autónomos*, roadblocks, and small acts of violence, are the clear signs that hope has been composted for too long and had begun to turn to rage. In terms of reality, the Santa Paz had a lot in common with Santa Claus.

I returned to San Cristóbal de las Casas to get ready to go to Guatemala to attend the Second Week for Biological and Cultural Diversity in Xela. The morning combi was late as usual, and I waited with a group of campesinos from Cerro and nearby communities. They, of course, wanted the full scoop on who the gringa was and began with a polite version of "so do you come here often?" Turning the conversation, I got one *viejito* from a tiny community to talk about changes in the forty years since he moved down from Margaritas. He described an environment of rich jungle with trees as round as truck tires and did a fine impression of a howler monkey yelling from up near Orilla del Bosque to those down on the river, the monkeys who left the day the big wind came. Monkeys, tigres the size of German shepherds, javelinas, and *tepescuintles* rounded out the land fauna. Add to this the *lagartos*, or small crocodiles, still rumored to live in a nearby lake. The jungle had been quite a place. This all amazed the youngest among the men. Once again, it was a problem of never asking those kinds of questions of the elders, something the autonomous schools promoted in their children.

From this innocuous opening, the conversation turned to coffee production. The Cerro *ejido* was certified organic, and all Cerro production was once organic. Once more, I was torn when I considered the *municipio*. Was there no way for this group to work together for mutual benefit before they all sold out to the latest additions to the government plans to bribe *ejido* farmers into individualizing their land? Our conversation turned to my pueblo, Carolina del Norte, and of course one of the men had a brother there. We made a per-cup comparison of the price of coffee at the farm gate and in the United States, with the conclusion that we were *chingados por los dos lados*. Finally, we turned to the usual discussion of opportunities for immigration, the trials of crossing the desert and the results of September 11.

September 11. During our first visit after the Torres Gemelos fell, Duncan must have told the story of the Twin Towers a hundred times. In Cerro, they knew that both of us had connections to New York, and so they had worried. Now, in the year since, we were seeing the results of the creeping terror, as checkpoints along the Guatemala–Chiapas border made a point of saying that they were involved in a permanent war against terror and drugs. We wondered during the long months that followed the massive Zapatista caravan to Mexico City in March 2001 how much their subsequent silence might be the result of an astute, strategic assessment by the *comandancia* that out of sight was out of mind. As Attorney General Ashcroft formalized his list of terrorist organizations, it would be counterproductive to do or say anything that might be misconstrued and catapult the Organization into Ashcroft's view and onto the list. A hundred Chiapas Project fund-raisers later, I breathed a related sigh of relief, setting to rest justifiable fear of guilt by association.

The buses bound for Guatemala left San Cristóbal carrying 180 Mexicans from all over the country and a few stray foreigners like me. Spanish, the language of the conquest of much of the Americas, became the language of unity as over 500 people met in Xela. Representing more than 350 grassroots organizations and at least fifteen different indigenous languages spoken in Mexico and Central America, the group gathered for four days to analyze and discuss ways to ensure the continued biological and cultural diversity of indigenous communities and plan alternatives to development models being imposed in Mesoamerica.

"Diversity does not mean divisionism. It means recognizing that there are different ways of life, philosophies," said Rigoberto Quemé, a Quiche Maya and the first indigenous mayor of Quetzaltanango, during the inauguration of the event.

Other speakers noted that the fight against globalization and for diversity and autonomy was a struggle without frontiers. Thus, the meeting of representatives of more than fifteen nations was an attempt to globalize socially and to design concrete proposals and actions including alternatives to PPP. At least 75 percent of those attending the forum were indigenous and campesinos named by their communities and organizations to speak for and about their needs, concerns, and problems in face of this threat and others.

"We are seated here for our people," began a Guatemala Maya, explaining that his purpose in coming to the forum was to bring back alternatives to PPP that would help solve growing crises in subsistence, especially among those dependent on coffee. For many, the most serious threat came from the imposition of a capitalist economic model through free-trade treaties such as NAFTA that legalized the right of transnational businesses to expropriate human and natural resources. Rather than a system of exchange where the goal is to gain the highest possible profit at the expense of human participants, they sought a model based on the relationship between the producer and the consumer, where the final objective is to improve the conditions of life for all.

"We need to change the concept of economy, not just in terms of money, but revalue the economy with other goals, that of the common good. We need to include these ideas in the education of our children."

For many, a key concept was the revaluation of culture, in language, worldview, and way of life. A growing threat to the basis of that way of life in Mesoamerica has been the introduction of hybrid corn imported from the United States both as seed corn and for food. In 2001, six million of the twenty-seven million tons of corn consumed by Mexicans was purchased from the United States. Since one of the conditions for investment in Mesoamerica set by international lenders is the removal of farm subsidies, corn produced by Mexican farmers is now too expensive for its own consumers to afford. In contrast, and in contradiction to its external policies, the United States continues to finance its agricultural industry, offering massive subsidies and artificially manipulating the market in its own favor. Mexicans are forced to buy imported corn, much of which is the result of genetic engineering. Using this corn reduces the diversity of genetic strains by contaminating native seed and increases the burden on producer/consumers since it can't be used for seed.

In relation to this, groups proposed the creation of native seed banks and registries on the regional level. They introduced proposals to halt "biopiracy" and regulate bioprospecting as international projects moved through their communities gathering plants and plant knowledge to be developed into pharmaceuticals in Europe and the United States. These gatherings and their offspring, the rural meetings that even PRIista Miguel attended in Santa Elena, show that campesinos remain unconvinced that highways and airports will do anything more than be catheters that suction out the wealth, without spilling a drop.

The Biological and Cultural Diversity Week in Xela ended and was followed almost immediately by the announcement of another huge gathering, this one called the Encuentro Por la Paz, held in early July in San Cristóbal de las Casas. The San Cristóbal Encuentro refocused waning international attention on civil society in action as it had been during the years immediately following the rebellion. The Encuentro was initiated and inaugurated by retired bishop Samuel Ruíz, who, like so many of us who keep returning to this place, admits that he was born here, in Chiapas, in the understanding of the struggle, in the accompaniment. The ex-bishop knows how to read the situation here better than any other observer. As international solidarity dwindled and civil society squabbled, as it often does in San Cristóbal, he was well aware of the fact that it was time for a periodic rite of intensification that would bring together the entire larger community to revalue, reinforce, and remember the things that bound them together in solidarity in the first place. Time for rebirth.

In the past, it has been the Zapatistas themselves who have called us to prayer, called us together to reflect and to act. After their long characteristic silences, they have hosted meetings, referendums, *consultas*, and *marchas* as refocusing activities that kept the interest and the support of the fickle alive. But this has been a long winter, when little news has passed from the strongholds of the Zapatista leadership to those in the support organizations here in Chiapas and the rest of the world. The official government amnesia that seemed to conveniently erase the entire conflict from recent memory also seemed to prevail in the Mexican NGOs. Mentioning the Zapatistas was a little like calling attention to a black-sheep relation, so the hallowed letters were not invoked. It made the various meetings I attended difficult: how do you explain what's going on in the community you accompany without mentioning the organizational structure and social programs that come to them from their continuing relationship with the folks living in that big cave behind Guadalupe Tepeyac?

In the long quiet months, my friends in the United States often inquired whether the silence extended to the communities themselves, whether they too had been left out in the cold. But we knew that the unfailing work of the autonomous municipalities bound those in the countryside to the movement that they have supported since the early 1990s. In Cerro Verde and Tulan, Alma and Carmen, Ramon, and the others continued to attend workshops and trainings as they have done for years in the areas of primary education, basic health care, and herbal knowledge. On the local level, they struggled to come up with a plan for countering the arrival of *transgénicos*, for conserving native seeds in low-budget seed banks. They sought to define acceptable compromises that would allow them to have vaccines for childhood diseases for the children who have gone without for the bulk of the overt war. Their leaders, like Camila and Martín, traveled across the state to investigate land-based disputes, expulsions, and reports of increased paramilitary and military activity. They returned to type up summary *denuncios*, explaining their right to act under the provisions of legal indigenous autonomy granted them by international law and the San Andrés Accords. In their isolated headquarters, wind-driven rain seeped through the slits between the boards of the office walls to dampen the workings of the municipal computer. It slowed to complete inutility, but *ni modo*, the electricity itself has failed, the single overloaded line gone as a failing branch shuts down the entire region.

The sky above San Cristóbal de las Casas cleared, and a distinct crescent moon rested against the cobalt blackness, with Venus right below it, the only point of light. It could have been Christmas, the star pointing definitively at the place where a contemporary Jesus might be found. The scene was so striking that one had to be really attentive to see the flashes of lightning in the background, momentary signals of greater turmoil in the *altos*, in the distance, in the communities. The night was much like Chiapas these days, where tranquillity seemed to prevail over the city and the tourists strolled in the plaza, where the faded graffiti's reminded them that ELZN was once something to support.

Isa had arrived back in the city, working to finalize plans for the Horizonte Program student visits to Cerro Verde and Tulan scheduled for January 2003. In Cerro, family meetings arrived at the consensus that Marta and Marisa, aged nine and ten, could accompany us from Cerro Verde to San Cristóbal, but with several cautions. Just two days before, Marta fainted during a graduation party at her Aunt Barbara's house, where her uncle still represented the opposite side of the conflict. It was one of the first mixed events that the children were allowed to attend, representing a normalizing of relations between the resistance side of the *ejido* and those still sucking at the tit of the *mal gobierno*. As community nurse, Ana pronounced that Marta still suffered the effects of the war, that she was catapulted back into remembering that it was these men, in their paramilitary hats, who had accompanied the blue meanies and the army as they destroyed the headquarters of the *autónomo* in 1998, wrecked the clinic and the schools, looted the offices, and arrested the men, including her Uncle Davíd.

Who knows the roots of Marta's inquietude? Is she made uneasy by the current presence of the *autónomo* offices in her sister's house? Does she, with the instinct of the innocents, fail to trust the new relationships in the larger community? If she does, then she is no less skeptical than much of civil society, which in the past weeks has come together in several locations to plan, question, and denounce the attitude and objectives of the Fox government. It is, indeed, a foxy government, allowing enough space for freedom of movement around the state by foreigners, retiring the army just behind the line of trees where there were once checkpoints, and babbling on publicly about the incredible improvements in the situation in Chiapas.

Where does the struggle continue, where do the faithful seek to look for balance? In the tiny autonomous school rooms, where junior high–aged boys analyze government documents concerning PPP? In the community assemblies, where the remaining members of the resistance communities vote to find some compromise that will allow them to have electricity? In the larger *autónomo* meetings, where women lead the committees to develop policy that will safeguard corn, their root of life? In the *Aguascalientes*, where representatives of groups try to design autochthonous development programs that will result in a viable countryside, not the sale of communal land, employment in factories, or migration to the United States?

The struggle continues in the minds and hearts of children raised in resistance like Marta and Marisa. During their first visit to the city, they played for hours in the running hot and cold water of our urban bathroom. We walked carefully to the market, holding hands as we dodged taxis and *colectivos*, trucks hawking *agua pura* and cylinders of gas. Finally, they dutifully compared life in the city to life in the country.

"In the city, there's so much more fruit and flowers, there's a market," said Marta.

And in the country?

"There's no market."

"So what is needed?"

"We need to set up our own markets!"

They talked about the lack of freedom in the city, where to leave the confines of the house means that you must be accompanied by an adult. The lack of a beautiful river. The availability of hot water. The need for cash in order to have food, a logic different from that in the country, where money is a means of exchange but not the only one.

The sight of preteens involved in economic and social reflection was something we had grown accustomed to experiencing. Girls and boys are included in shaping the development initiatives they will inherit.

What do we all really need to live, we considered, trying to separate out wants from needs. The exercise was as much for our understanding as for the girls, a reflection session that helped clarify what is really meant by self-sufficiency in the communities, what constitutes a solidarity economy.

"We need food, shelter, education, and firewood," said Marisa. Annotated, we need land to have both food and firewood. Her response was much like the *compañero* from Huitiupán, who had explained this to skeptical foreigners and Ladinos at the Encuentro in Xela.

We looked at a red EZLN bandanna, and together we read the Zapatista list of necessities: justice, food, education, health, liberty, shelter, democracy, equality, independence, peace, land.

Marisa had been drawing quietly, a multicolored picture of their autonomous school. "I should put the name on the roof," she said.

"No," countered Marta. "Just put EZLN."

Whatever is going on in the city, in the nation, in the communities, the children haven't forgotten where their ideals and ideology were refined. For the children brought up in "The Organization" and their families, this goes beyond an emotional commitment to an ideological position. In their economic and social behavior, they try to live their ideology. Resistance to programs that focus on monocropping at the expense of subsistence, as proposed in PPP, makes sense in the global marketplace, where flexibility and diversification provide the entrepreneurial edge. For them, cooperation and universal participation become the economy of scale, self-sufficiency a buffer against world market fluctuations. The failure of the coffee economy has made this lesson painfully clear, and in Cerro Verde families were planting experimental plots, ripping out coffee and replacing it with food, as they sought marketable alternatives. As jungle colonists, they have used a process of trial and error in the context of trying to find a balance between respect for their natural resources and keeping the family alive. Maximizing production may be one kind of efficiency, derived from an ideology where increasing profits is the primary outcome. But if long-term survival is the goal, then sustaining the environment at the expense of production is also efficient.

The summer flowed on, and August approached, another Zapatista anniversary date looming on the horizon. Luz confided that the silence was coming to an end. They would be traveling soon, local committees summoned to Realidad to prepare. Ramón and the children were practicing songs, making up new *bombas* and poems.

"Va a ver mucho movimiento," Luz whispered.

Aurelio was with the kids in front of the school, practicing martial arts.

My field season was over, and it was time to return to the United States to recruit students for Horizonte and begin the endless round of cookie sales and other fund-raisers.

Natalia gave her *abuelita* a big *abrazo*, and we all hugged good-bye.

Luz winked. "Maybe we'll see you in San Cristóbal before you go," she said conspiratorially.

Martín and Camila were nowhere in sight. Perhaps she was right.

Back in the Altos, the NGOs were whispering. "They're coming! The silence will be broken."

Excited, I stayed two extra days. In the third week of August, 18,000 people crowded the plaza to protest PPP, members of the autochthonous church group El Pueblo Creyente. But, at least formally, the Zapatistas never came. The work wasn't finished yet, the reorganization.

Poco á poco. Little by little. In their own good time.

NOTE

1. ALCA is Area de Libre Comercio de las Américas, the free-trade zone of the Americas, and is the latest incarnation of overarching plans for hemispheric "free trade" relationships.

Part 4

HORIZONS OF HOPE

CHAPTER 13

Acompañar Obediciendo

THE PULSING RHYTHMS OF TAPED *norteña* music cut through the damp night, topped in volume only by the constant laughter of twelve American women and their Zapatista hosts. The fiesta and dance were to honor the solidarity and sharing between the people of Cerro Verde and the students of our 2003 Wake Forest University/University of Texas–El Paso (UTEP) Horizonte Service-Learning Program. It was mid-January, and the coffee harvest had begun, a halfhearted effort thwarted by soft curtains of *selva* rain and potential prices that made picking the crop futile. Two low piles lay pushed back along the sides of the cement space in front of one of the houses, enough to make up a few *bultos*, fifty-four-kilo sacks that sold for 200 pesos. As the music came to a momentary pause, we looked up to notice a small pack of uninvited guests, all young men, their hair slicked back and secured by rolled bandannas, Los Angeles style.

"Who are those people?" Duncan asked Ana, as they finished a bouncing two-step.

"They come from across the river. They heard the fiesta. They are the sons of our enemies. We welcome them."

"And it's all right?"

"Of course," Ana said. "We welcome anyone who wants to join us. And maybe it will make them reflect on what they've done to us in the past; trying to expel us from the *ejido*; intimidate us with their armed patrols. Maybe they'll think twice about cutting off our electricity again, if it cuts off the music and their opportunity to get close to the gringas."

Ana's thumbnail analysis of what a visit from PRIista youth could mean in the big picture was second nature to her, an extension of the way she had been raised from toddlerhood, to reflect, analyze, act. Duncan sidled over to our students and quietly encouraged them to ask the young men to dance. It was a service program after all, and this was yet another definition of service. Jeanne watched as the young women strode across the coffee-drying patio turned dance floor to invite the other side into the fiesta. In Cerro Verde, no opportunity was missed to turn the personal into the political. Everything functioned on multiple levels. We marveled at the path the community had traveled in just over nine years, from a declaration of resistance to everyday acts of reconciliation. It has been a road riddled with topes—fear, hunger, imprisonment, outright attacks. If they learned to turn the other cheek as part of their religious reflection, their evolving political astuteness taught them to use that other cheek to make a practical statement. For the Zapatistas, every experience provided both a teachable moment and the possibility of service, something we were learning alongside our students, with each day of our program stay.

Jeanne had arrived before the rest of the group, making her way out to the jungle to be sure that all was in place for the upcoming visit.

"When was it exactly that you planned to arrive here with the students?" asked Don Francisco in Tulan, his voice nonchalant, noncommittal.

"We leave San Cristóbal on the second; arrive with you here on the third," she answered.

Francisco nodded. "Good. Good. That works. Then we will all be here, ready for you."

She looked hard at Francisco and caught the twinkle in his dark and serious eyes.

"Va a ver mucho movimiento," said Luz, later that day in Cerro Verde. This time she spoke with excited confidence, not the wistful anticipation of the last time she repeated that phrase. Something was in the air.

Martín, too, was inquiring but vague. "Do me a favor, Juanita," he said. "Don't leave San Cristóbal until the third. Better yet, I'll call you at the apartment."

Jeanne squinted skeptically at Martín. Camila was beside him, and she was pregnant and bursting, soon to give birth to her first child with Martín. But it was her eyes that were truly expectant, filled with anticipation and joy, a feeling that was palpable in winter air, first in Tulan, now in Cerro Verde.

"How many will there be?" Jeanne asked simply.

Camila smiled broadly. "Muchas, Doña Juanita. Muchas."

In the end, 22,000 Zapatistas, masked and carrying staffs and machetes, arrived in San Cristóbal on January 1, 2003, the ninth anniversary of the rebellion. Martín estimated that one in eight was allowed to go. Of the other 140,000 official members of the Ejercito Zapatista de Liberación Nacional, it was the children and the elders who stayed behind. Rodrigo was sad, falling in the later category for the first time in his life. But Dominga walked with the women, riding all night in one the huge trucks, then marching into the city, wearing her *paliacate* over her face.

We waited for them all day in the Plaza de la Paz, in front of the Cathedral. The Zapatista silence had been broken fitfully in the months between August 2002 and December but with little of substance. Just enough to say here we are, give us time to work, but not enough to get the Zapatistas on the growing Ashcroft terror list. Martín had been concerned that the Fox government would respond badly to the Zapatista reappearance, hence his warning to wait until the third to see what occurred. But San Cristóbal was eerily empty of any representatives of official Chiapas, federal, state, or local. As the day progressed, the San Cristóbal *coletos* retreated into their houses, closing the heavy wooden shutters over their barred windows. But for those who had accompanied the Organization throughout the years and for whom the silence had held a difficult loneliness, it was truly a new year. Our students experienced the excitement:

We had been in San Cristóbal, Chiapas for two days now, waiting for the go ahead from the Zapatista communities to come to their villages. Rumor had it, that something big was going to happen. Early that morning we were informed what that something was. The Zapatistas were coming to town in what would mark their first public gathering since March 2001.

Nobody knew at what time they were going to arrive so we took to the streets to see what was going on. In the main plaza, a podium complete with Zapatista paintings was set up in anticipation of the night events that would follow, along with other extraordinary, politically focused paintings strung to scaffolding outside of the church. Even with these additions to the Plaza, something was missing. The government's military that usually patrolled the corners of the streets and plaza were nowhere to be seen, an observation worth noting.

With nothing left to do, we bought a hacky sack from one of the street vendors with the intent of providing entertainment for ourselves. Unknowingly, we ended up sharing this entertainment with a rather large group who had gathered in a circle around us. This kept us and them busy for a good majority of the day.

It wasn't until after dinner that the Zapatistas actually made it to town and wouldn't be for another two hours until all that could physically fit, filed into the plaza. As the group came closer, we could hear the overwhelming sound of thousands of machetes, unyieldingly clanging together, sounding out the cries of their cause. "Clink, clink, clink . . ." Signs, protesting global terrorism and governments were held overhead. Trucks rolled in with loudspeakers. Men with ski masks, women, and children, faces covered with red Zapatista bandanas, paraded on foot. We moved back and forth from our pillar in the Plaza to one of the side streets watching this incredible demonstration as they came in.

Over twenty thousand Zapatista men and women gathered for this event, sacrificing days of work. With the help of our friends from El Paso, we were fortunate enough to understand the Spanish words that described the Zapatistas' commitment to their cause, and also what and who they were fighting for.

The sound of the machetes raised goose bumps on our arms that had nothing to do with the chill of the night. We were surrounded by banners proclaiming global sentiments: "No al terrorismo de Bush y Bin Laden." Jeanne was particularly taken by one that declared, "Long live the disobedient Italians!" We stood at attention in this city, abandoned by officialdom, in the now familiar blind eye of the Fox, while the Zapatistas sang first the Mexican national anthem and then their own lyrical cumbia hymn. As midnight tolled, bonfires blazed in the plaza, and then, as quickly as they had come, they were gone. In the early hours of the morning, as we took one last pass through the rapidly emptying plaza, we heard a soft voice call out, "Doña Juanita, Don Lucas!" It was Ramón and Alejandro, their *paliacates* pulled down and revealing tired but ecstatic faces. We hugged.

"See you tomorrow," Duncan said. We did.

LEARNING HOW TO HELP

It was the best service-learning program ever. Our mixed group of eleven students was getting along famously. We'd just completed a three-day stay in Tulan, and though the persistent winter rains dictated that one of our group's service activities was the continuous removal of mud from the cement patio in front of the compound's houses and health clinic, the climate did not dampen the enthusiasm of both our students and our host community. True to the theme, when we left, there wasn't a dry eye to be found. Now, we were downriver a few kilometers at Cerro Verde, and there was a short break in the rain. As we cleaned up from our usual breakfast of black beans, tortillas, and eggs,

Zapatistas enter San Cristobal, January 1, 2003

Isa, one of the two student assistants helping to run the program, met us, her face somber.

"We need to talk," she announced.

"Sure," we answered. "What's up?"

"Not here. We all need to talk. The group is waiting for you in the school."

We were staying in the Cerro Verde autonomous school, a product of our previous field programs. As we entered, we saw that the students were arranged in a circle on the wall-to-wall sleeping bags that lined the floor and on the hammocks that swung overhead. From the looks of it, there was mutiny afoot.

"We've been here four days now, and we're having a really wonderful time," began the group's spokesperson. "We enjoyed dancing and singing with the folks up in Tulan, and playing with the kids, and making tortillas, and yeah, well, we picked a few baskets of coffee. But . . ." She paused, and her tone grew ominous. "We aren't doing any service."

We looked at each other in stunned silence. Prior to departure and in our pre-jungle orientation, we'd had spent long hours discussing the nature of the service experience. This program was a result of years of preparation, the spin-off from our previous program, designed in collaboration and consultation with the Zapatista communities and their leadership. We were dancing and singing and playing with the children, making tortillas, and picking coffee. But they still thought that they weren't doing any service. It was back-to-basics time and a revisit to the theory, method, and practice developed with our community partners to guide anthropologically focused service learning in Chiapas.

The main thrust of Horizonte was to provide a community-authored service-learning experience in the Zapatista jungle communities of Cerro Verde and Tulan. In its focus, service learning meshed well with our goals as applied cultural anthropologists, following a venerable principle derived from 1950s Action Anthropology to learn and help in equal measures. But because Zapatista governance is guided by the precept *mandar obediciendo*, to lead by obeying, we were learning that to be involved with "helping" autonomous communities meant that we must accompany them on the basis of their strictures, or *acompañar obediciendo*. Like the Maya Summer Study Program, Horizonte was designed with the following goals in mind:

- Provide long-term accompaniment to communities in their process of autonomous and autochthonous development
- Understand service as a symmetrical, two-way process of learning, giving, and receiving
- Use our research skills and opportunities to assist communities in meeting their self-identified needs

- Learn about coffee production and assist in marketing
- Learn about plants and herbs from midwives and healers
- Examine the dynamics of change and choice in contemporary Mesoamerica
- Learn/improve Spanish
- Explore links to the broader Latino community in the United States
- Understand our own cultural, class, and ethnic biases
- Use what we have learned through service as a way of informing our own communities and as a basis for future fund-raising efforts

A unique characteristic of both programs remained the relationship between Wake Forest University, a private, historically homogeneous institution, and UTEP, a public university with a predominantly Mexican and Mexican American student body. As part of the program, students had the opportunity to share ideas and information with those whose life experience differed greatly from their own. For both groups, the learning process went beyond their experience in Chiapas and forced them to confront their own unidentified biases.

Student directors Teresa Sotelo and Liz "Isa" Story represented the polar extremes of life experience. Tere was a working-class firebrand Chicana and Isa a well-to-do and sometimes apologetic member of a privileged and conservative family. Veterans of the longer Maya Program each spent an additional period setting up Horizonte and doing research in Chiapas. Their adversarial relationship during the first program encapsulated what could be expected as the extremes of interclass, interethnic conflict. Of the students, they had the most growing to do. Their decision to accept the challenge to work together to develop the Horizonte initiative on their respective campuses was testimony to the life-changing effects of experiential learning.

As program directors, we negotiated these student conflicts during the Maya Program, developing a process for mediation as we went along. For Horizonte, the task passed to the two student leaders. Isa admits that she was more than slightly apprehensive about our decision to ask the two of them to be group leaders for Horizonte. She pointed out the irony of the situation, trying her best to make light of what she thought could turn to disaster. Building on the lessons learned from their own experiences, she and Tere worked with their student groups prior to departure to prepare them for possible conflict. But their December 29 meeting in the Mexico City airport was a refreshing new start. Their personal conflict and the nature of the whole Chiapas experience had made a profound impression on their lives in the intervening year. Perhaps following these cues, members of Horizonte formed immediate and strong bonds with each other, crosscutting all class and ethnic difference. It was these same intergroup bonds that turned the students into a solid front as they challenged our model of service and learning. As Isa recalls,

> Embarking upon this service-learning project I prepared myself to deal with potential problems: bickering between Wake and UTEP students (our group was entirely female), logistical complaints about food, sleeping, showers etc. Surprisingly, this was not the case, but I had many students, from both universities, approaching me with concerns arising from misconceptions about service. Even after our preparation, I found myself in the position of explaining what we were doing in these communities. Why were we there? So I thought to myself, "We are talking with them, picking coffee, playing sports, dancing, learning to make tortillas, playing the guitar, and building gardens . . . what does all of this mean?"
>
> But I knew that our "service" was so much more than these visible signs of our presence. Two years prior during the Maya Program I was first exposed to the idea of hermanamiento, which I understand as a brother/sisterhood between a community and an "outside" support such as ourselves. By definition, it is symmetrical and long lasting. This was the paradigm on which I was basing my notions of service. And I could see that many of the group members still perceived service as a tangible structure left behind as a testament to the "good will" of the group. We were clearly not building any structures. So what was the purpose of this trip? I gave the questioning few a brief account of the process that occurs in these communities. Schools and clinics do not get built because we want to build them. Projects occur according to their needs and in their time. If we came during coffee harvest, we picked coffee. At this particular point in time, the communities needed our presence. In a material world where humans cannot live without thinking of essential necessities, it is a rare and beautiful occurrence to appreciate physical accompaniment. Our presence represented solidarity and the earnest concern for community survival.

In 2001, the students had been forced to acknowledge that the community could do far better job building a school than we could ever do. What they needed from us was to build a model for future programs and relationships.

Horizonte students had been "introduced" to the Zapatistas before departure, through film, books, and lecture, but these materials could only superficially prepare them for their stay in the jungle. Then, while still on the "safe" touristy and urban turf of San Cristóbal, we were "invaded" by the people we would later go live with as 22,000 Zapatistas marched. We had an outsider's encounter with them as masked and anonymous crowds as they took over the colonial streets and plaza. Had this been our only encounter with the rebel organization, the students would have come away with the image of a well-disciplined but angry mob. Instead, in retrospect, the juxtaposed contrasts served to demarcate the difference between public social "performance" and everyday life. And if we had not seen them march, no amount of talking and meetings could have conveyed to us the importance they placed on remaining integrated in the larger Zapatista organization. Luckily, we had two days in which to reflect on all this before moving to the contrasting experience of living and working with them in their communities, and talk we did. With Isa and Tere, we'd done everything in our power to alert the Horizonte group to the ephemeral Zapatista definitions of service. Why, then, were they still so mired in the American model of helping?

What they still needed to learn was that what constituted service for people in the autonomous regions of Chiapas contrasted dramatically with their expectations for service work. Thus, a large focus of the program became learning how to serve in that context. Regardless, students still imagined service to be manual labor, like building houses, planting the fields, and picking coffee. In contrast, our Zapatista hosts defined manual labor projects such as these not as service but as learning. In their preparation for Horizonte, they worked together to construct culturally appropriate opportunities that would help us be able to help them. In Cerro Verde, they planned an excursion to the milpa so that we could have some sense of accomplishment while they taught us about their lives. After the students had thrown their backs into the exercise for about an hour, a twelve-year-old approached us to ask if they understood yet what planting was like. We said we thought they did; he immediately called to the others, and we packed our machetes and returned to the enclave. The time it took for them to "handle" us exceeded the value of any tangible service we could provide for them.

College students and Tulaneros relax together

In Tulan, we picked coffee and husked corn, making only a tiny dent in the actual work of the community. But we did a lot of singing and went with the children to the river to bathe, and they went with us to visit a cave. Perhaps the greatest contribution was that of Sharon, a registered nurse who was part of Horizonte. Her special skills were important in Tulan, where the small free clinic was doing a land office business for Zapatistas and PRIistas alike. The clinic was Francisco's and Carmen's own community service to those who lived around them. Sharon spent many hours exchanging information and experience and doing joint medical consultations. She was amazed to see how Carmen integrated the information she gave into a larger framework of low-tech, traditional healing. Sharon learned how to triage without technology. Carmen learned some new techniques as well, but what seemed most valuable to her was the social capital she gained when her patients were treated to a consultation that involved both healers, each obviously valuing the other's knowledge.

One morning in Cerro Verde, our students gathered with the Escuela Autónoma kids and did the English lessons Luz so dreaded. Joined eventually by most of the adults, they practiced basic phrases and did elementary school singing rhymes.

"Head, shoulders, knees and toes, knees and toes," sang the children, their accents almost perfect.

Singing was an important part of our sharing. When community members put on plays and sang to us, we were expected to reciprocate in kind. Make

College students help plant garden in Cerro Verde

sure you know something to sing. The Horizonte women did a rousing and emotional rendition of the song "Lean on Me," also translating it into Zapatista terms: Acompáñame. We all cried together.

In our stay in the Chayote Zapatista communities, our most important contribution was our very presence and sociability. To see an ethnically integrated group interacting equitably with each other and coming to understand their struggle and perspective provided a much needed service for them, especially in the midst of a sea of opponents, neighbors, paramilitaries, soldiers, hostile officials, and an enemy government. Our hosts define service as the visit itself. In addition, we lose sight of the fact that they know our culture only by reputation. Our service is to bring students who show by their own behaviors that there is hope across the border. In turn, the students provide the service of internalizing what they are doing, socializing within the community, playing with the children and the elderly, eating their foods with them, participating in their expressive activities, and generally giving their isolated lives the temporary feel of an international festival. In a note sent to the students in August 2003, Ramón reminded us of this:

> We wish to give you a thousand thanks for the school supplies you donated, which will help us a lot and are serving to help us move forward with autonomous education. All the children are very grateful for the help you gave us, but also they really miss your games and jokes . . . for us this is a gift, because the children need to enjoy themselves, because for them the work, the problems, the obstructions that their parents suffer, they feel, and they become desperate, up to becoming sick. For this, your presence is very important, and at the same time, very festive.

In Tulan, the joyous sound of shared laughter was often juxtaposed against the serious sound of reflection. We joined in a Sunday morning service where Francisco asked the students to contemplate and comment on the day's gospel: what did it really mean to love your neighbor as yourself? After, when Tere talked of writing about the theoretical implications of her experience in Chiapas, Francisco was firm.

"You cannot speak about theory until you have proved it in the practice."

For communities such as Cerro Verde and Tulan that are trying to subsist in a globalizing world, labor and work knowledge are abundant. Other resources, like usable supplies, were far scarcer, and our program helped provide these. Two of the women, Alena and Tracy, were soccer players. The team was changing from Adidas to Nike, so they commandeered enough jackets, jerseys, and shoes to outfit the *autónomo* team. But part of the service was also money. There were just so many sets of crayons, notebooks, and tubes of antibiotic cream that could be carried in luggage. Our Horizonte fund-raisers had in-

Students and teachers work in Cerro Verde school

cluded the venerable cookie sales. We'd also sold Escuela Autónoma embroideries and candy corn bearing information about genetically engineered seed. Isa applied for and received a project grant through Wake that provided a reasonable amount of cash. We were proud to pass the money, going through official channels, with a substantial cut for general *municipio* needs, following the rules we'd learned during our previous trips. But the money issue was touchy. As we learned the rules, we tried to live by them. But we hoped that some of our past involvements had been "grandfathered" in. How many times had Martín made oblique reference to the still-unfinished coffee project, wondering out loud where the money came from, arriving as it did before the *municipio* resurfaced in the immediate lives of Cerro Verde. What seemed safe were production projects, and this the students agreed to enter into. They would work with Tulan to develop a business plan for marketing their honey in the United States. Contracting for an initial delivery of 650 pounds of jungle pollen honey, Horizonte members obtained a small grant to cover shipping. Both the anthropologists and the autonomous municipality watched this experiment carefully. We sought to document the process of Zapatistas engaging with the market as they tried to do capitalism with socialist goals; they waited to see if the experiment could be a viable model for marketing honey from the entire region.

As the program came to its conclusion, writing was also on our mind. The proposal for *Uprising of Hope* had been with the Zapatistas for over six months. We were anxious to get on with the project. We already had a publisher. Suppose the *municipio*, acting on the wishes of its constituents, did not agree? There was other news as well. That strange office down in the basement of the World Bank was seriously considering the proposal for the regional vocational training school we'd developed with Martín the summer before. Would the new council of heads of autonomous municipalities accept it if it were funded?

The Horizonte women were still wrapped up in PRIista arms, dancing to the sounds of Los Tigres del Norte. We turned to see Camila beckoning to us and followed her into the house behind the Cerro kitchen.

Martín had been gone all day, finishing work in his milpa. Rebel leaders and their families still had to eat. As we entered the house's middle room and started to take seats in the small circle of chairs arranged in its center, Martín called to Duncan. In his hand, he had a small, plantain-leaf wrapped package.

"I was working in the milpa, and do you know, I found these slithering through my corn, first one, then the other."

He opened the package and placed the contents on the floor in the center of the circle. Two severed snake heads, one a little bigger than the other, stared at us from the floor.

"Embra y macho, no?" he said.

Female and male, they were *nauyacas*, pit vipers. This was the lethal snake of Duncan's long-past night of fear, swinging in a hammock somewhere near Nuevo Jerusalem, in the heart of the jungle.

"Nauyacas," he said.

Martín bent over and poked at the heads with a ballpoint pen. Ants crawled out of the fresh and bloody flesh. Duncan and Jeanne fell back on upstate New York learning.

"Salt," they said in unison. "You can cure them with salt."

Martín sat down and we followed suit, still looking at the snakes in the center of the circle. "Strange," he said. "They are on the move. All the burning and cutting. They are desplazados, moving deeper into the selva."

We thought about the monkeys that had been similarly displaced decades before and about the people of Chiapas still looking for land, moving deeper into the Montes Azules reserve.

Martín interrupted our reveries. "And so," he said. "About the book."

The room grew quiet.

We were all seated now, and in the silence we noticed a low peeping sound. Nestled in one corner of the room was a huge hen turkey. The peeping was coming from below her ample skirts. And in the other corner of the room, also making its own peeping sound, was the *municipio* computer. They'd finally moved it away from the outside wall. Jeanne thought quickly about the day she spent hunched over the monitor with Martín, reading instructions e-mailed to San Cristóbal from the Wake Forest tech guy at home. The screen was barely visible as they tried to defrag and scan the hard disk, suffering from too much humidity and the unseen fingers of curious children. They had, it seemed, succeeded.

"About the book, "Martín said again. He grinned. "Yes. We like it."

We smiled, broadly, happily, relieved.

Jeanne turned quickly to Duncan and whispered, "Is this a good time to bring up the Bank?"

Camila and Martín traded glances.

"What's up?" Martín asked in English.

Quickly, Jeanne outlined her relationship with the Bank renegades. It would be a coup, on both sides, if the Bank could see fit to give up total control of the grant and pass it to the *autónomos* without going through other hands, no indirects, no overhead. And it would be equally courageous if the council would accept it.

Martín thought for a moment.

"What can I give you to make this a reality," he asked?

"Information."

He turned to the computer and quickly inserted a disk, downloading the details, statistics, and accounts of a project they had with Spain, their only other *hermanamiento*.

We looked at each other; at the sputtering computer; at Martín, our multilingual jungle teacher; at the hen turkey with her brood of chicks; at Camila, pregnant and glowing; and at the circle with the two beheaded vipers in the middle. There was nothing else to say.

CHAPTER 14

Caracoles

Look, the stream is turning into a whirlpool there, and in its center the moon is shimmering its sinuous dance. A whirlpool . . . or a shell. They say here that the most ancient say that other, earlier ones said that the most first of these lands held the figure of the shell in high esteem. They say that they say that they said that the conch represents entering into the heart, that is what the very first ones with knowledge said. And they say that they say that they said that the conch also represents leaving the heart in order to walk the world, which is how the first ones called life. And more, they say that they say that they said that they called the collective with the shell, so that the word would go from one to the other and agreement would be reached. And they also say that they say that they said that the conch was help so that the ear could hear even the most distant word. That is what they say that they say that they said. I don't know. I am walking hand in hand with you, and I am showing you what my ears see and my eyes hear. And I see and hear a shell, the 'pu'y', as they say in their language here.

—Subcomandante Marcos (2003)

THE RAINS ENDED EARLY in the winter of 2003, even in the rain forest. In Tulan, they harvested the first crop of dark coffee flower honey, and then the blossoms ended. The bees were hungry, disconcerted at the lack of new flowers. Carmen, Micaela, and the other women sang to them, to keep them from deserting. It was a difficult winter in Tulan on other fronts as well, and we shared a particular hardship with them though separated by huge distances.

Early one morning, the phone beside Jeanne's bed rang, startling her from a deep sleep. She reached out from where she shivered beneath two down comforters and answered.

"This is Alena's mother," the voice on the other end said. "Do you know that all the girls who went to Chiapas are sick?" She carefully reviewed the symptoms: 103-degree fever, chills alternating with sweats, difficulty breathing.

"So am I," said Jeanne.

In El Paso, many of the students were also down. Between popping doses of ibuprofen to regulate his own fevers, Duncan wracked his brains to try to figure out what it was we had all done together. Could it have been something we ate? The only ones not sick were those who'd been away visiting Palenque during the final group dinner. But Isa wasn't sick, and she'd been there to eat.

What then? His mind wandered to a book written some years back by anthropologist Tim Knab. Called *A War of Witches*, the book told the tale of shamanistic journeys through a cave and into the realm of the underworld and a deadly disease spread by a fungus growing on the dung of bats. Histoplasmosis. We had visited a cave with the young folks from Tulan. Could this be it?

An e-mail to Knab produced both a diagnosis and a remedy, a wonder of the Internet age, as the shaman's realm pushed at the edges of tradition and practice. He suggested big cigars that would ward off evil while also changing the environment deep inside the lung, making it hard for organisms to grow. But he warned, whatever the symptoms and pathogens might be, the real cause was the theft of our souls by the little people, whom the Tzotzil Maya called *pukuj*. The only way to be truly cured was to meet up with them in our dreams and demand back our souls.

What had we done wrong? What cosmic error had we made? How could we confirm the diagnosis? Perhaps the spirit owners of the lands of resistance don't want to let go of all the pieces of our souls? Maybe, as Miguel would say, the owner has hold of us. Our two athletes, Alena and Tracy, were hospitalized as the doctors went bonkers doing tests trying to isolate the critters. Jeanne used a less excruciating tack. She e-mailed Ariana and asked her to go out to Tulan, where, it turned out, some of the Tulaneros were also terribly ill, the underworld pneumonia taking a serious and sorrowful hold.

That the Tulaneros were also ill was strange. They had entered the cave on numerous occasions, so why now? Doña Carmen was firm. The world was in a state of unrest, the Lords of Xibalba on the move. The Zapatistas were deep in difficult reflection. The United States was poised to invade Iraq. Like the sin eaters of Irish legend, we had presented ourselves as easy transport for evil, proxies for global pain. It was just not a good time to be at the mouth of the underworld. Carmen prescribed herbs, candles, and prayers. Ariana raced back to Comitán and sent an e-mail. Thousands of miles apart, we did the ceremonies simultaneously.

It was a long hard spring for all of us. The bat disease lingered, the jungle withered, and the Zapatistas demanded financial accountability from the communities we knew best, another facet of their continuing reorganization. Life was difficult in Ojo de Agua, too. Miguel's daughters were gone; his son Felipe turned into a sexist cowboy following his return from the United States.

We didn't return to Chiapas that spring, but Ariana worked with Francisco and Carmen to package the honey, and in late May they shipped it north. Alternating our visits, to make the experience more varied, Duncan returned to Chiapas alone in early June.

RETURN TO THE "EYE"

Duncan (June 2003): Here I was on my own again, as I had been when I started this work twenty-five years ago, when there was a quarter more jungle. Then, I had thought the new Chamula paradise would endure against the dialectic of Conquest, as an example, like Miguel's exemplary life, of how self-development can occur in a fragile ecology, a racist society, and with a defective government. What had I failed to see, back when it all seemed a development success? The shift to the Guatemalan workers? The loss of faith in the Catholics who could not attend them frequently or speak in Tzotzil? The Chamula-style Protestant sect, with the Bible in Tzotzil and quantities of hymns? The rise in income and quality of life, now followed by a collapse, a rural agricultural crisis, and downward mobility? I was grappling with what had seemed like a great example of self-development in Ojo, comparing it to these other Zapatista communities. Here I was, bouncing back and forth between the three and asking people why they joined and why others did not or left, what made those who did not join different, and what made Ojo with all of its promise so different.

As the *compas* answer these questions, most of the language to discuss this comes from religion, as political consciousness, as we have seen, appears a product of "reflection" in the context of everyday analysis of the relationship between God's world and this one. Religion finds its way into every conversation, for like political party, it serves as a social label to locate where people are in a total sense. The other subject that frequently frames discussion is health. Since there are still strong indigenous ties between these two, we should not find it strange in the conversations that they both come up.

I got the video camera rolling, taping answers, cutting off speakers at the waist. Alma, a Zapatista *promotor de salud*, is describing her grandfather, what a good man he was, with many talents, including the ability to serve as a midwife, and strong views against punishing children harshly. As his first granddaughter, she would go around with him a lot, and he would teach her the names of plants and how to find the trails. She told of how he decided to choose his day to die so as not to burden his children in his old age, after a nice meal, by jumping into the water he knew to be treacherous:[1]

"Before there were no people here. My father was the first, along with a man named Carlos Lopez, who was a good friend; they were the first to bring their cafetales down here by the river [from Orilla del Bosque]. There was no road then, just a path down the mountain, and to the hammock bridge, to go work on the other side, to Las Laureles. My grandfather died in 1980. My first husband died of a stomachache. In those days there was no ability to get to a doctor, no clinics, no medicine, just a few herbalists and massagers. And my husband, he did not like to go to the doctor. He said hospitals were places people went to die. He endured various months, but he died right here. Five years later, that is when I meet Davíd, he comes to work in the coffee, but he also went to the meetings of the church catequistas, and that is where we got together. Before, everyone here is Catholic, but now, there are Pentecostals, Presbyterians, 'Renovados,' and this is how they became more divided, with the sectos they got confused and went sprinkled across the landscape, now it is this family that serves as the core. Now it is pure singing . . . preaching, what they did not like about our religion was that we do a group reflection about the lives we are living, la realidad. They say this was not the word of God, it was just a talk, not from the text of the Bible, just talking, that is what they did not like. They study the Bible, and we no, we go into reflection, to reflect on what is the text saying, what is it saying to us, what is it talking about, and also how are we living in our community and region, what is this life about, what is happening, we speak a little about the government, and they do not like this.

"From this point they went dividing themselves up. One group I know, they divided into three, not long ago, with the Charismatic group, they divided even a house, they took it apart, in pieces. And they say they should not drink, but they do. And uglier things than that. They look for another woman, leaving their wives. This is what all the men did, not to judge them, just to say this is what happened. Their sect throws them out, then after a while they come back, get their pardon. It is ugly, *de por si*. Like children. No roots coming from their work, as if they are living in the air. They are looking up, but they do not see the other people here. The case of Natalia, from the Pentecostal pastor with the daughter-in-law, and then so they are not found out, they throw the infant away. *Dios mia*, who could want to throw away such a precious angel? So beautiful. And what is the purpose and meaning for us of this child? She has a destiny, a great purpose. What capacity, what abilities . . . this is what makes us reflect again and again. She has a purpose . . . like all of us. We hope one day they will see. As for right now, Dios mia.

"The problem is they do not see beyond the things close. Like the PRO-CEDE, they think it is great, private property, not you can sell it, get credit from the government. They are fooled by the pretty talk, and they just see what is given away, and looking down there they become bent over, *agachada*, and can't see the far horizon, the horizon of our hope, of what it is we dream of."

OJO, REVISITED

Hearing Alma's words echo, still wondering about the changes down river, I packed up the video camera and went to visit Ojo de Agua. The hammock bridge had a few more boards missing, holes in old and new and different places on the long, bouncy keyboard. Evidence of more decline in maintenance. Just because they now have that muddy roundabout road? The river is roiled chocolate milk, aching to get downstream into lazier lands, carrying the hefty sedimentations of deforestation, this jungle blood. Always attendant to the signs, the river bleeds the land, anywhere the middle, the green stories, has been removed. Vegetation—people, what are the ways to make people leave the land? I tossed about my thinking, knowing that however well or poorly the land here was managed, it was so much worse under private *latifundia*. Historically, this is self-evident; one always knows where the early fincas were, there are no trees.

The colonial legacy is well described by "cut and run, devil take the hind quarters," the way the Spanish crown administrators did in the former Aztec chocolate farms on the Soconuzco, in even less time than this by half (MacLeod 1973, 60–95). The irony of ecological damage in Chiapas, as Wasserstrom shows in his Altos critique of Collier's portrayal of Chamulas as promoting erosion (Wasserstrom 1983), is that it increases with *mestizaje*, or deculturation, and also with depth of history of *latifundia* or similar forms (in their case, the Church "hacienda" holdings, later abolished in the Reforms of Juarez). It is a "brown legend" that the indigenous are ignorant of their health of their native environments and cannot steward them. The problem comes with dislocation to other ecologies, such as occurred in the jungle colonies. Novel lands need different environmental knowledge (Nations 1970).

Jan De Vos's brilliant and beautiful *A Land for Planting Dreams* (2002) shows how under the right historical circumstances a jungle such as the Lacandon can be reduced by half in about fifty years. In such a colonizing process by the landless indigenous rain forest immigrant, De Vos's prognosis is not good, given the obvious demographic increases; the lack of local environmental knowledge of a new and fragile land; the internal, local conflicts; and the failure of Mexico to have a coherent and effective governmental plan to integrate people with landscape in a healthy, just, and equitable way. He waffles between hope, which is the discourse of Zapatismo, and pessimistic "realism," a discourse that speaks of intellectuality and ultimately Europe (personal communication, 2003).

Here on the far ridge above the slightly shabby *ejido*, I can see the deep vegetation, even some of the remaining big trees, out beyond the coffee. It is a still warming contrast with how badly things are upriver, a sense that this could be starter forest for reforesting at some point. Yet I know that such a stand of

God's milpa will call the heat, not the ritual heat of the elders but the attention of those seeking wood, global capital in the end. For it is not the jungle capitalism covets; it is the stuff in the middle—the trees, the water, the cultural and material resources—that can be marketed, as with ecotourism and archaeological sites and dams. It is no different than a generation ago, this battle between the campesino Indians and the ranchers and speculators, so what is different, why are they crumbling? Are we just at a low? Why is the resistance here less than before? What tapestry of ideology, economy, and moment can bring on such a change in trajectory, such a catastrophe in sustainability, threatening the end of paradise? I found I was swaying dangerously on the hanging bridge because someone, impatient with my drifting mind, was galloping my way. Whoa.

Crossing back on this bridge made the first time flash before my mind's eye again, with Inez, beyond the pasture, and it came to mind that the bridge was the line separating some basic divisions of here and there, like cattle and coffee, Ladino and Chamula, pasture and jungle, White Man's civilization and Chamula paradise, all the tropes and tribulations of the ethnographic eye that kept my categories clear. Now I crossed because I had taken a combi to Santa Elena and walked, just like the old days. Now the *Eye* before me was red with jungle blood, and I hung there trembling to see it. And over that bridge on cue came Felix, so as to illustrate the point, crossing the border between Santa Elena, the failed rebel county seat and its road to anywhere, and this island of nowhere, the annex. So taken was I with my thoughts and the view that his enthusiasm and bravado nearly tossed me in the water. I would not have survived it.

"Llegaste. Y las gringas? Andas solo?" You returned; and the gringas? Are you by yourself? Without time to answer, he went on, "Bad hour to come, no one is around."

He disappeared up the hill at a pace I once had mastered, leaving me to drift along the base of the rise, walking through the empty *ejido* streets of close-cut grass. Again the slightly shabby green, only a dozen sheep at work on the lawnscaping, my mind again engaged the significance of this new abandonment, the idea of their leaving. I thought of how the larger world is drawing off the autonomy these people once had, and their young people too, leaving children and the aged to fend without their most able members, who they raised or who were supposed to raise them. I thought of that huge social distortion of migration, how paradise could become a labor camp, raising the young, putting the elderly out to pasture, waiting in evangelical faith for the checks to come from El Norte or the cities. All hope now turned toward the global cities. The feeling of silence and abandonment of the settlement gave a chill of recognition, of what was at stake in this battle for autonomy in the jungle. Then a sigh as I begin to remember the date of the month, in the twelve-month calendar, where saints are commemorated.

And the song goes, "Vente cuatro de junio, dia de San Juaaaan . . ."

The tune always plays in my head regardless of where I am, when the date arrives, the twenty-fourth of June, San Juan's day, of the totem of the Chamulas, old San Shun. But I did not think that the determinedly Presbyterian Chamulas would be off to the titular fiesta in Pacayal. So it was a dark surprise to see the place next to deserted, no one I knew around, except lurking Felix. So they all went to Pacayal. That would have been a scene to see: how do non-drinking, nondancing Protestants celebrate San Juan? And why? Knowing what a growing roadside attraction Pacayal has become in the last years, I can only imagine the strange mixture of the sacred and the secular in that jungle three-day bash. Some fun for everyone under the San Juan sun, I guess. Does this reflect the still-operative power of an old ethnic and municipal identity, Chamula, before all other identities, now that there is a huge diaspora? Will this still be an ally in the struggle against pressures toward removal to Campeche, against falling apart as a functioning community? Could coffee prices and my faith rally?

My mind jumped back to where I was, in Sat Wo, the annex. People were home at Mingo's. Everyone was very warm and sweet, like I was some playful spirit who had emerged from the forest, for the amusement of the stay-homes. I let them play with my camera. There was a leanness here, always that sense of better times, of things overly worn, less laborers, more labor, attention to the corn. And always questions about how hard it is now to migrate: do I have any special knowledge of how to make a successful trip? The friendliness seemed tinged with disquiet. I'm anxious for Miguel's return; at least he will not ask about the road to the north.

I remembered how the women tried to get us to help with an alternative to their coyote, who bought embroidery from them, again struggling against a former individualism, in good times, to get something together now in the bad. So far, nothing had come of these organizational efforts, and the coyote still got his price. We are back to the model of Chiapas history, the structure of colonialism, people divided and then conquered, by one or another means, it seems. No one has approached me with a blouse yet, but the women behind Mingo must be thinking about the topic: cash in lean times.

MOL MIGUEL IS NOT WELL

Far down the street, a figure walks this way, a very slight limp and a labored pace. Seventy-something years of struggle, to have a home, to find prosperity, to raise up a family, to lead his people, to guide others when they go through the same struggle, and now hard times for this pioneer. Miguel and I exchange the old Tzotzil greetings, "Are you there?"

"I am here."

"Are you good?"

"I am good."

"Are you alive still?"

"Yes, I remain alive." And he is, still.

We sit on the portico. An elderly woman spins wool, using a gourd for a base and a stick spindle with a ceramic weight on it to make it go. Handfuls of wool become a stout yarn for another wool skirt like the one she and Miguel's wife both use, along with the signature Chamula blue blouse. The old clothes are not on Felix's two children; they have store-bought ones, flashy but not very sturdy. They each carry a new, light flesh-tone doll, from the day's fiesta. Felix's wife wears the black skirt but made of some synthetic, much cooler and cheaper, and a T-shirt. He talks to his children in Spanish, but everyone else is speaking Tzotzil.

Miguel has been seriously ill since the last visit, an old complaint that he has now suffered from for many years. Since the time of my study in 1979, the one dark spot in their self-development efforts at this *ejido* has always been in the area of health. In the old days, it was peddlers who sold coyote oil and other semimagical cure-alls. But these days, it is the huge government clinic, built after destroying the one run by Tierra y Libertad, which serves these people in the health arena. Miguel's right leg and ankle have suffered for years from some fungal infection, but this spring he became unable to walk. He went to the clinic, and they diagnosed him with enlarged prostate and suggested an operation, which he declined. I found him to have no bothersome prostate symptoms, and it seems even here in the United States there is debate about prostate operations for men over seventy unless things are dysfunctional—but most disturbing was that they never really addressed his systemic fungal problem.[2] For that, he was told, he would need a "specialist."

"A specialist with a saw," he half-jokes, and that was the end of his encounter with the world of government clinics.

But his father-in-law, Mingo, knew of a treatment that finally brought relief, using heated stones and heating up the legs as much as he could stand (*pulson*).

"The first time they were not so hot, with Domingo. The second time, with my wife helping, here, oh how the legs dripped sweat. That drove out most of the infection, although it does creep back from time to time in the form of itching. Today I feel good."

While he was laid up, he was not able to do the "*poda*," the work on the weeding and pruning of the coffee plants, nor was he able to plant his yearly milpa. Back in my dissertation, I spent some pages on the whole issue of "milpa logic," where it is part of a cultural ethic backed by sound defensive economics that Maya men should have their milpa, even if it did not suffice to feed a family all year. It expresses itself culturally in many domains of thought and action, but its material logic, a very old one, says, as the Zapatistas do today, that whatever else, grow most of your own food. A young man can raise enough for himself and a wife and toddlers on half a hectare, and for a robust family a hectare was usually sufficient, even on poorer soils. In the past, it was less. Mol Miguel says he normally would have his maize in.

"Let us see how it goes for the next year's planting, my milpa, my beans."

He does not tell me what has become of the coffee, I don't ask. It died, maybe. All those years of work.

"Now, those with some cattle still have some money, but that is declining too. Salvador, Mingo, Pedro Xilon, my father-in-law, they have quite a few."

"But the price has fallen?" I asked.

"Yes, but it is still a good business. Siempre. But they say it went down, five-six thousand for a big one, but now three thousand because the United States is sending lots of cows."[3]

Here I realize in horror that the ones who are making out best are the ones with a good-size herd of cattle. Cattle—the bane of the rain forest here and all through the tropics, in many areas the primary reason for rain forest destruction, the way the other half of the jungle died—cattle. Now Manuel spoke wistfully but keeping away any tone of envy. They had diversified in the worst way. Miguel goes on about my beloved nation's trade practices.

"Also maize, they say it will finish off our race of our maíz, what comes from there."

"This is the conflict," I reply. Silence.

"And what kind of corn is this?" he asks flatly.

I try to explain genetic modification and how it was already showing up in Mexican pollen and can change the seed, even make it not viable to plant without going to the store to buy new seed. He just said, "Ah bueno," like he always does when listening to another speak. How to really explain transgenics and what it may mean?

MAIZE LIFE

"The maize comes home in October, until December, before when the coffee was there, just December, January," Miguel begins, in storytelling mode. "But you have to check it, keep an eye on it. Like once, a few years ago, I went to see my milpa, and how beautiful, and almost coming out the ears. In ten days it will be ready the ears. I got delayed, I did not come by to check. Then when the hour of the desire hit me to eat my corn on the cob, I go and see the view where the milpa is, and it's all *clear*, what happened, the milpa, where is it, could it be the wind that knocked it down? How is this? I got closer, hell it was the Chitom [wild pigs] that swept it all away. If you can believe it, Lucas, three stalks of milpa still standing, from a quarter of a hectare. The pigs made off with the ears. Now if they are still there, you can get one, up to sixty kilos, with a bullet. But when they have cleaned out the milpa, no point in even looking for them. There are still herds in the monte, but they do not come down anymore like they used to."

I can tell he is enjoying telling tales that do not bring up the tough issues, the cattle, the coffee, the corn, the future. He has already dismissed my questions about his religious conversion, explaining on three counts that, first, they read the Bible in Tzotzil; second, no need for those priests, we have control; and third, the Bible does not preach Catholicism. Other than his spirited meetings, full of music, and saying a longer grace before eating, it seems the same. Back in my dissertation days, I had marveled at his clever way of mixing Catholic and Chamula traditional beliefs, the second in areas not covered by the first. Now it was no different. Miguel still believed that nature, the wilds, has its owners, some of whom can be made to respond to the presence of humans. This causes illness. So when I told him of our recent illness, from being inside a cave, and gave my Western medical model explanation, bat guano and fungal spores, Miguel answered, "It is the cave that is enchanted. It grabbed your soul. It is the owner of the cave who messed with you. They say there are some places we need not get close to. And who knows what illness we will be hit with, fever, I don't know what, but that cave has an owner."

Again, here was the tie with the past Maya view that all the important topography has an owner, although I do not think it would have a great reception with the mainstream Presbyterians. When Miguel talks about his agricultural life, with his milpa, that is where he is still most content, unlike the younger ones. He discusses the decline in fertility with concern, he laments his illness because he was not able to work, especially on his milpa. "El Café, ay, a loss, not a bean now, it is over. A year ago, still, but not now, does not make enough money to pay anyone. I was going to do the poda when I got sick."

When I asked him why Felix his son didn't help him with some milpa while he was ill, he told me Felix does not want to work.

"What are we if we do not have maíz,. Maíz, is what we eat. Si no tenemos maíz, con que podemos vivir? If we have no maize, by what means do we live? No."

"What does Felix say?" I asked.

"Nothing. He prefers to buy maize. But he is eating just by what he has worked, in El Norte. What happens if we do not have that work, and then we have no food? But if we have land to work, then we have food."

This, clearly, is the indigenous domestic productive system in hunkered-down stance and the political and economic basis of the sacred nature of corn. Miguel, no matter his advanced engagement with managerial labor relations, maintains a profoundly autonomous ethic of food security based in the milpa. For some of his many sons, the rigors of milpa have lost their attraction. This is in definite contrast with the Movement and even with the Cerro Verde *ejido* under the subtle influence of Movement philosophy.

PARADISE LOST

The price of coffee has fallen below the costs of production, so each year the coffee fields are fewer, as many die from neglect. The corn yields are still viable, if lower than before, as fallow cycles shorten and burns are reduced, but that is seen as food, not for commerce, where the price is also bad because of U.S. flooding of grain in the market along with cattle. The call of opportunities beyond the jungle strengthens as the hard work of jungle labors is of diminishing value. The period of 1980 to the early 1990s, when coffee peaked and then began to slide, were the boom years for jungle colonies. In Ojo, they were at about ten times the household wealth of their highland kin in poor Chamula. Now at two or three times the income of Altos villages, they see themselves as poor and in crisis, still land rich but with an almost solitary cash crop in market failure.

I saw this happen in Guatemala as well as they confronted declining rural economic viability after a prosperous period. Downward mobility is a double tragedy in that it suggests a disorganized and rapid growth and often misleads people into believing in a growth trajectory that cannot be sustained—one of the ideology of growth and development's cruel tricks. So here we have small-holding micro-*finqueros* in financial ruin, unable to even pick all the crop, just as the people had gotten used to their new standard of living, with the hope of even better. This combination one-two punch makes for the strongest migratory push, not simply poverty. It is like a whole nation full of monocrop gamblers who all lost it all. Even the younger Chamulas have difficulty returning to the field. Of the migrating son, Miguel says, "De por si, he has not liked the milpa work," as if to seek some way of naturalizing this transformation. Once freed from the milpa regimen, paying others to do it or buying corn, it is hard to go back as many have had to do. Surely this situation is widespread and has fueled political unrest as well as migration.

The sad irony of the message of diversification, as Miguel can see daily, is that the cattle option, once a very constrained and negatively viewed activity that only one or two men did, now has many followers and expanded pasture lands. So between cattle (environmentally destructive), milpa (low value, hard work, but edible), and coffee (dead?), the view of paradise seems clouded in a fog of dreams not sustainable. They are in a world way out of their control, in a society increasingly made up of individuals not able or willing to act in conjunction beyond the *ejido* obligations, which, if everyone is "PROCEDEd," they have as a memory only, a fiction. Chamula identity sometimes rejects Zapatismo because it is not reinforcing their chauvinistic ethnicity to the exclusion of others, with their pan-Indian, pan-Mexican, pan-people approach. In the end, the tragedy of this paradise at a loss is that Mol Miguel has to fend for himself again, in the cornfield and the coffee field, like an orphan.

A LAND TURNED INSIDE OUT

I caught the late afternoon micro for a quick run up to Tulan and joined a crowded cadre of Sunday afternoon riders. Two of these were Guatemalans, Maya refugees on the frontier, riding together. Both sat in the seat ahead of me, squirming with the heat of advanced intoxication, one of them swiftly swiveling his head around to look for any sign in my face, any hint of approbation, wavering. The floor plates groaned in some tectonic ballet of industrial decomposition—the road to Tulan had not been kind to this, its only bus. The second rider was more jovial, but the edge was there, the sense of difference, like I remembered from back on the coast. Suddenly he wheeled around, tilting radically and swooping close, "Vos no sos Español." You wouldn't be a Spaniard.

"No, Unitedstatesian," I responded amicably. Half the bus turned around to see, not so much that I could speak but that I would, and to these passengers—people out here try to circumvent the *borrachos* just in case they might become aggressive. Like the Ladino guy at the back of the bus, just look at him, and it's *pinche gringo jodido*, in between retching bouts out the window. He damned other nationalities as well, French, German, Italian, sending all to the same fecal location. But he is far gone, no real focus, no danger. The Guatemalan, in his late twenties, fit and tawny, sees my question in his fog and tells me that the Spaniards were the sons of the great whore, so he does not like them. "I am from Guatemala, and the Spaniards conquered us!"

Responding to the drama and volume of the statement, all the rest of the bus tunes in; the driver looks up into the cracked mirror. Big Eyes whips around and examines my face again. "We had a great place, we were a great people, and then, then they conquered us, they screwed us over. Now we are over here, not even in our house, this sad corner of the great nothing they left us!"

The heat is making the whole scene swim like an oily underwater dream and in the silence after his forceful declaration, making the baby cry across the aisle. We come around the bend in the road, pass by the old mill that belonged to the Tulaneros before the municipal destruction, and arrive at a little Eden in this sad corner of the great nothing, down below Doña Carmen's clinic.

This is the new best candidate for the title of Paradise, Francisco and Carmen's growing milpas, flocks of healthy poultry, herds of pigs, kept penned to keep them out of the young coffee. Because they already own their few hectares, they are not tempted by PROCEDE; they know about property taxes and the danger of borrowing against the land. They are both Zapatista and independent, and they live out each day with the ideology and goals of the Movement, but they are not constrained by the sometimes capricious tendencies of *ejido* decision making. They are individuals who live for the collective and sometimes critique their Zapatista brethren, calling them a collective that lives for the individual. It is a topsy-turvy world.

Even more so. With Tulan, we are in the process of recognizing the dream of an international market for their honey, but they are wary. How will the Movement, deep in reflection, view the notion of profit?

Downriver, in Cerro, the new PRIista *comisariado ejidal*, brother of Rodrigo, rules over the Cerro Verde ex-*ejido*. With the exception of the Zapatistas, it is completely PROCEDEd, and I remind him, as the Zapatista contingent often did, that they are technically no longer an *ejido*. *Pues, si,* but we have always governed ourselves this way, it is custom. But they are finding now that the government they supported has a truly *mal* side. To fight it, they must be organized, and it is the crazies in resistance who know how to do that.

Late one afternoon, just before leaving to return to the United States, the world twisted again, another politicoseismic shift. Alonso, the PRIista, ex-elected municipal representative, had come to speak to me hat in hand, with his wife Barbara and their eighteen-year-old son. The youth had just graduated from the Preparatoria and was interested in going to college in the United States. So here they were, calling shyly on Zapatista international contacts, to place their petition. Luz hovered purposefully, bringing coffee and *pan dulce*, the implications of the switch clearly evident in her proud stature. It was as Ana said, when the enemy came to dance with the gringas, a way to keep them reflecting on what they had done in the past so that it would never happen again, as all entered into an uncertain and difficult future.

THE ROSE-COLORED SHOE

Duncan returned home, and the springtime drought came to an end at about the same time that the Tulan honey crossed the border into El Paso, taking advantage of what we had begun to call ZAFTA, the Zapatista Autonomous Free Trade Agreement. As Tere turned her apartment into a full-time bottling plant, Jeanne returned to Chiapas for a short visit.

The Zapatista silence had been broken on January 1, but the content of spring communiqués issuing from the Sup remained equivocal and curious. Building on the promise to elevate the Movement's struggle to the global level, Marcos offered to act as a mediator between the Spanish and the Basques. International observers squabbled over the meaning of this harangue, a diversionary tactic keeping the Zapatistas in international eyes while they hurried to complete the real work.

Finally, in late July, the Zapatistas announced sweeping changes in their external and fiscal policy as part of the internal reorganization that Martín and the *municipios* had been working on for at least two years. It's not often that the recipients of development and humanitarian aid have the courage to speak out about the well-intentioned, uneven, and mission-directed assistance that arrives to "help" them. Spearheaded by the regional councils of municipalities such as Tierra y Libertad, they were striving to truly achieve a more equitable and effective development plan.

Since 1998, we'd watched the rebel organization work as an informal NGO, providing services and training to its constituents and support bases in education, health, production, commercialization, and tourism. For them, the changes meant another important step toward functioning autonomy. For us, it was a hint that the service and the learning we'd been involved in had been a true exchange. Now the real challenge was beginning.

As spokesperson for the autonomous councils, Marcos, sounding like his old, lyrical and satirical self, offered a lengthy critique of the provision of aid. He prefaced the five-part discussion with an excerpt of a communiqué he wrote just after the uprising, over nine years ago:

> We offer no reproach to those of civil society who reach our communities, we recognize they risk a lot to visit us and bring help to our people over here. It is not our poverty that hurts us, but rather seeing in others what they do not see in themselves, the same absence of liberty and democracy, the same lack of justice. . . .
>
> From what it is our people have received as a benefit of this war, I set aside an example of "humanitarian aid" for indigenous Chiapanecans, that arrived a few weeks ago: a rose colored, spike-heeled shoe, imported, size 6½, without its mate. I carry it with me always in my backpack, along with interviews, photo reports. . . . To these good, sincere people who sent us this rose colored, spike-heeled little shoe, imported, size 6½, without its mate, thinking that, as poor as we are, we will accept any little thing, charity and alms, how do we say to these good people, that no, we longer wish to live in shame in Mexico?

Noting that the other little rose-colored shoe never arrived and that the pair remained incomplete, Marcos continued,

> This was written in April 1994. We thought that it was just a question of time, and that the people would come to understand that the indigenous of the Zapatistas

have dignity and that what we seek is respect, not handouts . . . but piling up in the Aguascalientes are nonfunctioning computers, expired medicines, clothing too extravagant that not only can't we wear it, we can't use it in our theatrical productions, and yes, single shoes without their mates. . . . And this kind of thing keeps coming, as if to say to us, "poor folks, in such need, surely they will take anything, and this stuff is just in my way. . . .

Not only this. In large part, there is a kind of handout even more concerning. This is the approach of NGOs and international organizations that consists, broadly speaking, in that they decide what the communities need, without a thought towards consulting; imposing not just predetermined projects but also the time frame and form that they should take. Imagine the desperation of a community that needs drinking water and they are saddled with a library, those that need a school for the children and they are given a course in herb use. . . .

To no small number of people we have insisted that the resistance of the Zapatista communities is not in order to provoke pity, but rather respect. Here, now, poverty is a weapon that we have elected for our communities to use for two reasons: to prove that we are not seeking "assistance-ism" and to demonstrate, with our own example, that it is possible to govern and govern ourselves without this parasite that is called a "govern-er."[4]

In the series of articles appearing in *La Jornada* beginning on July 22, 2003, Marcos also asked civil society to set aside August 6–8, the anniversary of the 1994 National Democratic Convention in the Aguascalientes of Guadalupe Tepeyac and the birthday of Emiliano Zapata, for a special celebration. It was exactly a year since the people of Cerro Verde and Tulan had expected the organization to break its silence, an additional year working on the details of autonomous development. All were invited to Oventic to commemorate the formal passing of the Aguascalientes, the regional infrastructure centers, and the birth of the Caracoles. According to the communiqués, the five Caracol locations would provide space for the new Juntas de Buen Gobierno, where the work of development, adjudication, and conflict resolution would actually take place.

We applauded as we read the details of the proposed reorganization and chuckled out loud at the announcement of a 10 percent tax on all development aid coming into the Zapatista communities to be used as a discretionary fund. Embedded in the new policies were all of Martín's concerns about inequitable distribution of aid.

In spite of and because of all the changes taking place, Jeanne made her way out to Cerro Verde to seek clarification. Camila was in the kitchen, where a new smokeless cookstove had finally been installed, part of a *municipio* project. She held her new baby, Chul, born the same week as Jeanne's first biological granddaughter, Fiona. Martín was away dealing with details of the reorganization, as were most of the young men and the most involved of the women. As gray dawn broke, Jeanne was called to a short meeting up in the kitchen. Looking tired and unkempt from days on the road, Martín's successor, the new president of the new and reorganized municipal government, apologized for being unable to carry out their plan to take her to visit other communities. But on our next trip, we would be introduced to education and health projects in several other locales.

Though the shape of the reorganization was not completely clear, what was certain was that if we wanted to keep working in Chiapas, we too would have to follow the new rules. Now donors would no longer select the community they wished to support. One could select an area of interest, such as education, but the Zapatista Juntas would determine which educational program would get the money. Not only this. No longer could we select a site for our service-learning projects. With the aid of Cerro Verde's women, who developed workshops for other Zapatista communities in how to host gringo students, other more neglected sites would be developed to receive future programs. And because the Zapatista motto is "for each of us nothing, for all of us, everything," even the surplus earned from the sale of the Tulan honey would technically have to flow into the Junta office for redistribution. We wondered how the independent Tulaneros would handle this possibility. Or did it fall under the rubric of production and so might be exempted? Back in the United States, the honey was selling really well.

Our immediate response was to envision the nightmare logistical and safety briefing it would take to allay the concerns of parents sending students on a service program to some unknown location in the jungle. But, in good faith, we offered to use photos from the projected community visits to produce a multilanguage brochure describing the types of project to be given to potential development partners. We thought of the real tests of the new fiscal and foreign policies, as our individual donors would have to decide if they were willing to support, for instance, Zapatista health projects in general rather than just the Tulan free clinic as they might prefer. The Zapatistas were clear on this point:

> The aid to the indigenous communities shouldn't be seen as help to the mentally retarded who don't even know what it is they want (and therefore must be told what they need to receive) nor children who need to be told what they ought to eat, at what time and how, what they should learn, say and think. . . . This is the rationale of some NGOs and a good part of the international funders of community projects. . . . With the passing of the Aguascalientes there also dies the "Cinderella syndrome" [an attitude of deprecating charity; providing castoffs to the poor relations] of some civil society types and the paternalism of some national and international NGOs. . . . At least they die for the Zapatista communities, that, from this moment onward the communities will not receive leftovers nor permit the imposition of projects.[5]

A crucial piece of the fight in Chiapas is about gaining greater control over life and what happens in the shared future. Encouraging prospective donors and servers to disencumber their generosity means asking them to give up control. The Zapatistas took us seriously in our anthropological commitment to community-authored service and learning. Did we have the courage and humility to truly live out our theories of agency and act on our mutual learning experience to both *acompañar* and *consultar obediciendo*?

We were fascinated by the prospect of seeing how the new Junta would grapple with historically established social contacts such as ours that were never before mediated by the larger social movement. It could provide deep insights into the real nature of these "political reforms"—and the ways they benefit and constrain the actions of base communities. As the Mexicans loosened their restrictions, the Zapatistas were tightening theirs. We wondered what they were afraid of, spies and infiltration, insincere *hermanamientos*, NGOs run amok, creating some of the problems we had discussed and witnessed, like envy, favoritism, and so on? Or was there some sense that there are hundreds of communities out there who chafe at oversight and that they are seen as a threat to Zapatista hegemony and control? Or would this renewal process give the Juntas the material they needed to develop policy for the new Zapatismo, validating, refining, and empowering this tentative new organizational form? In any case, it invited a policy discussion. Could we get multiple entry visas, or must we start from scratch each time? What criteria were acceptable for visiting communities—would there be time constraints, or charitable donation restrictions? How available would the Junta members be when we sought to gain their *permiso*, especially for those of us who had to seek them out in Realidad, the home of Tierra y Libertad's Buen Gobierno? Was all this just about resource distribution equity, or was it also about insulating the masses from unpredictable aliens or beefing up homeland security?

Duncan returned to El Paso, Jeanne to North Carolina. As she was leaving, Camila handed her a gift, an embroidered baby bib. Martín had returned late and prepared to leave again in the morning. Doña Dominga quipped that if the work did not slow down soon, Cleenton, the ex-presidential mutt, would not recognize him and would refuse to allow him entry into the enclave. Martín responded that he'd slipped in and out of places for so many years it would hardly be a problem. He stayed long enough to help Camila with a little English: "Hello, Fiona, I'm You Friend," proclaimed the bib. Jeanne hoped fervently that the reorganization would let such friendships persist.

The due date for *Uprising of Hope* slipped away quietly. There was another chapter still to be written, and for our relationship with the Zapatistas, there was a new one to be started. The slate was clean, the past erased. As Horizonte students sold socially responsible honey for just prices, we made plans to return to Chiapas in December. Accompanied by Isa, representing Wake Forest, and Rachel, as proxy for UTEP, we would finally travel on the road to Reality.

NOTES

1. Alma's text is verbatim, taken from an interview in June, 2003.

2. Treatment of prostate problems in the United States has grown conservative, especially in the elderly. Periodic screening tracks the pace at which the disease is progressing. The operation would also be costly, unlike the clinic visits.

3. At the end of December 2003, Mexico banned shipments of U.S. beef because of the threat of mad cow disease.

4. Summarized and translated by Duncan Earle and Jeanne Simonelli, from the discussions of the Autonomous Councils, as reported by Subcomandante Marcos, "Autentico etnocidio, el modelo de Salinas: Marcos," *La Jornada*, July 25, 2003, pp. 6–7. Portions of this piece appeared in "Commentary," *Practicing Anthropology* 25, no. 4: 56–57.

5. See note 4.

Waking Up in Reality

THE FADING, PAINTED FACES of Marcos and Zapata stare across the little river as daylight cuts the dense winter mist. A few children with notebooks skip by on their way to the mural-draped school building, answering the call of shrill whistles that began at 6:00 A.M. Nearby, bony horses sing out greetings, and chickens peck around the edges of two cavernous latrines. It was morning in La Realidad Trinidad, the Zapatista capital and past site of everything from international gatherings and educational training programs to military encounters and *comandancia* strategy sessions. You could call it their Mecca.

We arrived in the darkness, a six-hour trip from Cerro Verde. Riding in the back of the official truck of the Municipio Autónomo Rebelde Tierra y Libertad, Jeanne, her daughter Rachel, and student Isa joined a few members of the *municipio*'s *consejo* bouncing and ducking as the truck made its way deeper into the *selva*. Some of the land was dense young rain forest, with solitary ceibas standing sentinel over the ghosts of forests now only memory. Other parts were picked clean, nothing but reeds and grasses, the remains of too much milpa, cutting, burning, and the sacrifice of the forests to lumber exploitations starting fifty years before. Duncan rode inside the cab with Martín, and they talked about the Zapatista reorganization that had mandated this mid-December trip back to Chiapas for us. Petul, a young Maya of good humor, held his own at the helm of the three-ton vehicle.[1]

It is a wonder that thousands of foreigners have come this far over the past ten years. The road into Reality degenerates gradually after the jungle colony of Nuevo Jerusalem, just off the spanking *selva*-border highway. It passes through or close to such localities as "Glint of Gold" and "Shade" and then to Guadalupe Tepeyac before its last torturous twelve miles to reach the Zapatista stronghold. It took almost two hours to make the final descent to the place they call the Caracol Madre de Los Caracoles del Mar de Nuestros Suenos, Caracol Mother of the Caracoles of the Sea of Our Dreams. But despite a road that required three-ton trucks just to get through the huge trenches in the roadbed, the impossibly steep and muddy climbs and descents, through the marred landscape that everywhere speaks of what humans can do to a rain forest, the children who greeted us showed by their singsong pleadings to buy an embroidered keepsake that this was a place that knew outsiders like us. This, too, was reality.

We had seen it before in pictures and videos, masked Zapatistas and the Sup lounging in front of the same murals that were now backdrop to our visit. We were met by the community's official greeter, passports checked and details recorded, then escorted to the old Casa Ejidal, the place kept for housing determined visitors and unwary tourists who happen off the odd truck coming down the long hill bound for San Quintín.

The Casa Ejidal is the one structure of the Triple Reality that is not for the locals. A large, long building of wood planks and a cemented floor—the feeling is of a horse barn more than a meeting place for the collectivity or, as it now has come to be for Mexico's most unlikely tourist location, the Hotel Perdido for visitors. The roof beams are well placed for hammocks, and the portico has a long bench everyone ends up sitting on, so we dubbed it the "Group W Bench," remembering an old Arlo Guthrie tune about misfits and strangers thrown together as we were in this jungle *ejido*. Our alien status came home with the first gray light of this *norteando* day as young heads appeared in the window spaces anxious for life to stir. We were marks to be sold the latest slogans of the struggle, wildly or neatly embroidered onto plain manta cotton, "Long live the Caracol, mother of the Caracoles of the sea of our dreams" and "We plant seeds of consciousness to harvest new societies."[2] The locals know the global!

The reference to Caracoles is part of the reorganization of the Zapatista political infrastructure, announced in August, the reason why we were here on this murky day. We were seeking an audience with the Junta de Buen Gobierno, the Council of Good Government, which has asserted itself as the current arbiter of all efforts to assist the Zapatista communities. This junta, called Hacia la Esperanza, Moving towards Hope, and also known by the less poetic but descriptive name Zona Selva Fronteriza, the Jungle Frontier Zone, is one of five regional councils. In territory, it covers the largest space of all, including Tierra y Libertad, itself divided into six districts for easier administration.

Caracoles are huge snail shells, an ancient Maya symbol of time, continuity and true speech, *la palabra*, the word. In this case, Caracoles have replaced Aguascalientes as the regional seats, sites of the infrastructure for large gatherings, including training programs and international encounters. The Juntas, it seems, do the work of setting policy for everything from development to internal peacekeeping, overseeing the lengthy process of consensus decision making as it moves up and down the ladder from the communities.

From the start, we knew we would be coming here, that to again approach our friends in the familiar and somewhat less (physically) remote communities we had come to love and admire, we must defend ourselves before an organization with an emerging sense of ownership of the development process. For over three years, they had insisted on our considering the priorities they were coming to agree on, not just those that had evolved out of the dialogic process at the grassroots level between us and Cerro Verde and Tulan. So we had dutifully prepared our letter of introduction, outlining our history of interaction, bringing students so they too could see firsthand the "reality" of Chiapas by way of their communities in resistance, and requesting the continuation of our siblinghood, our accompaniment, our preferential ties to those we had come to know. We say preferential because part of the problem we and they were trying to address was the contradiction between coming to know deeply a few locations, the basis of our dialogue and mutual trust and the place of security for our students, and the larger concern for equity, for having "no one be left behind." We had addressed this issue from the very first time we met with Martín, in the surprise appearance of authorities from an autonomous municipality we thought was dead. Now we were addressing it at the next level, and that level happened to be housed in the mother of all Caracoles, in Reality.

This trip was also our first look at Guadalupe Tepeyac, the sometime Zapatista center where Duncan's PRIista compadre Miguel imagined Marcos and the Marists residing together in a big, hidden cave. Until two years ago, the zone had been occupied by a huge military base, the bane of the region for rebel and nonrebel alike. But as part of the negotiations for peace based on the tattered San Andrés Accords, the base had been shut down. In its place were the offices of SEDESOL, the latest in a series of social development institutions the Mexican government used as their alternate weapon against Zapatismo. We passed by it on the way in, with a small trickle of campesinos coming and going from its incongruously huge buildings. It struck us that this was symbolic of the shift from Zedillo and the PRI approach of intimidation and violence, the Acteal Massacre and the crushing of Tierra y Libertad, to the more insidious approach of foxy Fox. As we had been told so many times before in the communities, the strategy was to nickel-and-dime people into staying away from Zapatismo with little gifts, handouts, and projects. As Martín said, as we passed through areas still divided in loyalties not far from Tepeyac,

No they are not with us because of the little sweets they get, just forty pesos or fifty pesos, but these are poor people in desperate times, what with the bitter price of coffee and the general isolation they suffer. If we could compete with the government, offering resources of similar value but with sustainable results, we would win them all over. This is what the government fears. Poco á poco, kun kun, this is our goal.

He smiled. "Little by little, no?" he added in his improving though accented English.

"Takal, takal," said Duncan, trying out the same phrase, learned the night before from Don Antonio in Tojolobal.

Clearly this intent added powerful import to their need for coordination of efforts at aid. The unwritten part of Marcos's parable of the single pink shoe is that effectiveness and equity in aid is the front line now of the battle for autonomy and against the oblivion that creeps in the dark shadows of smallholder failure. This green group of idealistic campesinos must uphold their part of the bargain with those who walk by the huge SEDESOL building and refuse their largesse from the current version of the still *mal gobierno*. And this means every effort must be thought of in terms of the whole so that no community becomes envious of others who may be more accessible or, like Tulan and Cerro Verde, just happen to accidentally gain patronage from resourceful outsiders. All must feel included. So here we were on the bench, waiting to see how this contradiction would be resolved, how the battlefield of alternatives in development would impact our small effort.

Office of Tierra y Libertad in the Casa de Buen Gobierno, La Realidad

The night before, Duncan's conversation with Martín showed signs of the direction things might take. He talked of the need for better communication systems and for a needs assessment of the sort we often did with the communities but this time on the level of the Junta. He talked of getting a truck to take the early corn from hot country up to the supporters in cold country, developing regional interconnections of mutual dependency within Zapatista territory. He talked of stores and products that might compete with those in the region, as did the co-op at Cerro Verde, and local production of honey, coffee, and other goods. He talked about the success of the welding shop in Nuevo Jerusalem now making many items used by the communities, how these things served to let people know they were working in the interest of the people. The war for the hearts and minds of Chiapas had shifted from bullets to beans, from militarism to developmentalism. This was the context we were to engage when we got the call to leave the bench.

We crossed the little bridge over the river that provides autonomous water-driven electricity for Realidad, walked down the razor-straight street of grass, past the peace camp compound of Spaniards and urban Mexicans, past a house with a sweat bath or *temascal* and the smell of copal, where a gray-haired man stood in front cutting wood, arriving finally at the Mother Caracol compound. It was a large square, ringed on three sides by single-story structures, with a huge bandstand at one end and a roofed, open-air area of seats at the other. We walked alongside of a string of buildings housing offices. The first was that of Tierra y Libertad, followed by the three other autonomous municipalities of this Junta, all neatly labeled. The last was an unassuming room with several tables in a row and chairs in front of them and along the wall.

As we approached, we noticed one of the young men from Cerro Verde lounging on a bench in the shadows. It is Luz and Rodrigo's fifteen-year-old son, Alejandro, who two months previously had decided to join the ranks of the insurgents, the Zapatista army. We were equally amazed to see each other. A good sign. Duncan recalled all the good signs the day before, birds mostly, always chirping in at propitious moments in the conversation as if to say yes, this is so, this is the true path, this is reality. The copal lingered in his head as we entered.

MADRE DE LAS CARACOLES

Almost nine years ago in San Cristóbal, the international viewing audience mumbled in perplexity and frustration as the Zapatistas left the dialogue to return to their communities for two months of consultation and discussion. The leaders were present, they groused, let them make a decision for the people. But the slow, revealing truth was that the people made decisions for the leaders, not the other way around, so each community was called to consider the proposals lying on the table of democratic decision making. Now, as celebrations continued for the tenth anniversary of the actual uprising and the twentieth year of the arrival of leftist intellectuals in the jungle, that process of consultation had become regularized, normal.

We could only marvel at the system of self-governance they have chosen to enact, the continually evolving process of democracy in formation. The basic structure is a sort of three-tiered representational consensus. It enjoys universal participation at the community level, a consensus system that is led by those who also represent them in their autonomous municipal councils, two people in rotation, for their four respective *municipios*. For Hacia la Esperanza, at the third level, one of those eight holds the office of spokesperson for two weeks, to be displaced by the next member from the next *municipio*, and so goes the round. Each one takes up the job of speaking before the other municipal representatives for that time and then having ninety-eight days of listening to the other seven speak. This process, we imagine, has a huge interactive effect, as each hears the others and sees how they represent the whole. From what we have gathered, the alternates, rather than following right after their partners, cycle through. This makes sense in the case one had to be absent in that the local *municipio* holds the cargo, not just the person.

Drawing on a quarter century of analysis of Maya custom, Duncan could not help but look at this rebel cargo of authority and compare it to what took place in Maya traditional times. Then, authority cycled between ranked groups of married men to be headed by elders who eventually retired from cycles of service. Here in the regional center, this has a distinct manifestation in the form of leaders whose service is overseen not by hidden elders but hidden troops, the army of the "*politico-militar*" sector. Cargos, then, are either for as long as it is decided that they are serving their community and wish to continue, in their civil system, or for as long as the army must still play a role in making space for autonomy, inside the EZLN. The soldiers themselves are within a cargo of much greater commitment, as we saw with Alejandro, a weighty and indefinite one. We know that the holders of the positions of leadership in the Junta will give way to others after a time in the consensus configuration, while there is no time limit for the soldiery. When we asked Martín what was the age of retirement from the army, he said they had not gotten to that issue yet, as there was no one at that point.

It was, as observers suspected, evolutionary revolution. In each case, those charged with leadership must await the actual situation in order to develop a response, a precedent stimulated policy. As Martín noted with a smile, the manual for development hadn't been written yet. In the same way, there is no certainty that the realities of the troop situation will continue to be the same. There might even come a true peace, but until then the threat of war is the only way to vouchsafe for the communities in resistance, and the army stands.

But Zapatismo does respond actively to what the world is doing, so for now this is their plan, but with all structures provisional and subject to change, as we saw with the passage of the Aguascalientes into the Caracoles. As we entered the Junta headquarters, we felt a sense of deep privilege to be both observers and participants in the process, the applied ethnographer's dream.

We were met at the door by Sebastian, a serious and well-spoken man whose turn it was to speak for the Junta. With him were what appeared to be a young secretary and our friend Martín. Along the far wall sat the representatives of the councils of the municipalities, the men who rode with us in the truck. They were mostly younger men but included a few elders, the *tíos*. Though today there were no women present, we knew that the rotating Junta representatives were not all men since Martín's wife Camila was about to come and take her own two-week turn.

Above the long twin desks where this cycle's Junta spokespeople sat was an original painting of Guadalupe, the dark-skinned virgin, wrapped in the Mexican flag, wearing the typical red Zapatista *paliacate* over her face, the Santa Revelde. We greeted everyone warmly. Duncan noticed how Martín seemed to be taking the role of the Yahval Tikil, the ritual adviser who has already held posts of authority and now guides others in that role as a kind of helpful second, a formal office in the traditional cargo system, as described years ago by anthropologists working in the Highlands (see Cancian 1965; Gossen 1999; Vogt 1969). Martín often restated our questions and statements to better facilitate their understanding of what we were attempting to communicate. We explained our dilemma. We were not an NGO or representatives of a large institution; our work was our own and that of those who followed, inspired by our example, mostly students, including Isa and Rachel, who were seated with us. We brought students so they could also talk about what it is like here to others who have not come, to their families, their community.

"O sea," piped in Martín. "They gain an experience you cannot get in books, only by living it with the compañeros, and then they take it back with them, to raise the consciousness of others."

"We have always taken the students to the communities that we know well, for in these places we have great confidence in their well-being," added Duncan.

"But all the communities have good people that can receive these students," responded Sebastian.

"Yes, but how can we say to the parents of these students, that we are going to place your child in a community somewhere in the jungle, but we don't know which one, or where. How many parents would accept that?"

Heads nodded gravely.

"What should be done," said Sebastian. "Is to identify and visit a number of communities in advance, and establish communication, so we can come to an accord."

In fact, that was where we were during Jeanne's August visit, about to go meet the children and members of other communities, when the announcement of the completed reorganization put foreign relations on hold. We talked about the whole notion of two stages of visitation, beginning with an orientation in the known communities, then trips out to new ones, and the idea of workshops on how to receive gringos, like those already done by the Cerro Verde women. A lot hinged on the improvement of communications and the arrival of a satellite phone to facilitate direct contact via the Internet with the Junta's planning body.

Finally, we moved to the touchy question of production projects, of the commercialization of goods and crops produced within the Caracol's boundaries. We understood from Martín that the infrastructure and policy was not yet in place to take charge of this issue. But we had just completed the successful international sale of Tulan honey, an issue too touchy to bring up here in detail. Since there was no existing policy, we didn't know if the surplus in excess of costs could legitimately return to the Tulaneros as it had done. It was a wonderful experiment, a success, but we couldn't speak directly about it.

We gave the scenario in honey anyway. What if, after we have provided a just price for the product and have covered the cost of shipping, labeling, and even a bar code there is still a surplus (remanente in the local lingo) of profit from the sale?

"We are not coyotes, or at least are coyotes sin dientes, toothless intermediaries," Jeanne added. Smiles all around. The dilemma is laid out: If we are not interested in pocketing the difference, what is the disposition of the rest? Ten percent to the Junta, ten to the *Consejo Municipal*, and the rest to the producer? The notion of a 10 percent tax has insinuated itself into Zapatista fiscal policy since we first raised it with Martín in 2001, to the extent of expecting 10 percent on government-financed projects as well, such as improvements to the road into Realidad. We talked about needing to maintain incentive on the part of the producers, but we also recognized that part of the demand for the product as a social responsibility commodity was tied to the Movement, and it is a Movement in need of cash flow. We conferred out loud, using our own term: social capitalism. Sebastian considered the question.

"We will need to start from the bottom," he told us. "The producer must be consulted, this must be something to which the producer agrees. There is no policy now since the situations have not yet arisen. It is something that must be taken to the communities."

But to begin, there must be a *consulta*, and here the Junta shows its stripes. They would bring this issue to the *compas*, in a process Martín later estimates will take two months, like the process of consultation during the earlier dialogue. A policy would emerge, we were assured. This important issue was on the table, and the slow gears of community consideration would soon begin to turn.

As we shook hands again all around, not missing any of the representatives, Duncan was reminded of the Waxak Men, the eight mythic holders of the four corners of the earth according to the Mayas of Zinacantan. Maybe this answers why four earth holders were called eight, *waxak*: like the Junta, they alternate (Vogt 1969). Structure is nested basically into two contrastive but integrated tiers, at two contrasting levels, emphasizing the ancient dualism of Mesoamerican cultures in which a complimentary, binary system of relations prevails at all levels and walks of life (Earle 1986; Tedlock 1992). At the top of the pyramid of civil authority, the place where we have come to petition, is an office, a cargo held in a rotation of four months total for the eight members. In this office, each is the Caracol, spokesperson to the outside and with the inside. This mirrors the cycling of the discussion, the negotiations inherent in community-based consensus governance, as each speaks to those who are their leaders and comes to agreement as to the destiny of their collective selves.

We see in this authority structure both a mirroring and a contrast as the few come to negotiate the *mandado* of the many, in numerous ways, as a small group of the Junta de Buen Gobierno reflects the ethos of the larger one that gave them life. In this way, through constant discussion, speaking, and considering, *la palabra*, the social landscape moves with the conversation. Because there is the ideal of autonomy, this often results in considerable variation when it comes to the actual details of their posture of resistance. This is the case in the two communities we know well enough to characterize, but we strongly suspect it exists within others, varying along the lines of the degree of collectivization and the use of subgroups of youth and women in arriving at consensus, among other characteristics.

The Junta is the rotating whole made up of the collective conjoining of the second tier of representatives of municipalities. All fall under the dictum of *mandar obediciendo* and are the facilitators of the political life of the people. This structure allows both the Zapatista military structure and the San Cristóbal Enlace Civil to pull away, the latter withering as its functions are purposefully usurped by the people they are helping, one of the goals of community development. It also means the army can focus on its own cargos more and serve only as an outside check against the development of *mal gobierno* habits within the new *buen gobiernos* while not involved in day-to-day or policy issues. Those who say the Juntas de Buen Gobierno just replace the Aguascalientes do not see the evolution clearly, how they morph to better fit current needs as more and more power flows through the civil arm. *Fuego y palabra*.[3] Like the ancient ancestors who remain present to give commentary on the way that their descendants rule, those who birthed the movement in fire remain to oversee its evolution through the word.

The meeting broke, and we emerged into the light of the Caracol space. We got permission to photograph some of the cloth artwork proclaiming the re-organization. A Tierra y Libertad representative who is a Chamula from "Glint of Gold" explains in Tzotzil to Duncan that we should wait for the result of de-liberations, but it is not very clear to us what this means. At the same time, we were relieved. A quiet sort of jubilation took hold, despite the gray, the stark accommodations, not knowing when we would be called, when we would set out again for Jerusalem, what more was afoot. We were at the end of a journey and a beginning too, the Maya place in the middle where transitions occur, where the topes smooth out and the road goes on. We had worked our way from darkness to light, as the Popol Vuh proclaims of creation, from the acci-dents of a fumbling effort to understand autonomy as lived out in everyday patterns of practice, to a clarification of ever larger territories, figurative and literal, of the structure of an emerging social and political movement. We had been led to the place where in this dialogical stance we spoke with growing un-derstanding to a people willing to help us to learn, a collectivity giving our voices greater and greater credibility. We were in the vortex of the Caracol spi-ral, listening, speaking, learning, offering, exchanging words and views and worlds, in the heart of this alternate reality. Like the Zapatistas themselves, we had crossed the sea that divides one creation from the next, one lived reality to the gradually solidifying dreams of another. We strolled back to the bench to see what was to happen next. The mid-afternoon truck from Tepayac had made it down the potholed road. Now, as we crossed the babbling tributary of the Rio Euseba over the plank bridge, we saw that other "Weros" (or *güeros*, light-skinned people) had arrived and were there waiting on the Group W bench.

We sat back down to pass the time with a French woman wanting to do a follow-up video study of children and education in San Juan del Rio six years after her first stay and two students from Mexico City working in Te-peyac trying to get people to raise chickens to fund education in that rebel *ejido*.

"Have you been here long?" asked one of the Mexicans. "Have you seen the Junta?"

We confirmed that, yes, the Junta was sitting and that we had completed our audience with them.

"How did it go? Did you get a positive response?"

Like us, they were trekking here in search of the *visto bueno*, the positive nod for a project they had conceived after almost a year of residence and in consul-tation with agronomists and other *técnicos* from Mexico City and surrounding universities. Long months of work with the community provided them with a sense of local and regional need, and they had prepared a neat booklet explaining their project to present to the Junta. Yet inspired as it was with months of ethnographic detail, it was still *proyectismo*, a scheme responding to an outside analysis of need. It involved raising chickens, this time on a much grander scale than the DESMU projects that had soon become *caldo* in the Chayote River communities and bordered on a free-range variant of the Purdue/Tyson model that employed migrants up in the United States. It wasn't a bad idea, but in our own minds we immediately morphed it into a way to start the vocational training center proposed by the multimunicipal council two years ago and still under consideration by the World Bank. In that iteration, the chickens and their economic bounty were a by-product of a larger initiative, that of training agronomists to know how to raise and promote healthy poultry, a capacity that could later be transferred to those in more distant communities. The young Mexicans had the means to secure the funding, but it was still their vision inspiring the project, not a dialogical process of needs assessment. We wished them well.

Time passed, but how much was hard to gather without a clock. It misted, it stopped, misted again, the *chipy chipy* drizzle typical of a *norte*. In a small ramada across the way from the Casa Ejidal, young Alejandro, the soldier in formation, relaxed with two of the five comrades of his plebe, his cohort of recruits completing basic training. We waved and went to join him, and he introduced us to the others, both young men. There were two women as well, but they were off on other errands. Fresh and hopeful, the little group faced years of discipline and separation from society. They were the ones who left society for society's sake, a still increasing number of adolescents who swelled the ranks of the Zapatista military.

Just the night before, we'd been with Luz and Rodrigo as they described their feelings about the departure of Alejandro and Martín's daughter Linda from Cerro Verde to join the military. Both fifteen, they were raised with the dream and floated purposefully within it. They had worked hard with the Movement through their early teens, the first generation whose conscious development had been in the arms and heart of resistance. That they left together was another example of the ever-present Maya duality, this time expressed in the joint decision of a young woman and young man seeking a greater involvement than the resistance life that their communities offered, to go put on the mask.

Luz's and Rodrigo's quiet tears expressed the pride they had in their children and the deep sadness of knowing that they would be gone indefinitely, that they had, in essence, chosen to enter the cloister of military preparation, taking vows of obedience and youthful stoicism. Luz acknowledged that they should be proud, that their children's decision was testimony to the depth of their preparation, the model set by community members daily maintaining their cargo and commitment to the Organization. At the same time, there was also a practical impact for Cerro Verde. Gone were two of the strongest of the youth, the most *capaz*, whose labor and contributions to the daily life of the group had been crucial. Without Linda, who would help with the cadre of toddlers and children? We had seen the impact of women's involvement in the development tasks of the Organization, as men and boys did day care for their absent spouses and mothers, carrying the babies in rebozos and cooking meals of eggs and beans for the remainder of the family. Linda's departure reinforced the idea of a feminism embedded in the rebalancing of society when women enter the army, so men can handle children. Roles become realigned in ways that add to diversity and adaptability and, ultimately, to resistance. It is part of the redrawing of responsibilities and activities within a larger vision, sometimes traditional like cooking and milpa and sometimes not, adjusting to the new times and conditions. With Alejandro gone and Ramón working as community educator, would it be Marta who helped with the planting and the harvest?

In a way, Cerro Verde and other resistance locales we knew replicated the demographic profile of agricultural communities throughout North America and increasingly in Chiapas. There were the comprised of the children and the aging, while the youth migrated away. But in this case, they had not gone to the cities to seek wage labor but instead followed their dreams across the sea of resistance to take up cargos in areas critical to the sustainable survival of a valued way of life. They migrated to become insurgents for the sake of all. For us, nothing; for everyone, everything.

We talked with Alejandro about the impact of his departure on his grieving parents, keeping the banter light so not to embarrass him in front of his peers. Isa shared current photos of the family stored on her digital camera. Bringing the other young men into the conversation, we showed pictures of a recent demonstration against George Bush that took place in Winston-Salem on the occasion of the president's $2,000-a-plate lunchtime appearance there. This allowed Alejandro to send love and an *abrazo* to his parents without losing face with those who might say something about sentimentality to unseen staff sergeants back in their mountain barracks.

It is a sad reality that for the space of autonomy to open, there must be a hidden standing army, but after years of peaceful struggle, they know that it was only the attention they gained as a fighting force challenging the Mexican army that led to these ten years of autonomous evolution. They also know it is the threat of political instability or the perception of it brought on by an armed group of Indians in confrontation with Mexican authorities that keeps the government respectful of their right to resist. With the concern for attracting foreign capital central to the Fox strategy for development, all parties understand that the resumption of hostilities would swiftly translate into the retreat of global investment dollars. With the peace negotiations perpetually stalled, the San Andrés Accords process violated by the Senate, the space exists nevertheless for constructing other worlds where the communities control the details of daily life and the hegemony of the state has little role in the reproduction of society.

We said good-bye to Alejandro, *hasta pronto*, and went back to the chitchat on the bench. We had no idea what our departure plans were and waited notification of whether we would brave the gradually worsening roads tonight, in the dark, or wait until the morning. The conversation was interrupted by the arrival of an older man, one of the *consejo* men from the Junta meeting. They wished to speak to us again. Now what? We again trotted behind this quiet man down the wet grassy lane to the Caracol afloat in seas of dreams painted on the sides of rustic buildings. Entering the room, we all assumed our prior positions. The Junta was back in session.

The deliberation among the Junta members had gone on for over two hours as they considered the call to do a textbook-model rapid-needs assessment. Both of us were presented with a beautifully printed one-page proposal describing the pressing concerns of the Junta in the area of education. Immediately after the new year, courses would begin to train four classes of educational facilitators (*promotores de educación*), the first ones already trained, the faster ones to learn quickly, the slower ones to learn in greater detail and the recent recruits starting from scratch. The proposal included the numbers of teachers to be trained (115 total) and the numbers of students impacted, an estimated 2,031. They had read our presence, our petition, and our understanding of the contradiction as a request for them to provide their first priority as a Junta. This was their primary and most pressing need, eloquently summarized in one compact paragraph, labeled in boldface capitals: "EDUCATIONAL NECESSITIES OF THE COUNCIL OF GOOD GOVERNMENT."

> The existence of formers (trainers) of the educational guides [*promotores*] of education in the service of the Council of Good Government, those who are among themselves compañeros in their four municipalities of General Emiliano Zapata, Liberty of the Maya People, San Pedro of Michoacan, and Tierra y Libertad, have the problem of passage (travel funds) for their relocation to the center for capacity-building, which is in the location of the CARACOL, and what is more they must leave their families so the training can happen. This is a problem for the trainers, the promotores, and the community, as all of them must directly deal with the costs of transportation, maintenance of the family, their training, and those costs associated with giving classes to the children.

So here was a request for support for teacher training, at a high-end estimate of $20 a teacher, for six months of training. In the space of a few hours, we had moved from the abstract to the concrete. It was for them a substantial request, but we saw immediate visions of an "adopt a promoter program," subscriptions at the $5 to $20 level, proposed in our local churches, on our campuses, even to our student bodies as they plunked down bar money on some upcoming Saturday night. We can do this, we said with confidence. It's Christmas, the end of the IRS fiscal year. American hearts and pocketbooks are wide open. Here was an effort that could reach into the far corners of Tierra y Libertad and three other municipalities, one we touched on with our first educational effort, disencumbering designated funds during the summer 2001 student project. Here was our first cargo for the Junta, our chore, our *servicio obediciendo*, so as to leave fewer people behind. Perhaps in this way we would earn our right to return to our friends and our field sites, to the first histories, that led us here, to our sisters and brothers back along another river.

It's been a long day for the Junta. Though they dealt with issues of external relations and foreign policy like ours and that of the other non-Zapatista petitioners, even more important was the need for them to resolve day-to-day problems of their own communities, coexisting in contested space. We'd shared our hammock space in the Casa Ejidal the night before with a couple from San Carlos del Rio who walked from across the *selva*. Even in this time of relative peace, the rivalries and conflicts still continued. The wife was a timid woman, providing support for her stern and concerned farmer husband. Like us, they were awaiting audience with the Council, seeking those with authority. But for them it was a petition against the continuing intimidation of those who opposed the Zapatista model.

A few days before, while the man was in his fields, some people came and threw fireworks under the kitchen window of this couple, a form of bomb. The children got very scared, and the woman frightened and the man angry by turns. He went to complain to the *ejido* "*suplente*," the local authority based on the *ejido* land-grant structure. The next day, he was confronted by armed men who threatened his life because he had complained. Now, like us, they were awaiting audience with the Council, seeking those with authority.

"I do not know the rules, the law, this is why I come, to speak with those who are the ones who know. They will settle this."

As darkness fell and we prepared to dig in for another night with the couple from San Carlos, the Mexicans and the French woman, the local hanging out with the global, word came quickly that the truck that we came in was about to leave. The continuing drizzle would only make the road worse by morning, we were told. We wondered whether even in this time of relative peace it was better for truckloads of Zapatistas to travel unannounced, to leave suddenly. We gathered our belongings and bid farewell and *suerte* to the others still there waiting. The night was damp but festive. Martín and Duncan got into the cab with Petul, the truck's "pilot," all chatting on and off again in Tzotzil. Jeanne, Rachel, and Isa climbed up into the back of the truck, joining two members of the *consejo*. With elder spokesman Tío Santiago and Antún, another highland Maya transplant, they braced themselves for the three-hour run to Jerusalem. As we rode lurching through the night, headed for the Zapatista iron workshop and hostel where we would sleep, Antún revealed that he spent part of his childhood in Ojo de Agua. He knew all of Duncan's field family, and we were not surprised when, with typical Maya serendipity, it turned out that his grandfather was the same Ojo-founding colonist who fought Duncan's acceptance into the community twenty-five years before. Once an active rival of Miguel's, he had died some years ago.

We arrived in Jerusalem and prepared to bed down together in the workshop bunkhouse. The ironworks and welding shop was the result of the *municipio*'s other *hermanamiento*, the one with the city in Spain. It was the product of a person-to-person linkage between Martín and a Spanish activist who died of cancer two springs ago. His name was also a variant on "Juan," and so Luz's baby Juanito, born on Jeanne's birthday, also commemorated that relationship.

The entire building was furnished in workshop creations, from the welded bunk beds with chain-link bottoms to hold the mattresses to iron pedestal armchairs. The Jerusalem *compas* were making everything from windows and door frames to the ironwork for the new concrete, smokeless stoves now featured in Cerro Verde kitchens.

Jerusalem itself was an interesting jungle *ejido*, almost unrecognizable as the little jungle colony where Duncan spent a night in 1979 during a walk across the *selva*. From Jerusalem we could manage by car and left just after breakfast. With Martín still in tow, at the edge of town we passed a Madonna-faced mother with her small careful child at her feet, both of them walking on a path by the road as if an apparition, evoking Guadalupana imagery of beauty, grace, and strength. Duncan remarked on this scene, and Martín noted it was his sister, one of seven.

"They all live here, and my father and brother, all very independent people here, as I have said. Not siding as a town with anyone, although we have supporters."

A storm brewed in his brow, the special silence of an impending story and as always a commentary on the subject at hand. We had been talking about the military's use of temporary roadblocks and how each of us had some close call, and this served as his touchstone for the subject.

"There was a man, out hunting on the ejido with his old .22. He was stopped at one of those retenes, they took his rifle. Told him it was federal law. The man took off to see the ejido leaders, who were in a meeting, everyone together.

Well they got into their trucks and off they went, but the roadblock was gone. They went farther, farther, then they come upon some military vehicles. Without a word, one goes ahead, cuts off the road, this way." With his hand, Martín shows a sideways blocking off of the road.

"Then, the other, the same, below, blocking them in between, stopping up their path. When they get out of the trucks the military commander is already restraining his troops, who brandish guns, spoiling for a fight. He demands to know what this is about.

"We simply have a man who was on this road not long ago, our road, and some people outfitted like you took his gun. We want it back, now.

"The commander begins to launch into chapter and verse on federal firearms laws when he is interrupted: 'Don't speak dung about the federal law here, we are an ejido with our own law and relations, this road we built without a federal peso, and on this ejido land the law says we are in charge. This man had his rifle when the sun rose, he will have it went it goes down, or we are all still here.'" The day was heating up.

Then the commander tried to tell them they were not the troop, that it must be others.

"Well, we can wait until they show up," was the reply.

Then they admitted they had the gun but claimed it was too late to give it back because it had been reported to the higher-ups.

"We don't give dung for what has been reported. The man gets his gun, then you get to leave, that is how it is here." More heat, the soldiers want to fight, the commander emerges with a box.

"Here is your rifle, now go away." But the rifle has been taken apart.

"Is this how it was before?" they solicitously ask the gray-headed man. He shakes his head. No.

"It was whole when he gave it over, whole he will receive it."

"Just take it, and go!" insists the commander. The *ejido* men get comfortable in the noon heat.

"As it left his hand . . ."

A circle forms around a sweaty soldier with a screwdriver, reassembling the rifle. But one screw is stripped in the process. When the old man takes up the gun, the *ejido* leaders ask with care, "Is it as before?" The man hands it back, pointing out the uselessness of the gun without the screw to hold it together. They hand it back to the military commander.

"You have got your gun, now let us through," the commander says.

"The gun is useless. You want to go through, you pay for the rifle."

They show their patience, Martín editorializes. They take the old man aside and ask him what the gun costs to replace, in Tzeltal, the language of Tenejapans. He says 4,000 pesos, some 400 dollars more or less. Then they go over to the commander.

"He wants 8,000 pesos."

"But we heard him say 4,000," remarks the commander, testily.

"That was in his language. When you translate it, it comes out 8,000."

By this time the soldiers are furious and want to fight. They are not recognizing the costs of all those men chasing them since they do so for nothing. But the commander calms them, and they get together the pesos to pay for the now pricey gun. As they rev their engines to leave, the *ejido* spokesman says, "It has always been by our leave you travel here. Tell your leader that we no longer are extending that privilege on this, our ejido road, and that if they must cross, it is allowed the use of helicopters to get over our ejido, to land at the far edge. But not on this road, not today or tomorrow, not ever."

"You see how independent they are," Martín said, the story concluded. "They support us without supporting us. Now that leaves the army only one ground approach from this side."

Duncan responds, "Must be even more disturbing for the military that the ejido is not affiliated, since it is further evidence of a generalized climate of autonomy, a kind of civil society in the jungle, sharing a conjunction of interests. Autonomous autónomos." He was reminded of the old days with Miguel in Ojo.

"Yes, exactly," Martín confirms in a tone of pride tinged with the sadness of his own exile from Jerusalem, the community of his birth.

It was a profound social contract, the agrarian reform, and its child, the *ejido*. One might even say that the bargain with the peasant after the 1910 revolution was an exchange of land rights and autonomy for political containment and conformity with the PRI. Now the historical amnesia that led to the Salinas betrayal and the PROCEDE trap has left the true believers in a simmering rage. No one in Jerusalem has had their land privatized; their lush green sea of dreams remains intact.

We drove back along the *selva* highway to Cerro Verde in our rental car, followed by the *municipio* truck. Earlier, Martín proudly displayed the sign that would eventually go on the door, announcing that the truck belonged to the Junta de Buen Gobierno from the Zona Frontera Selva Fronteriza. "Municipio Autónomo Revelde Zapatista, Tierra y Libertad," it read in big letters. As we crossed through the military checkpoint in front of Santa Elena, we watched as the soldiers took out the sign, read it, and put it quietly back in the cab, without comment. What a different world it was, at least on the surface. No longer did the military demand foreign passports, or harass professed Zapatistas. It had become a losing proposition.

The government was losing on other fronts as well. In precedents that included the resolution of the Cerro Verde *ejido* case and Jeanne's own rescinded expulsion, decisions were being documented on the government level that followed judicial process and ultimately did make a difference.

In one such case, a man lent his truck to another, and the second man sold it as if it were his own. The first man got the Junta de Buen Gobierno to detain the truck seller, in a situation that starts in the way that the first Tierra y Libertad ended. But things go very differently. The detained man is a member of a union, and the case also involves the mayor of the town of Margaritas, who seems to have been involved for reasons of profit. The government attempted to get the detained man released, and the case was put before the government authorities and the national human rights commission, both of which agreed that the truck should be returned, plus whatever contents were lost in it, so that the detainee could be freed and everything resolved. Making precedent like the case of Jerusalem, it represented the growing level of legitimacy of the autonomous authorities.

The union people, emboldened by local anti-Zapatista political relations, threatened the autonomous municipal authorities of San Pedro Michoacan, saying they would take the law into their own hands and free the man without paying for the truck and contents. They threatened to come once, twice, but never showed up. The old tactics of local political violence and intimidation did not work anymore. The Fox government, desperate for political stability for their own political purposes, finished the incident by allowing the autonomous authority to stand and obliging other local forces to do so as well. The man got full compensation. Ironically, the PAN's approach of negotiation and compromise has led to more Zapatista institutional legitimacy of the sort that would have been unacceptable in the past to the PRI. In this sense, once again we see the careful and plodding use of the structures of existing institutions to further the cause of their transformation and the irony as the marginalized appropriate the legal weapons of the strong. It is a strategy of good government.

We headed back to Cerro, stopping to visit another tiny town, where a rural clinic would be opened as soon as the needed supplies were acquired. This was one of the communities where students might be hosted, another of the places where, as Sebastian had assured us, good people would welcome visitors. We met with the children in their autonomous school, chatted with the health promoters, and ate scrumptious tamales.

Sebastian was right, and we were convinced. The Zapatistas and their supporters were quietly chipping away at *topes* in the path of indigenous and campesino autonomy, and it took different forms in different towns, as we had suspected. And that autonomy promised to have far-reaching ramifications, including better health and higher education, reaching far beyond the adjudication of stolen trucks and rifles. Like a snail from an ancient shell, slowly, patiently, *kun kun*, little by little, a new and ancient society was emerging into the growing light.

NOTES

1. For a translation of the communiqués that described the reorganization and for other texts from and about the Zapatistas, see www.zmag.org/chiapas1/index.htm.
2. In Spanish, *sembramos semillas de consciencia para cosechar nuevas sociedades.*
3. Fire and word; for a commemoration of the Zapatista anniversaries, see Muñoz-Ramírez (2003).

CHAPTER 16

The Sea of Our Dreams

Thus says God, the Lord, who created the heavens and stretched them out, who spread out the earth and what comes from it, who gives breath to the people upon it and spirit to those who walk in it: I am the Lord, I have called you in righteousness, I have taken you by the hand and kept you; I have given you as a covenant to the people, a light to the nations, to open the eyes that are blind, to bring out the prisoners from the dungeon, from prison those who sit in darkness. . . . See, the former things have come to pass, and new things I now declare; before they spring forth, I tell you of them. (Isaiah 42:5–9)

IN THE FIRST WEEK OF JANUARY 2004, ten years after the Zapatista uprising, we were one chapter short of a manuscript. We were racing to complete this book, heady from our experience in Realidad, but coming up on the start of the spring semester. It was time to get the course outlines done, outlines that had little to do with Chiapas or Zapatistas. And yet they did. Both of us teach courses about the greater southwestern experience, and in the preface to a text concerning the decline of the Chacoan Anasazi a millennium ago was the following:

> *. . . a powerful society . . . captures more energy and expends . . . it more rapidly than an efficient one. Such societies tend to be structurally more complex, more wasteful of energy, more competitive, and faster paced than an efficient one. Think of modern urban America as powerful, and you will get the picture. In contrast, an efficient society "metabolizes" its energy more slowly, and so is structurally less complex, less wasteful, less competitive, and slower paced. . . .*
>
> *In competitive terms, the powerful society has an enormous short-term advantage over the efficient one if enough energy is naturally available to "feed" it, or if technology and trade can bring in energy rapidly enough to sustain it. But when energy becomes scarce or when trade and technology fail, an efficient society is advantageous because its simpler, less wasteful structure is much more easily sustained in times of scarcity.* (Stuart 2000, xix–xv)

As scholars and academics, the themes that draw us, the repeating questions, are those that endure across time and the seas of geographical space. We were not surprised, then, to encounter this analysis in what seemed to be an unrelated text. Like Scott, Netting, and Bodley, this author provided support for a smallholder model, in this instance using archaeological evidence. We could hear Ramón yet again: *But Doña Juanita, why do we need electricity?*

Believing as we do in the potential for sustainable society, it is incredibly tempting to root for the slow and steady Zapatistas, seeing them as the only snails of our time. But much as we would like to conclude this book by predicting the fall of our technological age as it enters into an era of obsessed and fear-filled protectionism, that outcome is unlikely to happen, at least anytime soon.

Still, look at Mexico. The PRI has learned a powerful lesson from its defeat; the PAN has won little. September 11 exploded not just American buildings and airplanes but also the star to which Fox hoped to hitch Mexico's future. The PAN's victory was birthed in the Zapatista rebellion, in the courage to vote for change gained by the Mexican people because the indigenous and campesinos of Chiapas had the nerve to shout Basta! The PANistas tried to seize the moment but failed. Grandiose plans to cede the nation to global interests receded. The United States began to close its protectionist doors to the northward impulses of NAFTA and the actual movement of the Mexican people, even though President Bush moved to resurrect a sixty-year-old guest worker program. Then, as the protests and meetings in Chiapas and elsewhere said simply no to Plan Puebla Panamá (PPP), those plans also ebbed. The threat of bad press in a battle over a dam, for example, was a tope that Fox and the PAN did not want to pass over. Maintaining the Santa Paz was much better for business.

"Chiapas is at peace, as you can see," declared President Vicente Fox as the New Year approached. "The state has taken the lead in electronic government, and we've just opened a majestic new bridge that cuts four hours off the trip to Mexico City" (Stevenson 2004).

On New Year's Eve 2003, what was left of the international press in Chiapas went to Oventic, the closest Caracol to the tourist city of San Cristóbal, to report on the Tenth Anniversary celebration. According to the Associated Press story that resulted, the movement was "settling into an uneasy peace, closing itself off from progress and being bypassed by history."

"The movement hasn't stagnated," retorted a Zapatista spokesman in an interview. "We're moving forward. If the government won't give us autonomy, we'll just go ahead and apply it in practice."

The accompanying press synopsis of the thoughtful Junta process we'd just seen in action in the Marde Caracol was terse. "No outsiders are allowed into

Zapatista communities without extensive questioning. Government-issued property titles mean nothing, and justice is doled-out by rebel councils. Some concede there is little chance of a new uprising, but don't see much peace," the reporter concluded (Stevenson 2004).

The majority press analysis, like that of some of our colleagues, was about the lack of political show and drama so popular to our disquieted world. Unfortunately, for many of the international supporters, such drama is what motivates them to keep faith with the *compas*. But it should not be. The less-than-sexy message of the Zapatista tale about the pink shoe and their recent reorganization is linked to transformations within their own world, or worlds, and the evolution of how they relate to the outside world. For us, this is the ongoing story, the one that does not end with the term of an administration, the decline of a development strategy, or joint press conferences of neighbor presidents. In the ebb and flow of the Caracol, the tide is in, and the focus is on the next ten and twenty years and the reflective mirror of the last rather than great outward festivity. Now is a time of reaching inward, to grow.

Even Pablo Salazar, the current governor of Chiapas, sees the potential within the shell: "These Caracoles are the reaffirmation of the Zapatisas that they themselves want to make war no longer viable. Expressing this issue in hard and concrete facts, in almost ten years, we have more problems that come from structural conflicts in the state, as in land, religion, etc., while the Zapatista zone is the one place we do not have these problems, nor deaths, nor violence" (Clio Libros y Videos 2004).

For Salazar, the safest, most calm part of the state is within the Zapatista zone. His statement also recognized the relationship between the quality of government and the ability to live in peace, ironically putting Salazar's ability to govern in a more negative light, comparatively speaking. Most of all, it is a recognition by a sector of the local political class that autonomous *municipios* have earned their respect for the more or less orderly way they have managed things. In that sense, they have helped take some of the workload off a beleaguered centralized state.

We were not surprised that the 2004 celebrations were subdued. In Realidad, they were anticipating a January 2 start to their educational training program, not possible if the membership planned a foray to San Cristóbal. The year's end contrasted markedly with the spirited action at the start of 2003, occupying the city in a ritualized reenactment of the Zapatista takeover nine years before. This inversion of the dialectic of conquest, to symbolically conquer the colonial capital in a huge organized mass march (like the max monkey men of Chamula's Carnival),[1] signaled their linkages with the outside. Their signs and slogans made reference to Bush and bin Laden and many other international causes and outrages against the marginalized. There they tied the local to the global, on a platform before Samuel's cathedral, with a few *La Jornada* journalists running about in a delighted frenzy. But even a year ago, much of the press had already deserted. A solitary Italian satellite link had to fold up before the Zapatistas arrived since it was rented and only for a few hours. That was how 2003 started, a call out of the spiraling caracol to those still attentive after half a generation. Now, at the completion of the year, the movement is *pa' dentro*. After the initial nine years, they look inward, regestate; they shift as in rebirth. Like a fifty-two-year cycle in the Maya ceremonial calendar, those who parented the movement's membership step back to reconsider it, reborn as elders.

Duncan was reminded of a day during the summer when the drought was about to break. The night before had been the first hard rains. He looked up from where he was audiotaping an oral history with Doña Dominga, the tale of her courtship with Antonio, to the delight of her daughters and granddaughters, who'd never heard the story (for the actual story, see chapter 1). The whole yard was abruptly filled with giddy excitement. There was Antonio, prancing it seemed through the enclave, followed quickly by several of the other men, returning from a worrying day in the milpa. Others came onto the coffee-drying patio, as if driven by some mad fever, going this way and that, high and low, even the ducks and the dogs, each in their own worlds. It looked out of a Fellini film. The women rushed out to join them, equally mad, with the call, "cicim, cicim." To Duncan's eye, they all seemed to be plucking at the air, but when he looked closely, what he saw was the descent of a torporous swarm of huge, hairy flying ants. Before long, everyone was totally involved in the enterprise, the griddle was heated, and the male ants, called *cicim*, were being consumed like high-fat, high-protein popcorn, lightly salted and crispy. The following morning, the milpa was prepared, and that night, it rained again, hard so as to let you know the rains would stay.

The *cicim* come once a year, the sign of the impending rains, and when they come, all else stops. They figure in Maya history. When the Yucatec put down their arms on the brink of defeating the conquerors, they were listening to a higher logic, one that said that in the cycle of life, if you don't stop now to lay the groundwork for the future, come winter, there will be nothing (described in Reed 1967). Rebirth, renewal, reorganization. But now the Zapatistas must design the world as well as the milpa, in relation to Foxy capital, not Salinas/Zedillo politics, evolving as the techniques of hegemonic state power keep changing in the shifting global scene. The *cicim* have arrived.

In this year, the Zapatistas came together and consulted, and they deliberated and decided to do something new, to increase the flow of water through the sea of dreams. They let the Aguascalientes die since in the end these were betrayed the first time around in the Mexican Revolution.[2] They gave birth to the Caracoles, with their spiraling outer shell, their retractable appendages, and their little-by-little movement *hacia el horizonte*, toward the horizon. The symbolism is not trivial, and the change is palpable. The retaking of San Cristóbal in 2003 was political theater, right down to the machetes clanging in support of the *ejidatarios* of Atenco, who, like the potential of voices against dams and inundations, forced Fox to abandon his Mexico City airport plans. That technique was appropriate for the start of the year of changes, with its nostalgic aspect that reiterated and reenacted their pivotal politicomilitary act, a ritualized restatement of past military history like Gossen (1999) has described for the Tzotzils. Following Gossen's analysis, such collective actions invoke imaginings of the past for the possibilities of the future since for Mayas such things are closely tied in a spiraling historical sensibility. And then at midnight, the ritual ended, the people turned to the fields and the future where their dreams sail. It was time.

The bridges, roads, and infrastructure are all that seem to remain of the promise and threat of Central American megadevelopment. Beneath that veritable sea over which the Zapatista dreams skim, PPP receded, returning once again to the depths of developmental planning like a chance sighting of the Loch Ness monster. In its stead, the *autónomos* proposed a smallholder model, Plan Realidad-Tijuana, or Plan RealiTi. This was a proposal to tie the north of Mexico to the south without a hit from the great carnivorous coyotes in the center of the country. Described in the clever Marcos voice, it burst forth on the Internet and in the liberal press. It poked fun at the fact that under PPP, the south of the nation would be linked to Central America, while it is not yet linked to the north within Mexico, places like Tijuana on the U.S.–Mexico border.

There is not much drama for the prime-time news in planting and training teachers. But in the time frame of the snaily world of intentional social change, things are moving at a heady pace. In divided regions of Chiapas, in the waiting game, time may well be on the side of Zapatismo. Other scholars of the area have noticed small moves of reconciliation as practical issues and daily life contradict the polarities (Jan Rus, personal communication, 2003). The near expulsion of the Cerro Verde *compas* from their *ejido* was one of the few cases where people were not expelled, during an era when that type of practice was the rule rather than the exception. Times have changed. In fact, the political and legal precedent–setting of that epoch probably helped others, for after this period the practice went into decline, especially after the PRI lost the national and state elections. The Santa Paz makes poor copy, but it is a blessing for the people living on the front lines, the borderland where Zapatistas coexist with non-Zapatistas, the "divided communities" that characterize so many of the places holding out for the horizon.

It is in these places that new forms of cooperation are being tested. Privatization of land through PROCEDE can lead to abandonment of the rural lifestyle, or, in those who hold on, new forms of resistance, as in the case of *ejido* colony New Jerusalem. While not Zapatista affiliated, they nevertheless share a common spirit and common goals with their neighbors. They are autonomous in their own right, like Ojo's Miguel in the old days and even more recently when he attended anti-PPP workshops in Santa Elena. Perhaps if Miguel could have dreamed forward in 1994 or used biblical reflection to envision the new things springing forth, he might have seen his daughters employed as Coleto maids and his sons returning from El Norte with minimal money and maximum bad habits and would not have threatened to hang young people who asked to join the Zapatistas.

These spirited non-Zapatista communities move alongside the Movement, heading in the same general direction and feeding on all the possibilities for synergy. Like the larger national and global civil society, they are in search of balance between isolation and loss of control, wanting to be the authors of their own lives and, most especially, the lives of their children while still being tied in and tuned in to the larger world. This parallel trajectory is also part of the story. In all these cases, belief, political ideology, sociopolitical perspective, *usos y costumbres* and religion, a shared worldview, play a determining role in how people respond. If they are not all Maya, they are all campesino and are more or less in the same leaky economic boat. Almost more important than having Zapatismo to believe in is that Zapatismo believes in them. "When the poor believe in the poor, then we can sing of liberty," goes a favorite hymn. That is where the power of the Movement lies. Hope lives there.

ORIGINS AND ARRIVALS REVISITED

In writing about these continually growing skills, we must pay homage to the origins of some of what the Zapatistas now do so well. Activities and organizations sponsored or promoted by the government in the decades prior to the uprising served to give understanding and expertise to poor people who later used this against the government. Church groups of all denominations taught basic literacy, though it was the Catholics who taught the art of reflection. This base produced the dreams and energies that created the ideological power to motivate people against obstacles that at times seemed hopeless, taught them to keep their eyes on the horizon, to have faith, to become Zapatistas, as we saw in the stories told by those of Cerro Verde.

The way that people "see," the lenses they use in their social analysis, provides clues to why some became Zapatistas and others did not. A critical contrast in vision lies in their distinctive time frame for changes. The ones won by the government aid were the most desperate, the least informed about the outside world, the most hand to mouth, isolated and immediate, and though Zapatismo is ecumenical, here the Protestant sects parted company with the Catholics. Wrapped in a world of evangelical imminent apocalypse and otherworldly distractions, Protestantism encouraged shortsightedness, and generated a sense of paternalistic vicarious well-being, as in being taken care of by a patron. In their version, Jesus came to serve as spiritual analog to the party boss, the *finquero*, the *cacique*.

The Zapatista alternative required everyone to pull their weight, no patronage, no *caciques*, no sloths, no "*dulces*" or gifts. The progovernment worldview dovetails here with the Protestant because of its miraculousness and the focus of their lives in otherworld, not "earthly" matters. Martín confirmed this for us as he recounted the story of a debate with wandering Jehovah's Witnesses who happened to knock on his door one recent evening.

Responding to the Witnesses' condemnation of all things sinfully material and earthly, Martín said, "So isn't it supposed to be the same in heaven as on earth? Doesn't the Santa Biblia say just that? So if we make earth into a hellish place to live, how will that effect heaven? How can we be praising the sky and not have our feet on the holy ground? When we have perfected this world, then we will have honored God, don't you think?"

Liberation theology clarified in a new idiom a theme of great antiquity for this area, one of joining together the spiritual and material domains into a total epistemic whole. To organize to make the world better is to make things better for God rather than the evangelical vision of denial of the significance of this world for the next one. Thy kingdom come, thy will be done, on earth as it is in heaven, has never sounded so revolutionary or so Maya.

The very earthly concerns for social justice and economic inclusion of the largely Catholic rebels show the contrast in worldview between those focused on the afterlife, the elsewhere, the last apocalyptic ending point and the Zapatistas. And, as Isa pointed out in her parable of the baby crying in the kitchen, Protestantism also brought a kind of individualism that made this material life more difficult, especially for the women.

Nevertheless, some early earthly organizations also taught skills to the campesinos. Rodrigo credits ISMAM with providing training in the early days of coffee that is still state of the art. Groups such as PRONASOL are still at it, providing credit and financing public works, among other development projects (see Hernández Castillo 2001a, 201–3). Even more important, we must credit the government with creating many of the labor and other civil organizations. This alphabet soup of groups brought people together who later divided up and provided a steady stream of recruits to the other developing Organization. And if the government provided people, they also provided a more important precursor, the ideology of revolution.

Under the rhetoric of the PRI's institutionalized revolution, those in political control projected an idealized notion of the revolution and its heroes as a justification for their power. Though this was less in keeping with real practice than an ideological armature of state legitimization, it nevertheless taught the true believers that the Revolution and its Constitution were the defining social contract for rural Mexicans. The problem came not with the ideology but with the hypocrisy, a tender nerve in the indigenous psyche at least since the European invasion. One could maintain effectively that the single greatest cause of Chiapas indigenous uprisings is duplicity and betrayal, the failure of the state and other bearers of power to behave by their own rules. The cynical use of revolutionary doctrine as a form of state co-optation was not seen as such by those who truly believed in government promises, who thought all along they were sincere. The discovery that, in fact, the government was betraying the revolution, right on the heels of teaching its virtues and ideals, did not play well in rural, indigenous Chiapas. In fact, it remains such a bitter pill that some observers place no trust in the everyday acts of reconciliation that we see taking place in Cerro Verde, Tulan, and Jerusalem, among others, and see this as just another instance where the government will move to co-opt, seizing the successful practices of a rebellion they fought to suppress. At the same time, the use of the Constitution and legal precedent to uphold the rights of *ejidatarios* and foreigners alike came as an unexpected aftershock to the PRIista government of the late 1990s as the government ruled against the government in the judicial process. The Constitution did come to their defense.

MIXED HORIZONS

As much as we are optimistic as we close this chapter, we do not want to seem excessively upbeat. We know that the *compas* sail a very tiny boat across a vast ocean, a pirate ship in the jungle.[3] Thus, we would be remiss in our analysis if we did not also define the shape of the waves that threaten to submerge the ship. There are many forces, local and at larger levels, seeking to destabilize the fragile unity, just as there are moments of weakness among the Movement's members. This is to be expected. We emphasize the hopeful here, as do the Zapatistas, because the hard task is to imagine liberation after so many years of the colonial, to imagine autonomy after so many years under the patron, the *cacique*, the political boss. Hopeful as our community partners are, they also tell the stories of the pitfalls, acutely aware of what has passed and what their children face. So the path the children walk from their autonomous school, the path woven into the embroidery that makes up this book's cover, also has dark spots as it goes across the river toward the horizon. These, says Luz, are the holes the children risk falling into as they travel this difficult road.

Backslides and backsliders abound. In the height of the frenzy and xenophobia of the Albores administration, one week after the March 21, 1999 *Con-*

sulta at the time of Jeanne's expulsion, purported Zapatistas surrendered right and left, turning their arms over personally to the governor and then wandering off to eat chicken at a particularly nice restaurant in Ocosingo. So many guns were turned in that it bordered on exceeding the entire Zapatista arsenal. We speculated that it was the same fourteen rifles that the PRIistas accepted over and over again (Ross 2000, 306).

Half the people who entered the Movement a decade ago in Cerro Verde left, pressured by the others, facilitated by religious conversion, or in some cases bolting over the issue of drink and its aftermath. Don Antonio lost one of his sons to the government side over soccer because it placed his son in the company of non-Zapatistas, whose habit was to drink after a game, "to celebrate if they won and to forget if they lost." And as Alma pointed out, "Concerning all of this suffering and persecution of our community, envy and gossip is the worst thing that we faced, within the larger community. But at the same time, it fills us with bravery, motivation to persist." The 22,000 masked people who took San Cristóbal at the start of 2003 did not seem defeated, vacillating, or merely herded by their leaders. And they represented only a fraction of the total.

Time may be on the side of many in the rural backwaters because unlike those who embrace PROCEDE, they refuse to abandon the milpa, the domestic-based production that is their secret to surviving tough economic times. But there are other, really serious issues to be considered concerning education, regional economic interactions, and especially the environment. Can the Zapatistas get their followers to arrest the destruction of the remaining rain forest despite land scarcity and take up its protection as part of their militancy? Can they succeed in efforts to build production arrangements that do not excessively tax the fragile world around them while the forests remain, like the production of honey, where higher yields depend on better forestation?

The region we write about has been transformed in the past fifty years from near-virgin rain forest to a zone harboring 200,000 people. Half of it is no longer rain forest and will never be again. Another fifty years will kill the other half, even at current rates of growth, never mind the demographic explosion within the jungle communities. From nearly any point of view, the jungle is "full"—at or beyond carrying capacity. Thus, the real dilemma is to devise alternative productive activities and techniques to keep what is left of the rain forest from disappearing. In other words, far from pitting indigenous colonists against conservation efforts, the solution must be in supporting ways that they can exploit the rain forest while also keeping it alive.[4] That is the reality. Dreams of an empty, pristine jungle were never more than romantic projections, biosphere reserves notwithstanding. Like Stuart, writing about the Anasazi, archaeologists know how changed the region is. After all, the Classic

Maya sustained a civilization with a higher population in the same region a thousand years ago. What once was the largest and only significant rain forest in Mexico faces ever-increasing shrinkage, like taking out part of a lung, only for the whole planet.

At the same time as this ecological tragedy unfolds, so does a human one. Chiapas, the poorest Mexican state, has as its poorest region this same tropical zone. Exiled from the already depleted and crowded lands elsewhere, the poorest of the poor came here. After a twenty-year period of an emerging coffee boom and growing prosperity, the market has collapsed. Like Ojo de Agua, communities that imported labor in significant numbers twenty years ago now export it. The high demographics means that the side effect of this destruction, if nothing is done, will be to generate a new stream of desperate migrants or a new base of operations for those trafficking in drugs. This redoubles the importance of what we are writing about here. With no change, this is what we might call a lose-lose situation. Nobody wants that.

Standing to gain in this is the government in that the destruction of the remaining half of the rain forest would deprive many Zapatistas of a sustainable independent land base, a sad way to win a war. The apparent paradox is that, for the long run, truly sustainable development in the rain forest means keeping informed campesinos in it. The agribusiness plans of PPP are not really sustainable in the ecological sense of the term. Most businesses don't plan generations ahead since immediate benefits outweigh the long-run costs of permanent environmental harm. If we cannot find adequate rural stewards to take care of the green and blue parts of the world for us, then we all die, rural and urban.

Early one morning, we watched the crop dusters pass low above the Chayote drainage at dawn, alternating as they do with the military intelligence flyovers. The conflict in Chiapas still has several faces. The impact of pesticides and herbicides is well known, and the ramifications for health go far beyond contaminating the plots of those trying to raise organic coffee (cf. Quandt et al. 2001). It is hoped that we learn from our mistakes. At this point in the twenty-first century, we must come to see the world anew and realize that it is not the urbanites leading the poor peasants into the light but that it is we who must be learning from them about development and the survival of the planet. We see this truth because it is the remaining, less trammeled parts of our spaceship earth that hold the keys to the survival of us all. As apocalyptic as that may sound, like the destruction of the Lacandon rain forest, this is a "when" question rather than one of "whether."

LOCAL RENOVATIONS AND GLOBAL PLANS

On a misty winter morning in December 2003, we found Don Antonio down in the bottom of a six-foot-deep rectangular hole in the orange orchard out behind his house, not far from the Zedillo memorial latrine. At seventy something, Antonio's knees were bothering him, his bones ached, especially as the chill humidity of the *nortes* slipped in. He was, he told us, finally building a *temascal,* a Maya sweat bath. Duncan thought back to the day last summer when he encountered Don Antonio sitting in his patio on the floor with one pant leg up. A boot buffered his knee. As he approached, Antonio did something he never did. He explained he felt great embarrassment to ask, but he wanted a loan of fifty pesos. He explained that a ball had formed on the neck of his cow, and she was about to give birth.

"I think it is just on the surface, attached to the hide, but it would be best if someone could come, to take a look, and we don't have those trained to do this yet. Marta, someday. But for now, I don't want the cow to die, so close as she is to calving," he said.

Duncan could see some pain in his eyes.

"I haven't been to see her in three days," Antonio continued.

After yesterday's work in his hilltop *cafetal* where he weeded coffee for a few vigorous hours, his knee was too painful to go out to the pasture.

Duncan responded by placing his hands on Antonio's knee, where he could feel the sinews of aging power and the chill that gets in bones after a humid night of rains, especially in your seventies and up. He concentrated in the application of Reiki he had been taught some years back, warming the painful place with his touch. Then after a few minutes of this, as soon as he could feel some warming, he gave Antonio's thighs and knees and calves and feet a good rubbing. Antonio said that in the morning he had felt as if they were not there, which sounded like circulation problems. Duncan's immediate response, based on his time in Guatemala, was to think of how his compadre Lucas would have dealt with such problems using a sweat bath. A recent academic paper had also supported this method of healing.

Duncan raised Antonio's leg and got him to relax it with the foot off the ground. He slapped the bottom of the foot intently and firmly for a few minutes, then switched to the other foot and did the same.

"Do you feel anything different?" he asked Antonio.

Antonio smiled and said his legs felt warmer. Then Duncan took out his wallet and slipped out a hundred pesos and folded them and put them in Antonio's shirt pocket.

"I can't lend you money, Antonio," Duncan told him. "Because it might look like I was giving you money and that would be a donation, one without authorization of the Municipio Autónomo, and you know we can't do that, since we want to stay in keeping with the Organization."

Unreadable emotions slid across Antonio's weathered face but with a hint of a wry smile.

"So, this money you may use as you please," Duncan told him. "But I want you to do a service in exchange, I want to pay you to encourage you to do this service. I want you to build a sweat bath. Nobody is getting any younger around here, and this kind of ailment will be around more as time passes. Then there is the issue of women with their moonsigns, and when their uteruses shrink back to normal after a child is birthed."

Now, Dominga had joined them and was smiling, intent on the conversation. Duncan continued.

"There are the pains of the muscles after labor, the pain of the tendons and cartilage after an injury, the stiffness of the morning cold, even the cold suffered in the case of intestinal troubles, and the knitting of cuts and broken bones. The temascal stimulates circulation by opening up the veins and relaxing the muscles." Dominga was nodding rapidly.

Duncan could feel the tension in Don Antonio's legs, and it was a constant struggle for him to relax his muscles when they were massaged. Antonio needed the sweat bath bad, that was Duncan's take, after twenty years of knowing the impact of sweat baths and doing massages, and here was his bid.

He reached out to Antonio as he got ready to go, in the gesture to shake hands, as if to say, is it a deal? The cow gets looked at by a vet, the *autónomo* regulations are respected, and a *temascal* gets built. Antonio's eyes sparkled with understanding. This was not the first time money had been transferred in advance of a service yet to be rendered. The community's oral history had come months after the payment of the 7,000 peso reintegration fee after the Cerro Verde expulsion.

Dominga piped in that Antonio knew all about the *temascal*, as he was around them back in the old days. His hand hovered, and Duncan thought in that second of pause, here I am obliging this aged Tojolabal to re-create a dead institution, a locally waning cultural practice, because I think it would be good for him. What deep interventionalism. Could it be justified? Am I acting out notions of perceived authenticity? No, this was about healing.

This was a personal engagement with the body, one might say, of colonialism and its opponents. He could feel resistance in the surfaces of Antonio's gnarly, gaunt legs, in the craggy pads of his small, wide, and taut feet. There was a flecked stain of earth around his blackened toenails, such that the earth was always with his feet, as they poked out of sandals or wrestled with rubber boots. The energetic effort to carve a living out of this new land for a whole new community, from well before the time of Zapatismo and still every day deeply into it, could be read in the feel of his toughed and lean indigenous body. If this would bring a cure to Antonio's pains, methods didn't matter. Forget objective anthropology in this instance. This was about healing.

Duncan could feel the rightness of this contract in his bones. The sunny patriarch of this clan was faced with a truth he knew, that the old ways served to heal the body, and if it was that they did not know better when they lost the technique, they do now, it was obvious. The palpable enthusiasm of Antonio's wife and later his health *promotora* daughter gave him added motivation, to serve the community. This was the right thing to do.

The grip of a callused hand ended this reverie. Antonio was reaching up out of the hole, asking for a boost. The *temascal* was half done.

"What do we need to finish this?" Duncan asked Antonio. We were waiting around Cerro Verde for Martín to obtain a truck to haul us to our Junta meeting. We had a car as well.

"Well, I need to cut some more poles, and then we need rocks," Antonio said shyly.

Rachel, Jeanne, and Duncan followed Antonio to the edge of the orchard, where, with a few deft strokes of a machete, he felled trees three inches thick. We hoisted the logs up onto our shoulders, ignoring mud and mites, and hauled them back to the emerging *temascal*, saving Antonio two dozen trips. Then Duncan got the car, and he and Antonio crossed the river together to gather the rocks.

We remembered the project weeks later, thinking of Antonio steaming in his *temascal*, as we finished this text, hunched over our computers, scratching. The fiendish jungle chiggers dug deeply into our skin, keeping Chiapas alive in us, as we listened in amazement to an announcement by President George Bush reviving the old bracero program. Opening the door to legal, short-term immigration of foreigners, for the Zapatistas this guest worker plan was insidious, like the slow creep of jungle mites into the warm spots on the collective body of the people. They are wary of out-migration and its aftermath.

"Don't let yourself be deceived; stay here and fight for your country, for the motherland that gave birth to you . . . you don't have to leave. We lack a lot of things, and so we get addicted and then we have to look for money in the United States or somewhere else. But that doesn't help us. Instead we find death, drug and alcohol abuse and prostitution, and all that causes us to lose our beloved country."[5]

In our mind's eye, we were catapulted back to Cerro Verde, where the day seldom ends without listening to the late-evening news. In all likelihood, Luz would have been appalled at Bush's news, fearing the specter of immigration the way the women do. Having given her son and foster daughter over to the Zapatista military, would she now lose husband, brother, and brother-in-law to the army of the other side, the army of global capitalism?

According to Bush, this new version of an old program would allow those from the outside to fill jobs that purportedly remain empty because Americans are not interested in filling them. "I propose a new temporary worker program that will match willing foreign workers with willing American employers, when no Americans can be found to fill the jobs," said the president (MSN News Summary 2004). Without digressing into a soliloquy on unemployment in North Carolina and other states, suffice it to say that we find this curious in light of both statistics and anecdotal information.

The ways in which the State and its numerous allies can undermine a quietly growing Zapatismo are numerous and, like liberalized immigration laws, not always obvious. After all, aren't we providing valuable work and wages to our struggling neighbors from the south? Perhaps the changes will aid the two older brothers of El Chamaco, Cerro Verde's twelve-year-old truck driver, who remain in Virginia, packing chickens, calling Jeanne occasionally for a lonely chat with someone who has recently seen the family. But what of the three others from the Chayote valley who returned home from the United States in *cajas*, undocumented guest workers whose welcome and lives suddenly expired? And when immigrants return alive, like Felix in Ojo, they bring back many of America's worst habits, as the Zapatistas caution. There is a lot that is not positive about the journey to the north. But Bush was jubilant, laying out his gesture to the Hispanic voters as we entered the North American electoral season.

The immigration initiative was one of the topics brought to the table the following week during the Summit of the Americas held in Monterrey, Mexico. Though Fox, with little real choice, was supportive of Bush, other Latin American presidents spoke out against the U.S. agenda for Latin America. They were especially critical of ALCA, the free-trade area of the Americas, and mirrored the opposition against this proposal seen in Chiapas meetings. They pointed out that a free-trade agreement should "acknowledge differences" and "could not be a one-way street," as NAFTA appears to be.[6] The United States was urged to drop its farm subsidies, seen as responsible for serious economic hardship in many Latin American countries, as with the issue of corn in Mexico.

The keynote session at Monterrey was centered on three fundamental themes: economic growth with quality and equality, social development, and democratic governance. It is these very same issues that concern the Zapatistas in their Juntas de Buen Gobierno, but they seek solutions through the medium of investment in a viable rural economy. We wished we could invite Bush, Fox, and the other American leaders to travel with us to Tulan, where ZAFTA had resulted in a highly successful sale of their honey in American markets.

MILPA LOGIC: THE GLOBAL-LOCAL HELIX

In Tulan, Francisco and Carmen were thrilled at the outcome of the honey project but at the same time guarded. They, too, remained acutely cognizant of the rules they must live by to remain part of the Movement they believed in. The Tulaneros were remarkably productive. According to Francisco, the reason for their success is true collectivism, that they pool their resources, assets, and costs, buffering each participant from the blows of uneven individual luck. He maintains that the real problem in many of the *ejido*-based communities is too much individualism, which comes from the maintaining of autonomous household economies though acting collectively in social programs. In his case, the households make up a unity in areas of production, management, profit, and distribution. With no larger entity such as an *ejido* to insist on household differentiation, their private property situation allows for a resilient and profitable adaptation in part by taking Zapatismo into a fascinating experiment in kin-related collectivism. In this case, it is the owners of private property who are more communal and those involved in collective ownership who are more individualistic.

The Tulaneros are makers of this new form of communalism, reminiscent of that which created the stem of clan formation in pre-European times. They see themselves as a Zapatista model for a more aggressive autonomy, based on total surrender of independent resource management to a larger whole. The weakness of the model is in the key role that Francisco and Carmen play as patriarch and matriarch, creating vulnerability in that it is their energy that keeps things moving. They are in a race against time to both build the model base from which to promote bees, health, Zapatismo, and jungle conservation and at the same time train enough of their up-and-coming kin to take their place. This is even more difficult for Carmen because her calling as a healer is a "*don*," a gift from God as she sees it. Because of this spiritual basis of healing, it is not something one can teach to those without the gift. She followed her grandmother and was blessed and trained in the manner of participant observation. This can be reproduced only with great effort, in someone who also has the "*don*." But Carmen is not closed in finding a successor, knowing how important it is, as we saw when she worked with our student Sharon. If the calling is in a gringa, so be it.

It is the Tulaneros who are the experiment in social capitalism, in interfacing with the market while also turning its benefits inward. This winter we returned to Tulan with *remanente*, profit, yes, but also to discuss business concerns about consistency, quality, and transparency in market transactions. It is their case, acknowledged though unspoken, that has put the issue of commercialization on the table with the Junta. This is a continuation of the conversations begun between Jeanne and Martín when the prototype for the Juntas was created in the silent spring of 2002. Now that this pilot project has occurred, our piece of the work continues. We are hell-bent on a bar code for honey, to allow the entire Zapatista region to market theirs together, taking advantage of the niche that exists in organic foods supermarkets. A graduate student in business works in the background, making sure that shipments will be possible through the *mero* NAFTA.[7] And while all this plays out in the arena of global trade, behind the Tulan enclave, the milpa gets ever larger.

In the rural Maya ideal, all basic foodstuffs are produced in adequate amounts so that cash is not expended. Cash is important for items like machetes and matches, new radios, rubber boots, and transportation but not for what one's family is to eat. While in these hard times this ideal is hard to reach, the effort to supplement purchased corn with at least some straight from the land, as the *comisariado* of the topsy-turvy Cerro Verde *ejido* ordered members to do, is more than just an economic strategy. It the key to maintaining the skills to survive if necessary should cash-based alternatives evaporate. Zapatismo strives for this: if the global system went down, as the children assure us, they would not be greatly inconvenienced except for the loss of machetes and maybe those plastic jugs for hauling water. It would not be life threatening. *But Doña Juanita, why do we need electricity?*

This is a daunting challenge: to get everyone to be a part-time farmer while also bringing urban skills into the woods, construction, accounting, and small-appliance repair. But when compared with the options facing Don Miguel and others like him, we are far more confident of a positive outcome from the approach the Zapatistas are applying. As a live-in, culturally motivated aid agency, a GGO or "good government organization," the Zapatistas have a sound platform from which to do community development efforts. Miguel's future must always be tethered to the shifting faces of the *mal gobierno* and its minions, who, as PPP plans suggested, do not have the rural persons' best interest at heart if they wish to stay agrarian.[8] The millions of dollars the government has spent on romancing the non-Zapatistas in this decade, as well as the new roads and high-cost infrastructure, means that indirectly the Zapatista uprising has helped many people in Chiapas. But, though the handouts are designed to counteract what can be offered by the Organization, the welfare state has limits, especially in the eyes of international banking. Stuck between a rock and a hard place, hoisted by its own petard,[9] in a sense, Mexico needs Zapatismo to succeed.

Thus, the whole picture now shifts toward viability, including education and health as facets of the alternative of economic self-sufficiency. The viability of rural Zapatismo may win the Movement what they could not do by political means alone. Education and the maintenance of good health are key to this incremental revolution toward some sort of true autonomy, as a large social entity. Whether it is through autonomous schools that actually teach the children basic skills, free clinics such as that in Tulan providing services where there is neither health care or transportation, or a bevy of gringas available as dancing partners at a weekend fiesta, the Zapatistas are winning them over by example. But they are not too shy to try a little door-to-door promotion. In a hand-drawn poster on the outside wall of the Junta office in Realidad, an EZLN man is seen talking to a campesino in his milpa, explaining the fringe benefits of the Movement. "Insurgente recruiting a campesino," reads the caption, with speech scrolls, Maya codex style.

Last summer, both Luz and Alma dreamed our arrival in Cerro Verde in advance. Five days before we came, Luz saw a group of us and we went from the Cerro "*por abajo*" toward La Realidad with her and others, setting up hammocks by the little river. We had not gotten the resources we had wished to bring, but we were "happy" anyway, going to Reality together. "Yes," said Alma. "I dreamed of your arrival, the two of you, just last night." Predictive dreaming is not that uncommon with the traditional Maya. Compadre Lucas always knew about visits. But that was the first time we heard of such stuff at Cerro. They both commented, jokingly, that with dreamers like them, there was "no need to phone ahead."

Now, we ask you to dream ahead with Luz and Alma and imagine a world in which it is expected, aside from your career specialty, that you grow your own food. Such labor diversification is part of the agenda of Zapatista autonomy, alongside that of "grain autonomy," so everyone must know how to do a milpa—and something else as well. In the people's desire to build a vocational training center is an example of the intent to create "dual" workers who are both specialists in a specific technical skill, the basis of a lifelong profession, and part-time agrarian *milperos*. This is a dream that makes great sense. How we begged the rural New York school system to do just that, to allow our children to pursue a similar dual strategy that was both college prep and some real-life vocational skill, but to no avail. So we take our dreams southward, along with our students.

The binary work system the Zapatistas seek to build is reminiscent of Marxian notions contesting essential labor division but is also a bit suggestive of the cargos of civil leader and soldier in the Caracoles. The latter is a lifelong commitment just like milpa. In pre-European Mesoamerica, at least in the post-Classic period just before Columbus, we know that war was carried out seasonally to keep the rainy season free for milpa work. This truth took the Yucatec away from certain victory against Merida over a century and a half ago, with the sign of the *cicim*, those ever-so-tasty flying ants. Milpa logic is ancient in Mesoamerica, and its efficiency and "part-time" labor aspect was an attractive system for building civilizations then, with half your year or better free of required agricultural work, based on the security of allied households of households, families of families. It was a social and economic setup ripe for considerable autonomy, as with today's case. The fundamental material basis

of Zapatista notions of autonomy rests on the milpa logic, the idea of local production, hand right to mouth, as a way of being able to resist incorporation
into the globe on globalization's terms, or immigration, surrender to the city,
to *el norte*.

The household and its production and reproduction are the basic location
of the Zapatista revolution, the foundation and source of the Movement, but
how that household is constituted and how it relates to other households vary.
To understand how this movement is able to encase huge variation in unity
is to look at the ways people fit the variations in environment and setting that
they live in.

We can say that Zapatismo is a social experiment to discover alternative
ways to arrange people in space so no one is left behind. The Zapatistas have
immediate practical problems they are trying to solve, small pieces of deeper
theoretical questions about how and why societies and culture change. Hanging in the balance, in this text, and in our shared future is the promise that rural smallholders maintain for those inside spaceship earth. It is to be expected
that the moguls of late capital, hard fixed for growth options, gaze lustfully on
the green spaces rural people live in. The temptation is great, and we all wonder what the outcome will be. These are "science" issues of the first order.

As anthropologists, our contribution to an understanding of Zapatismo
comes from using everyday life as the starting place rather than Marcos's po-
etics or national political assessments. We understand Marcos's beautiful little
stories better from having shoveled the mud off the coffee-drying patio. We
see the impact of PRIista policy by living in the fallout of *ejido* envy and fear as
they contemplate PROCEDE. Without the overlay of the world of everyday
life, the autonomous movement might seem to be no more than impractical
rhetoric, a utopian dream.

TAJKOPONBATIK: AUTHORITY TO SPEAK[10]

This book hangs on the debates about how rural life can and should be organized for its survival and how anthropology can help in this endeavor without
causing damage or hurt. During these years, the Zapatista organization also re-
considered the impulse to help, dealing with some of the same issues as does
the discipline of anthropology concerning the place of informed activism. Zapatismo has always been about applied insurgency, even in its Marxist intellectual beginnings twenty years ago, just as we have always been applied
anthropologists. Because we entered into this research through the medium of
trying to understand development, doors opened that would have been invis-
ible to us had we only been sniffing out the political. Our discussions with our
Zapatista hosts and teachers and the actual projects that resulted have been
acts of reciprocal learning. There have been sticky points, where serious com-

munity reflection has been needed to reconfirm their joint vision of development and the role of outsiders in it or to reach consensus among women, men, and youth. It is a work in progress and must continue to be for all involved.

As ethnographers with particular interests, we have decided to notice some things more than others, creating a particular picture made vivid through our subjective impressions. Ours is but one way to learn from and document the Zapatista movement, and we advocate for more research from different perspectives. Our students have begun some of this work, research that the Zapatistas themselves are now requesting, concerning the regularization of their educational system and the health status of their membership.[11] We teach them the skills they ask for; they help answer the questions that inform our research. It is "methodology *obediciendo.*"

We wish there were more of us able to look deeper at other topics we've only touched on. When people are in the process of reinventing their society, there is lots to get involved with, lots to report on, lots to write about. We do our best to keep our particular interests, understandings, and perspectives transparent as we open ourselves to our reader through narrative, as characters in the book. We have agency in a social situation and are visible to the reader as "part of the picture," active in daily life, fairly well exposed. We believe the only way to stay honest with the reader is to be part of the tale for all to see.

In all this, we are compelled by the guidelines that have emerged from our mutual assessment of community development that views the process as having some logic, some preferred approaches for success.

Together we contribute to a social science of community development informed by both anthropology and Zapatista experience at a time in history when such a science and the funds of knowledge it can marshal have never been more critical. With our community partners, we coauthor a tale about autonomous development and authority, having been given the authority to tell this tale by them. "They say that they say that they said," wrote Marcos, in telling of the birth of the Caracoles. In like manner, we say it is a coauthorized tale of a coauthorized community development of which we (and they) speak here, with our decidedly coauthorial, nicely edited voices. We have intervened, yes, sold cookies and honey and tracked down project grants, first for a community, then for its municipality, and now for the larger regional organization. We are asked for seeds, we bring them, they plant them and replant them, in a milpa of their own choosing, and we watch to see how they grow. We share the authorial voice, we share the community dream. And since we speak to different audiences, we carry their story outward, and they carry our anthropological queries inward. This is our compromise between none of it and all of it, between doing nothing with our extensive field-based knowledge and doing something that might not be what our hosts see as important. It is a balance the Mayas appreciate. We hope you do as well.

Zapatista communities have begun to test the plausibility of using globalism to improve their entry position in the marketplace of value. By working with them, we can test our own understandings of autonomy and development in the processual laboratory of rural, indigenous experience. This analysis of actual behaviors will ground subsequent theoretical discussions of how small-scale producers are transforming and being transformed by the development experience. Just as the resistance communities face the challenge of moving beyond rhetoric to practical programs, we as anthropologists use their experience to move beyond discourse.

Finding ways to resist and still succeed in living a viable rural life is the struggle, the *lucha* that we have provided a glimpse of, a small, deep window into a tenuous future. To check the validity of this vision, we have created something of a dialogical test through the engaged discourse we have carried out with the Zapatista communities. Out of this five-year period of conversations arises the validation of our basic reciprocity, beginning in the community, growing through *hermanamiento*, and continuing into the Caracol. This was confirmed in the two meetings with the Junta: in Realidad we were given our visas, and policy concerns were discussed, with a plan for *consulta* feedback on commercialization, in exchange for the commitment to seek funds for training educators. We reached a compromise over our concerns about student placement with the notion of stages, training hosts, and meeting enough of a sample to feel confident about the whole. And most amazing, in these past months, the Zapatistas offered up a table on which to place policy questions we knew they needed to consider to move forward as they wished. And consider them they did, using the questions we asked as a vehicle, authorizing our work as they risked looking in new directions, with Martín's voice in the *consejo* risking the same, for his community, for the *municipio*, for Mexico, for the world. "Let's go, let's go, let's go, let's go forward," says the Zapatista hymn.[12]

The hot season is approaching once again, and the bees will soon begin to sip the jungle's nectar. The waters of the Lacandon rivers have not risen to inundate Miguel and the Ojo colony as he so feared, but the waters of global change are rising faster than his quiet, aging Tzotzil heart can cope with. Yet the Zapatista experiment shows us that these forces are not inevitable, inexorable, or irreversible. They are human creations. If there are 113 *topes* on the road from San Cristóbal to Tonina, there are an infinite number on the road from armed uprising to sustainable society. But those who learn to travel in Chiapas learn to negotiate the *topes*, just as they learn to negotiate the details of their lives.

In the gentle summer dusk of August 2003, Jeanne sat with little Natalia, then three and a half years old, reading a textbook on Chiapas history. Pointing to pictures of white-haired leaders of the 1910 Revolution, Natalia asked, "Abuelita, who are these old men?"

Jeanne thought for a moment, and then the history of Mexico was explained to a miraculous Maya child through the eyes of a curious and maturing gringa. Natalia turned the page.

"Campesinos," she said, pointing to another picture, annotating the story with her own toddler commentary on rural life.

It was a strange analysis, like this whole experience, but together we were writing history.

Into the swirl of the voices of a *consulta, asamblea,* meeting, goes a word, and it circulates through the ears and minds and voices, and what comes to be seen as the path, the right direction, the collective vision, rises up at the end, when the consensus emerges. Hope breathes slowly in the shell of the Madre Caracol, in the cave of the last North American rain forest. We honor the chance to participate in this breath, by this book, our inscribed document, and the commitment we share to see the journey through, to receive whatever the decisions are from the communities, the birth of new policy, when they are finished talking about it. The perseverance, patience, and good humor of these jungle communities in the face of monumental global *topes* are a wake-up call for those who view the search for alternative development as futile. Their continued efforts are the not just the horizon of hope, they are the globalization of hope.[13] We sail together on the sea of our mutual dreams.

NOTES

1. Chiapas has a long history of indigenous rebellions, all fairly swiftly put down, but not without impact on the Ladino population (see Bricker 1981; Earle 1994; Gossen 1999). The parallels in them are quite remarkable.

2. Pancho Villa and Emiliano Zapata met together at a town called Aguascalientes in central Mexico to establish the principles of the Mexican Revolution, which were later betrayed by the postrevolutionary government.

3. Ross (2000, 75–76) describes the actual Pirate Ship in the Jungle during the 1994 National Democratic Convention near Guadalupe Tepeyac.

4. The conservation-versus-occupation dichotomy is the basis of debate concerning Montes Azules.

5. Zapatista commandant, speaking at the August 8, 2003, celebrations in Oventic on the announcement of the Caracoles.

6. AFP (2004), President Nestor Kirchner of Argentina, speaking at the Summit of the Americas. Such distress at U.S. actions was reiterated in Brazil as the government of President Lula da Silva responded to the new U.S. tactic of fingerprinting and photographing visitors by doing the same to Americans entering Brazil.

7. Smith and Lindblad (2003). In an article appearing in *Businessweek*, the authors noted that "rightly or wrongly, a large proportion of Mexicans today believe the

sacrifices exceeded the benefits. The Mexican mood is infecting other Latin countries, which after 15 years of gradually opening their own economies to trade and investment are showing pronounced fatigue with the 'Washington consensus,' the free-market formula preached by the U.S. and the International Monetary Fund. In an August poll of 17 Latin countries carried out by Chile-based Corporación Latino-barómetro, just 16% of respondents said they were satisfied with the way market economics were working in their countries. Thus NAFTA's perceived shortfalls are giving fresh ammunition to free trade's opponents. 'Now you have a whole network of people organizing against the Free Trade Area of the Americas and globalization because of what has happened in Mexico under NAFTA,' says Thea Lee, the AFL-CIO's chief expert on international trade pacts."

8. At the urging of the diocesan group El Caminar del Pueblo, Bishop Felipe Arizmende arranged for a workshop concerning PPP. Held on July 3, 2002, in San Cristóbal, the meeting featured the then head of the PPP initiative for the Fox government. Jeanne was present during this meeting when the government representative admitted that there was no platform on agriculture and that the government was reconsidering its stance. Appalled by this and other aspects of PPP, 18,000 people thronged the plaza in protest on August 18, 2002.

9. *American Heritage Dictionary* (1981, 980). If you are not familiar with this saying, a petard is defined as a firecracker, and the saying means "to be injured by one's own cleverness" (from the French and Latin, meaning to break wind; to fart).

10. Tzotzil for "We'll talk later."

11. Most notable are ongoing research projects by now graduate students Elizabeth Isa Story and Marcial Martínez and Teresa Sotelo.

12. Chorus, "Himno Zapatista."

13. The original title of this book, as presented to Martín in the summer of 2002 for Zapatista approval, was "The Globalization of Hope." In a communiqué dated September 12, 2003, Marcos also used the term, calling out to civil society to "globalize hope."

Glossary of Spanish and Maya Terms

A

Abrazo: Hug
Abuelita: Granny
Acelga: Boiled bitter greens
Acompáñame: Lean on me
Acompañar Obediciendo: Accompany obeying
Acta: Protocol; agreement
Acuerdo: Agreement
Agachada: Bent over
Aguaceros: Downpour
Ahijados (das): Godson (goddaughter)
Algo mas: Something more
Altos: Highlands
Anexo: Annex
Aparato: Public address system
Artesanías: Crafts
Así es: So it is
Autonomías: The autonomous municipalities
Autónomo: An autonomous municipality

B

Balames: [Tzotzil] Jaguars
Balsa: Raft
Bases de apoyo: Support bases
Basta!: Enough!
B'atz: [Tzotzil] Howler monkeys
Bocina: Loudspeaker
Bolos: Drunks

Bolsas: Bags
Bombas: Short political rhymes
Bonito: Beautiful
Borrachos: Drunks
Bueno: Good
Buenos Dias: Good morning
Bultos: 54-kilo sacks
Busca un conejo: Look for a rabbit (look for a bathroom)

C
Cabecera: Head city of a municipality
Cabildo: Council room, town hall
Cacique: Locally powerful boss
Cadres: Groups
Cafetales: Coffee orchards
Cajas: Coffins
Caldo de Pollo: Chicken soup
Calle: Street
Camisas: Dresses
Campamentos: Refugee settlements
Campesinos: Farmers
Campo: Countryside
Cañadas: Canyons
Capacitación: Training
Capáz: Capable; to become aware
Capilla: Chapel
Caracol: Seashell; snail shell; for the Zapatistas, these are regional centers
Carácter Jurídico: Legal face
Cargo: Duty; responsibility
Catequistas: Catechist
Caxlan Ca'etik: Motorcycles
Ceiba: Mahogany
Central de Abastos: General market
Cerrado: Closed
César Chavez: Union organizer in the United States
Cleenton: Dog named after President Clinton
Coletos: San Cristobal residents who trace their origins to the Spanish
Comadres: Close woman friend; godmother
Comal: Clay or metal griddle

Comandancia: High command of the Zapatistas
Combis: Vans used in public transportation
Comercio Justo: Fair trade
Comida: Food
Comisariado: Elected ejido leader
Compadre: Close male friend; godfather
Compañeras/Compañeros: Companions in the struggle
Compás: Short for companions
Complementaridad: Complimentarity
Compradrazgo: Ritual kinship
Comunidad: Community
Comunidades Agrarias: Agrarian communities
Consejero: Councilman
Consejo: Council
Consejo Autónomo: Autonomous council
Construcción: Construction
Consulta Nacional: National referendum
Consultar Obedeciendo: To consult by obeying
Contabilidad: Accounting; accountability
Convenio: An agreement
Copal: Maya incense
Corridos: Story-songs; ballads
Costumbres: Customs
Coyote: Middleman
Cuarenta: Forty days of isolation after a birth
Cuarteles: Barracks
Cumbia: Waltz-like song
Cumplir es cumplir: To comply is to comply
Curandera(o): Healer

Ch
Chalupa: Coffee shade tree
Chamaco: Boy
Chayotes: Type of squash
Chile Ancho Adobada: Roast chilies
Chingados por los dos lados: Screwed from both sides
Chipy chipy: Drizzle
Chitom: Wild pigs
Chul na: [Tzotzil] Church

D

Definitivo: Final land title
Dentista: Dentist
Denuncias: Denunciations
De por si: In and of itself; actually
Desplazados: The displaced
Despulpador: Machine that removes the soft, outer skin from the coffee fruit
Dinero: Money
Dioses: Gods
Dios es Amor: God is love
Dios mia: My God
Disculpe: Excuse me, Pardon me
Duende: lucky magical dwarf

E

Educación: Education
Ee, Zeta, Ele, Ene: EZLN
Ejido: Communally owned land
Electricidad: Electricity
El Horizonte: The horizon
Elotes: Green corn; corn on the cob
Embra y Macho: Female and male
Empresa: Enterprise; business
Encuentro Por la Paz: Conference for peace
Engancho: Hook (to be hooked)
Engaño: Deceit; trick
Entre: To enter into
Envidias: Envies
Eres tu?: Are you?
Escuelita: School
Eso: That
Evangélicos: Evangelicals
Expulsados: The expelled

F

Fiesta: Party
Fincas: Hacienda-like farms
Finqueros: Owners of fincas
Foco: Lightbulb
Frayba: Abbreviation for Human Rights Center

Fuerte: Strong
Fútbol: Soccer

G
Galletas por gallinas: Cookies for chickens
Gracias (a): Thank-you
Gringa: Foreign woman
Gripa: Flu
Grupita: A little group
Guardias Blancas: Paramilitaries
Guatemaltecos: Guatemalans
Güeros: Light-skinned people
Guitarron: Type of guitar

H
Hamaca: Hammock
Hasta Lunes (Pronto): See you Monday (soon)
Hectare: 2.4 acres
Hermanamiento: Sister city
Hermanas: Sisters
Hermanos: Brothers
Hija: Daughter
Hijos de la Chingada: Children of the damned
Huipiles: Indigenous blouses

I
Iglesia Autóctona: Catholic Church in Chiapas
Incensario: Incense burner
Instituto: Institute
Inteligencia: Intelligence

J
Javelina: Wild pig
Jefe: Leader
Jesu Cristo: Jesus Christ
Jesús, mi Salvador: Jesus, my Savior
Jitomates: Tomatoes
Jodido y Justo: Between screwed and fair
Junta de Buen Gobierno: Council of Good Government
Juntas: Councils

K

Kaibiles: Jaguar warrior; killer elite army
Kanal: Star
Kun kun: [Tzotzil] Little by little; take it easy

L

La Franca Fincero: Agricultural zone near Ocosingo
Lagartos: Type of crocodile
La Jornada: The liberal Mexico City newspaper
La Lacandona: The Lacandon rain forest
La Ruta Maya: Tourist route through the Maya region
Las Abejas: The bees; survivors of the Acteal massacre
Las Citatorias: The cited ones
Latifundias: Expansive landholding by a single owner or family
Ley Indígena: Indigenous Law
Linea Revelde: Rebel line; revealed line
Los Tigres del Norte: Music group popular on the border

Ll

Llanta: Tire
Llanteria: Service station without gas
Llanto: A cry

M

Madera: Lumber
Maicito: Endearment for corn
Maíz: Corn
Mal: Bad
Mal Gobierno: Corrupt, bad government
Mandado: Errand
Mandar Obediciendo: To lead by obeying
Manta: Simple cotton cloth
Mapaches: Raccoons; masked paramilitaries in 1910
Maquiladoras: Factories
Marchas: Marches
Masa: Corn dough
Matitas: A few plants
Mero: True
Mesas de Reconciliación: Reconciliation boards
Mestizaje: Mixing of blood
Mestizos: Mixed blood
Mexicanos: Mexicans

Miel: Honey
Migración: Immigration
Milagro: Miracle
Milpa: Cornfield; field devoted to raising subsistence crops
Mole: Mexican dish of meat served with a chile gravy
Monte Ejido: Mountain ejido
Moreno: Brown; dark skin color
Muchas: Much
Municipios: Municipalities
Muy Alegre: Very festive
Muyuk: [Tzotzil] Negative, like Spanish "no hay"

N
Nan 2: A type of baby formula
Nauyacas: Pit vipers
Ni modo: But never mind; pay it no mind
Noche de Paz: Spanish version of the song "Silent Night"
No esta aqui: (He's) not here
Norte: North (United States); persistent light winter rains
Norteando: Drizzly
Norteña: Type of music from the U.S.–Mexican border
No Sirve Eso: This doesn't work
Noticias: The nightly news

O
Ojo: Eye; water hole; watch out!; [Spanish slang] disease of the soul
Ollas: Pots
Oratorio: Oratory
Originarios: Founders of ejidos
Orilla del Bosque: Edge of the forest
Oro: Gold; Fully processed, unroasted coffee
O sea: For instance

P
Pa'dentro: Inward
Padre: Father
Palabra: Word
Palabra de Dios: Word of God
Palacio: City hall
Paliacates: Red and black bandannas typically worn by Zapatistas over the face
Panadería: Bakery

Pan Dulce: Sweet bread
Paraje: Rural hamlet
Patrón: Hacienda owner; feudal lord
Paz y Justicia: Peace and justice; paramilitary group
Pequeños propietarios: Owners of small plots of land
Perdido: Lost
Pergamino: Coffee beans retaining their thin outer shell
Permiso: Permission; offering to the gods
Persona no Grata: Unwelcome individual
Peso: Mexican monetary unit (currently 11 to the dollar); weight
Pinche: Damned; screwed up
Pinche Gobierno: Damn government
Pisicultura: Fish farming
Plátano: Banana
Playa: Beach
Poco a Poco: Little by little
Político: Political; policy
Porque Somos en Resistencia: Because we are in resistance
Posada: Christmas play
Posh: Rum, Maya moonshine
Potrero: Fenced-in pastureland
Pox: Rum; Maya moonshine
Pozole: Corn-based beverage
Proceso: Mexican magazine
Profesores: Professors
Promotoras: Teachers
Promotor de Salud: Health care workers
Proyectismo: Project as object in development
Pueblos: Villages
Pues: Since; because; well
Pues por nosotros: Well, for us
Pukuj: [Tzotzil] Devil-like individual
Pulson: Type of Curandera
Puro Café: Only coffee

Q
Qué bueno!: How good!
Qué es?: What is it?

R
Ramada: Covered shelter
Ranchos: Ranches

Realidad: Reality; Zapatista capital
Rebozo: Shawl
Recorrido: Trip
Recurso de Revisión: Appeal
Refugiados: Refugees
Remanente: Profit
Remolino: Whirlwind; whirlpool
Renovados: Charismatic Catholics
Rio: River
Rústicos: Rustic cabin

S
Santa Paz: Tranquillity
Santo: Holy; saintly
Sat Wo: [Tzotzil] Water hole
Secretário de Gobernación: Secretary of state
Secto: Religious sect
Secundaría: Middle school
Seguimiento: Continuance
Seguridad Pública: State security forces
Selva: Jungle; Rain forest
Sexenios: Six-year presidential term in México
Si: If
Sí: Yes
Siempre: Always
Smajbil: [Tzotzil] Conflict
Sombreron: Ghostly figure
Son Nuestra Gente: They are our people
Sonrisa: Smile
Subcomandante Insurgente: Insurgent subcommander
Subprocuraduria de Justicia Indígena: Bureau of Indigenous Justice
Suelo: Soil
Sus Papeles, Por Favor: Your papers, please
Sus Pasaportes: Your passports

T
'Tabueno: It's okay; it's good
Takal takal: [Tojolobal] Little by little
Tambo: Drum
Tameshebat: [Tzotzil] Farewell; I go now
Tameshibat: Farewell; I go now

Ta siki osil: [Tzotzil] To cold country
Técnicos: Technical experts
Telesecondaria: School through television
Temascal: Sweat bath
Templo: Temple; church
Temporales: Rainwater-fed fields
Teoscuintles: Raccoon-like animal
Terrorismo: Terrorism
Tiempo de Dios: God's time (standard time)
Tiempo de Fox: Daylight savings time
Tiendas: Stores
Tierra: Land
Tierras Baldios (dias): Vacant lands
Tierras Nacionales: National lands
Tierra y Libertad: Land and liberty
Tios: Uncles; respectful address to elders
Tipografia: Typing
Todos Somos Marcos: We are all Marcos; we are all a rebellion
Tomatillos: Small green tomato-like fruits
Topes: Speed bumps
Topografía: Topography
Torres Gemelos: The Twin Towers
Trabajo: Work; labor
Tramites: Offical forms
Transgenicos: Genetically enginered plants
Tumpline: Headpiece used for carrying heavy loads

U
Una Molestia: An annoyance
Un Ratito: Wait a minute
Un Retén: A checkpoint
Usos y Costumbres: Tradition

V
Vestidos: Clothing; dress
Viejitos: Endearment for old folks
Vinik: [Tzotzil] Human
Vueltas: Returns

Y
Ya Estas Aquí: You're finally here!
Ya Llegaste: He's finally arrived

Z

Zapata Vive: Zapata lives
Zapatismo: Read the book!
Zocalo: Central Plaza
Zona de Conflicta: "Red zone," conflict zone
Zona Norte: North zone
Zona Sur: South zone

References

AFP. (2004, January 13). Bush Scrambles to Set Free Trade Plans on Track at Americas Summit. http://news.yahoo.com (accessed January 14, 2004).

Alianza Cívica. (2002). El Plan Puebla Panamá. *Poder Ciudadano*, April–May, 7.

American Heritage Dictionary of the English Language. (1981). Edited by William Morris. Boston: Houghton Mifflin.

Anaya Gallardo, Federico. (1997). Making Peace in Chiapas: The Problem of State Reconstitution (unpublished manuscript in author's possession).

Barreda, Andrés. (2001). Los peligros del Plan Puebla Panamá. In *Mesoamérica-los ríos profundos*, edited by Armando Bartra. México, DF: Instituto Maya, AC.

Bellinghausen, Hermann. (2002). Atacan paramilitares comunidad Zapatista de Montes Azules; hay siete lesionados. *La Jornada*, August 3, 2002.

Benjamin, Thomas. (1989). *A Rich Land of Poor People: Politics and Society in Modern Chiapas.* Albuquerque: University of New Mexico University Press.

Bodley, John. (1999). *Victims of Progress.* 4th ed. Mountainview, Calif.: Mayfield.

Bricker, Victoria R. (1981). *The Indian Christ, the Indian King: The Historical Substrate of Maya Myth and Ritual.* Austin: University of Texas Press.

Brokensha, David. (1989). Local Management Systems and Sustainability. In *Food and Farm: Current Debate and Policies.* Monographs in Economic Anthropology, no. 7, edited by C. Gladwin and K. Truman. Lanham, Md.: University Press of America, 190–218.

Brokensha, D. W., D. M. Warren, and O. Werner. (1980). *Indigenous Knowledge Systems and Development.* Lanham, Md.: University Press of America.

Brown, Pete. (1997). Institutions, Inequalities, and the Impact of Agrarian Reform on Rural Mexican Communities. *Human Organization* 56, no. 1: 102–9.

Burgerman, S. D. (1998). Mobilizing Principles: The Role of Transnational Activists in Promoting Human Rights Principles. *Human Rights Quarterly* 20, no. 4: 905–23.

Burgete Cal y Mayor, Araceli. (2002). *Indigenous Autonomy in México.* Somerset, N.J.: Transaction Publishers.

Calderon, Enrique A. (1998, May). Un documento rescatado en Tierra y Libertad. www.jornada.unam.mx (accessed June 19, 2003).

Cancian, Frank. (1965). *Economics and Prestige in a Mayan Community: The Religious Cargo System in Zinacantan.* Stanford, Calif.: Stanford University Press.

Cardoso, F. H. (1981). Towards Another Development. In *From Dependency to Development: Strategies to Overcome Underdevelopment and Inequality*, edited by H. Muñoz. Boulder, Colo.: Westview Press, 295–313.

CIACH, AC (2001). *Acuerdos de San Andres de la Mesa 1: "Derecho y Cultura Indígena."* Chiapas, Mexico: CIACH.

Clio Libros y Videos. (2004). México Nuevo Siglo [Television series]. México City: SA de CV.

Collier, George, and E. L. Quartatiello. (1994). *Basta! Land and the Zapatista Rebellion in Chiapas.* Oakland, Calif.: Food First.

Crewe, E. (1997). The Silent Traditions of Developing Cooks. In *Discourses of Development: Anthropological Perspectives*, edited by R. D. Grillo and R. L. Stirrat. New York: Berg Publishers, 59–80.

Croll, E., and D. J. Parkin, eds. (1992). *Bush Base, Forest Farm: Culture, Environment, and Development.* London: Routledge.

Davila, Enrique, G. Kessel, and S. Levy. (2000). *El Sur También Existe: Un Ensayo Sobre El Desarrollo Regional Mexicano.* San Cristóbal de las Casas: Ediciones Pirata.

Declaración Gobierno. (2002). Declaración Conjunta de la V Cumbre Del Mecanismo De Dialogo y Concentración de Tuxtla, Mérida, México, June 28, 2002 (summary prepared by México, Presidencia de la Republica).

De León Pasqual, Lourdes. (2001). *Costumbres, leyes y movimiento indio en Oaxaca y Chiapas.* Edited by Lourdes de León Pasqual. México, DF: CIESAS.

Desmi, AC. (2001). *Si Uno come, Que Coman Todos: Economia Solidaria.* México, DF: Grafia Editores Jalisco.

DESMU. (1998). Informe Sobre Las Actividades Principales Realizadas Durante 1997 (unpublished manuscript in author's possession).

De Vos, Jan. (2002). *Una tierra para sembrar sueños.* México, DF: CIESAS.

Duffield, M. (1997). The Symphony of the Damned: Racial Discourse, Complex Political Emergencies and Humanitarian Aid. *Disasters* 20: 174.

Diaz-Polanco, Hector, and Consuelo Sánchez. (2002). *México Diverso: El Debate por la Autonomia.* México, DF: Siglo Veintiuno Editores.

Duran Duran, Claudia. (2001). Trabajando Con Comunidades Diversos. Paper presented at the annual meeting of the Society for Applied Anthropology, Merida, Mexico, March 2001.

Earle, Duncan. (1984). Cultural Logic and Ecology in Community Development: Failure and Success Cases Among the Highland Maya. Dissertation, State University of New York at Albany.

———. (1986). The Metaphor of the Day in Quiche: Notes on the Nature of Everyday Life. In *Symbol and Meaning beyond the Closed Community: Essays in Mesoamerican Ideas*, edited by Gary Gossen. Albany, N.Y.: Institute for Mesoamerican Studies, 155–72.

———. (1988). Mayas Aiding Mayas: Guatemalan Refugees in Chiapas, Mexico. In *Harvest of Violence: The Maya Indians and the Guatemalan Crisis*, edited by R. M. Carmack. Norman: University of Oklahoma Press, 256–73.

———. (1992). Authority, Social Conflict and the Rise of Protestants; Religious Conversion in a Maya Village. *Social Compass* 39, no. 3: 379–90.

———. (1994). Constructing Refugee Ethnic Identity in Context: Guatemalan Mayas in Mexico and South Florida. In *Reconstructing Lives, Recapturing Meaning; Refugee Identity, Gender, and Culture Change*, edited by Ruth Krulfeld and Linda Camino. Basel: Gordon and Breach, 207–34.

Earle, Duncan, and Jeanne Simonelli. (2000). Help without Hurt: Community Goals, NGO Interventions and Lasting Aid Lessons in Chiapas, Mexico. *Urban Anthropology* 29, no. 2: 97–144.

Earle, Duncan, J. Simonelli, and E. Story. (2004). Acompañar Obediciendo: Learning to Help in Collaboration with Zapatista Communities. *Michigan Journal of Community Service Learning* 10, no. 3: 43–56.

Eber, Christine. (1999). Seeking Our Own Food: Indigenous Women's Power and Autonomy in San Pedro Chenalho, Chiapas (1970–1998). *Latin American Perspectives* 26, no. 3: 6–36.

———. (2000). *Women and Alcohol in a Highland Maya Town: Water of Hope, Water of Sorrow*. Rev. ed. Austin: University of Texas Press.

———. (2001) Cracking the Vessel of Oppression: Women and Change in San Pedro Chenalhó, Chiapas, Mexico. Paper presented at the 2001 meeting of the Latin American Studies Association, Washington, D.C., September 2001.

Escobar, A. (1991). Anthropology and the Development Encounter. *American Ethnologist* 18: 658–82.

———. (1995). *Encountering Development: The Making and Unmaking of the Third World*. Princeton, N.J.: Princeton University Press.

Esteva, Gustavo. (1992). Los ámbitos de comunidad y su cercamiento, en Opciones. *El Nacional* 25 (December 26): 9.

Expo-Inversión (2002). Que es el Plan Puebla Panamá? http://expoinversion2002.presidencia.gob.mx (accessed May 15, 2002).

Expreso Chiapas. (2002). En Chiapas hay tranquilidad: Fox. *Expreso Chiapas*, June 3, 16.

Falla, Ricardo. (2001). *Quiché Rebelde: Religious Conversion, Politics, and Ethnic Identity in Guatemala*. Austin: University of Texas Press.

Farmer, Paul. (2003). *Pathologies of Power: Health, Human Rights, and the New War on the Poor*. Berkeley: University of California Press.

Farris, Nancy M. (1984). *Maya Society under Colonial Rule: The Collective Enterprise of Survival*. Princeton, N.J.: Princeton University Press.

Fazio, Carlos. (1994). *Samuel Ruiz: El Caminante*. México City: Espasa Calipe.

———. (2001). El Plan Pueblo Panamá, arma al servicio de Estados Unidos para contener la migración. In Plan Puebla Panamá. San Cristóbal de las Casas: Ediciones Pirata, 1–6.

FBCDH (Fray Bartolome de las Casas Centro de Derechos Humanos), archives document PLS 00011, San Cristóbal de las Casas.

Ferguson, J. (1994). *The Antipolitics Machine: "Development," Depolitization and Bureaucratic Power in Lesotho*. Minneapolis: University of Minnesota Press.

FORO. (2002). Evaluación del Seminario. Seminario En Comercialización de Productos Agroecologios. San Cristóbal de las Casas: FORO Para el Desarrollo Sustentable, AC, July 20.

Foster, G. (1962). *Traditional Cultures and the Impact of Technological Change*. New York: Harper and Row.

Fuentes Muñoz, Fernando. (2002). Aclaración a nota sobre el Procede. *La Jornada*, June 18, 2.

Garza, A. M., M.F. Paz, J. M. Ruiz, and A. Calvo (1994). *Voces de la Historia: Nuevo San Juan Chamula, Nuevo Huixtán, and Nuevo Matzam.* Cuernavaca: UNAM-Centro Regional de Investigaciones Multidisciplinarias.

Gledhill, John (2002). The Reform of Article 27 and PROCEDE. http://les.man.ac.uk/multimedia/mexcase16a.htm.

Global Exchange. (1998). On the Offensive: Intensified Military Occupation in Chiapas Six Months since the Massacre at Acteal, Special Investigative Report. www.globalexchange.org.

———. (1999). *Foreigners of Conscience: The Mexican Government's Campaign against International Human Rights Observers in Chiapas, 1999.* San Francisco: Global Exchange.

Goodenough, Ward. (1970). The Growing Demand for Behavioral Science in Government: Its Implications for Anthropology. In *Applied Anthropology*, edited by J. A. Clifton. Boston: Houghton Mifflin.

Gossen, Gary H. (1996). The Religions of Mesoamerica. In *The Legacy of Mesoamerica: History and Culture of a Native American Civilization*, edited by Robert M. Carmack, Janine Gasco, and Gary H. Gossen. Upper Saddle River, N.J.: Prentice Hall, 290–320.

———. (1999). *Telling Maya Tales: Tzotzil Identities in Modern Mexico.* New York: Routledge.

Grillo, R. D. (1997). Discourses of Development: The View from Anthropology. In *Discourses of Development: Anthropological Perspectives*, edited by R. D. Grillo and R. L. Stirrat. New York: Berg Publishers, 1–23.

Gross, Daniel, and Stuart Plattner. (2002). Anthropology as Social Work: Collaborative Models of Anthropological Research. *Anthropology News* 43, no. 8: 4.

Guigle, Marcelo M., O. Lafourcade, and V. I. Nguyen. (2001). *Mexico: A Comprehensive Development Agenda for the New Era.* Washington, D.C.: World Bank.

Guiterrez, Gustavo. (1997). *We Drink from Our Own Wells: The Spiritual Journey of a People.* Maryknoll, N.Y.: Orbis Books.

Harvey, Neil. (1994). *Rebellion in Chiapas: Rural Reforms, Campesino Radicalism, and the Limits to Salinismo.* Transformation of Rural Mexico, no. 5. La Jolla, Calif.: Center for U.S.-Mexican Studies, 22

———. (1998). *The Chiapas Rebellion: The Struggle for Land and Democracy.* Durham, N.C.: Duke University Press.

Hernández Castillo, Rosalva Aída. (2001a). *Histories and Stories from Chiapas: Border Identities in Southern Mexico.* Austin: University of Texas Press.

———, ed. (2001b). *The Other Word: Women and Violence in Chiapas before and after Acteal.* Copenhagen: International Work Group for Indigenous Affairs.

Hernández Castillo, Rosalva Aída, Shannon Mattiace, and Jan Rus, eds. (2003). *Mayan Lives, Mayan Utopias: Indigenous Peoples and the State in the Wake of the Zapatista Rebellion.* Chicago: Rowman & Littlefield.

Herrera, Carlos. (2000). Familias prozapatistas podrían ser expulsadas. *Cuarto Poder*, March 11, 23.

International Development Bank. (2001). Plan Puebla-Panamá. Regional Operations Dep't #2. Inter-American Development Bank PowerPoint presentation, June 2001.
———. (2002). Plan Puebla-Panamá. Information, Consultation, and Participation Program. http://www.iadb.org/ppp/document/documentDetails.asp?document_id=144 (accessed May 2002).

Iribarren, Pablo. (1991). *Los Dominicos en la pastoral indigena.* México City: Imprentei.

Kearney, Michael. (1996). *Reconceptualizing the Peasantry: Anthropology in Global Perspective.* Boulder, Colo.: Westview Press.

Kovic, Christine. (2005). *Walking with One Heart: Indigenous Rights and the Catholic Church in Highland Chiapas.* Austin: University of Texas Press.

Lappe, F. M., J. Collins, and P. Rosset. (1998). *World Hunger: 12 Myths.* 2nd ed. New York: Grove Press.

Legoretta Díaz, Ma. Del Carmen. (1998). *Religíon, política y guerilla en Las Cañadas de la Selva Lacandona (1973–1995).* México: Cal y Arena.

Levya Solano, Xo'chitl. (1998). Catequistas, misioneros y traditiones en Las Cañadas. In *Chiapas, Los Rumbos de Otra Historia,* edited by Juan Pedro Viquiera and Mario Humberto Ruz. Mexico: UNAM Centro de Estudios Mayas, 375–406.

Levya Solano, X., and G. A. Franco, eds. (1997). *Cultura, y Sociedad.* México: CIESAS

Ley Agraria. (2002). *Nuevo Ley Agraria.* México, DF: Gobierno de México.

Linden, Eugene. (1976). *The Alms Race.* New York: Random House.

Luna, Daniel. (2001). Briefing on Ley Indígena and Plan Puebla Panamá. Coordinadora de Los Altos, Túmbala, Chiapas (field notes July 18).

MacLeod, Murdo J. (1973). *Spanish Central America.* Berkeley: University of California Press.

Mama Maquin. (1994). *From Refugees to Returnees.* Chiapas, Mexico: Mama Maquin CIAM.

Mattiace, Shannan. (2003). *To See with Two Eyes: Peasant Activism and Indian Autonomy in Chiapas, Mexico.* Albuquerque: University of New Mexico Press.

Mead, M. (1961). *New Lives for Old.* New York: New American Library.

México Presidencia (de la Republica). (2001). Plan Puebla Panamá. *Capitulo México Documento Base* 3: 20.

Meyer, Jean. (2000). *Samuel Ruiz en San Cristóbal.* México City: Tusquets Editors.

MSN News Summary. (2004, January 5–11). Mexico Solidarity Network Weekly News and Analysis. www.mexicosolidarity.org (Accessed January 12, 2004).

Mueller, A. (1986). The Bureaucratization of Feminist Knowledge: The Case of Women in Development. *Resources for Feminist Research* 15: 36–38.

Muñoz-Ramírez, Gloria. (2003). *EZLN: 20 y 10, El Fuego y la Palabra.* México: La Jornada.

Murdoch, Jonathan. (2000). Networks—A New Paradigm of Rural Development? *Journal of Rural Studies* 16, no. 4: 407–19.

Nash, June. (2001). *Mayan Visions: The Quest for Autonomy in an Age of Globalization.* New York: Routledge.

———. (2003). The Integration of Indigenous People in Civil Society. *Social Analysis* 47, no. 1: 102–9.

Nations, James. (1970). *Population Ecology of the Lacandon Maya.* Ph.D. diss., Southern Methodist University.

Nations, James, and Ronald Nigh. (1980). The Evolutionary Potential of the Lacandon Maya Sustained-Yield Tropical Forest Agriculture. *Journal of Anthropological Research* 36, no. 1: 1–30.

Netting, Robert M. (1993). *Smallholders, Householders: Farm Families and the Ecology of Intensive, Sustainable Agriculture.* Stanford, Calif.: Stanford University Press.

Nigh, Ronald. (1997). Implicaciones Regionales y Globales de la Colonización Agropecuaria de Las Selvas Tropicales del Sureste de Mexico. In *Colonización, Cultura, y Sociedad,* edited by X. Levya Solano and G. A. Franco. México: CIESAS, 173–209.

———. (2001). Legislación Indígena y Recursos Naturales. In *Costumbres, leyes y movimiento indio en Oaxaca y Chiapas,* edited by Lourdes de León Pasqual. México, DF: CIESAS, 159–67.

Nunez del Prado, O. (1973). *Kuyo Chico: Applied Anthropology in an Indian Community.* Chicago: University of Chicago Press.

Olivera Bustamente, Mercedes. (2001). Acteal: Effects of the Low Intensity War. In *The Other Word: Women and Violence in Chiapas Before and After Acteal,* edited by Rosalva Aída Hernández Castillo. Copenhagen: International Work Group for Indigenous Affairs, 105–17.

Oppenheimer, Andres. (1996). *Bordering on Chaos.* Boston: Little, Brown.

Ortiz, Teresa. (2001). *Never Again a World without Us.* Washington, D.C.: EPICA.

Pickard, Miguel. (2002). PPP: Plan Puebla Panama or Private Plans for Profit? www.corpwatch.org/issues/PID.jsp?articleid=3953. (accessed September 19, 2002).

Quandt S. A., T. A. Arcury, C. K. Austin, and L. F. Cabrera. (2001). Preventing Occupational Exposure to Pesticides: Using Participatory Research with Latino Farmworkers to Develop an Intervention. *Journal of Immigrant Health* 3, no. 2: 85–96.

Reed, Nelson. (1967). *The Caste War of the Yucatan.* Stanford, Calif.: Stanford University Press.

Reyes Ramos, Maria Eugenia. (1992). *El Reparto De Tierras y la Politica Agraria en Chiapas.* México, DF: Universidad Nacional Autonoma de México.

Rosenbaum, Brenda. (1993). *With Our Heads Bowed: The Dynamics of Gender in a Maya Community.* Austin: University of Texas Press.

Ross, John. (1995). *Rebellion from the Roots: Indian Uprising in Chiapas.* Monroe, Maine: Common Courage Press.

———. (2000). *The War against Oblivion: The Zapatista Chronicles 1994–2000.* Monroe, Maine: Common Courage Press.

Rus, Jan. (2004). Rereading Tzotzil Ethnography: Recent Scholarship from Chiapas, Mexico. In *Pluralizing Ethnography: Comparison and Representation in Maya Culture, Histories, and Identities,* edited by John M. Watanabe and Edward F. Fischer. Santa Fe, N.M.: School of American Research.

Rus, Jan, Rosalva Aída Hernández Castillo, and Shannan L. Mattiace. (2003). Introduction. In *Mayan Lives, Mayan Utopias: The Indigenous Peoples of Chiapas and the Zapatista Rebellion.* Chicago: Rowman & Littlefield, 1–27.

Scherer Ibarra, M., and J. C. Lopez. (2000). Las expulsions ilegales de extranjeros. *Proceso*, no. 1210, January 9, 22–26.

Schneider, Harold K. (1974). *Economic Man.* New York: Free Press.

Schumacher, E. F. (1973). *Small Is Beautiful.* New York: Harper and Row.

Scott, James C. (1985). *Weapons of the Weak: Everyday Forms of Peasant Resistance.* New Haven, Conn.: Yale University Press.

———. (1999). *Seeing Like a State: How Certain Schemes to Improve the Human Condition Have Failed.* New Haven, Conn.: Yale University Press.

Simonelli, Jeanne. (2002). The Scent of Change in Chiapas. In *Personal Encounters: A Reader in Cultural Anthropology,* edited by Linda S. Walbridge and April K. Sievert. New York: McGraw-Hill, 46–52.

Simonelli, Jeanne, and Duncan Earle. (2003a). Disencumbering Development: Alleviating Poverty through Autonomy in Chiapas. In *Here to Help: Combating Poverty: NGOs and Latin American Communities in Dialogue,* edited by R. Eversole. New York: M. E. Sharpe, 174–98.

———. (2003b). Meeting Resistance: Autonomy, Development, and "Informed Permission" in Chiapas, Mexico. *Qualitative Inquiry,* February, 74–89.

SLAA/Chiapas. (2000). Human Rights Group on Issues Facing Researchers in Chiapas. http://www.ucr.edu/anthro/slaa/slaachiapas.htm (accessed September 8, 2004).

Smith, Geri, and Lindblad, Cristina. (2003, December 22). Mexico: Was NAFTA Worth It? A Tale of What Free Trade Can and Cannot Do. www.businessweek.com (accessed January 6, 2004).

Speed, S., and J. Collier. (2000). Limited Indigenous Autonomy in Chiapas, Mexico: The State Government's Use of Human Rights. *Human Rights Quarterly* 22: 877–905.

Stavenhagen, R. (1981). The Future of Latin America: Between Underdevelopment and Revolution. In *From Dependency to Development: Strategies to Overcome Underdevelopment and Inequality,* edited by H. Muñoz. Boulder, Colo.: Westview Press, 207–23.

Stephen, Lynn. (2002). *Zapata Lives!: Histories and Cultural Politics in Southern Mexico.* Berkeley: University of California Press.

Stevenson, Mark. (2004, January 1). Zapatista Rebels Mark 10th Anniversary. http://news.yahoo.com (accessed January 15, 2004).

Stuart, David. (2000). *Anasazi America: 17 Centuries on the Road from Center Place.* Albuquerque: University of New Mexico Press.

Subcomandante Marcos. (2003, September 12). Globalize Hope. www.revistarebeldia.org (accessed January 17, 2004).

Tedlock, Barbara (1992). *Time and the Highland Maya.* Revised ed. Albuquerque: University of New Mexico Press.

UNHCR. (2001). Mission Statement. www.unhrc.ch/un&ref/mission/ms1.htm (accessed March 2001).

Villamar, Alejandro. (2002). Remarks presented at diocesan pastoral briefing, San Cristóbal de las Casas, Chiapas, July.

Vogt, Evon Z. (1969). *The Zinacantecos of Mexico: A Modern Maya Way of Life.* New York: Holt, Rinehart and Winston.

Wasserstrom, Robert W. (1983). *Class and Society in Central Chiapas.* Berkeley: University of California Press.

———. (1994). *Fieldwork among the Maya: Reflections on the Harvard Chiapas Project.* Albuquerque: University of New Mexico Press.

Yorail Maya. (2001a). La autonomía y la reforma constitucional sobre Derechos y Cultura Indígena. *Yorail Maya* no. 1 (July–September 2001).

———. (2001b). Cuadro comparativo entre los Acuerdos de San Andrés y la reforma constitucional sobre derechos y cultura Indígena" *Yorail Maya,* no. 1 (July–September 2001).

Index

accompaniment, 231
ACNUR. *See* UNHRC
Acteal massacre, 2, 96–97, 124
advocacy, viii, 10–11
agency, 10–13, 142, 253–54
agriculture: decline of profitability of,
viii; efficient production in, 19;
genetic engineering and, 212–13; land
tenure, 38–39; milpa logic, 246;
organic farming and, 213; small scale,
16, 290. *See also* Lacandon rain forest
Aguascalientes (Mexico), 295n2
Aguascalientes (Zapatista), 27n5;
replacement of, 264, 297
Albores Guillen, Roberto, viii, 88, 104,
106, 107
ALCA (Area de Libre Comercio de las
Américas), 222n1, 288
alternative development, 189;
agricultural economics, 19;
autonomy and, 14; JBGs, 260–66;
profit (remanente), 263; training, 21.
See also Zapatismo
Amparo Aguatinta. *See* Santa Elena
Anaya Gallardo, Federico, 40
anthropology: application of, 166, 292;
community studies in Chiapas, 6–7;
dependency theory, 22–23; and
development, 22–44; economic
theory, 189; evolutionism, unilineal,
22–23; Harvard project, 6–7;
institutional review board and, 12,

157; methodology, 10–13, 114, 253,
293; political neutrality, 69, 125;
progress models, 22–23;
representation (*see* agency)
Area de Libre Comercio de las Américas.
See ALCA
article 27, 1917 Constitution, 38;
development and, 191; modification
of, 149–50; tierras baldios, 38
autonomous municipalities: break-up
of, 103–6; formation of, 92. *See also*
Tierra y Libertad
autonomy: communities and EZLN
negotiate, 165; Convenio 169,
192–93; defined, 8, 95, 168, 192–93;
education, 196, 268–69; Ley Indigena
and, 192–93; participation in
government programs, 197; San
Andrés Accords and, 95;
self-sufficiency and, 290–91;
Zapatista silence and, 218. *See also*
Tierra y Libertad

Bodley, John, 20–21, 189
Burguete Cal y Mayor, Araceli, 104
Bush, George W., 188, 288

Calderon, Enrique A., 104
campesinos: activisim outside Chiapas,
215; against PPP, 186–89; organizing
and, 212
Candalaria, Chiapas, 44

Earle, Duncan, 19, 23, 25, 48, 57, 148; and Jeanne Simonelli, 22, 66, 139, 190
Eber, Christine, 7, 137
economic theory, 16
economies of scale, 19
education, autonomous, 167–68
Ejercito Zapatista de Liberación Nacional. *See* EZLN
ejidos, 34; in Chiapas, 39; founding, 31; origins and definition, 38–39; privatization and sale, 149. *See also* PROCEDE
electricity: Cerro Verde and, 185–86; Federal Electrical Commission, 179–80
Enlace Civil, 158
Escobar, A., 20, 23
ethnography, Chiapas, 6–8
expulsions, viii; of campesinos, 147; of foreigners, 63–74, 107
EZLN (Ejercito Zapatista de Liberación Nacional/Zapatista Army of National Liberation): alcohol and, 183, 212; bases de apoyo (support bases), 69; commercialization and, 235; discourse of development, 253; effect on financial markets, 90, 267; foreign participation in conflict, 70–71; formation of, 88; importance of military arm, 267; as informal nongovernmental organization, 149, 251; lead by obeying, 168, 229; march to Mexico City, 156; march to San Cristóbal de Las Casas, 226–28, 277; outmigration and, 287; reorganization of, 207, 219, 256–74; silence broken, 209, 226–28; silence of, 169, 185, 192–93, 207, 209, 216, 218; tax on development, 263; tenth anniversary, 276–77; terrorism and, 216; women in, 91

fair trade (comercio justo), 197
Fazio, Carlos, 128n5, 265n5, 265n7

feminism, 66, 100–101, 110, 136–38
FORO, 197
Fox, Vincente, 126, 156; Bush, George W. and, 276; opposition to, 220; and peace, 186, 276; privatization and, 179–80
Franca fincero, 35, 39

Global Exchange, 94
globalization, summit on, 288
Gossen, Gary, 50–53, 137
guardias blancas, 96, 113
Guatemala: nongovernmental organization projects in, 57–62; violence in, 52, 61–62
Guatemalan Mayas: becoming Mexican citizens, 146; as refugees in Chiapas, ix, 56–57, 65–69, 82, 120
Guillen, Rafael, 90

Hacia la Esperanza (JBG), 256–69
hermanamientos, 15, 158–59, 195, 230–32; renegotiation of, 258
Hernandez Castillo, Rosalva Aida, 27n3, 27n4
histoplasmosis, 239
Human Rights Center "Fray Bartolome de las Casas," 73–74; and Cerro Verde, 147–48, 151; monitoring troops, 114

Iglesia Autoctona: contrasts to Protestants, 281; reflection and, 186. *See also* liberation theology
ILO (International Labor Organization), 192–93
immigration to United States, 206, 287
Indians of the Sierra Madre of Motozintla. *See* ISMAN
Indigenous Congress (CNI), 81–82, 95
indigenous peoples. *See* Mayas
informed permission, 11–13, 162, 169
INI (Instituto Nacional Indigena, National Indian Institute), 41–43

INM (Instituto Nacional de Migración): expulsion of foreigners, 63–74, 107; as military arm, 105; Pulido, Rene, 63–74

INMECAFE (Instituto Mexicana de Café/Mexican Coffee Institute), 48, 49

Instituto Mexicana de Café. *See* INMECAFE

Instituto Nacional de Migración. *See* INM

Instituto Nacional Indigena. *See* INI

International Labor Organization. *See* ILO

intimidation of foreigners, 70

ISMAN (Indians of the Sierra Madre of Motozintla), 87, 93n7, 281

Jerusalem, Nuevo, 55, 270–72, 280

Jolom Mayaetik, 196

jungle. *See* Lacandon rain forest

Junta de Buen Gobierno (JBG), x, 5, 252; rules for engagement with, 253

Kearney, Michael, 16, 23

Kovic, Christine, 79–81

Labastida, Francisco, 64

Lacandon rain forest; cattle in, 37–38; climatic patterns, 35–36; colonization, 31–40, 41–49; destruction of, 37, 242, 283–84; development plan, 40; Guatamalan refugees, 48, 56–57; invasions of, 90–93, 103; Lacandon Maya in, 82; languages of, 38; lumber exploitation, 34, 49; militarization of, 86, 90–93; opposition to colonization, 45; physical description, 35–37; Protestants in, 83; sustainable development in, 284. *See also* Cerro Verde; Ojo de Agua

land ownership, 34–40. *See also* PROCEDE

Las Margaritas (Chiapas, Mexico), 31, 40–41

latifundia, 39

Ley Indigena, 156–92

Leyva Solano, Xochitl, 27n3

liberation theology, ix, 100, 186, 200, 240, 281. *See also* Iglesia Autoctona

low-intensity warfare, 91–92; defined, 93n9

Luna, Daniel, 193

mapaches, 35

Marcos (Subcomandante insurgente, EZLN), 15; commentary on Caracoles, 238; critique of development aid, 13, 26, 251–52; on PPP, 279

Marists, ix, 56, 78, 81–83

Marx, Karl, and economics, 189

Mayas: curing and sweat bath, 285–86; identity, 148, 203–4, 244; vision of the universe, 137, 260

Mexican Coffee Institute. *See* INMECAFE

Mexico: debt crisis and devaluation, 90, 282; land reform (*see* article 27, 1917 Constitution); 1917 Constitution, 282; racism in, 14; Revolution of 1910–1917, 34–35, 38–40

Miguel Hidalgo community, 69; as beekeepers, 97, 103; break-up of, 106; denunciation of army, 106; founding of, 100. *See also* Tulan

militarization, 94; of border zone, 169; impact on children, 106; peace camps and, 94; post-2000 troop movements, 156, 162, 171, 205, 213–14, 258; preventative counterinsurgency warfare, 94; troop movements, 117–18, 186; Zedillo and, vii

milpa, defined, 27n6; logic, 291

Montes Azules reserve, 129, 132n1, 205, 215

Morris, Chip, 144n3

NAFTA (North American Free Trade Agreement), 99; critique of, 217, 288, 295n7

sustainable agriculture: alternative
models, 128–29; and Zapatistas, 128

terrorism, 117, 216
Tierra y Libertad (Land and Freedom):
Arevelo, Camila and, 9–10; Arevelo,
Martin and, 9–10, 193–98, 256–71;
autonomous region, 9, 68–69; breakup of, 9, 103–6, 128, 159, 212; in
Cerro Hueco prison, 107;
communities in, 103; community
development projects and, 235;
consejo autonomo, 158; construction
of foreign policy, 209–10, 160–162,
165; Maya program and, 157;
resistance communities, 8; seeks
nongovernmental organization aid,
92, 121; usos y costumbres and, 105.
See also Hacia la Esperanza
Tojolabal: marriage practices, 34;
migration to Lacandon, 31–32. *See
also* Cerro Verde; Orilla del Bosque
Tulan: clinic in, 201, 233; collectivism
and, 288–90; commercialization and,
201–2; community development and,
111–16; feminism and, 100; fieldwork
of authors in, 115; honey export, 201,
235; nongovernmental organizations
and, 115; philosophical
underpinnings, 250; relationship to
Tierra y Libertad, 202; students in,

233–34. *See also* Miguel Hidalgo
community
Tzeltal catechists, 79–80

UNHRC (United Nations High
Commissioner for Refugees,
ACNUR), 62, 96, 105, 137, 139–40
United States, migration to, 206
Urbina, Erasto, 41–43, 45–46, 49n1
usos y costumbres, defined, 27n4

Vargas Mendoza, Javier, 82–86
Vogt, Evon Z., 7

Wasserstrom, Robert, 242
women, Zapatistas and, 267. *See also*
complementarity; feminism
Word of God. *See* Iglesia Autoctona
World Bank, 188, 208, 236

Xela, meeting in, 212–13, 217

Zapata, Emiliano, 15
Zapatismo, 16; and alternative
development, 20–22. *See also* EZLN
Zapatista Army of National Liberation.
See EZLN
Zapatistas. *See* EZLN
Zedillo Ponce de Leon, Ernesto, 104;
military response of, 96; San Andrés
Accords, 96. *See also* militarization

About the Authors

Duncan Earle is an applied cultural anthropologist who is currently associate professor of anthropology at Clark University. With over twenty-five years of continuing field experience in research and community development in Chiapas, in Guatemala, and on the U.S.–Mexican border, his vita includes extensive publications pertaining to that work. Recent publications include "Menchu Tales," in *The Rigoberta Menchú Controversy* (ed. Arturo Arias, 2001); "The Boundless Borderlands: Texas Colonias on the Edge of Nations," in *New Perspectives on Migration* (ed. Lillian Golden, 2000); and "The Border Colonias and Communication: Applying Anthropology for Outreach," in *Public Health and the US–Mexico Border; Asi es la Vida* (by Mary Bain and Martja Loustaunau, 1999). He is codirector of the Maya Study Program, which teaches undergraduates to do field research.

Jeanne Simonelli is an anthropologist and writer who is currently professor and chair of anthropology at Wake Forest University. Her field experiences are united by the broad theme of change and choice in difficult situations. Her principal publications include *Crossing between Worlds: The Navajos of Canyon de Chelly* (1997), *Too Wet to Plow: The Family Farm in Transition* (1992), and *Two Boys, a Girl, and Enough!* (1986). She continues to work in the areas of development and conflict resolution in Chiapas and will take this research to Israel in the spring of 2005. She received the 2000 Prize for Poetry from the Society for Humanistic Anthropology and publishes both poetry and short stories based on her field experiences. Simonelli is the current editor of the journal *Practicing Anthropology* and is codirector of the Maya Study Program.

Simonelli and Earle have coauthored several monographs concerning Chiapas. These include "Help without Hurt" (*Urban Anthropology*, 2000), "Meeting Resistance" (*Qualitative Inquiry*, 2003), and "Disencumbering Development" (2003), and "Acompaña Obediciendo" (*Michigan Journal of Community Service Learning*, 2004). They have also written a number of articles for the popular press. In addition, Simonelli is author of "The Scent of Change in Chiapas," a book chapter published in October 2002.